HISTORIES OF RACIAL CAPITALISM

COLUMBIA STUDIES IN THE HISTORY OF U.S. CAPITALISM

COLUMBIA STUDIES IN THE HISTORY OF U.S. CAPITALISM

Series Editors: Devin Fergus, Louis Hyman, Bethany Moreton, and Julia Ott

Capitalism has served as an engine of growth, a source of inequality, and a catalyst for conflict in American history. While remaking our material world, capitalism's myriad forms have altered—and been shaped by—our most fundamental experiences of race, gender, sexuality, nation, and citizenship. This series takes the full measure of the complexity and significance of capitalism, placing it squarely back at the center of the American experience. By drawing insight and inspiration from a range of disciplines and alloying novel methods of social and cultural analysis with the traditions of labor and business history, our authors take history "from the bottom up" all the way to the top.

HISTORIES
OF RACIAL
CAPITALISM

EDITED BY DESTIN JENKINS AND
JUSTIN LEROY

Columbia University Press   *New York*

Columbia University Press
Publishers Since 1893
New York   Chichester, West Sussex
cup.columbia.edu

Library of Congress Cataloging-in-Publication Data
Names: Jenkins, Destin, editor. | Leroy, Justin, editor.
Title: Histories of racial capitalism / edited by Destin Jenkins and Justin Leroy.
Description: New York : Columbia University Press, [2021] | Series: Columbia
studies in the history of U.S. capitalism | Includes bibliographical references
and index.
Identifiers: LCCN 2020024539 (print) | LCCN 2020024540 (ebook) |
ISBN 9780231190749 (hardback) | ISBN 9780231190756 (trade paperback) |
ISBN 9780231549103 (ebook)
Subjects: LCSH: United States—Economic conditions. | Capitalism—
United States—History. | Racism—Economic aspects—United States.
Classification: LCC HC103 .H58 2021 (print) | LCC HC103 (ebook) |
DDC 330.9730089—dc23
LC record available at https://lccn.loc.gov/2020024539
LC ebook record available at https://lccn.loc.gov/2020024540

Cover image: Watts Riot, 1966, Noah Purifoy.
© 2020 Courtesy of Noah Purifoy Foundation

Cover design: Lisa Hamm

CONTENTS

FOREWORD

Racial Capitalism and Law

ANGELA P. HARRIS, UNIVERSITY OF CALIFORNIA–DAVIS
SCHOOL OF LAW

A s the editors of this volume note, neither the *racial* nor the *capitalism* part of the term *racial capitalism* ought to be taken for granted. I admit: the term makes me nervous. I worry that using *race* as a keyword will increase the fraught divide between scholars of race and scholars of settler colonialism.[1] I also worry that the rightful association of the term with the pathbreaking work of Cedric Robinson, W. E. B. Du Bois, and Eric Williams will solidify a masculinist canon. And I worry that the word *capitalism* will not only trigger for some scholars the everlasting debate about how to define that term but also foreclose the relevance of the project to noncapitalist and/or anticapitalist times and spaces. But in this essay, I won't dwell on worries. Instead, I'll argue that my discipline, law, is a key site for the development of new scholarship in racial capitalism, and that alliances among racial capitalism scholars in the humanities and social sciences and racial capitalism scholars in law have the potential to fruitfully disrupt some of the discourses that sustain neoliberal governance.

As this volume illustrates, an important strand of the new racial capitalism literature traces the historical role of white supremacy in the processes of dispossession, extraction, accumulation, and exploitation that are central to today's capitalism. The editors' introduction articulates the bold premise of this work: Racial subjugation is not a special application of capitalist processes, but rather central to how capitalism operates.

The implications of this literature for legal studies are intriguing. Legal scholarship and teaching circulate simultaneously in the university and in the larger networks of the profession. Within the university, law interacts with many other disciplines, including those in the humanities and the social sciences. For example, critical race theory (CRT) emerged in the 1980s as a university-facing flow, drawing on critical legal studies and on Third World studies.[2] Over the next few decades, it moved into the social sciences and the humanities.[3] Through some combination of these paths, critical race theory has now filtered into the world of progressive social movements and the nonprofit industrial complex that supports them.[4]

In mainstream professional discourse, however, where legal codes structure the institutions and actors of capitalist democracy, law's most powerful disciplinary alliance has been with economics. The romance, moreover, is largely one-way. Enjoying remarkable prestige and power in both academia and governance, economics as a discipline takes little notice of any other non-"hard" discipline, save (in a limited way) cognitive psychology.[5] The fiefdom-defending capacities of economics extend to its offshoot in the legal academy, "law-and-economics," which continues to hold sway over research and teaching in all the fields that touch markets, from business associations to securities regulation to intellectual property to contracts to international trade. "Capitalism" doesn't exist in these fields. There are only markets and economic analysis, abstract systems obeying rules that are elegant, timeless, and inherently disconnected from matters of "distribution."

Lately, though, there has been a series of disturbances in the force. The shock of the Great Recession of 2008, the slow creep of climate change, and most recently the cascading assaults of the COVID-19 pandemic have all undermined the neoliberal political-economic consensus, as has the post-postracial rush of xenophobic and nationalist authoritarianism around the globe.[6] In the context of these shocks, the emergence of racial capitalism in the tiny world of the academic humanities might actually be big. Traveling through the fissures and networks of legal studies and social movements in the way CRT has, racial capitalism has the potential to amplify the shock waves from within and without.

Part I of this essay argues that legal scholarship and teaching form an important bridge between academia and the doings of state and market governance. Part II imagines some moves that racial capitalism and legal studies, developing together, might make in these spaces and in progressive organizing for noncapitalist futures.

I. The Law Is Everywhere

Economists, I have claimed, pay little attention to other disciplines, but they *really* ignore race. Even Thomas Piketty's 2014 surprise blockbuster *Capital in the Twenty-First Century*—lauded for not only actually noticing economic inequality but conceptualizing it as the result of a struggle between capital and labor—proposed universal solutions that overlooked the central role that differentials of race and gender play in shaping capitalism as a system of production.[7] More typical in economic analysis is either the assumption that issues involving racial inequality are a matter of "distribution" and thus not the business of economists at all,[8] or else earnest assurances that since racism is economically inefficient, it is bound, like other immaterial distinctions, to vanish like dew on a summer's day in the sunlight of free markets.[9] Economists wishing to take white supremacy seriously have thus been pushed into awkward models such as positing an individual "taste for discrimination."[10]

In contrast, race is everywhere in law. But it appears in legal doctrine through a "recognition" paradigm that assumes that the problem of white supremacy is exclusion. Antidiscrimination law, the primary place where race shows up in legal practice, provides individuals with tools with which to contest their exclusion from employment, education, and other institutions of the market and the state—when that exclusion can be proven to have been motivated by racial difference. But antidiscrimination law assumes that these institutions are otherwise race-blind and race-free. Moreover, the remedies available under antidiscrimination law are designed to forestall collective economic redistribution as a possibility.[11]

The insistence that racial rights can only be rights of recognition and assimilation has helped maintain an uneasy divide between "people of color" and indigenous peoples. Federally recognized Indian tribes have collective political and economic rights of self-determination, resting on their inherent sovereignty as a people that predates the formation of the United States. These powers of sovereignty, however, have been preserved in the contemporary era only through denial of their "racial" character. The Supreme Court has held, for example, that employment preferences for Indians in the federal Bureau of Indian Affairs are permissible because being an Indian is a "political" and not a "racial" identity.[12] If Indian identity were deemed racial, such preferences would be clearly unconstitutional.[13] The distinction between political and racial identity at once suppresses the racialized nature of anti-indigenous state and private action[14] and renders nonjusticiable black bids for remedies that sound like redistribution, such as reparations for slavery, because they are inherently "political." (How is it that racial rights are neither political nor economic?)

Antidiscrimination law and its rights of racial recognition are further embedded in an implicit division of labor in the legal academy. Scholarship in the legal fields that claim centrality in regulating capitalism, such as business associations, securities regulation, contract, and property (including intellectual property), has been largely untouched by CRT.[15] Instead, the law of capitalism is studied and taught primarily through the race-free lens of law-and-economics, an analytic code well suited to neoliberal governance.

Stephanie Mudge identifies three faces of neoliberalism: intellectual, bureaucratic, and political.[16] The political face of neoliberalism insists that market-oriented methods and institutions of governance are invariably preferable over state-oriented ones, justifying this policy bent in the language of "efficiency" and "moral hazard."[17] The familiar neoliberal trope that market relationships are efficient (and therefore better at allocating scarce resources), except to the extent that the state has introduced regulatory burdens on production and exchange, is part and parcel of a long-standing assignment of freedom to the sphere of the market and coercion to the sphere of the state.[18]

Law-and-economics, when it first emerged in the legal academy, adopted this story wholeheartedly, embracing economists' disregard for history and society. The legal scholar who did the most to establish law-and-economics in the legal academy, Richard Posner (a professor at the University of Chicago Law School and a judge on the federal Seventh Circuit Court of Appeals), conceived it as the application of economic principles to legal rules.[19] His popular and influential textbook, *The Economic Analysis of Law* (first published in 1973), sought to demonstrate that Anglo-American common law rules do and should operate to foster economic efficiency.[20] Posner's vision of the economic analysis of law, one contemporary reviewer wrote,

> provides a virtually distortion-free vision of individual behavior and the market, a fuzzier view of collective decisionmaking, and almost completely filters out issues of equity. . . . His basic premises are that legal rules and institutions should be designed to facilitate economic efficiency, that they should make the greatest use of competitive markets, and, in the absence of such markets, should "mimic" what competitive markets would do.[21]

Despite this reviewer's skepticism and the many scholarly attacks to follow, this version of law-and-economics quickly achieved hegemony in legal scholarship and teaching. Its fit with the professional mission of producing lawyers to serve political and economic elites was admirably close. Law-and-economics perfectly suited the position of neoliberal governance that "unfettered market competition produces incentives for maximizing overall resources and individual responsibility, thereby making society better off in the long run in spite of harsh short-term effects on some people."[22] Translated into "cost-benefit analysis," law-and-economics became an important regulatory tool in the neoliberal administrative state.[23] Allied with a right-wing distrust of "dependency," it helped discipline the presumably feckless receivers of government benefits.[24] Imparted to law professors and federal judges in summer camps and weekend workshops generously funded by the conservative Olin Foundation and the Heritage Foundation, and to law students, judicial clerks, and young lawyers attending Federalist Society events, law-and-economics became a lingua franca of governance.[25]

Neoliberalism, of course, represents only one position in a long-standing oscillation in liberal capitalist democracies over the proper relationship between state and market governance. Democratic socialism and social democracy (roughly represented in the 2019 presidential campaigns of Bernie Sanders and Elizabeth Warren, respectively) represent very different resolutions of the same challenge.[26] Important as this war of position is, however, the struggle over the relationship between "government" and "the market" leaves invisible the extent to which *both* state and market governance are embedded in raced and gendered subjection.

In the 1980s, critical race theorists began to explore the relationship between white supremacy and state governance in the United States. Derrick Bell, for instance, argued that fidelity to white supremacy is a bedrock value in the public spheres of American politics and American constitutionalism.[27] A torrent of CRT scholarship since then has tried to show how the Supreme Court has designed antidiscrimination law not only to avoid redistribution at all costs, but also to protect white supremacy by creating enclaves marked "private" or "social" in which it can flourish. But until very recently, precisely because of the success with which racial rights have been severed from economic rights and markets (rhetorically) severed from the domain of state power, critical race theorizing has remained largely disconnected from the law of capitalism.

II. Racial Capitalism and Legal Code

In the wake of recent multiple catastrophic failures of neoliberal governance, legal scholars have begun once again to conceptualize economic governance as historically specific, beholden to state power, and situated in cultural and social context.[28] In other words, for these scholars, there is a thing called "capitalism" again. Moreover, some of these scholars have begun to link the history of capitalism with the history of race—exploring, for example, how the legal tools of finance emerged in slavery and indigenous dispossession,[29] and how the law of private property has been a crucial tool for disrupting indigenous political economies and reshaping First Nations into clients of settler states.[30] Recent scholarship also shows how basic legal concepts—including nation-state, citizen, sovereignty, property, and person—emerged from the crucible of colonialism, imperialism, and slavery.[31]

As the literature of racial capitalism develops in history and the other humanities, its themes are ripe for development by legal scholars. Consider, for example, the story of the Great Recession of 2008. As Emma Coleman Jordan notes, the Federal Reserve has disclaimed any role in economic inequality in the United States; yet its failure to recognize the role of racial discrimination in shaping the U.S. housing market contributed to its policy failures before and after the catastrophic collapse of the U.S. housing bubble, and it ensured the continued disproportionate extraction of wealth from black households.[32] Mehrsa Baradaran's work exposes the myth of "black capitalism," showing how law and policy in housing, employment, and the banking system have made it impossible for institutions to close the racial wealth gap by capturing the black dollar.[33] Daria Roithmayr's work explores the "lock-in" effects of racialized dispossession and extraction.[34] Bernadette Atuahene's work on "dignity takings," as well as her writings on U.S. state and local governance through fines and fees as a system of racial extraction, dovetails with these accounts of how racial capitalism functions in the present day.[35] More work in this vein is needed—and more that moves beyond U.S. borders. Neoliberalism, after all, is a transnational project. For example, the industrial food system presents a riveting case study of the international nexus of capital, colonialism, and white supremacy; legal scholars versed in the laws of immigration, labor, human rights, and international trade have just begun to explore these connections.[36] As the COVID-19 pandemic unfolds, it similarly unveils the interaction of racial capitalism and public health within the United States and beyond.[37]

Finally, as political and economic governance "dematerialize" and become further datafied, it is important to understand how these dematerialized relations interact with prior regimes of racial capitalism. Critical race scholars and others have already begun to explore the codification of racism within seemingly neutral computer algorithms developed by commercial firms and sold or leased to government agencies.[38] What happens in other realms of governance where the dissolution of the individual and its replacement by the "dividual"[39] meet embodied necropolitics?

In addition to generating more case studies of the centrality of white supremacy to political and economic governance, scholarship on racial capitalism in law has the potential to make theoretical interventions into the underlying code of liberal capitalist democracy. Feminist legal theorists have already begun to do this work, arguing that a concept of gender as prepolitical has helped constitute legal governance of both the state and the market.[40] The idea is not just that women are discriminated against in labor markets, but that the conceptual space of "the market" is already gendered. Are there similarly systematic relationships between race and the law of capitalism? The new scholarship on racial capitalism opens a door to possible answers.

We are back in the territory of semantics—but words matter. Are the terms *racial* and *capitalism* capacious enough to realize the full potential of this scholarship? For example, another corner of the legal academy is beginning to investigate the ecological dynamics in which state, market, and society are embedded. Influenced by recent writing in political ecology, some legal scholars have called for "green critical legal theory."[41] Might the literature in legal racial capitalism connect this work to decolonial theory through, for example, genealogical accounts of the Human?[42] Other legal scholars are developing links to indigenous political philosophy, including from South America and from Aoteorora/New Zealand.[43] If racial capitalism is understood broadly, the uneasy standoff between people of color and indigenous people as legal subjects might finally be ended.

Beyond the possibilities of transdisciplinary scholarship in the academy, the emergence of racial capitalism in law has the capacity to hasten transformations within political economy. In recent years, for example, a series of social movements taking the form of "[x] justice" have emerged.[44] Movements such as environmental justice, reproductive justice, land justice, water justice, data justice, and climate justice make use of legal strategies and discourse but simultaneously exceed them. As these movements have built denser interconnections and more complex analytic frameworks, they have begun to converge on a vision that links liberation struggles across the globe with a robust critique of capitalism that centers on its inability to deliver a viable future.[45] From a legal perspective, this work involves not only fighting the bad, as movement lawyers have always done, but building the new, a project that includes promoting cooperatives in place of corporations as the default legal structure for economic production, promoting transformative justice processes as replacements for the carceral state, and developing new practices for the legal protection of the nonhuman entities and systems with which human life is interdependent.[46] Just as CRT, moving through capillaries within and outside law, has made *intersectionality* a common word, a racial capitalism literature that engages with law may help advocates dream into being new forms of governance adapted to a more just and sustainable future.

Conclusion

In its capacity as a tool for maintaining "order," the law has, in partnership with economics, ruthlessly adopted commitments that have fostered and protected racial capitalism. Yet the law is also porous and open-textured. Social movements and community lawyers regularly use the discourse of "justice," law's other face, in the service of liberation. In the academy, racial capitalism scholarship that engages with law can move forward the critical project of eroding the structures of power and knowledge that ally political-economic institutions and activities with white supremacy and settler colonialism. Outside the academy but in alliance with it, lawyers and organizers who understand the implications of racial capitalism have the capacity to smuggle at least some of its critical power into the citadels of political and economic governance—and, more important, to begin building the other worlds we know are possible.

NOTES

1. See, for example, Justin Leroy, "Black History in Occupied Territory: On the Entanglements of Slavery and Settler Colonialism," *Theory & Event* 19, no. 4 (2016), https://www.muse.jhu.edu/article/633276; Tiffany Lethabo King, "New World Grammars: The 'Unthought' Black Discourses of Conquest," *Theory & Event* 19, no. 4 (2016), https://www.muse.jhu.edu/article/633275; Manu Vimalassery, Juliana

Hu Pegues, and Alyosha Goldstein, "Introduction: On Colonial Unknowing," *Theory & Event* 19, no. 4 (2016), https://www.muse.jhu.edu/article/633283.

2. See Sumi Cho and Robert Westley, "Critical Race Coalitions: Key Movements That Performed the Theory," *UC Davis Law Review* 33, no. 4 (Summer 2000): 1377–1428.

3. See, for example, Edward Taylor, David Gillborn, and Gloria Ladson-Billings, eds., *Foundations of Critical Race Theory in Education* (New York: Routledge, 2009); Devon W. Carbado and Daria Roithmayr, "Critical Race Theory Meets Social Science," *Annual Review of Law and Social Science* 10: 149–67, https://doi.org/10.1146/annurev-lawsocsci-110413-030928; Rozena Maart, "When Black Consciousness Walks Arm-in-Arm with Critical Race Theory to Meet Racism and White Consciousness in the Humanities," *Alternation* 21, no. 2 (2014): 54–82.

4. See, for example, Marie Laperrière and Eléonore Lépinard, "Intersectionality as a Tool for Social Movements: Strategies of Inclusion and Representation in the Québécois Women's Movement," *Politics* 36, no. 4 (2016): 374–82, https://doi.org/10.1177/0263395716649009.

5. Marion Fourcade, Etienne Ollion, and Yann Algan, "The Superiority of Economists," *Journal of Economic Perspectives* 29, no. 1 (2015): 89–114.

6. For an argument that the new authoritarian "populism" visible in the United States is a reaction to intensifying economic and political inequality, see Jacob S. Hacker and Paul Pierson, "Plutocrats with Pitchforks: The Distinctive Politics of Right-Wing Populism in the United States," August 2019, https://www.law.berkeley.edu/wp-content/uploads/2019/09/Hacker_Pierson_APSA_2019.pdf.

7. Kathryn Moeller, "A Critical Feminist and Race Critique of Thomas Piketty's *Capital in the Twenty-First Century*," *British Journal of Sociology and Education* 37, no. 6 (2016): 810–22.

8. Paul Krugman quotes the economist Robert Lucas: "Of the tendencies that are harmful to sound economics, the most seductive, and in my opinion the most poisonous, is to focus on questions of distribution." Paul Krugman, "Why We're in a New Gilded Age," *New York Review of Books*, May 8, 2014, https://www.nybooks.com/articles/2014/05/08/thomas-piketty-new-gilded-age/.

9. As Milton Friedman wrote in *Capitalism and Freedom* (Chicago: University of Chicago Press, 1962): "It is a striking historical fact that the development of capitalism has been accompanied by a major reduction in the extent to which particular religious, racial, or social groups have operated under special handicaps in respect of their economic activities; have, as the saying goes, been discriminated against" (108).

10. See, for example, Gary S. Becker, *The Economics of Discrimination* (Chicago: University of Chicago Press, 1957). Since Becker's initial conception, law-and-economics scholars have posited that racial discrimination involves not just individual taste but coordinated action on the behalf of racialized "cartels." See, for example, Richard H. McAdams, "Cooperation and Conflict: The Economics of Group Status Production and Race Discrimination," *Harvard Law Review* 108 (1995): 1003–84. Nevertheless, even the cartel model predicts, under conventional law-and-economics analysis, that cascading defections will eventually cause racial discrimination to collapse. See Amanda P. Reeves and Maurice E. Stucke,

"Behavioral Antitrust," *Indiana Law Journal* 86 (2011): 1527–86 (1531): "The Chicago School's neoclassical economic theories teach that irrationality is irrelevant to antitrust doctrine: rational firms eliminate irrationality from the marketplace." See also Richard Epstein, *Forbidden Grounds: The Case Against Employment Discrimination Laws* (Cambridge, Mass.: Harvard University Press, 1992, 41–47, arguing that market forces cause racial cartels to crumble; and David E. Bernstein, "The Law and Economics of Post–Civil War Restrictions on Interstate Migration by African-Americans," *Texas Law Review* 76 (1998): 781–847 (825): "It is very difficult for a cartel, including a cartel of racist whites, to operate effectively unless the government intervenes on its behalf."

11. See, for example, Cass R. Sunstein, *The Partial Constitution* (Cambridge, Mass.: Harvard University Press, 1998), explaining that constitutional anti-discrimination remedies assume that the "baseline" of existing wealth and power distributions is just.

12. Morton v. Mancari, 417 U.S. 535 (1974).

13. Native Hawaiians, who lack federal recognition as "Indians" despite their indigenous identity, fell victim to this distinction when the U.S. Supreme Court struck down a voting scheme that gave only "native Hawaiians" the right to vote on trustees for the Office of Hawaiian Affairs. Rice v. Cayetano, 528 U.S. 495 (2000). In its opinion, the majority likened this state voting scheme, intended as a means of indigenous self-determination, to twentieth-century white attempts to prevent black people from voting such as poll taxes and literacy tests.

14. See Bethany R. Berger, "Red: Racism and the American Indian," *UCLA Law Review* 56 (2009): 591–656; Addie Rolnick, "The Promise of *Mancari*: Indian Political Rights as Racial Remedy," *NYU Law Review* 86 (2011): 958–1045.

15. There are, of course, exceptions, such as a hardy band of "critical tax" scholars and feminist- and/or CRT-informed incursions into corporate governance. See, for example, Karen B. Brown, Mary Louise Fellows, and Bridget J. Crawford, "The Past, Present, and Future of Critical Tax Theory," *Pittsburgh Tax Review* 10 (2012): 59–67; Darren Rosenblum, "Feminizing Capital: A Corporate Imperative," *Berkeley Business Law Journal* 6 (2009): 55–95.

16. Stephanie Lee Mudge, "What Is Neo-Liberalism?" *Socio-Economic Review* 6, no. 4 (2008): 703–31, https://doi.org/10.1093/ser/mwn016. Neoliberalism's intellectual face, Mudge argues, is distinguished by its "Anglo-American-anchored transnationality," its birth in the Cold War and the institutions of welfare capitalism, and, most notably, its "unadulterated emphasis on the (disembedded) market as the source and arbiter of human freedoms." Its bureaucratic face involves directions in state policy toward deregulation, privatization, and the commodification of goods conventionally understood as public, such as education and health care (704).

17. See Martha T. McCluskey, "Efficiency and Social Citizenship: Challenging the Neoliberal Attack on the Welfare State," *Indiana Law Journal* 78 (2003): 783–876. As a recent example, immediately after the first tranche of federal aid to individuals and businesses ravaged by the COVID-19 pandemic, commentators began to argue that

further relief would constitute a "moral hazard." See Neil Irwin, "How Bailout Backlash and Moral Hazard Outrage Could Endanger the Economy," *New York Times*, May 4, 2020, https://www.nytimes.com/2020/05/04/upshot/bailout-backlash -moral-hazard.html.

18. See Robert L. Hale, "Coercion and Distribution in a Supposedly Non-Neutral State," *Political Science Quarterly* 38 (1923): 470–94.

19. Ron Harris, "The Uses of History in Law and Economics," *Theoretical Inquiries in Law* 4, no. 2 (2003): 659–96 (664). As Harris notes, this project ignored other possible lines of inquiry for law-and-economics.

20. Pareto efficiency has been met when there is no rearrangement of resources that can make anyone better off without making someone worse off, where "better off" and "worse off" are defined in terms of each individual's evaluation of his or her own welfare. See A. Mitchell Polinsky, "Economic Analysis as a Potentially Defective Product: A Buyer's Guide to Posner's *Economic Analysis of Law*," *Harvard Law Review* 87 (1974): 1655–81 (1664). As this bemused legal scholar observed soon after the book appeared, "Posner argues his case in an adversary spirit, and although he initially concedes that his analysis has limitations, he virtually ignores them and their implications thereafter" (1657).

21. *Ibid.*, 1657.

22. McCluskey, "Efficiency and Social Citizenship," 785.

23. Like other neoliberal governance projects, cost-benefit analysis (CBA) is not promoted only by Republican administrations; one of its proponents, for instance, is Cass Sunstein, who ran the White House Office of Information and Regulatory Affairs under President Obama. See Cass R. Sunstein, "The Big Ideas Behind OIRA," *Regulatory Review*, September 9, 2013, https://www.theregreview.org/2013 /09/09/09-sunstein-big-ideas-oira/, describing OIRA's version of cost-benefit analysis as "humanized." Critics argue, however, that the more formal (i.e., mathematically rigorous) cost-benefit analysis is, the more it obscures policy choices under a false veneer of objectivity. See, for example, Amy Sinden, "Windmills and Holy Grails," *Legislation and Public Policy* 19, no. 2 (2016): 281–90. Sinden concludes that formal CBA is not only technically unworkable; it "undercounts the preferences of the poor vis-à-vis the rich, devalues the lives of our children and grandchildren, ignores distributional inequities, fails to account for low-probability catastrophic outcomes, and [. . .] rests on a vision of human nature and behavior that has been shown to be fundamentally flawed and internally inconsistent" (289).

24. As Martha McCluskey observes, from the assumption that first markets make and then citizens take flows "the deduction that redistribution tends to be the mark of non-citizens or subordinate citizens: those who are deemed inadequate to assume the responsibilities of freedom because of their incapacity or incivility." McCluskey, "Efficiency and Social Citizenship," 789.

25. See Richard Delgado and Jean Stefancic, *No Mercy: How Conservative Think Tanks and Foundations Changed America's Social Agenda* (Philadelphia: Temple University Press, 1996).

26. Erik Olin Wright usefully analyzes various governance assemblages as combinations of state, market, and social power. See Erik Olin Wright, "Compass Points: Toward a Socialist Alternative," *New Left Review* 41 (2006): 93–124.

27. See, for example, Derrick A. Bell, *Faces at the Bottom of the Well: The Permanence of Racism* (New York: Basic, 1992).

28. See, for example, Katharina Pistor, *The Code of Capital: How the Law Creates Wealth and Inequality* (Princeton, N.J.: Princeton University Press, 2019); Christine Desan, *Making Money: Coin, Currency, and the Coming of Capitalism* (New York: Oxford University Press, 2014); David Singh Grewal and Jedediah Purdy, "Introduction: Law and Neoliberalism," *Law and Contemporary Problems* 77, no. 4 (2014): 1–23; Amy Kapczynski, "The Law of Informational Capitalism," *Yale Law Journal* 129, no. 5 (2020): 1276–1599. These scholars are part of a new movement called "law and political economy," of which I am also a part.

29. See, for example, the essay by K-Sue Park in this volume.

30. Brenna Bhandar, *Colonial Lives of Property: Law, Land, and Racial Regimes of Ownership* (Durham, N.C.: Duke University Press, 2018); Aileen Moreton-Robinson, *The White Possessive: Property, Power, and Indigenous Sovereignty* (Minneapolis: University of Minnesota Press, 2015); Glen Sean Coulthard, *Red Skin, White Masks: Rejecting the Colonial Politics of Recognition* (Minneapolis: University of Minnesota Press, 2014).

31. See, for example, Antony Anghie, *Imperialism, Sovereignty, and the Making of International Law* (Cambridge: Cambridge University Press, 2005); Sarah H. Cleveland, "Powers Inherent in Sovereignty: Indians, Aliens, Territories, and the Nineteenth Century Origins of Plenary Power Over Foreign Affairs," *Texas Law Review* 81, no. 1 (2002): 1–284; Cheryl Harris, "Whiteness as Property," *Harvard Law Review* 106, no. 8 (1993): 1707–91.

32. Emma Coleman Jordan, "The Hidden Structures of Inequality: The Federal Reserve and a Cascade of Failures," *University of Pennsylvania Journal of Law & Public Affairs* 2 (2017): 107–84.

33. Mehrsa Baradaran, *The Color of Money: Black Banks and the Racial Wealth Gap* (Cambridge, Mass.: Harvard University Press, 2019).

34. Daria Roithmayr, *Reproducing Racism: How Everyday Choices Lock in White Advantage* (New York: New York University Press, 2014).

35. Bernadette Atuahene, "Dignity Takings and Dignity Restoration: Creating a New Theoretical Framework for Understanding Involuntary Property Loss and the Remedies Required," *Law & Social Inquiry* 41, no. 4 (2016): 796–823; Bernadette Atuahene, "Predatory Cities," *California Law Review* 108, no. 1 (2020): 107–82.

36. Charlotte S. Alexander, "Explaining Peripheral Labor: A Poultry Industry Case Study," *Berkeley Journal of Employment & Labor Law* 33, no. 2 (2012): 353–400; Andrea Freeman, "The Unbearable Whiteness of Milk: Food Oppression and the USDA," *UC Irvine Law Review* 3, no. 4 (2013): 1251–80; Carmen G. Gonzalez, "Markets, Monocultures, and Malnutrition: Agricultural Trade Policy Through an Environmental Justice Lens," *Michigan State Journal of International Law* 14, no. 2 (2006): 345–82; Guadalupe T. Luna, "Agricultural Underdogs" and

International Agreements: The Legal Context of Agricultural Workers Within the Rural Economy," *New Mexico Law Review* 26, no. 1 (1996): 9–56; Anne Orford, "Food Security, Free Trade, and the Battle for the State," *Journal of International Law and International Relations* 11, no. 2 (2015): 1–67; Anna Williams Shavers, "Welcome to the Jungle: New Immigrants in the Meatpacking and Poultry Processing Industry," *Journal of Law, Economics, & Policy* 5, no. 1 (2009): 31–86.

37. See African American Policy Forum, "Under the Blacklight: The Intersectional Vulnerabilities That COVID Lays Bare," https://aapf.org/aapfcovid.

38. Safiya Noble, *Algorithms of Oppression: How Search Engines Reinforce Racism* (New York: New York University Press, 2018); Bennett Capers, "Race, Policing, and Technology," *North Carolina Law Review* 95, no. 4 (2017): 1241–92.

39. Marion Fourcade and Kieran Healy, "Seeing Like a Market," *Socio-Economic Review* 15, no. 1 (2017): 9–29.

40. See Susan Moller Okin, *Justice, Gender, and the Family* (New York: Basic, 1989), noting that the family has been coded "private" and not subject to norms of justice; Frances E. Olsen, "The Family, the Market, and the State: A Study of Ideology and Legal Reform," *Harvard Law Review* 96, no. 7 (1983): 1497–1578, tracking the shifting designations of "public" and "private" in legal and political discourse.

41. See, for example, Michael M'Gonigle and Louise Takeda, "The Liberal Limits of Environmental Law: A Green Legal Critique," *Pace Environmental Law Review* 30, no. 3 (2013): 1005–1115; see also Carmen G. Gonzalez and Sumudu Attapatu, "International Environmental Law, Environmental Justice, and the Global South," *Transnational Law and Contemporary Problems* 26, no. 2 (2017): 229–42.

42. See, for example, Sylvia Wynter, "Unsettling the Coloniality of Being/Power/Truth /Freedom: Towards the Human, After Man, Its Overrepresentation—An Argument," CR: *The New Centennial Review* 3, no. 3 (2003): 257–337; Walter D. Mignolo, "Who Speaks for the Human in Human Rights?" *Hispanic Issues on Line* (Special Issue: Human Rights in Latin America and Iberian Cultures) 5, no.1 (2009): 7–25.

43. Daniel Bonilla Maldonado, "Environmental Radical Constitutionalism and Cultural Diversity in Latin America: The Rights of Nature and Buen Vivir in Ecuador and Bolivia," *Revista Derecho del Estado* 42 (2019): 3–24; Jacinta Ruru, "Finding Support for a Changed Property Discourse for Aotearoa New Zealand in the United Nations Declaration on the Rights of Indigenous Peoples," *Lewis & Clark Law Review* 15, no. 4 (2011): 951–74; D. Kapu'ala Sproat, "An Indigenous People's Right to Environmental Self-Determination: Native Hawaiians and the Struggle Against Climate Change Devastation," *Stanford Environmental Law Journal* 35, no. 2 (2016): 157–222; Kyle P. Whyte, "Indigenous Environmental Movements and the Function of Governance Institutions," in *Oxford Handbook of Environmental Political Theory*, ed. Teena Gabrielson, Cheryl Hall, John M. Meyer, and David Schlosberg (New York: Oxford University Press, 2016), 563–80.

44. Angela P. Harris, "Anti-Colonial Pedagogies: [X] Justice Movements in the United States," *Canadian Journal of Women and the Law* 30, no. 3 (2018): 567–94.

45. As the Climate Justice Alliance, a movement of movements in support of a just transition, explains ("What Do We Mean by Just Transition?," https://climatejusticealliance.org/just-transition/):

   Just Transition strategies were first forged by labor unions and environmental justice groups, rooted in low-income communities of color, who saw the need to phase out the industries that were harming workers, community health and the planet; and at the same time provide just pathways for workers to transition to other jobs. . . .

   Building on these histories, members of the Climate Justice Alliance, many of whom are rooted in the environmental justice movement, have adapted the definition of Just Transition to represent a host of strategies to transition whole communities to build thriving economies that provide dignified, productive and ecologically sustainable livelihoods; democratic governance and ecological resilience.

46. See Movement Generation Justice & Ecology Project, "Movement Generation Just Transition Framework Resources," https://movementgeneration.org/movement-generation-just-transition-framework-resources/; Sustainable Economies Law Center, "What We Do," https://www.theselc.org/what-we-do.

HISTORIES OF RACIAL CAPITALISM

INTRODUCTION

The Old History of Capitalism

DESTIN JENKINS AND JUSTIN LEROY

T he argument of this volume is simple. Racial capitalism is not one of capitalism's varieties. It does not stand alongside merchant, industrial, and financial as a permutation, phase, or stage in the history of capitalism writ large. Rather, from the beginnings of the Atlantic slave trade and the colonization of the Americas onward, all capitalism, in material profitability and ideological coherence, is constitutive of racial capitalism. In other words, we reverse the basic assumption that racial subjugation is a particular manifestation of a more universal capitalist system. The purpose of this argument is not to claim ownership over the field of capitalism studies or to narrow inquiries about capitalism to those that focus explicitly on race. To acknowledge capitalism as racial expands, rather than particularizes, our sense of what capitalism is. Racial capitalism also asks us to recognize that seemingly race-neutral archetypes of capitalism are in fact thoroughly racialized—after all, what is the ubiquitous "white working class" if not a subject of racial capitalism?[1]

Why Racial Capitalism?

It has become a kind of common sense that the 2008 financial crisis, subsequent bank bailouts, and the "second Gilded Age" of unprecedented income inequality helped generate interest in and support for academic work on the history of capitalism. For some historians who do not work on race, capitalism became a topic of renewed interest at a moment when the logics of capitalism seemed to be breaking down—in other words, when capitalism was no longer working for its presumptive, universalized white working- or middle-class subjects.[2] While a handful of scholars rigorously interrogated the racial dynamics at the heart of the so-called subprime mortgage crisis and the web of race, debt, and financial innovation at its heart, many commentators, both academic and popular, did not.[3] The notion that a racial critique of capitalism must always be subordinate to a more universal critique has been an analytical problem since Marx.[4] And much of the post-2008 scholarship on the history of capitalism has developed in ways that continue to reduce race to epiphenomenon, to superstructure, to particular example rather than general principle.

The financial crisis came as Americans were asking whether the election of Barack Obama meant the "end of race." That the question could be raised at all in the midst of a highly racialized economic crisis suggests the extent to which discussions of race and capitalism have been divorced from one another. If such questions did not seem disingenuous in 2008, they certainly do a decade later amid the resurgence of open white supremacy and racial revanchism under the presidency of Donald Trump. And although it is abundantly clear that we are not in a postracial era, the insistence that white support for Trump and his policies can be explained by economic anxieties confirms the need to separate race from capitalism operates as an analytical instinct and ideological strategy shared by liberals and some leftists alike.[5]

The devastating effects of the subprime crisis for communities of color, and the ways in which racialized economic predation was one of its major components, compelled scholars and activists to take up questions of racial capitalism. Even if it does not use the term explicitly, or uses it only in passing, recent work on the prison-industrial complex has illuminated the reinforcing processes of criminalization, labor extraction, and profit; the Movement for Black Lives has mobilized renewed understandings of the relationship between antiblack violence and economic immiseration; and indigenous movements have fought the logic of economic development in the name of Native sovereignty and environmental protection at the Dakota Access Pipeline, Alberta tar sands, and Mauna Kea. These and other examples suggest an urgent need to understand the intersections of white supremacy, race, colonialism, and capital. The purpose of this volume is to offer genuinely dynamic accounts of the historical relationship between economic relations of exploitation and the racial terms through which they were organized, justified, and contested. Put another way, we hope the flexible yet analytically rigorous uses of racial capitalism here—and the debates and arguments they elicit—will clarify the term and be of use to intellectuals and organizers in the political struggles of today and tomorrow.

Debating Racial Capitalism

Definitional debates are a hallmark of the historiography of capitalism, no less so in current than in classic scholarship. There are many varieties of capitalism, and an insistence on a pithy definition serves to obscure as much as it illuminates. To draw too sharp a distinction between capitalist and noncapitalist is usually to willfully mystify how capitalism works by ignoring that which is necessary but falls outside capitalism's own definitional terms. Among the recent work, an important—but contested— intervention has been to place an emphasis on explaining how capitalism works rather than setting out to define precisely what capitalism is; although resisting definitions completely can naturalize capitalism and render it ahistorical, overly narrow definitions produce an exclusionary effect.[6] That said, racial capitalism is the process by which the key dynamics of capitalism—accumulation/dispossession, credit/debt, production/surplus, capitalist/worker, developed/underdeveloped, contract/coercion, and others—become articulated through race. In other words, capital has not historically accumulated without previously existing relations of racial inequality. This process functions in two ways. First, the violent dispossessions inherent to capital accumulation operate by leveraging, intensifying, and creating racial distinctions. Second, race serves as a tool for naturalizing the inequalities produced by capitalism, and this racialized process of naturalization serves to rationalize the unequal distribution of resources, social power, rights, and privileges. Racial capitalism is a highly malleable structure. It has at times relied on open methods of exploitation and expropriation that wrench racialized populations into capitalist modes of production and accumulation, such as slavery, colonialism, and enclosure. But racial capitalism also relies on exclusion from those same modes of production and accumulation in the form of containment, incarceration, abandonment, and underdevelopment for a racial surplus population. The maintenance of racial capitalism can even rely on the limited inclusion and participation of racially marked populations; by extending credit and

political rights to these populations, the pervasive "racial" of racial capitalism recedes, entrenching itself through obfuscation.[7]

Cedric Robinson established the dominant critical understanding of
racial capitalism in *Black Marxism: The Making of the Black Radical
Tradition*. Originally published in 1983, *Black Marxism* remained a relatively
obscure text until its republication in 2000, which introduced a new generation of readers to the language of racial capitalism. But while Robinson
popularized the term, he did not invent it. The term first cohered around the
struggle to end apartheid and white supremacy in 1970s South Africa, pro-
voking contentious debate among intellectuals and activists. Some used
racial capitalism to explain the unique racial-economic conditions of South
Africa, while others dismissed it as a ruse by white Marxists seeking to make
race the invention of class conflict. The term eventually found some purchase, and in 1983, Neville Alexander—formerly imprisoned alongside
Nelson Mandela and cofounder of the National Forum, an amalgamation of
leftist organizations—included the language of racial capitalism in the
National Forum's founding manifesto:

> Our struggle for national liberation is directed against the system of racial
> capitalism that holds the people of Azania [South Africa] in bondage for the
> benefit of the small minority of white capitalists and their allies, the white
> workers and reactionary sections of the black middle classes. The struggle
> against apartheid is no more than the point of departure for our liberation
> efforts. Apartheid will be eradicated with the system of racial capitalism.[8]

Robinson drew from these debates and developed the concept of racial
capitalism "from a description of a *specific* system to a way of understanding
the *general* history of modern capitalism."[9] In *Black Marxism* he argued that
capitalism did not flatten, eliminate, or homogenize older forms of social
difference into more universal class differences. Quite the opposite, capitalism's emergence in Europe followed a path cut by feudal forms of social
particularity, heightening and transforming them into the modern notion
of race. For Robinson, "the creation of capitalism was much more than a
matter of the displacement of feudal modes and relations of production";
against classical Marxist accounts of the transition to capitalism, he argued
that "capitalism was less a catastrophic revolution (negation) of feudalist
social orders than the extension of these social relations into the larger
tapestry of the modern world's political and economic relations."[10]

Because capitalism emerged from a feudal society already rife with forms of ethnic, religious, and national division, and because capitalism did not erase but amplified these divisions, Robinson claimed that the "development, organization, and expansion of capitalist society pursued essentially racial directions."[11] Although medieval and early modern forms of difference were not unique to Europe, the fact that capitalism developed within Europe and in the context of its expansion into the Americas has given the processes of racialization that came out of this Atlantic crucible—exemplified finally in racial discourses about Africans and indigenous peoples—an exceptional place in the history of capitalism.[12] It was these processes that allowed Robinson to argue that the "historical development of world capitalism was influenced in a most fundamental way by the particularistic forces of racism and nationalism."[13] This influence was not incidental or momentary, but integral to the origin and operation of capitalism. In a final refutation of conventional theories of proletarianization, Robinson concluded, "the tendency of European civilization through capitalism was thus not to homogenize but to differentiate—to exaggerate regional, subcultural, and dialectical differences into 'racial' ones."[14]

For Robinson, the "racial" in racial capitalism was a capacious and often ambiguous analytic that sometimes bore an unclear relationship to modern forms of racialization. This linguistic challenge was exacerbated by a new preface to the 2000 edition of *Black Marxism*, in which Robinson identified Aristotle's denigration of women, non-Greeks, and laborers as the beginning of an "uncompromising racial construct." Centuries later, the European feudal order "reiterated and embellished this racial calculus."[15] Because of Robinson's use of the word *racial* to describe a staggering array of social categories across an equally staggering period of time, a reader might be forgiven for interpreting his claims about race as inattentive to historical specificity, or even as ahistorical. Yet word choice in the preface aside, *Black Marxism* resists such a reading. Robinson did not argue that race as we understand it today has existed since time immemorial, or that all forms of difference are reducible to race; he argued that the emergence of capitalism exaggerated older, precapitalist forms of social difference *into* racial difference.[16] Robinson was very clear, for example, that the early modern figures of the "blacke moore" and the "Ethiope" preceded that of the "Negro." The invention of the Negro was a historical process that came "at the cost of immense expenditures of psychic and intellectual energies in the West."[17] In Robinson's account, the successful Spanish revolt against

Muslim rule in Granada completed the process of removing "the Islamic intrusion into European history." Because Islam was long associated with Africa in the European mind, for Robinson the Reconquista represented the culmination of the European disavowal of Africa's role in its own history. Cleft from that history, Africans became empty vessels, and "for the Negro to come into being all what was now required was an immediate cause, a specific purpose."[18] That purpose, of course, was Atlantic slavery. Thus race making was a process driven by capitalist development itself in the form of the slave trade, and it was an "effort commensurate with the importance Black labor power possessed for the world economy sculpted and dominated by the ruling and mercantile classes of Western Europe."[19] The modern concept of race, in other words, built upon but was not identical to earlier forms of difference.

Robinson told an origin story about capitalism that made domination based on difference the main event, the lead character, the inciting incident. But if the manifestation of race, in its modern form, took a herculean effort on the part of capitalist forces to coax into being, why were the "racial construct" of antiquity and the "racial calculus" of the Middle Ages so central to the argument of *Black Marxism*? For Robinson, a key through line in European history was economic domination predicated upon, justified by, and rooted in social theories of deep, even existential, difference: "The function of the laboring classes was to provide the state and its privileged classes with the material and human resources needed for their maintenance and further accumulations of power and wealth. This was not, however, a simple question of the dominance of a ruling class over the masses. The masses did not exist as such."[20] The difference between the ruling classes and the lower orders, for Robinson, was not simply one of wealth, but rather one of culture, religion, ethnicity, and nationality. Thus "this European civilization, containing racial, tribal, linguistic, and regional particularities, was constructed on antagonistic differences," and capitalism calcified those differences into race.[21]

Robinson was part of a cohort of scholars who theorized and debated the relationship between race and capitalism through histories of slavery, imperialism, and beyond. This work spans the twentieth century. We might term this body of scholarship the "old history of capitalism" to further emphasize that the study of racial capitalism is not a reaction to or subfield within a "new" or "general" history of capitalism. The old history of capitalism offers two important insights. First, it helps to distinguish between the rather specific history of the *term* racial capitalism and the much broader *idea* of racial capitalism. Although these and other scholars did not use the specific language of racial capitalism, collectively their work and Robinson's laid bare the sedimented histories of race that developed alongside capitalism. Second, the old history of capitalism draws our attention to the remarkable range of thought concerning racial capitalism. Indeed, this intellectual cohort, composed primarily though not exclusively of black Marxists, did not always share an understanding of the precise nature of the relationship between race and capitalism.[22]

These differences are especially pronounced on the question of origins. Robinson argued that although capitalism effected the transformation of the African into the Negro, such a transformation ultimately represented an extension of older social dynamics rather than something totally novel. Others marked race in its modern form as a sharp break with what came before, the unambiguous creation of capitalism. Eric Williams, who famously argued that West Indian slavery was crucial to British industrialization, insisted that the origin of chattel slavery was "economic, not racial." Planters, he wrote, "would have gone to the moon, if necessary, for labor. Africa was nearer than the moon, nearer too than the more populous countries of India and China."[23] The Trinidadian-born sociologist Oliver Cromwell Cox argued in his first book, *Caste, Class, and Race*: "Racial antagonism is part and parcel of [the] class struggle, because it developed within the capitalist system as one of its fundamental traits. It may be demonstrated that racial antagonism, as we know it today, never existed in the world before about 1492; moreover, racial feeling developed concomitantly with the development of our modern social system."[24] In his 1972 classic on imperialism, *How Europe Underdeveloped Africa*, Walter Rodney came to a similar conclusion:

> It can be affirmed without reservations that the white racism which came to pervade the world was an integral part of the capitalist mode of production.... Occasionally, it is mistakenly held that Europeans enslaved Africans for racist reasons. European planters and miners enslaved Africans for *economic* reasons, so that their labor power could be exploited.... Oppression of African people on purely racial grounds accompanied, strengthened, and became indistinguishable from oppression for economic reasons.[25]

Historian Barbara J. Fields has made the most influential contribution to the origins debates in the context of the United States, challenging the long-standing notion that the relationship between slavery and freedom in

U.S. history represents a "paradox."[26] Fields took to task historians who wrote about slavery "as primarily a system of race relations—as though the chief business of slavery were the production of white supremacy rather than the production of cotton, sugar, rice, and tobacco." In one of the most pithy and incisive explanations for the raw necessity of race in American social and economic life, Fields wrote, "Those holding liberty to be inalienable and holding Afro-Americans as slaves were bound to end by holding race to be a self-evident truth. . . . When self-evident laws of nature guarantee freedom, only equally self-evident laws of equally self-evident nature can account for its denial." For reasons of culture, religion, nationality, appearance, and custom, the labor of Africans was easier to exploit than that of English indentured servants, "but that did not add up to an ideology of racial inferiority" until the language of universal liberty took hold. Put simply, for Fields, the economic exploitation of enslaved Africans preceded their racialization as black.

Other scholars in this tradition were not concerned with the precise origins of capitalism's entanglement with race, and instead theorized the nature and meaning of that relationship to offer radically countervailing explanations for the racial and economic violence that black people and even black nations experienced. In her groundbreaking writings on lynching, Ida B. Wells reversed the prevailing understanding that lynching was a response to black criminality unleashed in the wake of emancipation. She argued that lynching was in fact directed toward upwardly mobile black people, "an excuse to get rid of Negroes who were acquiring wealth and property and thus keep the race terrorized and 'the nigger down.' "[27] Wells framed lynching as a weapon of the Southern capitalist class, part of the arsenal they used to maintain the racial-economic order. Indeed, "threats of lynching were freely indulged, not by the lawless element upon which the devilry of the South is usually saddled—but by the leading business men, in their leading business centre."[28] In *Black Reconstruction*, W. E. B. Du Bois described whiteness itself as "a sort of public and psychological wage" that could quell discontent about the paucity of actual wages among white workers.[29] And in his classic account *How Capitalism Underdeveloped Black America*, Manning Marable described the United States as both a capitalist state and a racial state, arguing: "Capitalist development has occurred not in spite of the exclusion of Blacks, but because of the brutal exploitation of Blacks as workers and consumers. Blacks have never been equal partners in the American Social Contract, because the system exists not to develop, but to *underdevelop Black people*. . . . Because of its peculiar historical development, the U.S. is not just a capitalist state, but with South Africa, is a *racist/capitalist state.*" For Marable the results of such a state were clear: "A capitalist/racist state still attempts to resolve problems within the Black community via fraud rather than force, just as it does for whites. Nevertheless, there remains a greater reliance on the omnipresence of coercion aimed at Blacks than at whites." He thus concluded that life under capitalism is a constitutively different experience for black people, and that "it is in the interests of capital, in final analysis, that permits the climate of racist terrorism to continue."[30]

These analyses of capitalism also addressed the racial dynamics of imperialism. In "The African Roots of the War," Du Bois described European peace, prosperity, and nationality itself as a kind of dividend of colonialism: "It is no longer simply the merchant prince, or the aristocratic monopoly, or even the employing class, that is exploiting the world: it is the nation, a new democratic nation composed of united capital and labor."[31] Du Bois suggested the emergence of a new cross-class alignment between the bourgeoisie and the labor aristocracy within the global North. The new class compact was lived and articulated through racial knowledge (about the "Negro" and the "native") and racialized practices (of exclusion, violence, and murder). In his masterful account of the Haitian Revolution, C. L. R. James wrote: "The race question is subsidiary to the class question in politics, and to think of imperialism in terms of race is disastrous. But to neglect the racial factor as merely incidental is an error only less grave than to make it fundamental."[32] James here referred to the idea that one of the Saint Domingue revolutionaries' failures was to see their struggle against the capitalist planter class as one primarily of racial rather than class antagonism; for James, this understanding prevented them from seeing whites as allies, either reluctant (French bourgeoisie who remained on the island) or enthusiastic (French Jacobins who might have seen their own revolutionary aims as being in line with those of the enslaved). Rodney, on the other hand, wrote of imperialism as an extension of the division between capital and labor on the world stage, emphasizing "the actual ownership of the means of production in one country by citizens of another," which "from an African viewpoint . . . amounted to consistent expatriation of surplus produced by African labor out of African resources." In the same way that the capitalist grew wealthy by claiming the surplus value produced by wage laborers as his own, colonialism "meant the development of Europe as part of the same dialectical process in which Africa was underdeveloped."[33]

These old historians of capitalism probed the relationship between race and capitalism but did not define or utilize race in the same ways. These differences not only demand substantive engagement with the subtleties of their work but also reinforce our position that racial capitalism is expansive, malleable, and changes over time.

The Difference Racial Capitalism Makes

Racial capitalism makes a temporal claim upon the study of capitalism; to think with racial capitalism is to rethink the past, present, and futures of capitalism. Racial capitalism is not a moment anterior to deracinated capitalism, nor does capitalism's racial character diminish or disappear over time. It is also a methodological practice—a way of seeing—that asks practitioners to question the structuring idioms, themes, and subjects in the study of capitalism in the present. Finally, the analytic of racial capitalism also suggests a future-oriented political analysis that cautions against either a "race first" or a "class first" approach toward social justice.

The concept of racial capitalism is chronologically and sequentially disruptive. At stake in Robinson's argument—that through race, capitalism represented not a break with but a heightening of the social dynamics of feudalism—was a radical revision of Marx's own account of historical periodization and capitalism's emergence. In *Capital*, Marx wrote:

> The discovery of gold and silver in America, the extirpation, enslavement and entombment in mines of the aboriginal population, the beginning of the conquest and looting of the East Indies, the turning of Africa into a warren for the commercial hunting of black-skins, signalized the rosy dawn of the era of capitalist production. These idyllic proceedings are the chief moments of primitive accumulation.... The so-called primitive accumulation, therefore, is nothing else than the historical process of divorcing the producer from the means of production. It appears as primitive, because it forms the prehistoric stage of capital and of the mode of production corresponding with it.[34]

Marx recognized the critical historical importance of slavery and colonialism but categorized them as a form of "primitive" or precapitalist accumulation. For Marx these forms of racialized accumulation were the conditioning possibilities of capitalism even as he placed them before capitalism proper chronologically. Drawing upon indigenous and settler colonial studies scholars who have expounded on Patrick Wolfe's formulation that the invasion of indigenous lands is not a single moment in time but an ongoing structuring logic in all settler societies, our conception of racial capitalism frames primitive accumulation as an ongoing organizing principle of capitalist social order.[35]

Although the old history of capitalism put slavery under capitalism's purview even when Marx would not, racial capitalism is not coterminous with slavery, and its operation is not consigned to any particular historical moment. Rather, racial capitalism marks a historical intimacy among the slave trade, enslavement, and colonialism that often goes unacknowledged, but also captures the way slavery epitomized a racialized system of valuation and extraction that continues to this day. Alongside indigenous dispossession, slavery inaugurated that system, yet the system survived slavery's demise—and thrived.[36] Moon-Ho Jung has shown how the failed effort of Louisiana sugar planters to secure labor in the wake of the Civil War was intimately tied up with their irrational rendering of Chinese migrant laborers as possessing white traits in some instances and the insistence that in others they were "a sorry substitute for our former negro slaves."[37] Sarah Haley has argued that the economic modernization of the Jim Crow South was predicated on the racial and gendered ideology of black female deviance; through convict leasing, the firms of the New South secured cheap labor that literally paved the road for corporate capitalism.[38] The end of slavery signifies the malleability and resilience of racial capitalism despite the otherwise momentous nature of emancipation. To quote one writer and social critic, "while emancipation dead-bolted the door against the bandits of America, Jim Crow wedged the windows wide open."[39]

Few scholars of racial capitalism have taken up the question of the feudalist transition since Robinson. They have, however, offered other ways of theorizing historical continuities and repetitions under racial capitalism. We might think about the reproduction of racial capitalism through investment capital or through reparations paid to former slave owners, some of whom invested compensatory funds in efforts to recruit South Asian laborers— racialized as "coolies"—to the plantations of British Guiana.[40] Saidiya Hartman's notion of the afterlife of slavery captures how "black lives are still imperiled and devalued by a racial calculus and political arithmetic that were entrenched centuries ago."[41] And as Du Bois famously wrote of

Reconstruction, "the slave went free; stood a brief moment in the sun; then moved back toward slavery."[42] These temporal formulations reject the idea that the current entanglement of race and capitalism is an echo of the past that has diminished over time, or that it is a relationship born out of historical contingency rather than structuring essence. The temporality of racial capitalism is one of ongoingness, even if its precise nature is dynamic and changing. It is a process, not a moment, and several essays in this volume build upon these heterodox theories of temporality. For example, Jenkins makes racial ideologies and narratives about racial governance central to the tripartite temporality of debt (past borrowing actions, present fiscal conditions, and future economic performance), while Leroy argues that the image of forward linear movement, no matter how uneven, cannot account for the shape of black history or black disappointments with freedom.

Racial capitalism also invites us to reconsider the methods and archives of capitalism's history. The contributors to this volume answer this invitation in a variety of ways, as when K-Sue Park situates the mortgage as a tool of dispossession rather than accumulation. By reframing one of the legal cornerstones of property, Park shows us what it might mean to focus on theft, plunder, and expropriation rather than entrepreneurship, innovation, and investment as key terms for understanding capitalism. The field of racial capitalism, this volume included, has an unsettled relationship to quantitative methods. While the quantitative has been—and should be—important to the study of capitalism, it has also been a way for critics of racial capitalism to dismiss the field's claims without wrestling with the content of its arguments. Eric Williams's classic study *Capitalism and Slavery*, for example, has been endlessly debated and criticized. Williams's essential arguments are first, that West Indian slavery was crucial to the development of Britain's industrial economy, and second, that the decision to abolish the slave trade (and eventually slavery) was economic rather than moral. At stake in these arguments is the notion that the rise of the global North was predicated upon the immiseration of millions in the global South, and a rejection of the idea that capitalism produced any kind of moral orientation toward antislavery. With a few notable exceptions, critics have focused on precisely how Williams quantified slavery's contributions to the British economy rather than on the force of his more ideological claims.[43]

As scholars of racial capitalism, we wish to caution against the authority of the quantitative even as we recognize its usefulness. Numbers, like all forms of evidence, serve a performative function. As Mary Poovey reminds us, until the early modern period, rhetoric was the privileged mode of evidentiary adjudication, and double-entry bookkeeping—so important to the rise of slavery and the rise of capitalism—was in part a tool for merchants who used it to wrest a monopoly on knowledge claims from higher-status clergy and academics. Accounting served a social function as it helped to redefine what counted (and still counts) as evidence.[44] The right numbers will not prove the existence of racial capitalism to skeptics; the impossibly large sums calculated by scholars working on slavery reparations or the value of Native land treaties have never been authoritative enough to affirm the central importance of racial dispossession in building the wealth of the global North.[45]

Writers in the tradition of the old history of capitalism were also actively engaged in radical political organizing. As they wrote about capitalism's past, they were building and imagining an anticapitalist world yet to come. The framework of racial capitalism, then, makes two related claims upon the future. First, racial justice cannot be achieved by subsuming it under a generalized call for economic justice; the racially differentiated distribution of suffering under capitalism will not be rectified without a robust analysis of race. Second, capitalism cannot be rehabilitated through the inclusion of previously excluded groups; the racial violence of capitalism does not end where political and legal rights begin.

Du Bois famously described enslaved people's flight from plantations during the Civil War as "a general strike against slavery."[46] In applying the language of labor activism to the plantation regime, Du Bois was insisting the problems of labor and class were always also problems of race, and his conclusion is borne out throughout the historiography. Marx memorably wrote, "Labour in a white skin cannot emancipate itself where it is branded in a black skin."[47] A. Philip Randolph, leader of the Brotherhood of Sleeping Car Porters—one of the first black labor unions—updated Marx's maxim for the postemancipation world: "Negro workers are not yet fully free in the South. By the same token, white workers in the South are not yet fully free, because no white worker can ever become fully free as long as a black worker is in southern Bourbon bondage."[48] If capitalism seeks the cheapest labor costs, and black workers command the lowest wages, then racial inequality will limit the ability of white workers to demand higher wages.

For other writers, slavery represented not simply *a* labor problem, but *the* labor problem, a foundational structure for understanding economic justice in the United States. Oliver Cox wrote: "It should not be forgotten that, above all else, the *slave* was a worker whose labor was exploited in production for profit in a capitalist market. It is this fundamental fact which identifies the Negro problem in the United States with the problem of all workers regardless of color."[49] Like Du Bois, C. L. R. James saw enslaved people as antibourgeoisie agents during the Civil War, and while they might not have been familiar with strikes and unions, James argued, "the Negro people, we say, on the basis of their own experiences, approach the conclusions of Marxism."[50] And in the same address in which Martin Luther King, Jr. identified racism, capitalism, and war as "the triple evils that are interrelated," he argued: "A nation that will keep people in slavery for 244 years will 'thingify' them—make them things. Therefore they will exploit them, and poor people generally, economically."[51] For King, slavery was the blueprint for economic exploitation, the original experiment with human commodification that made callousness to poverty a part of American social ideology.

Yet the solution to capitalism is not to be found merely in formal racial equality and the extension of rights; important and necessary as those things are, they are not sufficient to address the racialized economic violence of capitalism. In her groundbreaking 1949 article on black women's militancy, "An End to the Neglect of the Problems of the Negro Woman!," the Trinidadian-born Communist Party leader Claudia Jones wrote, "the vaunted boast of the ideologists of big business—that American women possess 'the greatest equality in the world' . . . stops at the water's edge where Negro and working-class women are concerned."[52] Jones argued that the race/gender nexus revealed the deep and abiding inequalities that the capitalist pretensions to equality were meant to obfuscate. When American capitalists offered the rights of (white) American women as proof of capitalism's moral and economic superiority, Jones retorted with evidence of the "super-exploitation" of black women. The end of Jim Crow would not change the inability of rights to equalize or deracinate capitalism. In his 1968 foreword to *Negroes and Jobs*, Randolph argued: "Despite progress toward social and political equality, the Negro worker finds that his relative economic position is deteriorating or stagnating. . . . Long ago, during Reconstruction, the Negro learned the cruel lesson that social and political freedom cannot be sustained in the midst of economic insecurity and exploitation. He learned that freedom requires a material foundation."[53] As Jodi Melamed and Chandan Reddy caution, even the extension of rights can fall under the capture of capital when "racial capitalism repurposes the liberal idealization of 'individual rights' . . . to negate radical and collective uses of rights born from colonized and racialized peoples' movements." In other words, under racial capitalism, rights become abstracted and individuated, divorced from demands for justice (including economic justice). Rights are de-radicalized and transformed into "the right of capitalists and corporate 'persons' to be free from government (regulation and taxation) . . . individual rights concepts are recruited for the benefit of investor classes by amplifying new cultural norms on the part of government and business to dismiss the needs of others."[54] To reiterate Randolph, rights, like freedom, cannot be divorced from their material context.

To insist upon the inextricability of race and capitalism does not mean disavowing the transformative impact political and legal rights, on the one hand, and universalist economic reform, on the other, have had on communities of color. To embrace the concept of racial capitalism does not mean accepting the immutability or permanence of race. But the insights racial capitalism brings to the study of the past are also crucial for envisioning the future. If race came into being to justify the social dynamics of capitalism, then racial justice cannot thrive under capitalism.[55]

What This Volume Is and Isn't

This volume originated in a series of seminars, workshops, and writing groups at various institutions; it is the culmination of conversations between senior and junior scholars trained in the disciplines of history, American studies, race and ethnic studies fields (African American studies, Asian American studies, and Latinx studies), women's and gender studies, political science, law and political economy, and anthropology. Accordingly, the following essays engage with a wide range of sources and methods, a methodological mélange we take as foundational to the study of racial capitalism. The volume is arranged roughly in chronological order. However, because the contributors are attentive to what lingers and are deeply invested in the politics of the present and future, the essays have an unruly relationship to periodization, and, in some cases, speak directly to the struggles for multiracial democracy and against ecological crisis and violence in the present.

K-Sue Park offers the clearest formulation of what is at stake in the study of racial capitalism: What is the role of race in producing the economy? Park challenges the tendency to treat race as something that infects the market—an unfortunate externality, overflow, and incidental problem to an otherwise objective economy rooted in deracialized principles, practices, and conflicts. She disturbs this formulation by exploring the relationship between mortgage foreclosure and the production of racial difference between English colonists and Native people in seventeenth-century New England. Although the mortgage foreclosure was originally reserved for Native debt-holders, colonists soon turned the racially specific practice on each other, making foreclosure a generalized reality of debt. Park's story of racial capitalism is not one of primitive accumulation by financial means, but a probing meditation on what happens when a creative mode of racial violence expressed through financial instruments applies to an ever larger swath of the population.

Shauna Sweeney explores how gender produced ideological and material forms of value during the eighteenth and nineteenth centuries. Her essay is in part a meditation on the implications of gender as a category of analysis for theories of racial capitalism, in part an attempt to push beyond the masculinist framings of the black radical tradition. Focusing instead on black women's spiritual practices, Sweeney maintains that the preservation of self, family, and community was a heretical act of resistance in the face of racial capitalism's orthodoxy of black genocide. Drawing on the legacies of Atlantic world maroons, healers, and black female abolitionists and freedom fighters, the essay illuminates the distinctive ways black women resisted the "social death" of racial capitalism. Sweeney's essay provides a set of novel answers to the question, where is resistance in the history of racial capitalism?

Most of the contributions to this collection and the existing scholarship on racial capitalism remain focused on the Atlantic, and the North Atlantic in particular.[56] We take for granted the exceptionalism of Euro-American racial formations because of the European and American hegemony of the past several centuries and the ways those racial formations influence regions and populations that might never have been enslaved or subject to formal colonialism. Nevertheless, the overwhelming focus on the Atlantic raises important empirical and methodological questions. How well does the concept of racial capitalism travel to various global contexts? Is racial capitalism useful outside of the Atlantic?

Mishal Khan and Allan Lumba trace the routes of racial capitalism to India, the Philippines, and Hawai'i. Khan explores how debt bondage emerged and was nurtured by the limited vocabularies of freedom that lay beyond the world of abolition in the British Empire. Focused on the nineteenth century, her story moves from an exploration of the predicament of the Indian coolie, free enough to enter contracts and penalized for breach of contract, to the circulation of credit through racial logics to show how regimes of formally free labor in the Indian countryside were inflected through diverse ideologies of racial difference and inferiority. Khan examines the role that Indian labor played in a new expanding global economy—how Indian labor figured into the "vast and dark sea" of human labor, as Du Bois put it. But she does much more. Perhaps it is India, more than anywhere else, that affirms Robinson's contention that the advent of capitalism expanded feudal and precapitalist social relations of caste into race, rather than produce race as an a posteriori justification for economic exploitation.

Allan Lumba maintains that Cedric Robinson's analysis of racial capitalism resonates with transpacific experiences and relations within the contemporary world system. One need only look to two U.S. colonies, the extractive colony of the Philippines and the settler colony of Hawai'i, to see how the dyads of production/surplus were permeated by race, and containment befell a racial surplus population. Lumba not only expands the "where" of racial capitalism, providing something of a bridge between transpacific and transatlantic studies; through a focus on the recruitment and management of Filipino laborers, he also insists that in the Pacific there was no racial capitalism without settler colonialism. Racial capital accumulation did not occur without the militarized and administrative logics of colonialism.

Manu Karuka also theorizes imperialism in relationship to racial capitalism, by following the lines of the transcontinental railroad across the southwestern United States. It was here, in the agricultural and mining regions of an emerging industrial capitalist economy, that the contradiction between free land and free labor was resolved through the "counter-revolution of property," as Du Bois put it. Along the Colorado River and in the Arizona Territory, an alliance between the U.S. Army and finance capital during the Civil War presaged the rise of monopoly agribusiness in the decades to come. It also unlocked vast resources for corporations through the splintering effect of racial distinctions. These distinctions militated against worker solidarity, shaped a racial division of labor in railroad and mining, and depressed wages in the area's core industries.

Justin Leroy's essay troubles the slavery/freedom divide. Drawing on the writings of black thinkers who lived through and struggled against slavery, Leroy challenges our most fundamental understandings about historical change over time and the moral urgency of abolition. In his account, racial capitalism is more than an analytic. It also refers to more than a historical process and malleable structure. It is a philosophy of history, a rebellion against strict periodization that makes the notion of forward historical movement from slavery to freedom fraught. As a philosophy of history, racial capitalism helps us better frame the limits of emancipation as endemic to racial capitalism itself rather than failures of implementation or mere echoes of a previously destroyed system.

Running through a number of essays is a focus on debt. Perhaps it is the coercive terms, extended temporality, and redistributive consequences of debt that make credit and debt particularly revealing of transitions between different moments in racial capitalism's history. The essay by Destin Jenkins begins with the consequences of the Civil War and emancipation for southern municipal finance to underscore that the end of slavery was indeed a momentous event in the history of capitalism. It ends by exploring the "propaganda of history" and the ways racial difference was threaded through stories told by New South boosters to mobilize bond buyers. In between, Jenkins explores the paradox of Jim Crow. On the one hand, the stability of southern debt was effectively backed by a modern regime of racial terrorism and extreme labor control. On the other hand, racial violence, domination, and segregation could become a liability for bondholders. Striking black longshoremen and migrations could disrupt dependence on a steady labor force, the circulation of goods, and undermine the overall value of southern debt. With a focus on Mobile, Alabama, Jenkins directs our attention to the largely unexplored subject of municipal debt to offer a materialist history of race, labor, finance, and the ideological narratives surrounding racial capitalism.

Of the nine essays, Ryan Jobson's is the most ambivalent about the term *racial capitalism*. Jobson agrees that the crucial dynamics of capitalism have shaped and been shaped by racial differentiation, but he maintains that racial capitalism becomes less useful when we take it as a totalizing framework rather than a provocation to guide future research. When racial capitalism becomes the end rather than the beginning of our analysis, it becomes a political and intellectual dead end. Instead, he offers *racial capital* as a heuristic to explore the extractive complexes of the twentieth century. On this score, Jobson is clearly influenced by the theory of "fossil capital," but he departs from accounts that privilege various abstractions to account for the rise of fossil fuels, carbon emissions, and the Anthropocene. Drawing on the writings and personal papers of W. E. B. Du Bois—a "critical theorist of energy, race, and capital"—Jobson argues that the enslavement of African peoples constituted the broadest effort to consolidate stores of energy under private ownership, which should remind us that the private ownership of energy is a necessarily violent process, whether the source of that energy is fossil fuels, the harnessed energy of solar, wind, or water, or human labor power.

The story of racial capitalism is largely one of slavery, dispossession, theft, and plunder, but the malleability of racial capitalism is due in no small part to the participation of racially marked groups. With a focus on Puerto Rico and New York City, Pedro Regalado insists that we direct our attention to the nonwhite business of racial capitalism in the years since the 1960s. The rise and coherence of color-blind ideology belied the continued development of U.S. capitalism, and the political culture it molded, in essentially ethnic and racial directions. Latinx businesspeople, Regalado notes, embraced capitalism as both the "sword" that would lead to upward mobility and the "shield" that would protect the community from the racialized consequences of urban decline. They often wielded both in ways that reinforced racial and ethnic inequality. Through their ownership of Latinx banks and bodegas, some Latinx businesspeople were able to extract profit from Spanish-speaking communities and doubled down on their success by promoting procapitalist conceptions of social progress. Regalado's account is one of ethnoracial modes of accumulation, not unlike but distinct from black capitalism, that is also constitutive of the history of racial capitalism.

This volume is not the definitive history of racial capitalism. The plural title, *Histories of Racial Capitalism*, is deliberate, and the essays contribute to a larger intellectual pursuit that cannot be contained within a single collection. We have attempted to develop the analytical potential of racial capitalism by placing the concomitant development, operation, and legacies of chattel slavery and indigenous dispossession alongside one another. We have been motivated in part by the elision of colonialism in Robinson's discussion of racial capitalism and in part by an elision among midcentury black Atlantic thinkers who, despite offering a powerful anticolonial critique of slavery, "ignored the problem of dispossession so central to settler colonial formations."[57] As Walter Johnson reminds us, "the land that enslaved people planted in cotton and which their owners posted as collateral was Native American land: it had been expropriated from the Creek, the Cherokee, the Choctaw, the Chickasaw, and the Seminole."[58] Still, more work remains to be done on the potentially differential relationship of racial capitalism to slavery and colonialism.

Similarly, this volume does not fully develop what Sarah Haley has termed "gendered racial capitalism," or the relationship between the "carceral life of race and gender ideology" and "capitalist expansion."[59] Shatema Threadcraft has rightly queried "what a more sustained analysis of gender would mean for scholarship on racial capitalism."[60] Shauna Sweeney adds, "the answer, however, is not to incorporate black women into established frameworks but to ask a different set of questions . . . about the place of black women and gender in the construction of the very categories that scholars use to assess politics, economics, science, and medicine."[61] If capitalism did not homogenize but exaggerated older distinctions into racial ones, as Robinson claimed, did capitalism also exploit "existing gender-based hierarchies as it sought to establish itself" and, if so, to what effect? What is the work that patriarchy performs for racial capitalism?[62]

Writing through the analytic of racial capitalism should be a process of pushing, testing, and expanding its boundaries, not the elevation of race over other forms of social difference. Ultimately, our hope is to build upon the stunning work penned by the old historians of capitalism who treated the slave trade, slavery, antislavery, and slavery's afterlives as essential problems—the first causes—of modern history. They offered an analysis that militated against relegating race to a social or political problem that could be disentangled from capitalism through the extension of rights without first challenging capitalism's fundamental dynamic of domination through differentiation. Finally, we also hope these essays provoke consideration of how some arguments about the history and nature of capitalism become valorized, are elevated to common sense, or attain the status of the universal, while others remain controversial, particular, contingent, and subjective even in the face of compelling evidence.

NOTES

1. Cedric Robinson devotes an entire chapter to the racial nature of class consciousness among English workers. Cedric J. Robinson, *Black Marxism: The Making of the Black Radical Tradition* (Chapel Hill: University of North Carolina Press, [1983] 2000).

2. The "new history of capitalism" is quickly becoming a vast and porous field, but several excellent historiographical primers are Seth Rockman, "What Makes the History of Capitalism Newsworthy?," *Journal of the Early Republic* 34, no. 3 (Fall 2014): 439–66; Sven Beckert, "History of American Capitalism," in *American History Now*, ed. Eric Foner and Lisa McGirr (Philadelphia: Temple University Press, 2011), 314–35; Jeffrey Sklansky, "The Elusive Sovereign: New Intellectual and

Social Histories of Capitalism," *Modern Intellectual History* 9, no. 1 (2012): 233–48; Amy Dru Stanley, "Histories of Capitalism and Sex Difference," *Journal of the Early Republic* 36, no. 2 (2016): 343–50; Nan Enstad, "The 'Sonorous Summons' of the New History of Capitalism, Or, What Are We Talking About When We Talk About Economy?," *Modern American History* 2, no. 1 (2019): 83–95; Louis Hyman, "Why Write the History of Capitalism?," *Symposium Magazine*, July 8, 2013, http://www.symposium-magazine.com/why-write-the-history-of-capitalism-louis-hyman/; and Sven Beckert et al., "Interchange: The History of Capitalism," *Journal of American History* 101, no. 2 (September 2014): 503–36.

3. Of course, the notion of a "crisis" suggests that communities of color had not been trapped in cycles of debt and dispossession long before 2008—in other words, a crisis for whom? For an excellent introduction to these questions, see Paula Chakravarty and Denise Ferreira da Silva, eds., "Race, Empire, and the Crisis of the Subprime," special issue, *American Quarterly* 64, no. 3 (September 2012).

4. Although Marx would not have agreed with our argument that all capitalism is racial capitalism, he was far from an unsophisticated commentator when it came to race. See Kevin B. Anderson, *Marx at the Margins: On Nationalism, Ethnicity, and Non-Western Societies* (Chicago: University of Chicago Press, 2010); Karl Marx and Friedrich Engels, *The Civil War in the United States*, ed. Andrew Zimmerman (New York: International Publishers, 2017); and Walter Johnson, "The Pedestal and the Veil: Rethinking the Capitalism/Slavery Question," *Journal of the Early Republic* 24, no. 2 (Summer 2004): 299–308.

5. For an example of hostility toward the framework of racial capitalism in the left press, see Michael Waltzer, "A Note on Racial Capitalism," *Dissent*, July 29, 2020, https://www.dissentmagazine.org/online_articles/a-note-on-racial-capitalism. Waltzer's article is a response to a much more sympathetic piece by K. Sabeel Rahman, "Dismantle Racial Capitalism," *Dissent*, Summer 2020.

6. For a sense of the ongoing debates about the usefulness of defining capitalism, see Rockman, "What Makes the History of Capitalism Newsworthy?"; Beckert et al., "Interchange: The History of Capitalism"; Jonathan Levy, "Capital as Process and the History of Capitalism," *Business History Review* 91 (Autumn 2017): 483–510; and John J. Clegg, "Slavery and Capitalism," *Critical Historical Studies* 2, no. 2 (Fall 2015): 281–304.

7. For other important definitions of racial capitalism, see Jodi Melamed, "Racial Capitalism," *Critical Ethnic Studies* 1, no. 1 (Spring 2015): 76-85; Andy Clarno, *Neoliberal Apartheid: Palestine/Israel and South African After 1994* (Chicago: University of Chicago Press, 2017); and Walter Johnson, *The Broken Heart of America: St. Louis and the Violent History of the United States* (New York: Basic, 2020).

8. Peter James Hudson expertly unearths the South African genealogy in "Racial Capitalism and the Dark Proletariat," in "Race Capitalism Justice," special issue, *Boston Review*, Winter 2017. For more on this history, see Neville Alexander, "An Illuminating Moment: Background to the Azanian Manifesto," in *Biko Lives!: Contemporary Black History*, ed. Andile Mngxitama et al. (New York: Palgrave, 2008), 157–70. The quotation is from Neville's speech, in *Biko Lives!*; see also the

published version, "Azanian Manifesto," South African History Online, https://www.sahistory.org.za/archive/azanian-manifesto, which has slight variations in the quoted portion, most notably the omission of the word "black" before "middle classes." In the American academy, sociologist Robert Baluner used the term *racial capitalism* in his *Racial Oppression in America* (New York: Harper Collins, 1972).

9. Robin D. G. Kelley, "What Did Cedric Robinson Mean by Racial Capitalism?," in "Race Capitalism Justice," special issue, *Boston Review*, Winter 2017.

10. Robinson, *Black Marxism*, 10. Robinson indirectly intervened in debates about the transition from feudalism to capitalism, and whether capitalism first emerged as a result of agrarian transformations or as a result of changes in trade. References contemporary with Robinson include Paul Sweezy et al., *The Transition from Feudalism to Capitalism* (London: Verse, 1978); Fernand Braudel, *Civilization and Capitalism 15th–18th Century, Volume 1: The Structures of Everyday Life*, trans. Siân Reynolds (New York: Harper, 1981); and T. H. Aston and C. H. E. Philpin, eds., *The Brenner Debate: Agrarian Class Structure and Economic Development in Pre-Industrial Europe* (New York: Cambridge University Press, 1985).

11. Robinson, *Black Marxism*, 2.

12. Robinson argues that the "lower orders"—slaves, mercenaries, domestics—that provided rulers and merchants "the material and human resources needed for their maintenance and further accumulations of power and wealth" were not merely of a different class, but were attached to existential forms of distinction, such as the biblical myth of descent from Ham, attributing to these "lower orders" a natural inclination toward servitude. Robinson notes that nineteenth-century race scientists also used the myth of Ham to support chattel slavery and claims of natural African inferiority (*Black Marxism*, 21–24). On Ham in the nineteenth century, see Bruce Dain, *A Hideous Monster of the Mind: American Race Theory in the Early Republic* (Cambridge, Mass.: Harvard University Press, 2002).

13. Robinson, *Black Marxism*, 9.

14. Robinson, *Black Marxism*, 26.

15. Robinson, *Black Marxism*, xxxi.

16. For more on race in the medieval period, see William C. Jordan, "Why 'Race'?," *Journal of Medieval and Early Modern Studies* 31, no. 1 (Winter 2001): 165–73; Helmut Reinz, *History, Frankish Identity and the Framing of Western Ethnicity, 550–850* (New York: Cambridge University Press, 2015); Denise Kimber Buell, *Why This New Race: Ethnic Reasoning in Early Christianity* (New York: Columbia University Press, 2005); Geraldine Heng, *The Invention of Race in the European Middle Ages* (New York: Cambridge University Press, 2018). For the relationship between medieval and nineteenth-century conceptions of race, see Matthew X. Vernon, *The Black Middle Ages: Race and the Construction of the Middle Ages* (New York: Palgrave, 2018). And for the misuses of race and the medieval in the context of modern white supremacy, see the Medievalists of Color statement "On Race and Medieval Studies," https://medievalistsofcolor.com/statements/on -race-and-medieval-studies/.

17. Robinson, *Black Marxism*, 4.

18. Robinson, *Black Marxism*, 100.

19. Robinson, *Black Marxism*, 4.

20. Robinson, *Black Marxism*, 21.

21. Robinson, *Black Marxism*, 10.

22. Charisse Burden-Stelly has done important work putting the framework of racial capitalism into conversation with the work of twentieth-century black radicals. See Burden-Stelly, "Modern U. S. Racial Capitalism," *Monthly Review* 72, no. 3 (July-August 2020): 8–20.

23. Eric Williams, *Capitalism and Slavery* (Chapel Hill: University of North Carolina Press, [1944] 1994), 19–20.

24. Oliver Cromwell Cox, *Caste, Class, and Race: A Study in Social Dynamics* (New York: Doubleday, 1948), xxx.

25. Walter Rodney, *How Europe Underdeveloped Africa* (Washington, D.C.: Howard University Press, [1972] 1982), 88–89.

26. Barbara Jeanne Fields, "Slavery, Race, and Ideology in United States History," *New Left Review*, May/June 1990. Fields was responding to, among others, Winthrop Jordan's *White Over Black: American Attitudes Toward the Negro* (Chapel Hill: University of North Carolina Press, [1968] 2012) and Edmund Morgan's *American Slavery, American Freedom* (New York: Norton, 1975).

27. Ida B. Wells, *Crusade for Justice: The Autobiography of Ida B. Wells*, ed. Alfreda Duster (Chicago: University of Chicago Press, 1970), 64.

28. Ida B. Wells, *The Light of Truth: Writings of an Anti-Lynching Crusader*, ed. Mia Bay and Henry Louis Gates, Jr. (New York: Penguin, 2014), 61.

29. W. E. B. Du Bois, *Black Reconstruction in America, 1860–1880* (New York: Free Press, [1935] 1998), 700.

30. Manning Marable, *How Capitalism Underdeveloped Black America* (Cambridge, Mass.: South End Press, [1983] 2000), 1, 10, 107–108, 249.

31. W. E. B. Du Bois, "The African Roots of the War," *Atlantic Monthly*, May 1915.

32. C. L. R. James, *The Black Jacobins: Toussaint L'Ouverture and the San Domingo Revolution* (New York: Vintage, [1938] 1963), 283.

33. Rodney, *How Europe Underdeveloped Africa*, 22, 149.

34. Karl Marx, *Capital, Volume 1* (New York: Penguin, 1992), 915, 874–75.

35. Patrick Wolfe, "Settler Colonialism and the Elimination of the Native," *Journal of Genocide Research* 8, no. 4 (December 2006): 387–409 (388). See also Jodi A. Byrd et al., eds., "Economies of Dispossession: Indigeneity, Race, Capitalism," special issue, *Social Text* 135 (June 2018) and Nick Estes and Roxanne Dunbar-Ortiz, "Examining the Wreckage," *Monthly Review* 72, no. 3 (July-August 2020): 1–7.

36. For recent scholarship on slavery that is engaged with the framework of racial capitalism, see Jennifer Morgan, *Laboring Women: Gender and Reproduction in New World Slavery* (Philadelphia: University of Pennsylvania Press, 2004); Stephanie E. Smallwood, *Saltwater Slavery: A Middle Passage from Africa to American Diaspora* (Cambridge, Mass.: Harvard University Press, 2007); and Walter Johnson, *River of Dark Dreams: Slavery and Empire in the Cotton Kingdom* (Cambridge, Mass.: Harvard University Press, 2013). Influential work in the new

history of capitalism and slavery includes, in particular, Sven Beckert and Seth Rockman, eds., *Slavery's Capitalism: A New History of American Economic Development* (Philadelphia: University of Pennsylvania Press, 2016); Caitlin Rosenthal, *Accounting for Slavery: Masters and Management* (Cambridge, Mass.: Harvard University Press, 2018); Sven Beckert, *Empire of Cotton: A Global History* (New York: Vintage, 2015); Seth Rockman, *Scraping By: Wage Labor, Slavery, and Survival in Early Baltimore* (Baltimore: Johns Hopkins University Press, 2009); Edward Baptist, *The Half Has Never Been Told: Slavery and the Making of American Capitalism* (New York: Basic, 2014); Daina Ramey Berry, *The Price for Their Pound of Flesh: The Value of the Enslaved, from Womb to Grave, in the Building of a Nation* (Boston: Beacon, 2017); and Calvin Schermerhorn, *The Business of Slavery and the Rise of American Capitalism, 1815–1860* (New Haven, Conn.: Yale University Press, 2015). The debate over whether slavery is capitalist is long and vicious. In the British West Indian context, it dates back to Williams's *Capitalism and Slavery* and Seymour Drescher's critical response in *Econocide: British Slavery in the Era of Abolition* (Pittsburgh: University of Pittsburgh Press, 1977). In the U.S. context, the debate stretches back even further, to the early days of the historical profession. For slavery as noncapitalist see Confederate apologist Ulrich B. Phillips, "The Economic Cost of Slaveholding in the Cotton Belt," *Political Science Quarterly* 20, no. 2 (June 1905): 257–75. For slavery as capitalist, see Alfred H. Conrad and John H. Meyer, *The Economics of Slavery and Other Studies in Econometric History* (New York: Routledge, [1964] 2017). Another classic debate was sparked by Robert William Fogel and Stanley L. Engerman, *Time on the Cross: The Economics of American Negro Slavery* (Boston: Little, Brown, 1977). Noteworthy contemporary detractors from the consensus that slavery was indeed capitalist are James Oakes, "Capitalism and Slavery and the Civil War," *International Labor and Working-Class History* 89 (Spring 2016): 195–220; and Alan L. Olmstead and Paul W. Rhode, "Cotton, Slavery, and the New History of Capitalism," *Explorations in Economic History* 67 (January 2018): 1–17.

37. Moon-Ho Jung, *Coolies and Cane: Race, Labor, and Sugar in the Age of Emancipation* (Baltimore: Johns Hopkins University Press, 2006), 87.

38. Sarah Haley, *No Mercy Here: Gender, Punishment, and the Making of Jim Crow Modernity* (Chapel Hill: University of North Carolina Press, 2016).

39. Ta-Nehisi Coates, quoted in Sheryl Gay Stolberg, "At Historic Hearing, House Panel Explores Reparations," *New York Times*, June 19, 2019.

40. Eric Williams, "The Historical Background of British Guiana's Problems," *Journal of Negro History* 30, no. 4 (October 1945): 357–81 (379); Cedric J. Robinson, "Capitalism, Slavery, and Bourgeois Historiography," *History Workshop Journal* 23, no. 1 (Spring 1987): 122–40 (125); Moon-Ho Jung, "Outlawing 'Coolies': Race, Nation, and Empire in the Age of Emancipation," *American Quarterly* 57, no. 3 (September 2005): 677–701 (679–80).

41. Saidiya Hartman, *Lose Your Mother: A Journey Along the Atlantic Slave Route* (New York: Farrar, Straus, and Giroux, 2007), 6.

42. Du Bois, *Black Reconstruction*, 30.

43. See in particular Drescher, *Econocide: British Slavery in the Era of Abolition*. The best assessment of Williams and his legacy is Barbara Solow and Stanley Engerman, eds., *British Capitalism and Caribbean Slavery: The Legacy of Eric Williams* (New York: Cambridge University Press, 1987). For an incisive rebuttal to Williams's critics, see Robinson, "Capitalism, Slavery, and Bourgeois Historiography." For two notable exceptions to the critics' focus on the quantitative in favor of an emphasis on the ideological sympathy of capitalism and antislavery, see Thomas Bender, ed., *The Antislavery Debate: Capitalism and Abolitionism as a Problem in Historical Interpretation* (Berkeley: University of California Press, 1992); and David Eltis, *The Rise of African Slavery in the Americas* (New York: Cambridge University Press, 2000).

44. Mary Poovey, *A History of the Modern Fact: Problems of Knowledge in the Sciences of Wealth and Society* (Chicago: University of Chicago Press, 1998).

45. See Hillary Beckles, *Britain's Black Debt: Reparations for Caribbean Slavery and Native Genocide* (Kingston, Jamaica: University of the West Indies Press, 2013); Nicolas Draper, *The Price of Emancipation: Slave-Ownership, Compensation, and British Society at the End of Slavery* (New York: Cambridge University Press, 2010); and Emilie Connolly, "Indian Trust Funds and Compensatory Justice: A Long View," paper presented at the American Historical Association Conference, Washington, D.C., January 2018.

46. Du Bois, *Black Reconstruction*, 57.

47. Marx, *Capital*, 414.

48. A. Philip Randolph, "The Struggle for the Liberation of the Black Laboring Masses in This Age of a Revolution of Human Rights," in *Black Liberation and the American Dream: The Struggle for Racial and Economic Justice*, ed. Paul Le Blanc (Chicago: Haymarket, 2017), 136.

49. Cox, *Caste, Class, and Race*, xxxii (emphasis original).

50. C. L. R. James, "The Revolutionary Answer to the Negro Problem," in *Black Liberation and the American Dream*, 223.

51. Martin Luther King, Jr., "Where Do We Go From Here?," accessed April 26, 2020, https://kinginstitute.stanford.edu/king-papers/documents/where-do-we-go-here -address-delivered-eleventh-annual-sclc-convention.

52. Claudia Jones, "An End to the Neglect of the Problems of the Negro Woman!," *Political Affairs*, June 1949, accessed April 26, 2020, http://ucf.digital.flvc.org /islandora/object/ucf%3A4865.

53. A. Philip Randolph, foreword to *Negroes and Jobs: A Book of Readings*, ed. Louis A. Ferman, Joyce L. Kornbluh, and J. A. Miller (Ann Arbor: University of Michigan Press, 1968), v.

54. Jodi Melamed and Chandan Reddy, "Using Liberal Rights to Enforce Racial Capitalism," *Items: Insights from the Social Sciences*, July 30, 2019, https://items .ssrc.org/race-capitalism/using-liberal-rights-to-enforce-racial-capitalism/.

55. For an important and nuanced debate on whether it is possible for capitalism to shed its racial characteristics, see Nancy Fraser, "Is Capitalism Necessarily Racist?," *Politics/Letters* 15 (May 20, 2019), and responses by Jordan T. Camp,

Christina Heatherton, and Manu Karuka ("A Response to Nancy Fraser") and Bruce Robbins ("The Answer Is No: A Response to Nancy Fraser") in the same issue; http://quarterly.politicsslashletters.org/is-capitalism-necessarily-racist/.

56. For a notable exception, see the extremely compelling comparative study of racial capitalism in South Africa and Palestine in Clarno, *Neoliberal Apartheid*.

57. Adom Getachew, *Worldmaking After Empire: The Rise and Fall of Self-Determination* (Princeton, N.J.: Princeton University Press, 2019), 86.

58. Walter Johnson, "To Remake the World," in "Race Capitalism Justice," special issue, *Boston Review*, Winter 2017.

59. Haley, *No Mercy Here*, 4–5.

60. Shatema Threadcraft, "Intersectional Capitalism?," unpublished paper, Race and Capitalism Project's History Group Writing Retreat, Atlixco, Mexico, June 2019.

61. Shauna Sweeney, "Black Women in Slavery and Freedom: Gendering the History of Racial Capitalism," *American Quarterly* 72, no. 1 (2020): 277–89 (287). To focus on black female sex workers in early-twentieth-century Chicago, for instance, is to explore the making of the formal and informal economies, both as discrete domains of study and as spheres of economic, social, and political activity. Cynthia Blair, *I've Got to Make My Livin': Black Women's Sex Work in Turn-of-the-Century Chicago* (Chicago: University of Chicago Press, 2010).

62. Threadcraft, "Intersectional Capitalism?"

CHAPTER 1

RACE, INNOVATION, AND FINANCIAL GROWTH

The Example of Foreclosure

K-SUE PARK

W hat is the role of race in producing the economy? The more familiar iteration of this question—namely, what is the role of racial discrimination in producing economic inequality?—captures the predominant and equally familiar answer: race is a form of bias that infects the market to produce outcomes that are unfortunate, but incidental. This formulation presupposes that "race" and "economy" are independent phenomena: it conceives of the first as wrongful, invidious, complexion-based discrimination, a background factor to an economy that otherwise functions more or less according to objective principles. This prevalent idea does not explain the work that racialization performs within the market. Rather, by its very terms, it tends to exclude the idea that it does and therefore fails to disturb the conceit that the existence of subordinated racial minorities is a phenomenon distinct from the predatory practices that plague them.

In this essay, I turn to the example of foreclosure in early America for the way it illustrates the dynamic relationship between race and economic growth. In a prior work, I described how colonists in America introduced novel practices of foreclosure in the seventeenth century in order to expropriate lands held by Native nations; how, by doing so, they deviated from an old English tradition of protecting families from land loss due to the nonpayment of debts.¹ Here, I return to this historical episode in order to highlight three different aspects of the significance of this innovation for shaping the colonial American economy. As I have already shown, the new foreclosure it introduced was a tool of indigenous dispossession.

Here, I explore what this innovation, made possible by the parameters and presumptions of the colonial enterprise, suggests about the relation between race and financial innovation, especially as it spread across the colonies to become quotidian practice in transactions between Europeans in the colonies. First, I describe how the practice of indebting Native people in order to take their lands combined two of the principal resources for experimentation that colonists had at their disposal to try and make their settlements sustainable—namely, racialization and debt creation. Second, I explain how this new practice helped inaugurate a two-track local economy, one based on different treatment for different, racially demarcated groups; after this practice began early in the seventeenth century, for several decades colonists reserved it for use only on Native borrowers. Third, this racially delimited practice functioned, in retrospect, as a beta test for a practice that would become widespread across colonial society as a whole. In the late seventeenth century, colonies increasingly began to pass laws permitting the extension of this new practice of foreclosure to transactions between settlers, and eventually Parliament passed an act sanctioning the practice between whites across the British Empire.

The history of foreclosure shows that the opportunities presented by racial differentiation fostered experiment and innovation that yielded new predatory practices that shaped the market in America. These practices, which racially bifurcated the colonial economy, therefore advanced the development of racial ideology and the economy in tandem. In other words, the essential, catalytic role of racialization in economic development during this period produced "races," as we have come to know them, as much as they produced the economy. Debt creation was a central economic tool for the production of both: it acted on both Native people and their homelands to dispossess the former of the latter, subordinating the people and converting the lands first into capital and then, in the eighteenth century, into a critical means of credit formation.

I offer thoughts on the significance of these events to invite readers to question prevalent ideas about race and the economy that continue to wield tremendous structural and affective power in the material world. The dream of a profitable real estate market that works for all still powerfully controls the collective American imagination today, and that market depends on simple and routine mortgage foreclosure. Foreclosure enables lenders to recuperate the value of their loans, ensures they will continue to lend, and remains indispensable because most people still rely on credit to buy property. Property ownership in turn facilitates access to credit, and owning property continues to be key to building household and intergenerational wealth in the United States.[2] Because real estate is such an important asset, nearly all property owners hope its values will rise, so they can sell their property on demand if they need to do so; they cannot help but feel solicitous of the cash value of the real estate they possess. Another undeniable feature of the real estate market is the racial inequities that pervade it. Minorities lack access to the market and face predation on it; property ownership remains a key source of the racial wealth gap in the United States, and evictions and foreclosures hit minorities the hardest.[3] Many who place their hopes in and praise the market also decry and condemn its inequities.

The early history of foreclosure suggests that racialization and foreclosure evolved together to develop crucial elements of the land market and make this market central to economic growth—as it remains now. Between the present and the early evolution of foreclosure in America, I suggest, lies a long and complex story of how the economy came to rely, fundamentally and structurally, on the sale of land, unequal bargaining power as a resource, and racialization as a key process for producing productive disparities. This essay describes one small episode in this broader story to highlight a generative dynamic between race and economic innovation, which scholars may recognize in other historical episodes. This dynamic belies the idea that the land system fundamentally works but that racism unfortunately and unnecessarily ails it. It demonstrates, rather, that the intransigence of racism is tied to the unequivocal commitment to the market's constitution and that race fuels and is fueled by power disparities that produce advantages, opportunities, and profit.

Race and Debt in the American Colonies

Two basic aspects of the English colonization enterprise are critical for understanding the kinds of transactional relationships that colonists developed with Native peoples after arriving in their territories: the centrality of *race* and *debt* as structuring principles to these ventures. More specifically, colonizing expeditions were premised on the use of force according to a fundamental distinction between Europeans and non-Europeans, which would become elaborated as "race" over the course of colonial experience; furthermore, they were financed by private lenders, which led colonists to manage trade in the settlements in large part by shifting the debt burdens with which they arrived and which they continued to incur to one another. In the colonies, race and debt functioned oppositely in one sense, for racial distinctions expressed colonists' sense of entitlement in the colonies while debt burdened their experiences there. In another, they operated in the same vein, for the possibility of shifting debt burdens and creating profitable equivalencies through debt meant that race and debt formed two critical resources that colonists could "spend" at will and at little cost, to their advantage.

To elaborate, the English first launched their ships under the overarching authority of a legal framework now known as the Discovery Doctrine, which used the guiding principle of a fundamental, hierarchical distinction between Europeans and non-Europeans to order European nations' efforts to conquer non-European territories among themselves. The Virginia Company's first charter, for example, in 1606 granted lands in America to groups in Virginia and Plymouth and also expressed the hope that the colonists would "in time bring the Infidels and Savages, living in those Parts, to human Civility, and to a settled and quiet Government."[4] The Discovery Doctrine's primary distinction between peoples of the world authorized the use of force against indigenous peoples and steered the use of that force in the colonies, providing a framework for developing the practical and ideological dimensions of European colonizing enterprises even before "explorers" set sail. In other words, the Discovery Doctrine unleashed the constraints of European society upon colonists' use of violence in transactions with Native peoples, giving them wide berth to experiment creatively with different forms of coercion. This license to use racial violence presented an especially malleable and nearly inexhaustible resource for colonists, as it cost little beyond their willingness to transgress familiar boundaries placed on the treatment of other humans, and was therefore one over which they had a relatively high degree of control.

Second, colonists sought charters from the Crown under the auspices of joint-stock companies, so that their ventures were financed by private entities rather than by the public fisc.[5] Because credit and investment vehicles structured the channels of these contributions, colonists sailed for America with debt burdens and a plan to engage in racial violence to satisfy them. From its founding, for example, Plymouth Colony began in a "mortgaged condition" due to its obligations to the Company's various investors;[6] the resources that colonists extracted during the first years were earmarked for repayment to them. The pressure that these arrangements placed on colonists to make settlements not only self-sustaining but profitable first incentivized colonists to shift their debt burdens both to one another and to Native peoples. It also incentivized flexibility and innovation as colonists used a range of techniques to interpret these mandates, from open warfare on Native nations to their use of creative and coercive tactics in economic transactions. That is, colonists channeled their use of force through transactions that did violence both by their terms and in their consequences, such as pursuing "agreements" to purchase land that were characterized by deception about the terms and fundamentally different viewpoints about what could be alienated through such a transaction.[7]

The racial framework of the Discovery Doctrine combined with the structure of debt-based financing to toxic and alchemical effect as colonists shifted their debt burdens to Native peoples and used that burden to force an equivalence between money and land. Given how completely the colonial market was structured by credit, it is unsurprising that colonists chose to cultivate debts in their transactions with Native people. As historian Bernard Bailyn tells us, "the key to [the] formation" of the import market upon which settlers depended "was credit, for it was by credit alone that the necessary goods were brought from Europe to America."[8] Colonial New England merchants quickly acquired political and social power through their monopoly on goods and the leverage they acquired over settlers who could only obtain the household goods they needed from lines of credit—leverage that was quickly compounded by their new ability to charge interest.

Land, too, quickly became centrally important in the colonies, not only because of the necessity of engrossing a site for settlement but also because it presented a solution to the challenge of building a settler population. The headright system, pioneered by Virginia in 1618 and quickly adopted by practically all of the colonies, provided incentives to migrate by promising an amount of land, frequently fifty acres, for every "head" a person transported to the colony, including his own. Richard Pares has identified assembling, transporting, and sustaining a population of colonists, in addition to identifying a site, as among the key challenges of a colonization project.[9] Colonial governments' promises of land solved many of these problems by luring people to the colonies, inducing them to transport others, building the labor force to procure food and other resources, and enlisting them directly in the process of locating residential sites and trade routes. The colonists who came for land also occupied it against other Europeans, spread disease, and provided the labor of "defense," or removing Native people from their lands. Moreover, as more people arrived and populated colonial settlements, the sale value of the lands rose, creating a powerful feedback loop between migration, occupation, and profit. For this reason, colonists became obsessed with what they viewed as abundant, available, and plentiful lands.

The stage on which the new American foreclosure so enduringly hitched land to credit was therefore set by conditions that had already powerfully elevated credit as a tool for expanding the economy and that came relatively quickly to fix land as a primary commodity within it. The use of foreclosure to expropriate Native peoples' lands in colonial America began almost as soon as the English arrived in the early seventeenth century and continued over its course. This practice, as several scholars have highlighted, represented a major departure from the practice as it existed in England. English law did not allow a creditor's claim to land to automatically trump a debtor's in the event of default but, rather, posed steep challenges to a creditor's ability to alienate land from families.[10] In transactions with Natives, merchants dispensed cloth and other goods on "credit" to *manufacture* debt and claim a "mortgage"; by foreclosing, they seized assets that increasingly came to represent value as capital in the colonial world.[11] This foreclosure on Native peoples' lands was strikingly unlike situations in which colonists pledged land as security for credit and understood the risks and consequences for doing so. In these English-Native transactions, there existed no mutual understanding of debt between lender and borrower, nor the possibility of alienating land, nor the possibility of alienating land as security for a debt. The distinct kind of coercion that colonists used in this new, racially targeted form of foreclosure stripped communities of assets as never before. The Discovery Doctrine's distinction between peoples both licensed and guided this transgression.[12] Above all, the new racial foreclosure reflected a new openness to trespassing upon a dimension of human life and over a boundary that the English had long protected: preserving the sustaining function of a community's homelands.

Race and the New American Foreclosure

Because Native people did not view land as a form of capital, it was the transition to English possession that paved the way, over time, for land's conversion into capital and made indigenous dispossession a mode of capital accumulation. But land's conversion into capital did not occur immediately upon the beginning of English occupation in the seventeenth century. Rather, colonists' land use at first resembled traditional English land use, creating barriers to foreclosure to protect the continuity and stability of colonists' own estates—precisely the aspect of English estates that anchored its communal, social function. This protection flags how colonists bifurcated their foreclosure practices in early America following the distinction between Europeans and non-Europeans; these practices appeared to lead the development of racial ideologies as colonists made innovative use of violence to pursue financial growth. Critically, though "religious and ethnocentric ideas of European superiority over the other cultures, religions, and races of the world"[13] constituted the premise given by the Discovery Doctrine, this premise remained general and vague as applied to all the diverse peoples whom colonists from different European nations might theoretically encounter outside of Europe. The specific content of ideological elaborations about the nature of non-European peoples developed through their evolving interactions and relationships on the ground.

The structure that protected a family's interests in land was comprised of English legal safeguards against foreclosures on mortgages, which colonists retained in transactions between themselves for several decades. That is, colonists continued to utilize English practices that preserved land for families while they began to engage in a harsh form of foreclosure in transactions with Natives. In some ways, their practices differed from contemporary practices in England: heavy reliance on credit in the colonies meant, for example, that colonists relied more heavily on mortgages to obtain lines of credit and goods than was usual in England;[14] they also applied mortgages to lands that had not long belonged to their owners, and on which individuals frequently did not intend to stay permanently.[15] Nevertheless, laws created obstacles against colonists' loss of these mortgaged lands by foreclosure, in contrast to the foreclosure on Native peoples' lands that jettisoned such protections for a debtor and his or her kin.

Colonists displayed considerable commitment to this segregated mortgage practice. Even when colonial markets suffered greatly, settlers became unable to pay their debts, and merchants pressured colonial governing bodies to make land liable for debts, courts and legislatures resisted this change. In 1640, for example, the infusion of import goods and cash nearly stopped with the stream of migration to New England, and the stilling of ship traffic threatened to destroy "the embryonic economy of the Puritan Commonwealth."[16] Yet both Massachusetts and Connecticut took measures during this period to prevent settlers from losing land and thereby suffering "total impoverishment at the hands of creditors."[17] As legal scholar Claire Priest has shown, many colonies, including Virginia, Maryland, and the island colonies of Jamaica and St. Kitts, created remedial schemes that "were even more protective of land than the English regime" in that they omitted a measure that would have allowed creditors to take a temporary possessory interest in land.[18] The new American foreclosure remained racial, or reserved for use against indigenous people, through the middle of the seventeenth century.

Foreclosure practices in colonial America therefore split into two variants, marking a racially divided economy that reflected the structuring impetus of the Discovery Doctrine and the colonial enterprise itself. Again, the plan for racial hierarchy laid out by the Discovery Doctrine and its authorization of racial violence, together with the debt-based structure of private financing, created a fecund environment for financial innovation in the American colonies. The new racially targeted form of foreclosure illustrates how colonists channeled the doctrine's license to use coercion against populations considered to occupy a lower tier of humanity through a debt instrument designed for land seizure. The example of foreclosure, in keeping with a panoply of colonial approaches to transactions with Natives, thus exhibited, extended, and developed a tendency that Cedric Robinson described as a key dynamic of European capitalist development in general: "not to homogenize but to differentiate—to exaggerate regional, subcultural, and dialectical differences into 'racial' ones."[19]

The dynamic and ongoing process of racialization, this history suggests, developed through the interplay between racial practices and racial ideas. Indeed, the racial divide in colonists' practices appears to have preceded and presaged their specific ideological elaboration of the racial justifications for these practices. As Nancy Shoemaker has noted, during the seventeenth century, Europeans and Native people transacted with one another upon a "foundation of shared concepts and practices,"[20] and it is not until the eighteenth century that we observe the rampant amplification of ideas about the nature and sources of racial differences—in tandem, uncoincidentally, with surges in colonists' land speculation and indigenous land dispossession. Though, as Wesley Frank Craven observed, "the subject of the Indian's color

was one of very great interest to Europeans at the time of Virginia's first settlement and for many years thereafter,"[21] colonial records relay that English
and Native agricultural practices bore many resemblances to one another.
At the same time, within this field of similitude, as Peter Thomas observes,
colonists' social practices of hiring farm labor, fencing fields, and constructing mills to facilitate these practices "gave the illusion . . . that the European
and native subsistence adaptations were far less similar than they were in
reality."[22] Yet while Europeans and Native people undeniably had different
languages, customs, and relationships with the land on which they resided,
as Shoemaker emphasizes, those differences did not correspond to the kinds
of ideological notions about fundamental, hierarchical differences in their
human attributes and capacities that would develop over subsequent years.

Nonetheless, the seeds of the ideological and institutional waxing of
racial ideology that would occur later are apparent in these early bifurcated
approaches to economic transactions with groups understood to be different
in a hierarchical scheme. As I have noted, in foreclosing on Natives in one
way and on colonists in another, colonists not only reflected the difference
they perceived between these two groups in practice but *broadened* the differences between the English and American mortgage, as well as between
English and Native understandings about the alienability of land.[23] These
gaps grew from the leap in the ways Englishmen were willing to disregard
certain structural safeguards on human communal life and expand their
notions of how it was possible to use land for commercial gain. Implement-
ing categorically different treatments for different groups created divisions
that each group would come to understand and explain as stemming
from the characteristics of the people in question, rather than the systemic
logic that made such divisions profitable. Through such practices, colonists
enacted their fundamental perception that the difference between English
and Native communities was hierarchical, thereby giving the ideological
framework of the Discovery Doctrine rudimentary but specific content that
would later find the fuller elaborations that Shoemaker has carefully tracked.
The specialized colonial practices for interacting with non-Europeans and
the concomitant, developing racial ideologies about them appear to have
formed a feedback loop in the sense that each motivated and played a justifi-
catory role for the other.

Out of this process emerged an instrument that would come to take pride
of place in the American system of real estate. It is worth emphasizing that

the mechanism at the heart of that device was and remains the violence of dispossession, the separation of people from land—land that is, very frequently, still their home. The context of resorting to this specific violence as a means for enlarging the economy was, again, the Discovery Doctrine's broader mandate to pursue economic growth using violence upon the premise of a divided world. This colonial structure organized colonists' initiatives to wage wars in America and to engage in financial transactions over which the specter of war always hung heavy. Furthermore, this violence imbued and drove colonists' racialization of Native peoples, which both facilitated and motivated new practices of enacting disparate degrees and kinds of coercion on groups distinguished hierarchically by racial categories. Colonists' narrative elaboration and exaggeration of these categories further licensed their use of experimental coercive techniques to build an economy organized by the premise of different treatment for different groups and designed to yield collective advantage for colonists at Native peoples' expense.

Foreclosure for indigenous groups thus bore the hallmarks of the financial and legal structures of colonization: it was a debt-based financial instrument that operated along the racial divisions given by the Discovery Doctrine, within an embryonic two-track economic system designed to reap collective advantage for settlers. Neither the effort to seize land through force and coercion nor the attempt to replace indigenous systems of land tenure distinguished the English enterprise from other European colonizing ventures. However, the development of foreclosure in the English colonies uniquely deployed racial violence to deeply entangle the growth of sovereignty and property together with *debt*.[24] As Greer notes, colonists' early use of the mortgage to foreclose on indigenous land did more than just secure debt: it "documented an assertion of jurisdiction over indigenous lands."[25] This assertion, which transferred jurisdiction with land, made debt an instrument for limiting one group's sovereignty in order to enlarge the power of another. This use of foreclosure therefore astonishingly channeled the racial violence of conquest, dispossession, and displacement through mortgage foreclosure in a manner that would soon become a quotidian part of the colonial market in lands.

Adapting Racial Foreclosure for General Use

Toward the end of the seventeenth century, several colonial governments began to eliminate the traditional provisions that had theretofore protected settlers' lands from foreclosure. In legislation that Claire Priest describes as "revolutionary," for example, in 1675 Massachusetts passed an unprecedented law that explicitly permitted a creditor to take an individual's freehold interest in land to satisfy colonists' unsecured debt;[26] over the next few decades, West New Jersey, Pennsylvania, Connecticut, and New Hampshire all took steps that followed suit, making it easier for creditors to seize land for a debtor's unsecured debts.[27] This colonial legislation indexes a remarkable shift: it brought foreclosure practice between colonists into alignment with a practice that had theretofore been reserved for Natives. The fact that this practice, which would become an essential element of the land system, emerged as a specifically racial practice and was hailed as an astonishing innovation, helps us perceive that racialization can foment innovation. By making easy foreclosure on land a general practice, in a context where land was increasingly acquiring importance as a capital asset, colonists committed to exploring the catalytic power of making land alienable through debt. The general availability of simple and routine foreclosure then made the practice a means by which colonists could obtain and generate credit as well. At the same time, extending the new American foreclosure to white colonists did not level but rather exacerbated a racially divided economy. Finally, as it accelerated Native communities' land loss, the status of indebtedness itself, endowed with new powers of making debtors desperate, appears to have become racialized in enduring American tropes.

As my analysis here does not investigate every cause of this extraordinary shift, it is worth noting relevant concurrent developments for future inquiry. It appears that the earliest experiments with making colonists' land susceptible to foreclosure occurred in Barbados, as part of a series of changes to the legal liability of land and enslaved persons for unpaid debts. These changes, which shifted liability back and forth and between these two categories of assets, reflected concerns shared by several of the Caribbean colonies about sustaining the flow of credit to the islands while protecting the interests of plantation owners, who worried about being left with only land and no enslaved labor to work it, or the reverse.[28] On the mainland, the New England colonies, which were less concerned with maintaining an enslaved workforce to make lands productive, led the shift from resisting to eventually acquiescing in foreclosure on colonists' lands, suggesting that independent factors prompted their parallel experiments.

During the preceding decades, a number of other factors in New England had already heightened colonists' focus on engrossing land, including mass migration from Europe, ensuing disease among Native groups, and interracial warfare that erupted as a result of the growing contest over space. As the promise of land ownership steadily induced a stream of migrants to America, increasingly dense settlement also caused the land's monetary value to rise. Yet furs remained the principal commodity that colonists sought to accumulate, until the supply began to wane in the 1650s[29] and individuals who had received credit upon the promise of returning pelts, both English and Native, found themselves unable to deliver on their agreements. The decimation of the beaver in New England by around 1660 entailed the loss of one of the most important sources of remittances to creditors[30] and further elevated land as an alternative primary commodity as creditors began to seize colonists' lands when they fell short on pelts.[31]

The tiered impact of the consequences of this shortfall again followed the Discovery Doctrine's hierarchical lines, which were reflected also in the structure of trade. In the homelands of the Woronoco, Agawam, Norwottock, Pocumtuck, and Squakheag people, now called the Connecticut River Valley, the Pynchon family's famous monopoly illustrates how the credit-based trading system operated on two levels:[32] between colonists— that is, between Pynchon and his subtraders– and between colonists and Natives, or between Pynchon and his subtraders and local Native groups. In general, the subtraders replicated the Pynchons' tactics. One year after the fur trade had become "strikingly depressed,"[33] John Pynchon began to give goods to the Norwottock sachem Umpanchela on "credit" in 1659, as I have described in detail elsewhere, only to impose a mortgage and foreclose on Norwottock lands the following year.[34] Under pressure from Pynchon to pay their debts to him, his subtraders did likewise: in the year 1660, for example, the subtrader Samuel Marshfield was unable to produce even one pelt to pay Pynchon what he owed, but "did, however, acquire a mortgage deed from most of the Indian families who were still living in Springfield which covered his immediate losses."[35] In April 1661, Marshfield thereby extracted all the Native-held lands left within Springfield's borders from Agawam leaders Cuttonis, Coe, Mattaquallant, Menis, Wallny [Wallump], and Taqualloush, who, in a parallel circumstance as Marshfield himself, could not repay their debts to him in beaver.[36] The terms were dubious enough that following the foreclosure, Cuttonis and the others denounced his acts. Eventually, Elizur Holyoke and other settlers submitted a petition on their behalf to the Massachusetts General Court that stated, "by virtue of a deed of mortgage" Marshfield "hath gotten into his hands," they had become "impoverished," had "little or nothing left to plant on," and were rendered entirely dependent on the English for food. They agreed to cease their complaints after the court ordered Marshfield to lay out fifteen acres for their use.[37] Though Marshfield displaced some of his desperation onto these parties, he could not thereby escape his own chronic indebtedness, for which Pynchon foreclosed on his house and lands in 1667 and because of which he surrendered another 120 acres of land and his share in the town sawmill to Pynchon in 1686.[38]

At least three of Pynchon's seven subtraders mimicked this practice to obtain Native groups' lands over the next few years,[39] frequently spurred by their own debts to Pynchon. For example, Thomas Cooper, a subtrader who had been frequently indebted to Pynchon since the 1650s,[40] obtained a mortgage for significant landholdings from a Woronoco man named Amoakussen, alias Nacowagallant, in October 1660 for a £12 debt.[41] After Cooper foreclosed, families from the river village Pojasick contested this action, claiming that Amoakussen had no right to alienate lands to Cooper, eventually presenting their grievances to the Massachusetts General Court in 1671.[42] This ongoing dispute did not prevent Cooper from selling his holdings in 1664 to Henry Glover and other "Proprietors" who planned to settle on the land.[43]

The racially divided economy remained the backdrop of these first steps to extend the previously racially exclusive new form of foreclosure to colonists. The patterns of simple price gouging in John Pynchon's account books provide an example of what these distinctions looked like in concrete terms: though Pynchon inflated prices for other colonists and Native people alike, he imposed a further markup of 55 percent for coats, 66 percent for shirts, 71–100 percent for "Bilboe rug," and 37 percent for shag cotton in sales to Native people, as compared to other colonists. These price gaps represent categorical differences in the degree of hardship he imposed on these two groups and show how much more quickly Native people would have faced foreclosure under otherwise identical circumstances. Of course, when those debts resulted in foreclosure of lands, the consequences for Native groups and settlers were profoundly different. The colonists who lost land to foreclosure understood land as an equivalent to the money they owed. Further, the land was land they had only lately and barely acquired, which frequently represented only a temporary residence and a monetary investment, rather than the basis of their sense of family and nation. Though the parcel of land in some cases could be the same, the difference between what Native communities lost and what colonists lost was qualitative; the incommensurable harm to Native peoples included negating the value of their homelands and assaulting their material ways of living and being together, their ancestral traditions, and their political futures.

The extension of the racial mortgage to transactions between colonists, like its parent model, relied nonetheless on creating leverage through a specific form of violence: severing people from land and, consequently, leaving them homeless and without means of independent subsistence. Further, foreclosure brought racialization to bear, for some European debtors who lost their lands for failure to pay debts, in metaphors. One sympathetic observer decried the insecurity and hardships that resulted for settlers, writing that they

> must enter into the Merchants books for such things as they stand in need off, becoming thereby the Merchants slaves, and when it riseth to a big sum are constrained to mortgage their plantation . . . and stock of Cattle, turning them out of house and home, poor Creatures, to look out for a new habitation in some remote place where they begin the world again.[44]

It is notable that this observer likened the colonists who fell victim to the same violence they had leveraged on non-Europeans to "slaves." The association of indebtedness with the subordination of being nonwhite in America appears to have become a lasting American discursive tradition: other commentators later likened the treatment of debtors to that of "savages" and "pigmies,"[45] and during the eighteenth and until the mid-nineteenth century, it would remain common for whites to protest oppressive creditors and their threats of eviction or foreclosure by dressing in Indian costume, and even darkening their skin.[46] This tradition of racializing the stigma of indebtedness performatively articulated how executing foreclosures functioned to further subordinate individuals at the bottom of governing social hierarchies; indeed, the first settlers to lose their lands to foreclosure, such as Marshfield and Cooper, were men who occupied the lowest social strata within the settler community. Of all Pynchon's subtraders, only two, Joseph Parsons and David Wilton, had significant social standing.[47] The historian Peter Thomas describes the others as "blatant failures" who "could be taken advantage of," with no political prominence in the community and "little capital to invest," who "likely . . . entered the Indian trade with the expectation of making quick profits to clear existing debts."[48]

The eventual new, widespread use of foreclosure raised the stakes of being powerless and poor in colonial society, in respects captured by Thomas: it left colonists without a home or means of independent subsistence, and wholly at the mercy of a market economy. Beyond the profound, qualitatively unique harms to Native communities discussed earlier, as the consequences of the new violence that debt transactions could inflict spread across society at large, they also hit Native communities the hardest in a quantitative sense. After the use of foreclosure on poor white colonists, the colonies, beginning with Massachusetts in 1675, passed legislation allowing the general foreclosure of lands for unpaid debts, and landholdings increasingly became a way of obtaining credit. Subsequently, colonists sought to accumulate more lands to get more credit. The way they obtained more land was to take it from Native peoples, through forced sales, often to settle debts, often incurred by predation, as well as by foreclosure. Native people had even fewer opportunities to engage in settler markets than poor whites and on that count, too, frequently fell victim to predation, dependency, and destitution. A wave of foreclosures in the 1670s had a "virtually catastrophic" effect on the Woronoco, Agawam, Norwottock, Pocumtuck, and Squakheag: Thomas describes how colonists' land hunger threatened these communities with starvation, and how food shortages, as settlers took possession of nearly all arable lands, ultimately forced their migration from the area.[49]

By the end of the seventeenth century, the accessibility of foreclosure to creditors in several northern colonies multiplied the incidence of mortgages where credit was already "a way of life."[50] In his study of Boston, the historian G. B. Warden found that the "remarkable" extent of borrowing recorded in mortgages suggests that "the mere possession of property, while important, was probably not so important as being able to exchange it rapidly as conditions changed, and to convert property into credit or cash."[51] Both land's new liquidity and its capacity to expand credit reached new heights after 1732, when Parliament made general foreclosure of lands the rule across the British Empire by passing the Act for the More Easy Recovery of Debts in His Majesty's Plantations and Colonies in America (also called the Debt Recovery Act or Credit Act). Jean O'Brien's description of how the Native people of southeastern New England who lived in the Praying Town of Natick became submerged in debt during the 1730s and 40s provides a clue about the effects of this Act. By that time, Native people in Natick had been forced to sell lands to discharge debts incurred with colonists over several decades[52] and adopted the English system of individualized land ownership, though they had to petition the General Court to sell their lands. O'Brien reports that petitions citing indebtedness as cause for the land sales rose threefold from the 1720s to the 1730s; whereas debt was a factor in only 33 percent of land sale requests prior to 1730, it rose to 74 percent between 1730 and 1740.[53] Sales to English purchasers "accelerated so rapidly after 1740 that the General Court took notice" and took some minor steps to prevent Native people from being "imposed upon by designing and ill-minded men in the dispossessing of their Lands."[54] Between 1741 and 1790, English creditors filed increasing numbers of lawsuits to attach lands; the vast majority of petitions cited debts as cause for the sale, including medical debts, debts due to financial overextension, lawsuits, and others.[55] O'Brien writes that English doctors, caregivers, and undertakers pressed "the threat of lawsuits . . . when they knew Indians owned land" and "may have extended credit and services to Indians in order to pry parcels of land away from them"; English neighbors, too, "occasionally intervened in the legal troubles of Indians, most likely knowing their land would serve as security against their investments."[56]

The successive iterations of this novel form of foreclosure in America used the radical nonequivalence between what Native peoples lost and what colonists acquired to usher in more than one new form of market value. First, as racial foreclosure imposed a new equivalence between money and indigenous lands and colonists took possession of lands as an asset that could produce more monetary value, they at once deployed debt to limit Native nations' sovereignty and expand their own, and also to produce capital.[57] In the first iteration of the new foreclosure, colonists manufactured debt that never even theoretically constituted potentially generative "credit" for indigenous borrowers. Though credit is commonly conceived as value extended, and foreclosure as a way to recuperate that value, colonists initiated the credit relationship by creating debt, which had the sole function of producing value through the foreclosure of lands to convert them into capital. Second, as creditors gained the ability to foreclose on this new capital asset for nonpayment of debts, and land increasingly became a way of generating credit, obtaining land for this purpose made that commodity—its acquisition, production, and trade—a primary driver of the colonial market. The new capacities of land motivated colonists to build ever larger estates, offering credit for land and using land to obtain more credit, causing land values to rise from demand. Foreclosure grew more common as colonists pursued more credit and used foreclosure to acquire security for this pursuit. The futurity introduced by credit not only widened opportunities to generate profit through interest but also motivated colonists' continuous use of racial violence to "cheaply" expropriate indigenous lands that could help them secure further credit, through a process of indigenous dispossession that they appeared to view as inexhaustibly productive for financial growth.

Conclusion

Over the course of the seventeenth and eighteenth centuries, an evolving relationship between racialization and innovation transformed the instrument of foreclosure from a rarely used option of last resort to a quotidian practice and a central part of the machinery ensuring the liquidity of real estate. Its debut as a racial practice first highlights the way racialization, and the use of violence that it licensed, furnished a resource for colonists that spurred their creativity and powers of innovation. Eventually, colonists adapted this device to convert it into a tool of general use, within an economic environment characterized by different treatment for different groups, where racial practices fertilized the ideologies that came to justify them. Foreclosure, in its subsequent iterations, combined the racial structure of the colonizing project and the debt-based structure of finance on which it relied to bring the enclosure to the core of the market by giving it unprecedented liquidity. Beyond the economy, these practices also shaped the social world in which they transpired, to generate lasting social, cultural, and political consequences that in many ways overshadow the institutional and economic thread with which they are entangled.

Thus, the premise of racial division made violence a variable and open factor susceptible to creative innovation in the colonists' hands, and the racial practices they pursued created a strong material context for the elaboration of racial difference: colonists came to explain their different treatment of European and Native peoples as the consequence of biological or cultural characteristics of the groups. Racially stratified economic practices, that is, encouraged racial ideological elaboration, which in turn justified and encouraged the racial development of the economy. The productive potential of racial violence fed this loop, in which racial practices and racial ideology were neither preordained nor remained stable but, rather, appeared to mutually evolve in a dynamic process of racial formation.

This innovation spread and made common a practical innovation born of the Discovery Doctrine's license to experiment with degrees and kinds of coercion that could be used against Native people, beyond the norms that had been established for transactions with Englishmen. This technical innovation, by incorporating foreclosure into regular practice, brought an unprecedented treatment of the human relationship to land. It operated within a racially divided economy that categorically, unevenly distributed loss and advantage, in both qualitative and quantitative ways. In this world, the advancement of one community depended on the destruction of another, creating collective advantage for one group at the expense of targeted groups' ability to survive. As the economy grew, it developed in tandem a social world riven by racialized inequality and violence. The eventual general iteration of this practice retained the kernel of the first innovation—a highly profitable violation of human well-being that is derived from the security of having a home. Although innovation need not originate nor feed on racial violence, or violence in general, foreclosure specifically fostered a real estate market founded on the powerful capacities of coercion in an uneven, colonial, extractive economy.

Over the course of the seventeenth century, as easy mortgage foreclosure went from a racially specific practice to a general one, the instrument transformed from a device for accumulating capital to one crucial for opening the flow of credit to and within the English colonies. The second transformation gave wholly new meaning to land as capital, raising its value in a variety of ways. Land was no longer a static asset: economic growth came to depend on tying debt to land, not just one's ability to alienate it, and the frenetic possession and dispossession of land became a principal way of obtaining more credit as well as land.[58] This debt instrument, which both depended on and facilitated colonial land expropriation, had the effect of liquifying land; by giving land the capacity to spur the creation of value through its attachment to debt, it ensconced land, as real estate, at the foundation of the market and financial growth—in today's language, made it "available for full economic use." Yet as the economy approached its "full" growth capacity, the adaptive normalization of easy mortgage foreclosure also spread a qualitatively new form of loss, in addition to the risk of financial loss. The absorption of this technique of conquest into everyday life preserved a forced equivalence between land—home—and money that would work to the detriment of all. The Debt Recovery Act traded lenders' security for the security of individuals' homes, and collective economic growth for individuals' ability to flourish.[59]

The effort to understand the intrinsic relationship between race and financial innovation faces steep barriers in the enduring explanation for racial inequality in the arena of housing, which casts the problems of the real estate market and racial division as separate and their convergence as incidental. In that account, practices, both predatory and regulatory, from subprime lending to foreclosure, have a disproportionate impact on the most economically vulnerable groups; and the most vulnerable groups in the United States are nonwhites, because these groups carry historical burdens of exclusion and discrimination that disadvantage them still. The early history of mortgage foreclosure suggests that although this articulation is not wrong, it is incomplete. Racial practices and the concomitant processes of racialization were key to producing the mechanisms of the market, the values and commodities it circulated, its viability, and its success.

This relationship is particularly critical to understand at a time when racism and innovation are flourishing wildly together under conditions of dramatic deregulation. Further, even before the Trump presidency, the federal regulations that forced big banks to formally abandon direct subprime lending after the financial crisis of 2008 merely shattered and dispersed a fairly centralized activity, conducted by a relatively small number of major actors. Now, countless entities take advantage of the same category of borrowers affected by subprime lending in hazardous work-around schemes that have only spread and diversified the problem. Small to medium-size lenders creatively exploit myriad legal loopholes to make high-risk loans to borrowers, in schemes that often escape the understanding of affected individuals and their attorneys. The old actors are not far from the action, though insulated from legal liability: big banks have removed themselves just one step from subprime lending and now lend money to nonbank firms that make the subprime loans. Meanwhile, investors, from local lenders to

Wall Street firms, are refashioning predatory racial innovations of the past for a new era, as in their embrace of the idea of securitizing high-risk contracts for deed, notoriously used to target African Americans during the era of redlining, and rampant in colonias ever since.

The historiographical erasure of conquest, in particular, has produced narratives about the market in America that diminish our interpretive capacities and ability to comprehend our inheritance of history under the present circumstances. The colonial history of the mortgage illuminates the close relationship among race, innovation, and financial growth in the field on which these actors contrive new schemes and play: a real estate market that constitutes a lion's share of world financial markets, which still privilege "collective" financial growth above widespread individual losses, both financial and more profound in nature. Though this market has grown infinitely complex in its higher strata and now derives profit chiefly from the pooling and trading of mortgage debt, it has built this precarious tower on the fundamental ability to routinely foreclose on individual parcels of land for nonpayment of debts. The race of the people who live on or around these parcels continues to determine their value, the racial distributions of land ownership, predatory lending, and foreclosure are still stark, and the payoff for producing profit from racial violence remains high. Across racial divisions, hunger for land ownership continues to propel credit and financial markets, just as the demand for access to credit and wealth continues to drive people's quest for land ownership. In this deeply racially riven society and economy, riddled with violence, foreclosure constantly and ubiquitously threatens to sever an enormously debt-burdened population from their homes. Under such pressures, this population is incentivized and largely permitted to pursue land usages that are most profitable to them in the short term—even if to the detriment of their neighbors, the environment, and society as a whole. They have no financial disincentives to engage in racial practices, but the origin story of this unhappy dynamic warns us that these choices, though individual, have aggregate effects—that are likely to stoke ongoing processes of racialization, to encourage the elaboration of new ideas about racial difference, and to exacerbate racial division and inequality. The power of racial violence to normalize violence is likely to foster ongoing creativity, generating new techniques of trespassing upon human life and dignity in ways that may at first seem beyond contemplation but, under the beacon of profit and through a racially marked separate entrance, will seep into the very fabric of the everyday. Racial practices enable the development of novel regulatory and market practices that eventually reshape quotidian market practices to the detriment of people beyond members of the group whose disposability occasions such innovations—of society as a whole.

NOTES

This piece has benefited greatly from generative conversations with the members of the Old History of Capitalism workshop, as well as with Paul Frymer, Cheryl Harris, Dirk Hartog, Willy Forbath, Beth Lew-Williams, Noah Zatz, and other members of workshops hosted by the American Studies Program and Program on Law and Public Affairs workshop at Princeton University and the Law and Political Economy collective's working group on Racial Capitalism. I am also grateful to Michael Dawson, David Freund, Darryl Li, and Robert Nichols for reading and providing helpful feedback at different stages of the project. Thanh Nguyen, Jeremy McCabe, and Lauren Konczos of Georgetown Law Library provided helpful research and editorial support.

1. K-Sue Park, "Money, Mortgages, and the Conquest of America," *Law and Social Inquiry* 41, no. 4 (Fall 2016): 1006–35.
2. James H. Carr, Michela Zonta, and Steven P. Hornburg, *2018 State of Housing in Black America* (Lanham, MD: National Association of Real Estate Brokers, 2018), 1.
3. The literature is wide and deep, but see, for example, Deena Greenberg, Carl Gershenson, and Matthew Desmond, "Discrimination in Evictions: Empirical Evidence and Legal Challenges," *Harvard Civil Rights–Civil Liberties Law Review* 51, no. 1 (Winter 2016): 115–58; Jacob S. Rugh and Douglas S. Massey, "Racial Segregation and the American Foreclosure Crisis," *American Sociological Review* 75, no. 5 (October 2010): 625–51, https://doi.org/10.1177/0003122410380868.
4. "The First Charter of Virginia; April 10, 1606," Avalon Project, Yale Law School, 2016, https://avalon.law.yale.edu/17th_century/va01.asp#1. See also Jeremy Depertuis Bangs, *Indian Deeds: Land Transactions in Plymouth Colony* (Boston: New England Historic Genealogical Society, 2002), 2–3.
5. Robert J. Miller, Jacinta Ruru, Larissa Behrendt, and Tracey Lindberg, *Discovering Indigenous Lands: The Doctrine of Discovery in the English Colonies* (Oxford: Oxford University Press, 2010), 33.
6. Bangs, *Indian Deeds*, 44.
7. See, for example, Lisa Brooks, *Our Beloved Kin: A New History of King Philip's War* (New Haven, Conn.: Yale University Press, 2018), 41.
8. Bernard Bailyn, *New England Merchants in the Seventeenth Century* (Cambridge, Mass.: Harvard University Press, 1979), 34.
9. Richard Pares, *Merchants and Planters* (Cambridge: Cambridge University Press, 1960), 1.

10. See Claire Priest, "Creating an American Property Law: Alienability and Its Limits in American History," *Harvard Law Review* 120, no. 2 (December 2006): 385–459; Park, "Money, Mortgages, and the Conquest of America"; David J. Seipp, "A Very Brief Legal and Social History of Mortgage," in *Mortgages Across Cultures: Land, Finance, and Epistemology*, ed. Daivi Rodima-Taylor and Parker Shipton (Boston: African Studies Center at Boston University, 2017), 19–25; Allan Greer, *Property and Dispossession: Natives, Empires and Land in Early Modern North America* (Cambridge: Cambridge University Press, 2018).

11. See Park, "Money, Mortgages, and the Conquest of America."

12. As historian Peter Thomas put it, for English colonists, "'American savages' were simply outside the bounds of moral obligation." Peter Allen Thomas, "In the Maelstrom of Change: The Indian Trade and Cultural Process in the Middle Connecticut River Valley, 1635–1665" (Ph.D. diss., University of Massachusetts, 1990), 65, ProQuest (7920903).

13. Miller et al., *Discovering Indigenous Lands*, 2.

14. Bailyn, *New England Merchants*, 48.

15. In Essex, for example, David Konig writes, "Many o[f] the first generation [of landholders], in fact, did not even contemplate permanent relocation, and regarded New England as only a temporary exile." David Thomas Konig, "Community Custom and the Common Law: Social Change and the Development of Land Law in Seventeenth-Century Massachusetts," *American Journal of Legal History* 18, no. 2 (April 1974): 137–77 (140), https://www.jstor.org/stable/844964.

16. Bailyn, *New England Merchants*, 46; see also "John Tinker to John Winthrop, Downes, May 28, 1640," in *Papers of the Winthrop Family*, vol. 4 (Boston: Massachusetts Historical Society, 2020), https://www.masshist.org/publications/winthrop/index.php/view/PWF04d227#PWF04d227n1.

17. Bailyn, *New England Merchants*, 47.

18. Priest, "Creating an American Property Law," 409.

19. Cedric Robinson, *Black Marxism: The Making of the Black Radical Tradition* (Chapel Hill: University of North Carolina Press, 1983), 26.

20. Nancy Shoemaker, *A Strange Likeness: Becoming Red and White in Eighteenth-Century North America* (Oxford: Oxford University Press, 2004), 12.

21. Wesley Frank Craven, *White, Red, and Black: The Seventeenth-Century Virginian* (Charlottesville: University Press of Virginia, 1971), 40.

22. Thomas, "In the Maelstrom of Change," 95. Thomas observes that one primary difference was the way the English depended on domestic animals for protein and manure, while Indians practiced hunting, fishing, and gathering to supplement their cereal diets (95). He also suggests that native agricultural practices may have been superior: "In terms of yields per unit of labor . . . early records suggest that native productive capacity was at least equal to that of the permanent fixed-field agriculture of the English settlers. Swidden systems throughout the world have frequently produced equal, or even higher, returns than fields under continuous cultivation" (113).

23. Park, "Money, Mortgages, and the Conquest of America," 1030.

24. For commentary on this close relationship made in the wake of England's own abandonment of feudal modes of land transfer some three centuries later, see Morris R. Cohen, "Property and Sovereignty," *Cornell Law Quarterly* 13, no. 1 (1927): 8–30, comparing the political sovereignty held by modern large property owners to that of feudal ones.

25. Greer, *Property and Dispossession*, 222.

26. Priest, "Creating an American Property Law," 414; General Court Enactment of May 12, 1675, in Nathaniel B. Shurtleff, ed., *Records of the Governor and the Company of the Massachusetts Bay in New England*, vol. 5, *1674–1686* (Boston, 1854), 28–29.

27. Acts and Laws of the General Free Assembly, chap. 12 (1682) (West Jersey), in *The Grants, Concessions and Original Constitutions of the Province of New Jersey*, ed. Aaron Leaming and Jacob Spicer (Somerville, N.J.: Honeyman, 1881), 442, 447; Penn's Charter of Liberties of 1682, Laws Agreed Upon in England §14 (Pennsylvania), in *The Federal and State Constitutions, Colonial Charters, and Other Organic Laws*, vol. 5, *New Jersey—Philippine Islands*, ed. Francis Newton Thorpe (Washington, D.C.: Government Printing Office, 1909), 3047, 3061; Act of 1700, chap. 48, §1, 1700 Pa. Laws 7, 7 (real estate liable to be sold for payment of debts); Act of 1705, chap. 152, §2, 1705 Pa. Laws 57, 58 (yearly rents and profits from land may be used to satisfy debts without seizing the land, but only if the debt can be satisfied within seven years); Executions Act, in *Acts and Laws of His Majesties* [sic] *Colony of Connecticut in New England* (Boston, 1702), 32; Act of May 14, 1718, chap. 20, 2 N.H. Prov. Laws 247 (making land and tenement liable to the payment of debts).

28. Priest, "Creating an American Property Law," 413.

29. Between 1658 and 1663, the returns dropped to just 41 percent of what they had been between 1652 and 1657. Thomas, "In the Maelstrom of Change," 321.

30. Bailyn, *New England Merchants*, 60.

31. Bailyn, *New England Merchants*. See also Thomas, "In the Maelstrom of Change," 321: "Land ceased to be a minor supplemental resource in the Indian-English exchange system and became a major replacement item for pelts."

32. Thomas, "In the Maelstrom of Change," 186, 313. Thomas notes that the Pynchons "reintroduced" the practice of extending credit to natives by the mid-1640s.

33. Thomas, "In the Maelstrom of Change," 323.

34. Harry Andrew Wright, ed., *Indian Deeds of Hampden County* (Springfield, Mass., 1905), 37–38, 44–45; *Pynchon's Account Books, 1652–1702* (Springfield, Mass.: Connecticut Valley Historical Museum, 1958), 2:218–19; Carl Bridenbaugh and Juliette Tomlinson, eds., *The Pynchon Papers, Vol. II: Selections from the Account Books of John Pynchon, 1651–1691* (Boston: Colonial Society of Massachusetts, 1985), 283–88.

35. Thomas, "In the Maelstrom of Change," 282.

36. Wright, *Indian Deeds*, 46–47.

37. Thomas, "In the Maelstrom of Change," 327–28; Nathaniel B. Shurtleff, ed., *Records of the Governor and the Company of the Massachusetts Bay in New England*,

vol. IV, part 2, *1661–1674* (Boston, 1854), 153; *The Probate Records for Hampshire County, 1660–1820, in the Hampshire County Registry of Probate, Northampton, Massachusetts*, vol. I, *1660–1690* (Holyoke, Mass.: Connecticut Valley Historical Museum, 1939), 63; *Hampshire County Waste Book* (Springfield, Mass., 1663–1677), 26–28.

38. *Pynchon's Account Books*, 1:107–8, 110, 2:108–9, 6:188–89; Bridenbaugh and Tomlinson, *Pynchon Papers*, 2:315.

39. Thomas, "In the Maelstrom of Change," 324.

40. *Pynchon's Account Books*, 1:78–82, 221; Bridenbaugh and Tomlinson, *Pynchon Papers*, 2:71–81, 275.

41. Wright, *Indian Deeds*, 40.

42. Thomas, "In the Maelstrom of Change," 328–29. Ultimately, Pynchon presided over the case and granted them a settlement of wampum that was greatly reduced by a bill owed by Whalehwhaet to Cooper for caring for his broken bones. *Hampshire County Waste Book*, 87.

43. Wright, *Indian Deeds*, 42.

44. Bailyn, *New England Merchants*, 99; John Josselyn, *An Account of Two Voyages to New England, Made During the Years 1638, 1663* (Boston: W. Veazie, 1865), 162.

45. Farah Peterson, "Constitutionalism in Unexpected Places," *Virginia Law Review* 106, no. 3 (May 2020): 559–609 (577, 578).

46. Peterson, "Constitutionalism in Unexpected Places," 561, 582.

47. Both men operated out of Northampton, held public office, arrived with wealth, and profited from the fur trade; Parsons and Pynchon were likely distantly related. Thomas, "In the Maelstrom of Change," 277–78.

48. Thomas, "In the Maelstrom of Change," 281.

49. Thomas, "In the Maelstrom of Change," 314.

50. G. B. Warden, "The Distribution of Property in Boston, 1692–1775," *Perspectives in American History* 10 (1976): 86–98 (95). At this time, mortgages were still rarely used to purchase property; rather, people used mortgages to obtain loans for small and large commercial ventures or to cover "some pre-existing indebtedness." The stated term for most was one year, though it took most debtors six to eight years to pay them off (92–96).

51. Warden, "The Distribution of Property in Boston," 90.

52. Jean M. O'Brien, *Dispossession by Degrees: Indian Land and Identity in Natick, Massachusetts, 1650–1790* (Cambridge: Cambridge University Press, 1997). As early as 1685, native Thomas Awassamug sold his inheritance of sagamore land to discharge the medical debts he had incurred after his father fell ill (80).

53. O'Brien, *Dispossession by Degrees*, 109–11.

54. O'Brien, *Dispossession by Degrees*, 171.

55. O'Brien, *Dispossession by Degrees*, 172–75 and accompanying notes for particulars of the cases.

56. O'Brien, *Dispossession by Degrees*, 174.

57. It is difficult to imagine a clearer illustration of the creation of debt, *ex nihilo*, than the situation in which the concepts of monetary equivalence, especially applied to land, were so unknown to the debtor as to the indigenous debtors upon whom colonists foreclosed.

58. The deeds and mortgages in the registry of Boston suggest that "the housing and credit markets remained highly active, frenetic, and unpredictable." Warden, "The Distribution of Property in Boston," 100.

59. Priest, "Creating an American Property Law," 447.

2.1 Ieshia Evans protesting the murder of Alton Sterling in Baton Rouge, LA.

Source: Jonathan Bachman for Reuters, 2016.

CHAPTER 2

GENDERING RACIAL CAPITALISM AND THE BLACK HERETICAL TRADITION

SHAUNA J. SWEENEY

On a warm summer day in July 2016, Ieshia Evans confronted the Baton Rouge police department while protesting the judicial murder of Alton Sterling. Unarmed and in a summer dress, Evans stood face to face with dozens of police officers in full riot gear. She wanted to look past the masks and helmets into the eyes of fellow human beings deputized to take black life. For Evans, the killing of Sterling was a breaking point. She later wrote, "Enough was enough. I had to do something. Too many people are being slaughtered by those who are employed to serve and protect us. . . . Baton Rouge was enlightening. It opened my eyes. I had been sleeping for years. I have been sleeping and now I am awake."[1] Evans' refusal to cooperate with police led to arrest and a short stint in jail, but her embodied opposition to state violence came to epitomize a contemporary antilynching movement born in response to the murders of Trayvon Martin in 2012, Michael Brown in 2014, and Alton Sterling in 2016, among so many others.

Nearly four years later, in the Spring of 2020, the murders of George Floyd and Breonna Taylor, among others, sparked a new wave of Black Lives Matter protests that provoked a global reckoning with the enduring social, economic, and political legacies of colonialism and transatlantic slavery. The overwhelming police force on display in the viral photograph of Ieshia Evans now seems a harbinger of what would await protestors participating in the Floyd uprisings. The 2016 image reflects the saintly calm of a woman moored to her own convictions in the face of state violence. It recalls earlier portraits of women who stood quietly resigned to their unjust fates, whether accused as witches, adulteresses or other heretics. Evans is peaceful but resolute, resigned to the likely consequences of her actions, but the silent power of her fearless stance makes a loud mockery of police who swarm a single, unarmed protestor. Visually, Evans retains her moral authority in the face of the brute force and arbitrary commands of police officers. Her actions, and the snapshot resulting from them, simultaneously illustrate the enduring centrality of women to the black radical tradition and point to the gendered nature of racial capitalism.

Black death at the hands of police officers and white vigilantes is the logical conclusion of an antiblack political economy. Although racist violence is as old as the United States, neoliberal capitalism compounded the historical underdevelopment of black Americans during the last three decades of the twentieth century. The 1970s witnessed the rise of a carceral state predicated on solving various political and economic crises through what Ruth Wilson Gilmore calls the "prison fix."[2] Thanks to a bipartisan law-and-order consensus, millions of African Americans were policed, prosecuted, and banished behind prison walls.[3] Despite recent calls for decarceration, bail reform, and an end to mass incarceration, municipal governments have developed regimes of predatory accumulation and debt-bondage that explicitly target poor black communities.[4] Police officers are still incentivized to harass black people and justified in using lethal force during these encounters. Ieshia Evans thus stood opposed to an entrenched set of social relations epitomized by the murder of one black man.

Black women too are victimized by the carceral state as both targets of punitive policies and as caregivers. They are the fastest growing incarcerated population, and, as the murder of Breonna Taylor illustrates, are perpetually in danger of being killed by police even as they sleep in their own beds. Black women also care for loved ones who are deported to rural prisons and work to sustain families left behind. Mass incarceration even exacerbates racial disparities in health outcomes, such as disproportionately high maternal and infant mortality rates. In a 2018 investigation, *New York Times* journalist Linda Villarosa concluded that, even taking into account class background and formal education, simply living as a black woman in the United States was the single most important factor accounting for the staggering number of black infant and maternal deaths.[5] State-sanctioned violence merely reinforces broader patterns of organized social abandonment that render black communities – and black women in particular – vulnerable to premature death.[6]

Black Lives Matter is both a critique of a racialized political economy and a philosophical affirmation of black ontology. It calls attention to the disposability of black life under neoliberal capitalism and refuses that disposability. When Patrisse Cullors, Alicia Garza, and Opal Tometi created #BlackLivesMatter, they crafted a metaphysical response to the material realities of state violence (police and prison) and predatory finance capitalism. Black Lives Matter is spiritual warfare. Patrisse Cullors explains: "When you are working with people who have been directly impacted by state violence and heavy policing in our communities, it is really important that there is a connection to the spirit world." The immaterial realm provides one route to comprehending and surviving racial capitalism. "People's resilience," Cullors continues, "is tied to their will to live, our will to survive, which is deeply spiritual. . . . The fight to save your life is a spiritual fight."[7]

Cullors's insight sheds light on the postmortem struggles over Michael Brown's body and the memorialization of his life in Ferguson, Missouri. Following the murder of Brown by police officer Darren Wilson, the police officers left his body in the street for hours and refused to let Brown's parents even see or identify their son. His lifeless body served as a reminder to a community under siege that black life simply did not matter in the eyes of white cops. This soon gave way to battles over a makeshift memorial set up by friends and residents at the site where Brown's body lay. While police officers desecrated the memorial, Brown's family members fought to ensure his life and passing were marked. They refused to let the erasure of life translate into the vanquishing of memory.[8] The contestations over Michael Brown's body and his memorialization exemplify what the historian of Atlantic slavery Vincent Brown calls "mortuary politics."[9]

The spiritual dimensions of black insurgency are very familiar to historians of the African diaspora. Slave owners across the Americas appealed to the Christian Bible to justify the torture of human beings, invoking their "sacred authority" to rape women, sell children, and reap profits. They even presumed to colonize the black imagination and lay claim to the African ancestral realm. Enslaved people, meanwhile, fashioned new cosmologies out of African, indigenous, and European spiritual practices. Syncretic religions provided a tenuous refuge from the ordeal of slavery and, at times, was invoked to wage war against slave owners in places as diverse as Brazil, Mexico, Jamaica, St. Domingue (Haiti), and the United States. During the 1831 Baptist War in Jamaica, for example, enslaved rebels claimed their actions were merely "a matter of assisting their brethren in the work of the lord ... this was not the work of man alone, but they had assistance from God."[10] Nearly two centuries later, speaking of her arrest, Ieshia Evans claims "This was the work of God, I am a vessel. Glory to the most high!"[11] African and African-descended women sustained black spirituality during slavery just as they do in freedom. This, as Alicia Garza notes, is because "black women continue to bear the burden of a relentless assault on our children and our families and that assault is an act of state violence." It is hardly coincidental then that George Floyd's last words were "Momma ... Momma, I'm through," calling upon his deceased mother in the moments just before his own passing from one world to the next.[12]

A meditation on black women's spiritual politics may seem amiss in a volume on racial capitalism, but the seeming contradiction presupposes a distinction between the political-economic and the spiritual that makes little sense to working-class black people today and would have made even less sense to their enslaved ancestors. To think about racial capitalism and the black radical tradition as hermetically sealed off from one another is ahistorical and politically dubious. They were mutually constitutive phenomena. This is precisely what Cedric Robinson posits in his foundational text *Black Marxism: The Making of the Black Radical Tradition*.[13] Frequently cited in discussions of either racial capitalism or the black radical tradition, Robinson's goal was actually to get us to see the connection between these two phenomena. This essay attempts to resurrect Robinson's dialectical formulation through a gendered analysis of racial capitalism and what I call the black heretical tradition. Women like Evans, Cullors, Garza, and Tometi—black heretical woman—reappear over and over in the archive of slavery and freedom.

In particular, this essay traces the various ways narratives about the pathological black woman played midwife to racial capitalism and, conversely, the radical implications of black women's spiritual politics. The denigration of black women, who were portrayed as simultaneously masculine, hypersexual, and deviant, facilitated the consolidation of chattel slavery, just as liberal narratives about the irredeemable black matriarchal household facilitated black exploitation following its abolition.[14] Indeed, the notion of a pathological black family acquired additional significance in moments of emancipation, when racial capitalism was reconstituted in accordance with "free labor" ideology, since the absence of slave law necessitated new techniques for justifying state-sanctioned and extralegal violence. Whereas a gendered racism once propped up chattel slavery in the United States, it subsequently underpinned Jim Crow capitalism and eventually served to justify the warehousing or outright murder of surplus labor in postindustrial America.[15] The immiseration of black women under racial capitalism in the United States and much of the world is correlated with their status, devised during slavery, as the progenitors of blackness.

Black women's dishonored status under racial capitalism, however, has never been the sum total of their experience. The second and third sections of this essay borrow concepts from Cedric Robinson's own thinking to suggest one way in which we might gender the black radical tradition. First, Robinson's engagement with *marronage* as an early birthplace of this tradition provides an opening for reconstructing women-centered *marronage* practices and their embodiment of a particular kind of oppositional praxis that defied the social relations of slavery.[16] The history of runaway women under slavery resonates with contemporary black fugitivity in the era of mass incarceration.[17] Next, I revisit one of Robinson's lesser known works, *An Anthropology of Marxism*, in which Robinson offers a feminist genealogy of socialism rooted in medieval peasant rebellions against the early Christian church.[18] The centrality of pious women to these movements illustrates, for Robinson, the sacred nature of early socialism. Condemned as witches by the Church, these heretical women enunciated a radical refusal of private property that resonates with the black radical tradition.

Enslaved women, like the pious women of medieval Europe, were conscripted into and dominated by a world where the accumulation of wealth took precedence over Christian charity or virtue. The commodification of African women was nothing less than an early profession of capitalist faith. This orthodoxy insisted that it was possible to excise labor, value, and future productivity from a human body through its transformation into a person with a price in the "market of slavery's future."[19] Enslaved Africans who refused to accept their status as chattel were therefore among the earliest heretics of Atlantic capitalism. Highlighting women's role in providing space for what Robinson called the preservation of ontological totality, the essay concludes with a reflection on the spiritual dimensions of the black radical tradition.[20] My analysis throughout is necessarily informed by a rich black feminist scholarship, especially its socialist variants, that has centered the struggle for black liberation within a diverse range of intellectual projects. These thinkers do not necessarily share the same ideological and political commitments—some focus on the material conditions of black life and politics while others seek to tease out the spiritual dimensions of black history and politics—but collectively they have bequeathed an indispensable canon that can help us unpack the gendered nature of racial capitalism and the black radical tradition.[21]

Gendering Racial Capitalism in Slavery and Freedom

In *Black Marxism*, Cedric Robinson offers a theory of racial capitalism that challenges liberal and Marxian political economy.[22] For Robinson, social differentiation is not epiphenomenal to but rather constitutive of the productive process and the social relations of production under capitalism. Consequently, what divides the ruling and lower orders is not simply ownership of the means of production but asymmetrical ontologies. This differentiation even operates within the lower orders, as between white and nonwhite workers. Early in the text, Robinson revises E. P. Thompson's interpretation of the making of the English working class by centering the Irish and Scottish workers whose labor propelled the Industrial Revolution but were excluded from the English nation.[23] Thompson's use of the appellation "English" obscured deep divisions among even nominally white workers through the universal of class, excising Irish nationalism, for example, from the history of the British labor movement.

Indeed, Robinson draws attention to the workings of racial ideology within medieval and early modern Europe in order to demonstrate that race naturalized class relations. Ideologies of difference shaped who could be enslaved, dispossessed, imprisoned, and exploited. Yet nothing encapsulated this dynamic better than Atlantic slavery, which played midwife to both modern capitalism and the global color line. Robinson's corrective highlights the folly of an orthodox political economic critique that concerns itself with class at the expense of race or other axes of difference (nation and religion). Racial capitalism rejects radical political philosophies that conceptualize race as a troublesome consequence of capitalism. Robinson understood that such formulations consigned the "Third World" and black people to the "waiting room of history."[24]

Black Marxism reimagines the genealogy of capitalism and illuminates alternative terrains of political struggle. But while Robinson insisted on the co-construction of race and class, he was less attuned to the inextricability of gender, race, and class.[25] The naturalization of male supremacy through a fictional grounding of inequality in biology was no less central to the processes of differentiation that Robinson so carefully historicized.[26] Gender has been indispensable to justifying the ability of rulers to exploit, injure, and dispose the ruled. I want to focus on the ways the gendered exploitation of black women was as significant—both materially and ideologically—as race to the development and propagation of capitalism.[27] The groundbreaking work of scholars such as Jennifer L. Morgan and Alys Eve Weinbaum reveals that the race/reproduction connection—women's capacity to literally reproduce racialized labor power—cannot be divorced from any story about the birth of capitalism.[28] A gendered analysis of racial capitalism is not only compatible with Robinson's formulation but further elucidates the process of differentiation inherent to capitalism and the black radical tradition.

Atlantic slavery required the commodification of human beings and speculation on the future profitability of their progeny. As slave ship cargoes, enslaved people became numerical abstractions that filled shipping logs, manifests, and margins as exchange values.[29] After a grueling and often deadly middle passage, having survived sickness, terror, and grief, enslaved people disembarked—often more than once—in the Americas to be warehoused or prepared for sale.[30] Next, enslaved Africans encountered the auction block, a site at which value was once again affixed to their souls, with considerations taken for age, sex, and (dis)ability.[31] The violence of sale was accompanied by extreme alienation and dislocation as this economic system attempted to wrest commodity from human form.[32] Race came to function as both a transatlantic currency and a theology, tethering physiognomy and a belief in intrinsic difference to the concept of enslaveability.[33] The acceleration of the transatlantic slave system welded together race and the chattel principle. If race became the self-evident mark of hereditary slavery at the heart of eighteenth-century racial capitalism, black women's wombs were the incubators of capital accumulation.

Atlantic slavery depended upon reproductive as well as productive capacities. Even in particularly deadly slave societies in the Caribbean and Brazil, where enslaved people experienced perpetual population decline, custom and legislation regulated the "issue" of enslaved women.[34] In slave societies as diverse as Virginia, Barbados, South Carolina, and Cuba, planter-legislators looked to enslaved women to enlarge their profits through "natural increase." The Roman principle *partus sequitur ventrem*, or "offspring follows belly," shaped English and Spanish slave codes and served to clarify the racial messiness endemic to slavery.[35] Slavery's legal architects in the

English empire used *partus* to settle the racial uncertainty of children of whose parents were increasingly seen as separate racial beings.[36] The racial nature of the slave law drew upon legal precedents concerning property and livestock rather than those that governed claims of familial lineage or bastardy.[37] The intention of the law was therefore not only to create a secure legal foundation for settling disputes about the ownership of human beings; *partus* also created that very property by enacting "the legal and material substitution of a thing for a child."[38] This legal transubstantiation became key to white supremacy under slavery and was an essential prerequisite for racial capitalism. The codification and casual acceptance of *partus sequitur ventrem* constituted enslaved women's wombs as a secondary site of production under slavery, akin to a sugar estate or cotton plantation. Early iterations of futures speculation inhered in merchant, trader, and planter considerations of enslaved women's bodies.[39] To reconcile their financial investment in black women's flesh with their humanity, slave owners denigrated the person of the black woman.

European observers represented enslaved African women as monstrous.[40] In the eighteenth- and nineteenth-century Anglophone Caribbean, for example, figures such as planter-historian Edward Long, Scottish traveler Mrs. Carmichael, and Maria Nugent, wife to the governor of Jamaica, were simultaneously fascinated and revolted, terrified and titillated by enslaved black women.[41] The racial intimacies of slave societies, in which rebellions were frequent and death commonplace, only strengthened white presumptions of black malevolence. These ideologies nurtured an image of black women that was at once licentious, lascivious, and prone to theft, laziness, and conspiracy.[42]

Racist discourses about black women rooted in slavery account, in part, for the enduring image of the pathological black family. The impossibility of keeping one's kin close and children together was a hallmark of chattel slavery. The twin specters of death and the auction block haunted enslaved people and were a constant reminder of their familial precarity.[43] Nuclear families were not the "natural" choice for enslaved people (nor are they for anyone else), but proslavery ideologues cited the fracturing of enslaved kinship networks caused by slavery as evidence that they lacked familial bonds. Runaway advertisements and court proceedings that suggest enslaved people ran with and to family, however, belied the paranoid discourses of owners. Enslaved people enthusiastically maintained their own property and trading relationships even when they became fugitives. In one example of many from Jamaica, in 1781 an enslaved woman named Rose was supposed to be "harboured by some person" in Montego Bay and had "been lately seen selling goods in country."[44] This fragment of Rose's life points to the social life of the enslaved—to be "harboured" presupposes social and economic relations beyond the master-slave relationship. Rose's ability to survive by "selling goods" points to Jamaica's robust internal marketing system as a commercial refuge from slavery. Enslaved people sought out the smallest cracks in white domination to protect and spend time with their families and care for their homes and gardens, if they had them. Enslaved people's property relations and economic practices also suggest that even under slavery's crushing weight, they were not just theorizing but enacting alternative visions of life.

As the British abolition of the slave trade began to stifle imports of enslaved Africans into colonies like Jamaica, enslaved women's reproductive capacities took on even greater importance. Parliament promoted ameliorative policies in its colonies that centered on women's childbearing, and even British abolitionists anxiously debated the capacity of black women to steward healthy families.[45] Presuming that enslaved people had no viable forms of family, reformers, inaugurating what would become a signature ideology of racial capitalism, argued that the system of slavery had so degraded enslaved people that only severe discipline could ensure nuclear family units. While wage work promised to liberate freed people from private bondage, they believed patriarchal nuclear families could stimulate habits of industry and transform slaves into modern workers and consumers.[46] Throughout the Atlantic world, emancipation schemes, such as apprenticeship in the British colonies, sought to train formerly enslaved people how to be free laborers. Apprenticeship forced freed people to continue to work long hours for their former masters—now "employers"—while laying the groundwork for extensive systems of state surveillance and carceral control.[47] The notion that slavery did permanent psychic and structural damage to black people, rendering their families forever incomplete, unnatural, and deformed, was entrenched during the era of emancipation.

The explanatory power accorded to slavery to account for black pathology emerged out of vigorous transatlantic debates. Abolitionists and planters were united, though toward very different ends, on the question of black people's comportment. Planters pointed to innate African backwardness, whereas abolitionists believed it was slavery that dehumanized black people and debilitated the black mind.[48] For them, slavery disrupted the natural

nuclear family structure that could only be salvaged through direct intervention in women's lives and bodies.[49] Just as early racial discourses justified
enslavement, racial liberalism justified the drudgery of wage labor and state
regulation of nominally free black families as well as a general condemnation of blackness.[50] The rapid decline in sugar production and fluctuating
prices in the British Caribbean accelerated the devaluation of black labor as
freed people left plantations and British capital turned its attention to
domestic industry and trade with Asia.[51] The refusal to recognize black
freedom dreams articulated with a shifting imperial economy.[52]

In the post-Revolutionary United States, black women's reproductive
capacities were explicitly incorporated into the legal process of slave emancipation in several northern states. Both Pennsylvania (1780) and New York
(1799) passed gradual emancipation laws that freed the children of enslaved
mothers after a certain date provided that they continue to serve their masters as "servants" for extended periods, ranging from eighteen to twenty-eight
years. Slave owners who preferred to abandon enslaved children rather than
pay for their upkeep relinquished title to the overseers of the poor (i.e., the
state). This scheme, which Robert Fogel and Stanley Engerman have called
"philanthropy at bargain prices," anticipated developments in Cuba and
Brazil later in the century.[53]

Slave emancipation in the United States and the British Empire crystal-
lized racist assumptions about the capacities of black people and the dangers
of black freedom associated with the Haitian Revolution. Ironically, it also
precipitated a "second slavery" in Latin America and accompanied the
domestic slave trade and the rise of cotton capitalism in the U.S. South.
American slaveholders exercised significant power over domestic and foreign policy in antebellum America, producing a series of political conflicts
that culminated in the Civil War. The fratricidal violence of 1861–65 made
recourse to the black womb less necessary, but gender colored the actions of
every major protagonist in the war and shaped the contours of freedom.[54]
In Cuba and Brazil, meanwhile, the inextricability of race, gender, and legal
status reached its logical conclusion in the "free womb laws" that governed
emancipation. As Camilla Cowling notes, "the wombs of enslaved women,
previously vessels for transmitting enslavement, became spaces in which
freedom was, literally, conceived."[55]

Abolition everywhere marked a significant transformation in the history
of racial capitalism. Black women continued to reproduce blackness, but
black life was increasingly stripped of the fluctuating monetary value

associated with slavery. This was coupled with the rise of biological racism. Black women, whose bodies were grounds for speculation and experimentation under slavery, were now reconfigured as economic burdens or dangerous labor.[56] Describing developments in the U.S. South, Talitha LeFlouria notes that female prisoners were "economically valued only for their ability to produce labor, not laborers."[57] In charting this "dramatic shift from conception to conviction as a means of growing bound labor forces in the new South," LeFlouria captures the arrival of Jim Crow racial capitalism.[58] Even after the triumph of the modern civil rights movement, the ever flexible regime of racial capitalism endured in the United States. By the late twentieth century, black women's economic and symbolic devaluation was enshrined in their unique vulnerability to premature death in a host of post-slavery societies.[59] *Partus sequitur ventrem* in late-stage capitalism means that poor black women bear black children with "no intrinsic value," a surplus, disposable population subject to judicial murder or the slow death of incarceration and poverty.[60]

Despite changes in tone and content, discourses about black women as monstrous nonwomen first precipitated their enslaveability and now account for their disposability. The violence of being excluded from the category of persons worthy of protection stands in stark contrast to the reputation of white women, whose purity an entire society is duty bound to secure.[61] As bearers of the hereditary mark of slavery, black women held the dubious distinction of bringing black life into a world that needed it as much as it despised it. In slavery, this meant that black life was to be commodified; after freedom, black life is to be monitored, constrained, or ended with impunity.

Marronage and the Black Radical Tradition

For Robinson, the racial nature of capitalism—its nonobjective character—helps explain why black political struggle necessarily exceeds the boundaries of class struggle as formulated by Marx. Racial capitalism not only alienates human beings from their labor but alienates them from each other through its grammar of immutable difference. While all workers at a factory, for example, are exploited by their employer, they experience the social relations of production (i.e., class) through the modality of race[62]—hence the explicitly race-conscious politics of white, almost white, and nonwhite workers. All this is not to say that Marx or Marxism is tangential to the black radical tradition. As Robinson noted, perhaps no other political theory—and its many (sometimes contradictory) historical iterations—has so deeply informed black opposition to capitalism.[63]

Black radicals have been central to developing and deepening Marx's critique of capitalism. By centering the lived experiences of Africans and their descendants, they have remapped the sites of capitalism's inaugural factories, proletarians, and revolutionary negations.[64] The processes that Marx located in Europe were relocated to European colonies in the Americas and Africa by black scholar-revolutionaries, who configured an Atlantic world long before the concept gained currency among white North American academics. But the specificity of black history—and its connections to the birth of capitalism in the Atlantic world—called for an entire rethinking of Marxist categories and political programs.

For Robinson, black liberation necessarily includes the struggle to preserve ontological totality, something fundamentally different from, though not unrelated to, class struggle and proletarian revolution. The dimensions of this struggle are beyond the material, because the alienation experienced by Africans and their descendants went beyond the physical and into the spiritual.[65] The process of commodification and the murderous character of daily life under slavery produced a kind of elemental spiritual alienation that remains unaccounted for in Marx's consideration of workers' plight under capitalism.[66]

Robinson's notion of ontological totality fleshes out an important thread in black philosophy on questions of being, articulated by Frantz Fanon and W. E. B. Du Bois.[67] Their philosophical treatments of ontology understood black being as fractured by processes of racial capitalism. The unification of this fractured being, or the preservation of ontological totality, can be achieved only through political struggle informed by the specificity of black history. What Du Bois famously describes as black "twoness"—"two souls, two thoughts, two unreconciled strivings; two warring ideals in one dark body, whose dogged strength alone keeps it from being torn asunder"—is not only about the tension between blackness and Americanness. This twoness also represents a division between the commodified, dishonored black self in itself and what we might call the black self for itself.

For Fanon, the fact of blackness and its historicity produces the ontological condition of being able to recognize oneself only through the eyes of others, or what he calls "crushing objecthood."[68] This ontological rupture precedes and stains interactions with the nonblack world. For both Fanon and Du Bois, even within the relatively closed worlds of black folks, only partial respite from the daily agony of living as fragmented beings is possible.[69] The recovery of ontological wholeness was and is central to any black political project in the aftermath of the transatlantic slave trade, even if it is not named as such.

Fanon and Du Bois' masculinist theories of blackness, however, must be read alongside feminist theories of black ontology. The philosophical contributions of Claudia Jones, the Combahee River Collective, and Audre Lorde, for example, draw attention to the specific sociological position of black women – as workers, mothers, lovers and friends—under racial capitalism. Their work elucidated the triple bind or 'super-exploitation' of black women in a capitalist society, but they also fashioned radical horizons of possibility from this unique embodied location. Forging community and solidarity is necessarily material—the provision of shelter, food, and warmth—but these exist alongside forms of relief that are also immaterial.[70] Audre Lorde, for example, foregrounded the somatic, sensual experiences of women—what she called the "erotic"—as key to black reparation. Here, pleasure en route to revolution became a negation of capitalism. For black feminists like Lorde, the political could never come at the expense of the personal precisely because exploitation—wage theft in secular terms—penetrated mind and body. They prioritized the preservation of individual and community ontology within broader revolutionary projects.

The creation of space for love, self-affirmation, commiseration, and communion are facets of political preservation that exist in tandem with or submerged within the more overt acts of rebellion upon which the historiography of slavery has tended to focus. Systematic and discrete instances of ontological preservation, especially led by women, ought to be analyzed for what they can teach us about how black politics enhances but also diverges from Western radical humanist traditions. In the sixth chapter of *Black Marxism*, "The Historical Archeology of the Black Radical Tradition," Robinson locates the origins of this tradition in the "the actual terms of [black] humanity." This consisted of "African cultures, critical mixes and admixtures of language and thought, of cosmology and metaphysics, of habits, beliefs, and morality."[71] One of the earliest expressions of this consciousness was the seemingly mundane act of running away from slave owners. Flight from slavery, or *marronage*, Robinson believes, indexed an enslaved political philosophy at odds with racial capitalism.[72]

Grand Marronage was endemic to slave societies throughout the Americas from the fifteenth though the nineteenth centuries, in places as diverse as Mexico, St. Domingue, Brazil, Jamaica, and the United States.[73] Robinson argues that maroons fled bondage not only to escape slavery but also for the purpose of constructing something new.[74] These fledgling societies in the belly of slavery kindled the embers of what would become the black radical tradition. Maroon communities needed not only space, food, and shelter to fend off re-enslavement but also military strategy and spiritual sustenance. The healing traditions of Africanized religions like *Obeah* and *Santería* intersected with African political affiliations and cosmologies, providing something like freedom outside of eighteenth- and nineteenth-century Enlightenment categories but more closely approximating preservation.[75] The purpose of maroon communities was the preservation of one's self and community, no matter how fleeting.[76]

Large maroon settlements represented one expression of enslaved refusal. Broadening the category of maroon community beyond established settlements, *quilombos*, or *palenques*, however, can reveal the ways the subterfuge and hidden geographies of enslaved women were and are critical to quotidian black politics.[77] *Petit marronage*, or truancy, for example, constituted essential breaks that enslaved people took to come up for air in a system in which they were drowning daily.[78] In my own research on enslaved women and the informal economy, I have found that less permanent, more flexible forms of *marronage* enabled some enslaved women to carve out semiautonomous space within slavery. Specifically, some women fled slavery to become market women who used the banality of their bondage to take refuge in plain sight. I call this fugitive freedom within slavery's internal economy, market *marronage*.[79]

As much as runaway advertisements lamented the ability of absconded people to "pass as free," what was even more infuriating to owners was the ability of some fugitives to perform their enslavement in order to remain free. Reading the archive of runaways shines a light on the forms of community and mutual aid that were often hidden in plain sight. In one nineteenth-century runaway advertisement, a master seeking the return of his human chattels unwittingly reveals both the violence that characterized slavery and the novel arrangements that enslaved people could devise to escape, if even for a brief moment. The advertisement reads:

> Ranaway from the subscriber, some time ago, a Negro Man Slave, named John, by trade a sailor; and lately, a Negro Woman Slave, named Ann, a

relation of his; The former is of short stature, full eyes, has a scar on his chest from the break of a tumour, and a cataract coming over one eye; he has been two or three times in different parts of the Parish, but escaped being take from his plausibility and he is supposed to have a false ticket:— The latter is a middle-aged person, of a yellow complexion, slim made, long visage, and much pitted in the face with small pox; she absconded from the vicinity of Lacovia, where she was selling Shads.

In this ad, Isaac Sams, John and Ann's owner, revealed his inability to control their lives and livelihoods. As a sailor, John may have had knowledge of the island's ports, and Ann was capable of selling fish to survive on the run. Their attitudes also facilitated their ability to live as fugitives. Their "plausibility" and the false ticket John was suspected of having suggest their forethought about how to live freely. Maroons not only established societies, but individuals, couples, and groups of kin (blood-related or not) practiced the kind of collective preservation that characterizes the black radical tradition.[80]

Understanding the complexity of *marronage* within slavery lends a deeper appreciation to the nature of refusal in the context of capitalist hegemony. Maroon communities were never completely independent from the slave societies of which they formed a part.[81] There was constant military pressure on maroons to negotiate the terms of order within which they managed to secure a modicum of freedom. Some communities policed enslaved people on behalf of colonial authorities, returning runaways and serving alongside colonial militias tasked with suppressing slave revolts. Market maroons, too, relied upon an internal marketing system that ultimately sustained plantation slavery. Historicizing maroon communities and *marronage* in all of their complexity reveals that the preservation of ontological totality necessarily exists within racial capitalism as an immanent critique.

Market *marronage* also suggests alternatives to traditional narratives of enslaved politics that emphasize masculine militarism.[82] Although militarism and guerilla warfare were critical to black politics under slavery, conceptualizing *marronage* purely in military terms obscures other routes by which fugitives from slavery might have sought and achieved interstitial freedom.[83] Further, slave rebellion and maroon sovereignty were at times in opposition.[84] Acts not typically associated with resistance to slavery, such as the tending of provision grounds and trading goods in the informal economy, conjure different images of what the black radical tradition might look like. Recognizing forms of resistance that do not exclusively conform to revolutionary tropes augments the concept of the black radical tradition, which Robinson equates with the preservation of ontological totality.

The Black Heretical Tradition:
A View from *An Anthropology of Marxism*

Black Marxism's excavation of maroon communities leaves room for a deeper consideration of the ways market *marronage*—or other forms of woman-centered preservation—constituted the black radical tradition. Robinson's most substantial engagement with gender and women's history, however, is to be found in *An Anthropology of Marxism*. There, Robinson thinks through a political genealogy of socialism that predates the cotemporaneous rise of Western socialism with a modern bourgeoisie in the late eighteenth century.[85] Specifically, Robinson argues that nonelite pious women and their radical rejection of the established church's worldliness were an early precursor to socialism.

The peasant uprisings of the thirteenth and fourteenth centuries were revolts against the church and the feudal ruling class. The dualist belief that things of the world were corrupted and only God-in-heaven was righteous laid the foundations for heretical revolt, as dissenters confronted the hypocrisy of the church's primary concerns of landholding and wealth accumulation.[86] Many poor women rejected dualism and manifested signs of their faith through the renunciation of property, stigmata, bodily miracles, and ecstatic worship and connection with the divine. These women, who were central to larger theological debates from the thirteenth century onward, exemplified and practiced the communal impulse and shifted the terms on which the church engaged the poor.[87] Women were seen as special threats to the ruling order, and even though the historiography of medieval heretical women has largely focused on elite women, they were greatly outnumbered by unfree and peasant women, characterized by contemporary observers as "whores and fornicators among the dissenters and heretics."[88] Their criticism of church wealth and the corruption of institutional religion was often conveniently construed as witchcraft by the powerful and punished accordingly.[89]

Robinson's examination of radical women in medieval Europe offers some clues for how we might reconstruct the black heretical tradition. If gender structured racial capitalism, *An Anthropology of Marxism* points to a specifically gender-based anticapitalism, one that was rooted in the bodily experience of exploitation on the basis of "womanhood" that preceded modern socialism. Black women, too, revolted against a system that conscripted them to be bearers of chattel rather than their own children in ways that reflected their specific bodily experiences and political perspectives. Following emancipation, they perceived the limitations of liberal freedom.[90] If capitalism's hegemony has made it, perhaps, the world's most consistent religion since the sixteenth century, then it might be useful to understand black women not only as radicals in opposition to it but also as heretics of its orthodoxy.[91] Black heretical women do not necessarily seek to overthrow the class system and replace it with a dictatorship of the proletariat, but rather work toward the simpler but no less radical task of preserving self, family, and community in communion with ancestors on solid ground in a society where such presence is perpetually under threat. This mystical and spiritual dimension always has an earthly resonance in the black radical tradition.[92]

Perhaps no literary figure is greater at exemplifying the unification of *marronage* and heretical refusal than Baby Suggs, Holy, in Toni Morrison's *Beloved*.[93] Baby Suggs is a survivor of slavery whose freedom was purchased by her son, Halle, but who can find no rest in free Ohio. Her radicalism is not shown to us in formal protests against slavery or freedom's failures, but rather in the quieter but no less profound moments of spiritual leadership, catharsis, and communion. Her hatred of the rotten system in which she lived and into which she brought children was also tied to her recognition that if, in the free present, black people were to really be free, then they would have to heal and "re-member" their humanity.[94] In one of the most powerful passages of the novel, Sethe, the protagonist and grieving daughter-in-law of Baby Suggs, remembers her preaching. Suggs's transcendental sermons took place in a forest clearing filled with freed men, women, and children, risking their lives, one presumes, to partake in this necessary ritual. Suggs convened gatherings that reflected her zealous belief in the full humanity of black people and her refusal to believe the racist ideologies foisted upon them. Suggs, though "uncalled, unrobed, [and] unanointed," held worship services that were as much about the people present as any god.[95] Her words from Sethe's remembrances are worth quoting in full:

In this here place, we flesh; flesh that weeps, laughs; flesh that dances on bare feet in grass. Love it. Love it hard. Yonder they do not love your flesh.

They despise it. They don't love your eyes; they'd just as soon pick em out. No more do they love the skin on your back. Yonder they flay it. And O my people they do not love your hands. Those they only use, tie, bind, chop off and leave empty. Love your hands! Love them. Raise them up and kiss them. Touch others with them, pat them together, stroke them on your face 'cause they don't love that either. You got to love it, you! And no, they ain't in love with your mouth. Yonder, out there, they will see it broken and break it again. What you say out of it they will not heed. What you scream from it they do not hear. What you put into it to nourish your body they will snatch away and give you leavins instead. No, they don't love your mouth. You got to love it. This is flesh I'm talking about here. Flesh that needs to be loved. Feet that need to rest and to dance; backs that need support; shoulders that need arms, strong arms I'm telling you. And O my people, out yonder, hear me, they do not love your neck unno-osed and straight. So love your neck; put a hand on it, grace it, stroke it and hold it up. and all your inside parts that they'd just as soon slop for hogs, you got to love them. The dark, dark liver—love it, love it and the beat and beating heart, love that too. More than eyes or feet. More than lungs that have yet to draw free air. More than your life-holding womb and your life-giving private parts, hear me now, love your heart. For this is the prize.

The prize of which Suggs, via Morrison, speaks is the preservation of onto-logical totality. It is a refusal to be completely vanquished by a system designed to wring labor from its subjects and discard the rest. Morrison, of course, was mining a deeper truth from a broader diasporic history of black women's spiritual and material struggles.

John Gabriel Stedman's eighteenth-century account of African religious practices in Surinam confirms the prevalence of similar assemblies in Caribbean plantation societies. After noting the generally "superstitious" nature of enslaved people, Stedman proceeds to offer an account of a gathering of women spiritual leaders:

The slaves have amongst them a kind of Sybils, who deal in Oracles; these sage matrons dancing and whirling round in the middle of an assembly with amazing rapidity until they foam a the mouth and drop down con-vulsed. Whatever the prophetess orders to be done during this paroxysm is most sacredly performed by the surrounding multitude which renders these meetings extremely dangerous, as she frequently enjoins them to murder their masters or to desert to the woods.

This "scene of excessive fanaticism is forbidden by law . . . upon pain of the most rigorous punishment," Stedman noted, "yet it is often practiced in private places."[96] While syncretic ceremonies could be conducive to political violence, they more often served the immediate spiritual needs of enslaved people. Across the African diaspora, enslaved women convened sacred gatherings that facilitated survival, pleasure, and, at times, political transcendence.[97]

Black feminist scholars have theorized most clearly the ways black women's metaphysical and philosophical concerns have shaped their politics.[98] Faith, ancestral connections, and millenarian divination have guided their struggles for dignity, civic recognition, and material resources.[99] While the secular orientation of Western Marxism and most intellectuals has lent itself to a bifurcation of black women's sacred strivings and anticapitalist critique, their spiritual practices inaugurated the black radical tradition and continue to be a font from which it gathers strength. Scholars who fail to appreciate the metaphysical dimension of this tradition miss one of its key attributes and, consequently, the conflict between European radicalism and black radicalism that Robinson first identified in *Black Marxism*.[100]

Grappling with the spiritual dimension of black women's politics illuminates the lives of black women activists who are usually considered only as feminists, abolitionists, or political radicals. For women such as Sojourner Truth, Ida B. Wells-Barnett, Mary Church Terrell, and Nanny H. Burroughs, the terrain of their struggle was as much spiritual as it was material.[101] Sojourner Truth's refrain from her 1851 speech at the first National Convention on Women's Rights in Akron, Ohio, "ain't I a woman?," is particularly instructive. The phrase is remembered by liberal accounts as Truth's plea for inclusion into the largely white movements of suffragists and abolitionists. In radical readings of Truth's speech, the broader context of her claim contains an indictment of her white movement sisters and abolitionist brothers. Both readings miss an obvious point about Truth's own contention about what gave her politics meaning: her understanding of the divine. As Truth gave her speech, she demanded that her audience look at the muscles in her arm and then went on:

I have ploughed, and planted, and gathered into barns and no man could head me! And ain't I a woman? I could work as much and eat as much as a man—when I could get it—and bear the lash as well! And ain't I a woman?

I have borne thirteen children and seen them most all sold off to slavery, and when I cried out with my mother's grief, *none but Jesus heard me!* And ain't I a woman?[102]

Truth proceeded to call out the false prophets in the audience—namely, the gathering's white men who protested and guffawed when she first took the stage. She spoke to one in particular: "That little man in black here, he says women can't have as much rights as men, because Christ wasn't a woman. Where did Christ come from? Where did your Christ come from? From God and a woman! Man had nothing to do with him."[103]

Truth reminded her audience that, as a black woman, she bore the lash as well as her own children, who were later sold away into slavery. "Ain't I a woman?" was not just a rebuke of sexist social reform circles, but a public indication of how Truth's own unorthodox faith animated her flight to freedom and her struggle to be made whole.[104] Truth embodied a black heretical tradition at odds with secular orthodox Marxism but nevertheless thoroughly anticapitalist in orientation. Truth, just like Harriet Tubman, Nanny of the Maroons, and civil rights leaders like Fannie Lou Hamer were each standard bearers of the black heretical tradition as were millions of other lesser known black women.[105]

The popular framing of the spiritual dimensions of black politics as "religious"—whether Western or "Africanized"—misses the fundamental political work of black spirituality. The persistence of working-class faith, often led by women and as profane as it is sacred, points to a vernacular refusal of racial capitalism. The particular metaphysical grammar of this struggle, as Robinson identified, revolves around ontological preservation and should not be conflated with the insurrectionary overthrow of class exploitation. Professions of faith by black women have functioned not only as incantations of protection and healing but also as historically informed attempts to make whole that which was divided by racial capitalism. Black women's contributions to the black radical tradition were enshrined in their preservation of self, articulated through language and action that emphasized that inviolability of human life. Black women gave birth, literally, to modern racial capitalism, but they also contested, fled, and refused its assault on black life when and where they could. The black heretical tradition continues to infuse the quotidian struggles of black women throughout the diaspora and the global #BlackLivesMatter movement, which demands nothing short of the preservation of ontological totality.

NOTES

1. Ieshia Evans, "I wasn't afraid. I took a stand in Baton Rouge because enough is enough." *Guardian*, July 22, 2016, https://www.theguardian.com/commentisfree /2016/jul/22/i-wasnt-afraid-i-took-a-stand-in-baton-rouge-because-enough-is -enough.

2. Ruth Wilson Gilmore, *Golden Gulag: Prisons, Surplus, Crisis, and Opposition in Globalizing California* (Berkeley: University of California Press, 2007).

3. Elizabeth Hinton, *From the War on Poverty to the War on Crime: The making of Mass Incarceration in America* (Cambridge: Harvard University Press, 2016); Loic Wacquaint, *Punishing the Poor: The Neoliberal Government of Insecurity* (Durham, NC: Duke University Press, 2009).

4. Elizabeth Jones, "Racism, Fines and Fees and the US Carceral State," *Race and Class* 59, no. 3 (2017): 38–50; "Policing and Profit: Developments in the Law," *Harvard Law Review* 128, no. 6 (April 2015); Jackie Wang, *Carceral Capitalism* (South Pasadena, CA: Semiotext(e), 2018), chap. 2.

5. Linda Villarosa, "Why America's Black Mothers and Babies Are in a Life-or-Death Crisis," *New York Times Magazine*, April 11, 2018; Elizabeth Swavola, Kristine Riley, and Ram Subramanian, *Overlooked: Women and Jails in an Era of Reform* (New York: Vera Institute for Justice, 2017). According to the Centers for Disease Control and Prevention (CDC), black mothers accounted for 43.5 deaths per 100,000 live births during 2011–2013, compared to 12.7 deaths/100,000 live births for white women and 14.4 deaths/100,000 live births for women of other races. CDC, "Trends in Pregnancy-Related Mortality in the United States: 1987–2013," accessed April 26 2018, https://www.cdc.gov/reproductivehealth/maternalinfanthealth/pmss.html. A 2010 study highlighted the material impoverishment of black women compared to women of other races. Single black women between the ages of thirty-six and forty-nine had a median wealth of five dollars, compared to $42,600 for white women. Insight Center for Community Economic Development, "Lifting as We Climb: Women of Color, Wealth, and America's Future," Spring 2010, http://ww1.insightcced.org/uploads /CRWG/LiftingAsWeClimb-WomenWealth-Report-InsightCenter-Spring2010.pdf/.

6. For the concept of "social abandonment," see Clara Han, *Life in Debt: Times of Care and Violence in Neoliberal Chile* (Berkeley: University of California Press, 2012); Joao Biehl, *Vita: Life in a Zone of Social Abandonment* (Berkeley: University of California Press, 2005).

7. Hebah H. Farrag, "The Role of Spirit in the #BlackLivesMatter Movement: A Conversation with Activist and Artist Patrisse Cullors," *Religion Dispatches*, June 24, 2015.

8. See Keeanga-Yamahtta Taylor, *From #BlackLivesMatter to Black Liberation* (Chicago: Haymarket, 2016), 154.

9. Vincent Brown, *Reaper's Garden: Death and Power in the World of Atlantic Slavery* (Cambridge, Mass.: Harvard University Press, 2008).

10. As cited in Mary Reckford, "The Jamaica Slave Rebellion of 1831," *Past and Present*, No 40 (July 1968), 115. See also Vincent Brown, "Spiritual Terror and Sacred

Authority in Jamaican Slave Society," *Slavery & Abolition* 24, no. 1 (April 2003): 24–53; Kate Ramsay, *The Spirits and the Law: Vodou and Power in Haiti* (Cambridge Mass: Harvard University Press, 2011).

11. "Nurse in photo describes her arrest in Baton Rouge as 'work of God,'" Reuters, July 11, 2016.

12. Alicia Garza, "A Herstory of the #BlackLivesMatter Movement," The Feminist Wire, https://thefeministwire.com/2014/10/blacklivesmatter-2/. October 7, 2014. Lonnae O'Neal, "George Floyd's Mother was not there but he used her as a sacred invocation," National Geographic, https://www.nationalgeographic.com/history/2020/05/george-floyds-mother-not-there-he-used-her-as-sacred-invocation/. May 30, 2020.

13. Cedric J. Robinson, *Black Marxism: The Making of the Black Radical Tradition* (Chapel Hill: University of North Carolina Press, [1983] 2000).

14. On race and black womanhood and its American particularities, see Hortense J. Spillers, "Mama's Baby, Papa's Maybe: An American Grammar Book," *Diacritics* 17, no. 2 (Summer 1987): 64–81.

15. On the idea of warehousing black bodies, see Gilmore, *Golden Gulag*, 14; and Tara Herviel and Paul Wright eds., *Prison Nation: The Warehousing of America's Poor* (New York: Routledge, 2003).

16. Robinson, *Black Marxism*, 132–40.

17. Cedric J. Robinson, *An Anthropology of Marxism* (Burlington, Vermont.: Ashgate, 2001).

18. Alice Goffman, *On the Run: Fugitive Life in an American City* (New York: Picador, 2014).

19. Walter Johnson, "Introduction—The Future Store," in *The Chattel Principle: Internal Slave Trades in the Americas*, ed. Walter Johnson (New Haven, Conn.: Yale University Press, 2004), 2. See also Daina Ramey Berry, "'We'm Fus' Rate Bargain': Labor, Value, and Price in a Georgia Slave Community," chap. 3 in the same volume.

20. Robinson, *Black Marxism*, 168–71. The black radical tradition necessarily encompasses both the material and the metaphysical aspects of collective black politics. In brief and somewhat mysterious passages, Robinson describes the black radical tradition as "the continuing development of a collective consciousness informed by the historical struggles for liberation and motivated by the shared sense of obligation to preserve the collective being, the ontological totality."

21. Black feminist scholarship cannot be represented in a single footnote, but some of the groundbreaking texts from this canon that have shaped my analysis here include Claudia Jones, "An End to the Neglect of the Problems of the Negro Woman," *Political Affairs*, June 1949; Michele Wallace, *Black Macho and the Myth of the Superwoman* (New York: Dial Press, 1979); Spillers, "Mama's Baby, Papa's Maybe"; Paula Giddings, *When and Where I Enter: The Impact of Black Women on Race and Sex in America* (New York: Harper Collins, 1984); Audre Lorde, *Sister Outsider: Essays and Speeches* (Trumansburg, N.Y.: Crossing Press, 1984); Crenshaw, "Demarginalizing the Intersection of Race and Sex" A Black Feminist Critique of Antidiscrimination Doctrine, Feminist Theory and Antiracist

Politics," *University of Chicago Law Forum* 1989, no. 1, article 8; Cheryl I. Harris, "Finding Sojourner's Truth: Race, Gender, and the Institution of Property," *Cardozo Law Review* 18 (1997): 309–409; Angela Y. Davis, *Women, Race, and Class* (New York: Random House, 1981); Dorothy E. Roberts, *Killing the Black Body: Race, Reproduction and the Meaning of Liberty* (New York: Vintage, 1997); Hazel V. Carby, *Reconstructing Womanhood: The Emergence of the Afro-American Woman Novelist* (New York: Oxford University Press, 1987); Toni Morrison, ed., *Race-ing Justice, Engendering Power: Essays on Anita Hill, Clarence Thomas, and the Construction of Social Reality* (New York: Pantheon, 1992); Selma James, *Sex, Race, Class: The Perspective of Winning, Selected Writings* (Oakland, Calif.: PM Press, 2012); M. Jacqui Alexander, *Pedagogies of Crossing: Meditations on Feminism, Sexual Politics, Memory and the Sacred* (Durham, N.C.: Duke University Press, 2005); Akasha Hull, Patricia Bell Scott, and Barbara Smith, eds., *All the Women Are White, All the Blacks Are Men, but Some of Us Are Brave: Black Women's Studies*, 2nd ed. (New York: Feminist Press, 2015); Cherrie Moraga and Gloria Anzaldúa, *This Bridge Called My Back: Writings by Radical Women of Color*, 4th ed. (Albany: State University of New York Press, 2015); Keeyanga Yamahtta-Taylor, ed., *How We Get Free: Black Feminism and the Combahee River Collective* (Chicago: Haymarket, 2017). On the idea of the superexploitation of black women, see Carole Boyce Davies, *Left of Karl Marx: The Political Life of Black Communist Claudia Jones* (Durham, N.C.: Duke University Press, 2008), esp. chap. 1; Davis, *Women, Race, and Class*, esp. chap. 1, 5. On the concept of intersectionality, see Crenshaw, "Demarginalizing the Intersection of Race and Sex."

22. Robinson, *Black Marxism*, 2; 9. Robinson was building on the pioneering work of black sociologist Oliver Cromwell Cox. See Cox, *Caste, Class and Race: A Study in Social Dynamics* (Garden City: Doubleday and Company, 1948).

23. Robinson, *Black Marxism*, 23–24, 41–43; E. P. Thompson, *The Making of the English Working Class* (New York: Vintage, [1963] 1966).

24. Dipesh Chakrabarty, *Provincializing Europe: Postcolonial Thought and Historical Difference* (Princeton, N.J.: Princeton University Press, 2000), 8. The "Third World" was a political formation that remained highly relevant in the 1980s when Robinson was completing *Black Marxism*. See Vijay Prasad, *The Darker Nations: A People's History of the Third World* (New York: New Press, 2008); and Peter James Hudson, "Racial Capitalism and the Dark Proletariat," *Boston Review* (Feb. 20, 2018).

25. Angela Davis, *Women, Race, and Class* (New York: Vintage, 1983); and The Combahee River Collective, "A Black Feminist Statement," in *All the Women are White, All the Blacks are Men, But Some of Us are Brave*, ed. Akasha (Gloria T.) Hull, Patricia Bell Scott and Barbara Smith (New York: The Feminist Press, 1982).

26. Joan W. Scott, "Gender as a Useful Category of Historical Analysis," *American Historical Review* 91, no. 5 (1986): 1053–75.

27. Recent work that engages with the history of gender and capitalism includes Catherine Hall, "Gendering Property, Racing Capital," *History Workshop Journal* 78, no. 1 (Autumn 2014): 22–38; Ellen Hartigan-O'Connor, "Gender's Value in the History of Capitalism," *Journal of the Early Republic* 36, no. 4 (Winter 2016):

613–35; Amy Dru Stanley, "Histories of Capitalism and Sex Difference," *Journal of the Early Republic* 36, no. 2 (Summer 2016): 343–50.

28. Jennifer L. Morgan, *Laboring Women: Race and Reproduction in Atlantic World Slavery* (Philadelphia: University of Pennsylvania Press, 2004); Alys Eve Weinbaum, *Wayward Reproductions: Genealogies of Race and Nation in Transatlantic Modern Thought* (Durham, N.C.: Duke University Press, 2004). On women's attempts to control reproduction to better preserve their well-being, see also Barbara Bush-Slimani, "Hard Labour: Women, Childbirth and Resistance in British Caribbean Slave Societies," *History Workshop Journal* 36, no. 1 (Autumn 1993): 83–99.

29. Stephanie E. Smallwood, *Saltwater Slavery: A Middle Passage from Africa to American Diaspora* (Cambridge, Mass.: Harvard University Press, 2008), esp. chap. 1, 2; Ian Baucom, *Specters of the Atlantic: Finance Capital, Slavery, and the Philosophy of History* (Durham, N.C.: Duke University Press, 2005).

30. Gregory E. O'Malley, *Final Passages: The Intercolonial Slave Trade of British America, 1619–1807* (Chapel Hill, N.C.: University of North Carolina Press, 2014); Sowande' M. Muskateem, *Slavery at Sea: Terror, Sex, and Sickness in the Middle Passage* (Urbana: University of Illinois Press, 2016); Marcus Rediker, *The Slave Ship: A Human History* (New York: Viking, 2007); M. NourbeSe Philip, *Zong!* (Middletown, Conn.: Wesleyan University Press, [2008] 2011); James Walvin, *The Zong: A Massacre, the Law, and the End of Slavery* (New Haven, Conn.: Yale University Press, 2011).

31. Walter Johnson, *Soul by Soul: Life Inside the Antebellum Slave Market* (Cambridge, Mass.: Harvard University Press, 1999). See also Anne C. Bailey, *The Weeping Time: Memory and the Largest Slave Auction in American History* (New York: Cambridge University Press, 2017).

32. On how violence was recorded and reproduced in slavery's archive, structuring the limits of historical knowing, see Michel-Rolph Trouillot, *Silencing the Past: Power and the Production of History* (Boston: Beacon, 1995), esp. chap. 1; Stephanie E. Smallwood, "The Politics of the Archive and History's Accountability to the Enslaved," *History of the Present* 6, no. 2 (Fall 2016): 117–32; Marisa J. Fuentes, *Dispossessed Lives: Enslaved Women, Violence, and the Archive* (Philadelphia: University of Pennsylvania Press, 2016).

33. Jared Hickman, "Globalization and the Gods, or the Political Theology of Race," *Early American Literature* 43, no. 1 (2010): 145–82.

34. Morgan, *Laboring Women*, chap. 3.

35. Jennifer L. Morgan, "*Partus Sequitur Ventrem*: Law, Race, and Reproduction in Colonial Slavery," *Small Axe* 22, no. 1 (March 2018): 1–17 (4). See also Joseph C. Dorsey, "Women Without History: Slavery and the International Politics of *Partus Sequitur Ventrem* in the Spanish Caribbean," in *Caribbean Slavery in the Atlantic World*, ed. Verene Shepherd and Hilary McD. Beckles (Kingston, Jamaica: Ian Randle, 2000), 634–58.

36. Morgan, "*Partus Sequitur Ventrem*," 6.

37. Morgan, "*Partus Sequitur Ventrem*," 5.

38. Morgan, "*Partus Sequitur Ventrem*," 5.

39. Jennifer L. Morgan, "Some Could Suckle Over Their Shoulder: Male Travelers, Female Bodies, and the Gendering of Racial Ideology, 1500–1770," *William & Mary Quarterly* 53, no. 1 (January 1997): 167–92.

40. Some prominent early histories that describe black women for white audiences are Edward Long, *History of Jamaica* (London: T. Lowndes, 1774); M. G. Lewis, *Journal of a Residence Among the Negroes in the West Indies* (London: J. Murray, W. Clowes and Sons, 1861); Mrs. Carmichael, *Domestic Manners and Social Condition of the White, Colored, and Negro Population of the West Indies* (London: Whitaker, Treacher, 1834); Verene Shepherd, "Gender and Representation in European Accounts of Pre-Emancipation Jamaica," in *Caribbean Slavery*, ed. Shepherd and Beckles, 702–12.

41. Shepherd, "Gender and Representation," 706–7.

42. Anthropologist Clara Han notes that "precarity is the differential distribution of bodily destruction and grievability that emerges through specific social and political arrangements." Han, "Precarity, Precariousness, and Vulnerability," *Annual Review of Anthropology* 37 (October 2018): 331–43. The precarity of the slave, broadly conceived, thus foreshadowed the underbelly of modern civilization. On the importance of slave families and neighborhoods, see Dylan C. Penningroth, *The Claims of Kinfolk: African American Property and Community in the Nineteenth-Century South* (Chapel Hill: University of North Carolina Press, 2003); Anthony E. Kaye, *Joining Places: Slave Neighborhoods in the Old South* (Chapel Hill: University of North Carolina Press, 2009); Rashauna Johnson, *Slavery's Metropolis: Unfree Labor in New Orleans During the Age of Revolutions* (New York: Cambridge University Press, 2016). On gender and family formation in Caribbean slave societies, see Marietta Morrissey, "Women's Work, Family Formation, and Reproduction Among Caribbean Slaves," in *Caribbean Slavery*, ed. Shepherd and Beckles, 670–82. On enslaved marriage in the U.S. South, see Tera W. Hunter, *Bound in Wedlock: Slave and Free Black Marriage in the Nineteenth Century* (Cambridge, Mass.: Harvard University Press, 2017).

43. Shauna J. Sweeney, "Market Maronnage: Fugitive Women and the Internal Marketing System in Jamaica, 1781–1834," *William and Mary Quarterly* 76, no. 3 (April 2019): 197–222 (208–9).

44. Sasha Turner, *Contested Bodies: Pregnancy, Childrearing, and Slavery in Jamaica* (Philadelphia: University of Pennsylvania Press, 2017); Camillia Cowling, *Conceiving Freedom: Women of Color, Gender, and the Abolition of Slavery in Havana and Rio de Janeiro* (Chapel Hill: University of North Carolina Press, 2013), 53–39.

45. Edward E. Baptist, *The Half Has Never Been Told: Slavery and the Making of American Capitalism* (New York: Basic, 2014).

46. Catherine Hall, *Civilising Subjects: Colony and Metropole in the English Imagination, 1830–1867* (Chicago: University of Chicago Press, 2002), 115–120; Thomas C. Holt, *The Problem of Freedom: Race, Labor, and Politics in Jamaica and Britain, 1832–1938* (Baltimore: Johns Hopkins University Press, 1992); Natasha J.

Lightfoot, *Troubling Freedom: Antigua and the Aftermath of British Emancipation* (Durham, N.C.: Duke University Press, 2015).

47. Diana Paton, *No Bond but the Law: Punishment, Race and Gender in Jamaican State Formation* (Durham, N.C.: Duke University Press, 2004). For a rare and powerful narrative from a former apprentice, see James Williams, *A Narrative of Events Since the First of August, 1834, by an Apprenticed Laborer in Jamaica*, ed. Diana Paton (Durham, N.C.: Duke University Press, 2001).

48. On the wrongheadedness of the "dehumanization" narrative, see Walter Johnson, "To Remake the World: Slavery, Racial Capitalism, and Justice," *Boston Review*, February 20, 2018.

49. On abolitionists and their interventionist, pronatalist strategies during amelioration and abolition, see Turner, *Contested Bodies*, chap. 1.

50. Khalil Muhammad, *Condemnation of Blackness: Race, Crime, and the Making of Modern Urban America* (Cambridge, Mass.: Harvard University Press, 2010). On missionary-supported free villages as training grounds for freed people, see Hall, *Civilising Subjects*, 120–39; Holt, *The Problem of Freedom*, 154; 126–27.

51. Holt, *The Problem of Freedom*, 126–27.

52. Robin D. G. Kelley, *Freedom Dreams and the Black Radical Imagination* (Boston: Beacon, 2002).

53. Robert William Fogel and Stanley L. Engerman, "Philanthropy at Bargain Prices: Notes on the Economics of Gradual Emancipation," *Journal of Legal Studies* 3, no. 2 (June 1974): 377–401.

54. Willie Lee Rose, *Rehearsal for Reconstruction: The Port Royal Experiment* (Oxford: Oxford University Press, 1964); Thavolia Glymph, *Out of the House of Bondage: The Transformation of the Plantation Household* (Cambridge: Cambridge University Press, 2008), chap. 4.

55. Cowling, *Conceiving Freedom*, 10.

56. Hall, *Civilizing Subjects*; Deirdre Cooper Owens, *Medical Bondage: Race, Gender, and the Origins of American Gynecology* (Athens: University of Georgia Press, 2017); Daina Ramey Berry, *The Price for Their Pound of Flesh: The Value of the Enslaved, from Womb to Grave, in the Building of a Nation* (Boston: Beacon Press, 2017). On black women's attempt to embrace freedom on their own terms, see Tera W. Hunter, *To 'Joy My Freedom: Southern Black Women's Lives and Labors After the Civil War* (Cambridge, Mass.: Harvard University Press, 1997).

57. Talitha LeFlouria, *Chained in Silence: Black Women and Convict Labor in the New South* (Chapel Hill: University of North Carolina Press, 2015), 98.

58. LeFlouria, *Chained in Silence*, 190. See also Sarah Haley, *No Mercy Here: Gender, Punishment, and the Making of Jim Crow Modernity* (Chapel Hill: University of North Carolina Press, 2016).

59. For "premature death," see Gilmore, *Golden Gulag*, 28.

60. Daina Ramey Berry and Jennifer L. Morgan, "#Blacklivesmatter Till They Don't: Slavery's Lasting Legacy," *American Prospect*, December 5, 2014.

61. Implicit in Jennifer Morgan's theorization about the (re)production of blackness is a converse argument about the function of white reproduction. There is much

work to be done in order to examine the ways white women under racial capitalism are charged with the duty to reproduce hypervalued, precious children and white supremacy. One of the solutions to the intractable problem of whiteness in contemporary sexual politics and "lean-in" feminism might be the historicization and desacralization of the white womb.

62. This is Stuart Hall's formulation. Hall, et al., *Policing the Crisis: Mugging, the State, and Law and Order* (London: Macmillan Press, 1978), 394.

63. While Robinson is highly critical of Western Marxism's Eurocentric orientation, on the one hand, and its failure to grapple with questions of racial, ethnic, and cultural divisions within Europe, on the other hand, not to mention its marginalization of the colonial world, he acknowledges the significance of Marxism to the black radical project. Robinson, *Black Marxism*, chap. 1–3, esp. pp. 18–28.

64. W. E. B. Du Bois, *Black Reconstruction in America: An Essay Toward a History of the Part Which Black Folk Played in the Attempt to Reconstruct Democracy in America, 1860–1880* (New York: Oxford University Press, [1935] 2014); C. L. R. James, *The Black Jacobins: Toussaint L'Ouverture and the San Domingo Revolution* (New York: Vintage, [1938] 1989); Eric E. Williams, *Capitalism and Slavery* (Chapel Hill: University of North Carolina Press, [1944] 1994); Walter Rodney, *How Europe Underdeveloped Africa* (Baltimore: Black Classic Press, [1981] 2011).

65. Brown, "Spiritual Terror." It is worth noting that Robinson's formulation of the black radical tradition as the "preservation of ontological totality" – or, a collective being that includes soul and spirit in addition to labor capacity – diverges sharply from Hegelian and Marxian understandings of freedom. Hegel believed freedom comes only when the slave abandons his fear of death and prioritizes liberty over survival. Marx and Engels develop this idea in the *Communist Mannifesto* when they declare that workers have "nothing to lose but their chains." The black radical tradition, by contrast, prioritizes survival over insurrection.

66. Marx's thinking on alienation, human nature, and the idea of species-being (*Gattungswesen* or "species-essence") evolved from his engagement with Ludwig Feuerbach's work, especially *The Essence of Christianity* (Leipzig, 1841). The most complete articulation of Marx's views on alienation or estrangement from the self (*Entfremdung*), which was then applied to the worker's own labor and product, is found in the *Economic and Philosophical Manuscripts of 1844* (Moscow: Progress Publishers, 1959). For considerations of the process of alienation beyond European borders, see Michael T. Taussig, *The Devil and Commodity Fetishism in South America* (Chapel Hill: University of North Carolina Press, [1980] 2010); Dipesh Chakrabarty, *Rethinking Working-Class History: Bengal, 1890–1940* (Princeton, N.J.: Princeton University Press, 1989).

67. W. E. B Du Bois, *The Souls of Black Folk* (New York: Vintage, [1903] 1990); Frantz Fanon, *Black Skin, White Masks*, trans. Charles Lam Markmann (New York: Grove Press, 1967).

68. Fanon, *Black Skin, White Masks*, chap. 5, "The Fact of Blackness," 82–83.

69. Though support could be found in black communities, Du Bois and Fanon were also careful not to romanticize them. The self-estrangement wrought by capitalist

exploitation followed workers back into their communities upon which violence was projected, intensified by poverty and state violence. Communities can be havens only to the degree that they are momentarily and episodically shielded from the ravages of racial capitalism (which is to say, not very often). Preservation requires that space to do so.

70. Double consciousness and the fact of blackness are not simply abject conditions but are in dialectical tension with the project of preserving ontological totality. The struggle for preservation can be both formal-political and aesthetic-cultural. On the aesthetics of the black radical tradition as illuminated in jazz, see Fred Moten, *In the Break: The Aesthetics of the Black Radical Tradition* (Minneapolis: University of Minnesota Press, 2003).

71. Robinson, *Black Marxism*, 121–22.

72. For a philosophical treatment of *marronage* as a cornerstone of black politics, see Neil Roberts, *Freedom as Marronage* (Chicago: University of Chicago Press, 2015).

73. The literature on Atlantic world maroon communities is vast and rich. See, for example, Sylviane Diouf, *Slavery's Exiles: The Story of the American Maroons* (New York: New York University Press, 2014); Richard Price, ed., *Maroon Societies: Rebel Communities in the Americas*, 3rd ed. (Baltimore: Johns Hopkins University Press, 1996); Alvin O. Thompson, *Flight to Freedom: African Runaways and Maroons in the Americas* (Kingston, Jamaica: University of the West Indies Press, 2006).

74. Jessica Krug, *Fugitive Modernities: Kisma and the Politics of Freedom* (Durham, N.C.: Duke University Press, 2018).

75. Diana Paton, *The Cultural Politics of Obeah: Religion, Colonialism, and Modernity in the Caribbean World* (Cambridge: Cambridge University Press, 2015).

76. Yuko Miki, "Fleeing Into Slavery: The Insurgent Geographies of Brazilian Quilombolas (Maroons), 1880–1881," *The Americas* 68, no. 4 (April 2012): 495–528; Barbara K. Kopytoff, "The Early Political Development of Jamaican Maroon Societies," *William and Mary Quarterly* 35, no. 2 (April 1978): 287–307.

77. Katherine McKittrick, *Demonic Grounds: Black Women and the Cartographies of Struggle* (Minneapolis: University of Minnesota Press, 2006), x–xiii.

78. Stephanie M. H. Camp, *Closer to Freedom: Enslaved Women and Everyday Resistance in the Plantation South* (Chapel Hill: University of North Carolina Press, 2004), chap. 2.

79. Shauna J. Sweeney, "Market Marronage: Fugitive Market Women and the Internal Marketing System in Jamaica, 1781–1834," *William and Mary Quarterly* 76, no. 2 (April 2019): 197–222.

80. Sweeney, "Market Marronage," 219–220. Original advertisement in *Royal Gazette*, May 17, 1818, CO 141/12, National Archives.

81. Maroon communities can be usefully thought of as communities that represented an immanent critique of slave society. See Theodor W. Adorno and Max Horkheimer, *Dialectic of Enlightenment* (New York: Verso, [1947] 1997).

82. Krug, *Fugitive Modernities*; Mimi Sheller, "Sword-Bearing Citizens: Militarism and Manhood in Nineteenth-Century Haiti," chap. 7 in *Haitian History: New Perspectives*, ed. Alyssa Goldstein Sepinwall (New York: Routledge, 2012).

83. A number of prominent maroon warriors were women, including, perhaps most famously, Jamaica's Nanny. Nanny's leadership during punishing campaigns of guerilla warfare against British forces, combined with her role as a spiritual leader, left an indelible mark on the history of enslaved rebellion. See Karla Gottlieb, *The Mother of Us All: A History of Queen Nanny, Leader of the Windward Jamaican Maroons* (Trenton, N.J.: Africa World, 2000). On the concept of interstitial freedom, see Melanie J. Newton, "The King v. Robert James, a Slave, for Rape: Inequality, Gender, and British Slave Amelioration, 1823–1834," *Comparative Studies in Society and History* 47, no. 3 (July 2005): 583–610 (585).

84. Recent work by historian Vincent Brown demonstrates that enslaved people understood and navigated competing jurisdictions. During Tacky's revolt in Jamaica (1760–61), insurgents followed paths between lowlands controlled by whites and mountains patrolled by maroons, underscoring that black geographies were crucial to resistance to slavery. Vincent Brown, *Tacky's Revolt: The Story of an Atlantic Slave War* (Cambridge, Mass.: Harvard University Press, 2020). See also Vincent Brown, "Slave Revolt in Jamaica, 1760–1761: A Cartographic Narrative," revolt.axismaps.com/project.html.

85. Robinson, *An Anthropology of Marxism*, Introduction.

86. Robinson, *An Anthropology of Marxism*, 49.

87. The poverty vows of the Dominican order, for example, were intended to replicate and therefore absorb the critique that was expressed through mass peasant mobilization against the church's landholding and patronage of the wealthy. Robinson, *An Anthropology of Marxism*, 50.

88. Robinson, *An Anthropology of Marxism*, 52.

89. Silvia Federici, *Caliban and the Witch: Women, the Body, and Primitive Accumulation* (Brooklyn: Autonomedia, 2004).

90. Hunter, *To 'Joy My Freedom*; Saidiya Hartman, *Wayward Lives, Beautiful Experiments: Intimate Histories of Social Upheaveal* (New York: Norton, 2019); and *Scenes of Subjection: Slavery, Terror, and Self-Making in Nineteenth Century America* (New York: Oxford University Press, 1997), esp. Ch. 4.

91. See, for example, Patricia Hall Collins, *Black Feminist Thought: Knowledge, Consciousness, and the Politics of Empowerment* (New York: Routledge, [1990] 2002), 213–14, 261–66.

92. Womanism and black liberation theology engaged with the distinctness of black politics outside of dominant European framings of feminism and Christianity, respectively. See Alice Walker, *In Search of Our Mother's Gardens: Womanist Prose* (New York: Harvest, 1983); Clenora Hudson-Weems, *Africana Womanism: Reclaiming Ourselves* (New York: Bedford, 1994); James H. Cone, *A Black Theology of Liberation* (Maryknoll, N.Y.: Orbis, [1986] 2010).

93. Toni Morrison, *Beloved* (New York: Vintage, [1987] 2004).

94. Jessica Krug argues that slavery might be usefully thought of as a system that profoundly dismembered its victims, both their bodies and their communities. Shared rituals and political idioms that predated slavery were used as a means to remember and "re-member," or reconstitute, natal communities. Preservation, as a signature characteristic of the black radical tradition, is similar. Jessica Krug,

"Social Dismemberment, Social (Re)membering: Obeah Idioms, Kromanti Identities and the Trans-Atlantic Politics of Memory, c. 1675–Present," *Slavery and Abolition* 35, no. 4 (February 2014), 540.

95. Morrison, *Beloved*, 102.

96. John Stedman, *Narrative of a Five Year's Expedition against the Revolted Negroes of Surinam . . . from the year 1772 to 1777*, vol. 2 (London, 1796), 262–63.

97. Diana Paton, *The Cultural Politics of Obeah: Religion, Colonialism, and Modernity in the Caribbean World* (Cambridge: Cambridge University Press, 2015); Randy Browne, "The 'Bad Business' of Obeah: Power, Authority, and the Politics of Slave Culture in the British Caribbean," *The William and Mary Quarterly* 68, no. 3 (2011): 451–80; Diane Watt, "Traditional Religious Practices amongst African-Caribbean Mothers and Community Othermothers," *Black Theology* 2, no. 2 (2004):195–212. For the post-emancipation context, see Mimi Sheller, "Quasheba, mother, queen: Black Women's Public Leadership and Political Protest in Post-emancipation Jamaica, 1834–1865," *Slavery and Abolition* 19, No. 3 (1998): 90–117. For black women's spiritual practices and the Haitian Revolution, see Ramsay, *The Spirit and the Laws*, 44.

98. This is particularly true of the "womanist" subfield of feminist thought. First articulated by Alice Walker, this branch of feminism was taken up with particular enthusiasm in the 1980s and 1990s. Patricia Hill Collins defined womanism's spirituality as "not merely a system of religious beliefs similar to logical systems of ideas. Rather, spirituality comprises articles of faith that provide a conceptual framework for living everyday life." Patricia Hill Collins, "What's in a Name? Womanism, Black Feminism, and Beyond," *Black Scholar* 26 (1996): 9–17. See also Walker, *In Search of Our Mothers' Gardens*. On the importance of transnational black women's feminism and spirituality, see M. Jacqui Alexander, *Pedagogies of Crossing: Meditations on Feminism, Sexual Politics, Memory, and the Sacred* (Durham, N.C.: Duke University Press, 2006).

99. The literature on liberation theology and the black church is important and vast. For the most part, this work thinks about religious practice and its history in relative isolation from black anticapitalism.

100. One suggestion to address Robinson's "gender problem" in *Black Marxism* might be to add black feminist Marxists to his analysis, perhaps in place of Du Bois, James, and Wright. However, adding black feminists into the black radical tradition does not resolve the fundamental tension identified by Robinson between the self-referential and sometimes contradictory Western political traditions and the historical alterity of the black radical tradition. For Robinson, the subjects of the second half of his text were not apotheoses of "black Marxist" thought; rather, as intellectuals and political activists, these men attempted to resolve, in their lives and work, the disjuncture between Marxism as a liberatory praxis and the lived experiences of the black majority. Indeed, as intellectuals committed to socialist theory and politics, Du Bois, Wright, and James came to an understanding, particularly in their later work, about how intellectuals as a class—left or not—became estranged from black politics on the ground. I think by highlighting these thinkers

Robinson is, at least in part, trying to demonstrate not only their crucial revisions of supposedly objective political theories, but also how the positionalities produced by studying these theories were inimical to the task of black liberation.

101. Davis, *Women, Race and Class*. See also Nell Irvin Painter's definitive account of Truth's life and political significance: Nell Irvin Painter, *Sojourner Truth: A Life, A Symbol* (New York: Norton, 1997).

102. Sojourner Truth, quoted in Stanton et al., *History of Women Suffrage*, 1:115–17, as cited in Davis, *Women, Race and Class*, 63 (italics added).

103. Sojourner Truth, as cited in Davis, *Women, Race and Class*, 63–64.

104. On Sojourner Truth's flight to freedom as motivated by a calling from god, see Painter, *Sojourner Truth*, Ch. 3-6. Claudia Jones, "An End to the Neglect of the Problems of the Negro Woman," *Political Affairs*, June 1948, 29. Carole Boyce Davies explains Jones's theory of super-exploitation as well as her interest in a communist-oriented black feminist group called the Sojourners. Carole Boyce Davies, *Left of Karl Marx: The Political Life of Black Communist Claudia Jones* (Durham, N.C.: Duke University Press, 2007), 37–39.

105. On the spiritual and material philosophy of Hamer, see Julia Cox, "Never a Wasted Hum: The Freedom Singing of Fannie Lou Hamer," *WSQ: Women's Studies Quarterly* 46, no. 3/4 (Fall/Winter 2018): 139–57; Priscilla McCutcheon, "Fannie Lou Hamer's Freedom Farms and Black Agrarian Geographies," *Antipode* 51, no. 1 (2019): 207–24; Monica M. White, " 'A Pig and a Garden': Fannie Lou Hamer and the Freedom Farms Cooperative," *Food and Foodways* 25, no. 1 (2017): 20–39.

CHAPTER 3

THE INDEBTED AMONG THE "FREE"

Producing Indian Labor Through the Layers of
Racial Capitalism

MISHAL KHAN

O ver the course of the nineteenth century, Indian labor
emerged as a vital commodity, as the British Empire adjusted
to a new, "free," global order after slavery was abolished in
1833. Racial discourses abounded as colonial agents constructed elaborate
taxonomies of peoples, vociferously measuring and orientalizing in grand
comparative projects of imperial knowledge production. Yet in order to fully
grasp the multiple valences of the worlds of labor that emerged in this imperial moment, we must properly link these larger dynamics to the particularities of precapitalist social formations. In this chapter I shift focus inward to
colonial India and argue that it is imperative to pay attention to a series of
racial projects that occurred on multiple scales. The discursive ordering of
races itself drew on contingent and possibly infinite manifestations of racialization as they unfolded in colonial contexts. Only by fully grasping the
interlocking scales on which human distinctions were produced and capitalized on can we apprehend the forces that were required to bring bodies into
the service of global commodity production in a capitalist world order.

This essay provides an account of racial capitalism that speaks not of
racialization, but rather of racializations in the plural. By focusing on two
separate figurations of the indebted Indian laborer in colonial India,
I elucidate how both were produced by distinct forms of racial ordering.
I argue here that abolition was a racial project—the left hand of global
capitalism, if you will. Indians were a racialized category of labor not because
of *slavery*, but because of processes set in motion by the particular constellation
of labor demands called into being by British *abolition*. This project was

global in its scope and ambition, clearly distinguishing, ordering, and assigning roles to populations based on the exigencies of imperial labor demands and cultural tropes reified into biological and scientific truth.

I follow a range of scholars who have asked various forms of the question: how were "new forms of bonded labor engendered by the vocabulary of freedom?"[1] This perennial question has now emerged with a renewed sense of urgency. Analyzing the postabolition landscapes in Jamaica, East Africa, and Cuba, Cooper, Holt, and Scott shift attention from the legacies of slavery to the problems of freedom, noting that abolition "did not break the association between race and labor, but in some ways deepened the racialization of the labor question."[2] Similarly, Eric Foner invites us to think about the "political economy of freedom," and Saidya Hartman pays attention to the "burdened individualism" of the world that lay in wait for freed ex-slaves in the Reconstruction Era South.[3] In this essay, I focus attention on one particular geographical location, tracing how multiple forms of debt bondage emerged directly from the deep interconnections between global abolition and racial capitalism in colonial India. Indeed, these connectivities and shared legacies were being pondered a century ago by W. E. B. Du Bois, who saw the effects of global capitalism, and the very definition of freedom itself, as a shared project for the "basic majority of workers who are yellow, brown, and black."[4]

Colonial India provides a unique opportunity to examine the workings of racial capitalism in a context where labor formations were truly staggering in their variety, manifesting in intense and often violent forms. These included subjugated untouchable labor, low-status kinship groups with tenuous to nonexistent claims to land, complex household economies where servitude, slavery, and marriage were almost indistinguishable, and new forms of coolie labor working on European-owned plantations in India. Scholars have noted that all these regimes were shaped in some way by debt, but the particular form these took and how they relate to one another is rarely elaborated. How were different forms of indebted labor framed amid imperial discourses that positioned Britain as the global standard-bearer of free labor and antislavery? How were these discourses bound up in racial projects that circulated, rehashed, and reverberated back repertoires around the African slave, the white master, and the East—and South—Asian coolie? What was the relationship between different iterations of debt bondage and forms of racialization as seen from the vantage point of colonial India?

As Robinson asserts in the opening of *Black Marxism*, "feudal society is the key."[5] Following Robinson's lead, Chhabria notes it is imperative to see the subcontinent's own history as one "shot through with a fundamental antagonism between capital and unfree labor" and suggests it is the "distinction between peoples rather than distinction between places that gives capital its power, everywhere."[6] Scholars of racial capitalism have highlighted that the "production of capital occurred in tandem with the production of difference," arguing that these processes were endemic to the spread of capitalism.[7] In other words, at all moments, "capitalism *is* racial capitalism."[8] I draw attention here to the layers of racialization that undergirded how labor was produced for the global capitalist order. There were always multiple repertoires at play in ranking human activity and, ultimately, civilizational and moral worth. It is crucial, therefore, to pay attention to the scales upon which racial processes were occurring in tandem—fluctuating between a more expansive notion of pre-modern iterations of racialization, as insisted upon by Robinson, and the more particular, emergent forms of racialization forged in the crucible of Atlantic modernity.

India is a site where we can interrogate how racial capitalism operates in a context where "race" as a category fits uneasily with prevailing notions of difference and inferiority—a site where we can think about "diverse genres of human difference."[9] To remain coherent in this engagement with *racial* capitalism, I step back to subsume two such "genres" under the umbrella of "racialization." Historians today debate tirelessly over labels and terminology, fearing the reification of modern concepts such as race in other times and places. Similarly area studies specialists insist on the contingent and unique ideologies of human difference in each of their contexts. Capitalism has no such concern for the vicissitudes of contemporary debates over biological-racial-religious-caste difference. It may be true that modern racial ideologies, best represented by the devaluing of black life before, during, and after the slave trade, were the most virulent and powerful drivers of modern capitalism. I argue, however, that capitalism has demonstrated remarkable flexibility historically, exploiting each new frontier's unique logics of exclusion and exploitation, where and how it finds them.

I focus on two interrelated processes. First, this essay takes global "racial" discourse as its empirical object, examining how it emerged over the course of imperial discussions around labor before and after abolition. Important scholarship has highlighted the global scale on which "races" were discursively constructed in broad strokes—the emergence of Asian-ness, Indian-ness, African-ness and White-ness, each of these categories as fictitious as the biological truths that were imputed to them.[10] I show that the global construction of "Indian labor" took place in a context of ideological comparisons with African slave labor. As Lowe reminds us, "the placement of peoples at various distances from liberal humanity—"Indian," "Black," "Negro," "Chinese," "coolie," and so forth—are integral parts of the genealogy of modern liberalism."[11] Constructing Indian labor as "free" was not only a crucial abolitionist strategy in the first instance, but became laden with meaning for a variety of actors thereafter.

The most pernicious aspect of the construction of Indian labor as free was the fiction that it conjured about relations *between* Indian subjects. These broad processes of demarcating and categorizing "races" embedded within them a simultaneous muting of internal forms of subordination from view, even as they continued to operate, quietly assigning unequal value to groups as capitalism expanded. This could be an epistemic assault on many levels, representing sets of truths about Indians, Chinese, or Africans in one-dimensional terms. In this case, I am interested in representations of Indian hierarchy and subordination. In India, relations of subordination were at all times mediated by caste or kinship, even if they were not always reducible to these categories. The particular role that Indian labor was called on to play in the new, expanding global economy was reserved, therefore, for particular Indians already embedded in internal feudal, caste, and service relations that were governed by their own sets of differentiating logics. All laboring bodies were forced to join the world of "free" wage labor, a scaffolding erected by colonial powers and the structures of global capitalism—but this process was enabled in the first place by dispossessions that started much closer to home.

I anchor this comparison by examining two distinct regimes of debt that both produced and subordinated Indian labor by drawing on racial discourses, in different ways. Both these legal regimes were enabled by a set of cultural discourses that read Indian slavery as benign and contractual relations between Indians as reciprocal and paternalistic. I first focus on the fiction of the Indian coolie laborer as the "free" self-possessed individual, a legal status that legitimized moving Indian bodies to work on plantations in India as well as the coolie indenture trade across the Indian and Atlantic oceans. Master-servant legislation criminalized breaches of work contracts involving a cash advance, turning what would have been a civil debt into a criminal offense. Court magistrates upheld these contracts by either mandating fines or, even more problematically, ordering the specific performance of work.

Through the Indian coolie, we examine how a particular form of debt bondage emerged from the global political vocabularies of free-market individualism and the ascendance of contractual forms of labor control.[12] The "entrapments" of liberal discourses of freedom have long been a subject of interest and debate among South Asian historians.[13] However, in this essay, I embed this constellation of policies in a particular set of racial assumptions that we can trace to Indian labor's role in empire—free enough to enter contracts, yet devoid of the industrial spirit that made them willing workers without the aid of coercive legal mechanisms.[14] I focus on the coolie trade within India, particularly labor imported to tea plantations in Assam, but given the close connections with the overseas indenture trade, the logics and discourses around both were closely intertwined.

Then, shifting focus away from plantations, I turn to the rural countryside where debt operated in an entirely different way and was not always visible as a form of labor control. I show how indebtedness was constantly kept alive as a specific problem to be addressed, but that reform efforts were redirected to conversations around concern for "peasant" debt—a category that privileged landowning agricultural classes rather than landless, low-status groups. Capital and credit were already channeled into the hands of groups that had benefited from preexisting forms of domination. Through this discussion around debt I demonstrate how these discourses were justified as natural and tied to the value of labor and moral worth of different subjects. This not only created the very conditions that made labor desperate enough to have to work on distant plantations but also strengthened forms of labor control that agrarian capitalistic projects rested on in the global countryside, increasingly integrated into global commodity markets. These racializing discourses were the foundations upon which groups were seen as landed in the first place, deemed creditworthy thereafter, and finally considered worthy of being rescued from the evils of indebtedness. Through an exploration of this second kind of debt regime, focusing on one particular case in the Bombay Presidency—relations between sharecroppers and landowning peasants in Sindh—I highlight the more nuanced and less visible workings of racial capitalism.

The Slavery/Freedom Divide in India

The abolition of slavery in India took place in a broader imperial context, as Great Britain assumed the lofty responsibility of carrying the torch of freedom when it became the first nation to abolish the slave trade in 1807.[15] Soon after, with the passage of the Slavery Emancipation Act of 1833, the British Parliament officially abolished slavery in British colonies. In a single day, almost a million slaves in the British Empire were called from "social death" to "life"[16]—with little concern for the caveats and limits that would burden this new mode of living. The triumph of the moment was attenuated, however, when the British public turned their gaze eastward and discovered to their horror the sheer number of slaves in British India. India, still officially under the East India Company (EIC) rather than the empire proper, had been excluded from the 1833 imperial decree. According to numbers circulating around abolitionist circles, there were more slaves in British India than had been emancipated in the entire British Caribbean.[17] While the existence of slavery in India was a shock to the British public, it was certainly no secret to members of the EIC, who been enforcing legislation and regulations around the slave trade in India for decades.[18]

Prior to 1833 British abolitionists, too, had been invested in de-emphasizing the ills of Indian slavery. The "discovery" of slavery in India took place in the first decades of the nineteenth century, as debates raged over abolition in the British Carribbean.[19]Abolitionists and industrialists looked to India as the promised land of plentiful and free labor—the palatable alternative to slave labor. Ironically, it was George Saintsbury, an active member of the West Indian planter association, who first published the widely circulated pamphlet *East Indian Slavery* in 1829.[20] This was part of a concerted campaign to highlight not only Indian slavery but the downtrodden position of the Indian laboring poor in general. Highlighting both the abuses of the EIC and the inherently unfree nature of the Indian laborer was designed to thwart abolitionist arguments to promote Indian "free" labor as an alternative to African slave labor. Abolitionists had been arguing that Indian labor was not only cheaper but a more ethical option that would align with the British Empire's emerging moral commitments. Focusing in particular on sugar, the commodity that William Fox famously compared to a "pound of human flesh,"[21] abolitionists were intent on promoting India as the answer to the labor shortage crisis that plantation owners dreaded.[22]

Plans to both invest in plantations in India, and ship labor out of India were floated periodically throughout the nineteenth century, to produce not only sugar but also cotton. India figured prominently as the solution to Britain's ever-increasing need for raw cotton to supply its textile factories.[23] In the decades leading up to the Civil War, abolitionists, keenly aware of the global monopoly enjoyed by the American South, pressured the British government to consider India as a free-labor alternative for cotton production. As Florio notes, the Indian poor were thus "supposed to do emancipatory work on behalf of America's slaves"[24]—not merely physically, but also ideologically.

British abolitionists, therefore, insisted on the benign nature of Indian slavery. The EIC was more than happy to go along with these assertions, keen to underplay their own complicity in Indian slave trading, and to promote capital investment in British India. This was an unlikely partnership, as the EIC was a symbol of British mercantilism and monopoly power, imperial policies that abolitionists had often railed against. Both found themselves on the same side of the table, arguing that slavery in India was governed by a uniquely paternalistic logic, particularly when it came to domestic regimes of slavery and servitude. What had already emerged by the time of abolition in India in 1843 was the peculiar idea of the "Indian contract" defined by a "warm feeling" toward the familiar attachments and domestic life of Indians.[25] Unlike the position of African slaves in the Caribbean, who were notoriously prone to uprisings and resistance and in need of brutal regimes of disciplining, Indian slavery, it was said, was a protectionist institution, the equivalent of an Indian poor law.

Once the 1833 Act was passed, however, British abolitionists soon began to see India as the new frontier for their antislavery fervor—even though they more or less held on to the notion that Indian slavery was qualitatively different from West Indian slavery. In light of mounting pressure and increased British and Foreign Anti-Slavery Society (BFASS) advocacy, the British Parliament assembled a commission to investigate the full extent of Indian slavery. The Indian Law Commission was instructed to solicit evidence from magistrates and district-level officials, as well as Muslim *qazis* and Hindu *pundits* (religious legal authorities), about the prevalence of Indian slavery. In this sweeping review of the state of Indian slavery, it became clear that "slavery" took a bewildering variety of forms. These included children sold to wealthy families during times of famine, household slaves imported from outside British India, agricultural slave castes "attached" to the soil—bought and sold as appendages to landed property—and poor Indians who sold themselves into slavery.

Important for our purposes is the fact that agricultural laborers trapped in cycles of debt were frequently cited as "debt slaves," or indebted bondsmen. For example, the *halees* in Gujarat were described thus: "a halee is a hereditary bondsman, almost the only description of slaves" in the region, "employed in agricultural labor . . . these bondsmen are compelled personally to work out their debt."[26] The state of being trapped in cycles of debt, with the debt transmitted hereditarily and the indebted reduced to having to serve in perpetuity, was the clearest example of a degraded state of slavery and unfreedom. Although these reports have been criticized as haphazard and unsystematic in their method, they are still critical documents.[27] These reports provide some of the most incisive accounts of forms of servitude and labor subordination in Indian society. As Dharma Kumar noted many decades ago, perhaps they tell us more about agricultural bondage than they do about the state of slavery per se.[28] In fact, she argued that what colonial officers were seeing was really caste-based servitude rather than "slavery." Notwithstanding the murky terrain of defining slavery in India, what these reports demonstrate was a willingness to read debt as a key form of unfreedom among the Indian population prior to abolition.

Importantly, even while documenting these different forms of slavery and indebted labor, the report noted that, in general, "there is nothing more remarkable than the fact that most slavery in this country is voluntary in origin."[29] Indian labor, it was argued, was governed by customary traditions of reciprocal exchange that included patronage and care in exchange for provision of service, honor, and of course, labor. This reading of Indian labor relations was thus a crucial part of constructing a discourse around Indian labor as free, laying the groundwork for new imperial labor regimes, such as the global indenture and contract labor systems, that would emerge after abolition.

In addition, this reading made it easier to legitimize the particular form that abolition took in India. In 1843, the EIC finally caught up to the rest of the British Empire and passed the Indian Slave Act—Act V. Unlike the dramatic Emancipation Act of 1833 Act, Act V merely delegalized slavery. This did not include any direct legal imperative to free slaves; rather, British courts were simply instructed to cease recognizing rights over slaves. This clearly relied on the problematic assumption that that the power relations within which Indian slavery operated relied on colonial legal institutions for their legitimacy. Indrani Chatterjee has famously, and aptly, described this move as abolition by denial, or by semantics.[30] Colonial courts would no longer use the word *slavery* to describe attached or traded peoples and, in fact, would reprimand official uses of the term.[31] Act V thus erased the official comparison between debt bondage and slavery. The widespread regimes of debt, resulting in cycles of poverty and sometimes violence, which the Law Commission had been clear in labeling as slavery one moment, thus ceased to be read in these terms. To do so would fly in the face of the empire wide designations of Indian labor as "free," clearly demarcated from black African labor as "slaves."

Coolie Labor—The Debts of the Free

Discourses insisting that Indian labor fell somewhere on a spectrum between "free" and subject to the dying hold of a benign slavery had global repercussions. The Indian "coolie" was thus called into being to serve the demands of plantations in India and across the colonial world. As Jung has argued, "coolies were a conglomeration of racial imaginings that emerged worldwide in the era of slave emancipation, a product of the imaginers rather than the imagined."[32] While he focuses on East Asian coolies, a similar argument can be made about Indian coolie labor.

The Indian indenture system spanned the globe, creating the legal scaffolding for circuits of labor from India to far-flung regions such as Reunion, Mauritius, Natal, East Africa, Fiji, South Africa, and Brazil.[33] The long voyages, threat of death, and starvation they faced could be waved off with the refrain that they had "freely" entered these contracts. At the same time, within India, particularly in Assam and Travencore, novel plantation complexes were springing up. Scholars such as Kris Manjapra connect these complexes with the rise and fall of plantations in the Caribbean, showing how capital generated on West Indian plantations in the Caribbean moved eastwards to India.[34] In exchange for their capital investments in India, the EIC guaranteed planters and entrepreneurs a docile and steady supply of labor. Others show how technologies of violence and discipline perfected on slave plantations were transported to India.[35] This was the new world of free labor that the death knell of African slavery had ushered in.

The shifting discourse around Indian labor, debt, and slavery began to recalibrate the contractual terrain in India almost immediately after abolition.

For instance, in 1843 the district magistrate in Konkan in the Bombay Presidency wrote to the commissioner asking whether any special measures were to be taken in regard to debt contracts in light of the recent abolition legislation. After examining several exemplary cases of debt bonds, they concluded that "the Judges are of the opinion that the term slavery is altogether misapplied in these cases, they being merely contracts of service which are nowhere forbidden by Law . . . it being fair to assume that such would not be entered into except as a *mutual convenience* to the parties concerned."[36] Indeed, this perspective became juridical common sense after 1843. This new contractual regime was signaled by the passage of key legislation from the Workman's Breach of Contract Act, (Act XIII) in 1859, sections 491 and 492 of the Indian Penal Code (Act XLV) in 1860, the Indian Contract Act (Act IX) in 1872 and a series of provincial-level legislation to enforce labor contracts, particularly around plantation complexes.[37] The same moment that Indian slavery vanished, therefore, was the moment when the juridical conceit of Indian laborers being free enough to enter contracts was rendered sacrosanct.

The construction of the free Indian laboring subject only strengthened over the course of the nineteenth century. These ideas emerged in full force as both plantation owners and officials in London debated the merits and risks associated with using labor from different colonial populations. The emergence of strictly demarcated racial categories, each with assigned labor roles, took place in various settings where populations were migrating and mixing with each other—on plantations, on the high seas, and within colonies such as India and South Africa. Mawani shows how in British Columbia different racial populations were "constituted dialectically against one another in a shifting and unstable global order."[38] These global and local projects of racial governance served to reify and conjure "truths" regarding the "racial" distinctiveness of Indian labor, calling upon particular policy interventions and modes of disciplining. In the Caribbean, studies have shown how anxieties over racial mixing between different laboring categories reified divisions between groups, making it crucial to demarcate the boundaries between free Indians and African ex-slaves.[39] Planters hoped "industrial labourers from India would eventually uplift the 'moral character' of the local African-derived workers."[40]

While contingents of British navy vessels stopped, searched, and freed African slaves carried on ships on the Arabian Sea, others were quietly shipping "batches" of Indians to plantations in Suriname, Jamaica, Fiji, and Reunion.[41] Sue Peabody traces how Indians and Africans faced distinct legal identities and possibilities for freedom as they wove their way through British and French legal regimes.[42] Within India, African-origin groups were singled out as "self-evident" slaves and freed, unlike Indians, who were trafficked with impunity.[43] The conceit of the Indian laborer as free, therefore, was integral to both the initial drive for British abolition and the myth that allowed the engine of capitalist production to keep on churning out imperial global commodities.

The above scholarship demonstrates the discursive production of the Indian coolie across colonial sites. Turning inward to British India, this construction affected contractual and moral discourses around labor on the Subcontinent. Debt was a critical part of the apparatus set up to control and discipline the migrant Indian coolie within India. Cash advances were crucial modes for recruiting Indian laborers to work on plantations and the basis upon which contracts became enforceable. Indians were often reluctant to sign on to work on plantations; among themselves, they used the term *phataks* (meaning jail) to refer to the Assamese tea plantations. To overcome this problem, recruiters handed out advances in cash, one of the few sources of cash outside of the credit advanced by the local moneylender as I will discuss in more detail below.

Once this cash advance had been distributed, the labor contract became subject to the laws governing debt contracts, with even stricter rules for defaulting and absconding. This tactic was couched in rationalistic language that claimed to be based on shrewd economic logic.[44] According to planters, they incurred heavy expenditures in importing immigrant labor, and the Act was devised to "in short, to give the employer the penal contract as security for his outlay, while it ensures to the labourer complete protection by the government."[45] Such measures were therefore justified as being beneficial to both parties. This kind of strict interpretation established the "coolie" as a particular category of laborer under the law, subject to uniquely harsh penalties for violating debt contracts.

Methods of recruiting labor to work on plantations, particularly in Assam and Travencore, were often highlighted for their particular cruelty. Professional native recruiters, known as *arkattis*, or *sardars* rounded up illiterate Indians or sometimes kidnapped and illicitly trafficked them to numerous depots across the country.[46] These middlemen were notorious for the potentially violent and duplicitous methods they used to obtain labor. Reports detailed what was known among recruiters as "coolie-raiding," the widespread kidnapping of women, and the obscuring of contract terms and working conditions from illiterate and vulnerable villagers.[47] On arrival at designated depots, laborers would be made to sign a contract—with their consent taking the form of a mere thumb imprint. Both the overseas indenture system and the internal coolie trade to plantations drew on similar recruitment structures.[48]

Indian labor was thus subject to a specific set of racial discourses in the minds of planters tallying profits and deliberating the merits of slave versus free labor, and by magistrates and colonial agents making decisions about the nature of contracts between Indians. These judgments were tied to the global exigencies of empire, bringing order to increasingly connected populations and sorting them in line with assigned roles. This particular form of debt bondage—a term rarely deployed by those involved—was bound up in a contractual regime that criminalized defaulting on loans by Indian coolies with particularly harsh penalties. This form of bonded labor thus emerged directly out of the vocabularies and discourses of freedom.

Rural Debt Regimes

The racialization of the Indian coolie as a particular laboring subject in the new world of global commodity production occurred at various sites across imperial spaces—in Jamaica, Mauritius, Fiji, British Guiana, Natal, and on the high seas. These sets of discourses circulated across continents and were etched into the bureaucratic apparatus of the Indian colonial state, as the ambiguous status of the coolie between free and unfree permeated into debates over how to manage the plantation complexes within India. These global constructs were forged in an ongoing dialectical relationship with more discrete and contingent racial logics as they unfolded on South Asian soil. Returning to that most controversial of Cedric Robinson's claims, this essay insists that older processes of racial structuring shaped the distribution of capital, land, and credit as India became more and more integrated into the global capitalist order. As Robinson asserts, "capitalism was less a catastrophic revolution (negation) of feudalist social orders than the extension of these social relations into the larger tapestry of the modern world's political and economic relations."[49] Using this insight, we refocus attention away from the Indian plantation towards the feudal social structures that had already in many ways predetermined who would collaborate, who would profit, and who would labor in India and beyond.

Scholars have emphasized the intimacies of continents—how plantation technologies traveled across the globe and how commodity production for the world market brought diverse geographies into the same temporal rhythms. However, the local skirmishes of feudal relations and the dusty, almost arcane, world of agrarian relations have somewhat fallen to the sidelines of these global histories writ large. Manjapra, among others, has noted that as the plantation complex traveled, this did not "flatten the customary land tenure systems of Asia, but rather it created new relationships between land, labor, capital, and international markets for commodities."[50] While acknowledging that the relationship between broader land regimes and the plantation is crucial, it is imperative to acknowledge that these causal processes also moved in the other direction—that underlying social relations with their own discrete logics continuously structured capitalist transformations.

Indeed, the very ability of capitalists and plantation owners to lure coolies away from their villages and communities was premised on Indian landless or land-poor peasants being trapped in webs of debt to the local shopkeeper, the moneylender, and of course the landlord. While many actors were involved in loaning, enforcing, forgiving, and accruing debt, "dependence on loans meant a structural subordination to . . . money capital in general."[51] At the same time that legislation trapped coolies into "free" debt contracts with plantation owners and industrialists, debt was already being wielded as a crucial mode of controlling agrarian labor outside the plantation. The manner in which landless groups were pushed into increasingly fragile sharecropping arrangements—exemplified by the haris, discussed below— was the product of a regime that produced its own kinds of racial assumptions about labor, status, and "natural" occupational hierarchies. These regimes, embedded in local myths and discourses around kin and caste, were reified by the colonial state in grand projects of knowledge production such as the census, and a truly voluminous arsenal of travel writings, and compendiums on caste and tribes.[52]

Over the course of the nineteenth century, rural debt slowly became a dominating feature of the agrarian economy in India.[53] Peasants borrowed money against their land to help meet expenses for the year between crop cycles, to pay for weddings, funerals, implements needed to grow crops, and basic food and subsistence. In return, peasants pledged a certain percentage of their crop to their creditors, relying on the transferability of legal titles in property to guarantee their loans. Meanwhile, low-status landless laborers, who had no land to pledge, had to rely on patronage networks with elites to access credit. David Hardiman aptly describes the prism through which groups were deemed capable of paying back loans and safe to lend to as "hierarchies of honor."[54] Debt bonds certifying shares in crops over money borrowed from the local storekeeper, moneylender, merchants, and landlord overwhelm the records of district and city courts.[55] Indeed, rising colonial taxation regimes and years of famine often increased the burden on agricultural laborers, who had to either borrow greater sums or enter new debt contracts to survive in an increasingly precarious rural economy.[56]

Initially, the colonial administration saw the *bania*, or moneylender, as a crucial source of credit in the agrarian economy, providing the capital needed to encourage technological developments as well as cash crop production.[57] However, after decades of peasants' losing their land after defaulting on payments, colonial policy shifted to a more protectionist stance against the moneylender. The growing concern was that moneylenders did not make good agriculturalists, so that land alienated from a skilled peasantry would lie wasted and uncultivated. In the Deccan in the 1870s, there were riots over the problem of peasant indebtedness, indexing debt as a real social issue that could incite social unrest. Comparisons between debt and slavery became commonplace as the public outcry against strict enforcement of debt contracts became more virulent. One article in the *Times of India* noted: "the complaints of multitudes of debt-slaves for reform must be attended to . . . the existing law aims at the relief of insolvent debtors—first by releasing from prison all who give up the whole of their property . . . millions of wretched men have still to take their choice of binding themselves to be slaves to usurers, or of going to prison and leaving their families to starve."[58] These concerns led to the passage of the Deccan Agriculturalists Relief Act of 1879 and later, in Punjab, the Punjab Land Alienation Act of 1901. In Sindh, the Encumbered Estates Act, or Act XX, of 1896 was enacted to protect zamindars who were in debt and had mortgaged their land.[59]

These reforms were limited in scope, however, and meant to protect only specific categories of Indians. The social problems caused by indebtedness seemed visible only when they involved agricultural peasants losing their land. The commentator in the *Times* article above, like so many others, mourned that debt condemned landed peasants to the ranks of the landless—with little concern for those who were landless to begin with. It was landless groups who were confronting the ever increasing burdens of unremunerated labor in an increasingly cash based economy. In other words, these policies did not target the "debt bondsmen" that the Indian Law Commission had been so concerned about decades before. There were times when missionaries, rebel members of the judiciary, and district officers sporadically brought attention to the ill fate of the indebted "slave" caste laborer.[60] Yet these actors had to insist on these labels against discourses produced by the colonial state.

What options did an indebted landless laborer have? One possible way to procure a livelihood was to work as a coolie on a plantation or some other small-scale industrial or extractive site. When this option was not available, or when news of the terrible conditions on plantations reached their ears, they could but continue to work as sharecroppers for a landlord to try to pay off the debt. This "choice" was often made even when this relationship involved violence and the extraction of extra forms of unpaid labor. Meanwhile, debt not only rendered the indebted labor immobile but also meant quite immediately that he and his family would not have enough for subsistence after laboring an entire crop season.[61]

Therefore, by and large, the official conversation around rural indebtedness was driven by the feared pauperization of landed peasants. This was in line with a general policy of protecting customary agrarian relations—once again, an offshoot of discourses around benign Indian social relations.[62] This was so, even though widespread transformations were taking place throughout British India—from factories opening up in cities to the increasing infusion of money into the countryside, large-scale public works projects, an increasingly sophisticated railway system to facilitate long-distance trade, and a growing orientation toward production for export to the global market.

Hierarchies of Indebtedness: Other Racializations

In Sindh, as in much of British India, anxieties about debt were inextricably linked to the colonial state's concerns about increasing revenues from the land and cultivating a class of flourishing "peasants proprietors."[63] Indeed, the definition of peasant in this instance meant the *zamindar*, or landlord, rather than the people who actually cultivated the land. Zamindars held lands of varying sizes—some were petty cultivators, and others commanded large, unwieldy estates.[64] The colonial state viewed zamindars as key allies when it came to managing and modernizing the rural economy and relied on them to invest in capital-intensive methods of agrarian production. As one officer put it, "It is unnecessary to insist upon the retention and preservation of the zamindar. He has long been looked upon as an integral part of our administration. In times of flood and disaster, in times of crime and disorder, in times of need, we look to him to help, and he is never wanting to our call."[65] Zamindars were solely responsible for paying taxes and were entitled to receive *lapo*—translated as manorial due—from those subsisting off his land.

In the 1840s and 1850s, the early days after Sindh was annexed by the EIC, colonial surveyors went to painstaking efforts to record the name of the official cultivator in settlement records. The colonial state thus introduced a specific, legally enforceable regime of property rights that bestowed privileges and coopted the authority of landowning groups. The vast majority of agricultural laborers, however—those who ploughed land, built roads, served touring colonial officers, fixed breaches in canals and in their "spare" time performed extra work for the landlord in return for his generosity—were not given the status of official tenants except in exceptional circumstances. The people who actually performed the labor in Sindh were known as *haris*—derived for the Sindhi word, to plow. Hari was the term used to describe a landless laborer, or sharecropper, who entered into agreements with the zamindar, sometimes on a yearly basis and sometimes generationally. Haris were mostly removed from direct interaction with the colonial state.

What does it mean to use "racialization" to describe the phenomenon encountered here? In most cases agents relied on "self-evident" logics upon which to demarcate the landed from the landless. When agents surveyed the Sindhi countryside to determine who the "real" landowners were, families who displayed status and wealth were recognized as entitled to the land and its produce. One way this was determined was through a group's connections with the previous ruling dynasty, established through reputational networks and wealth. Such measures such as the size of a zamindar's *autak* or guesthouse where he would meet and entertain guests and followers was often a measure of status.[66] Landowning families were described more often than not as reputed simply for *being* great families, proclaiming myths of migration from Central Asia or Arabia, and particularly being connected to the bloodline of the Prophet.

However, while these external markers helped colonial agents distinguish categories of people, the status of the zamindar was inscribed most viscerally and immediately in behaviors and comportments—on his body and the bodies of those around him. State recognition of status was based not only on ostentatious displays of wealth but also on the strength, and the subservience, of laboring entourages and followers.[67] Haris knew all too well that the zamindar required the hari to publically and ostentatiously perform obedience and subservience. Therefore they "bowed" to the zamindar to demonstrate their allegiance to him, and his standing in the community. Indeed, as Abu Shaukat, an early twentieth century poet who supported the hari movement, lamented that all a hari had to do was fail to bow low enough, clasp his hands tight enough, or forget to call the zamindar "sain"— and he was beaten, jailed, or worse.[68] "Wealth in people,"[69] was correlated to entitlements to wealth in landed property.

G. M. Syed, famous leftist leader of the hari movement, contrasted the "helpless, heavily indebted, overworked, overstrained malaria-stricken, famishing farmer (hari) who marched on the moods, fancies and caprices of his landlord" with the "wealthy, healthy, idle, scheming, sporting, polygamous, hospitable host of the touring district satrap."[70] Abu Shaukat points out that the haris lived in a state of wilderness, providing us insight into how haris were described and devalued in the vernacular. He describes them as drudging under the sun alongside their donkeys, drinking from the same dirty river—donkeys with their mouths and the haris with their hands. The haris "look like people but in reality they are animals."[71]

The haris as a category made up the vast majority of the rural population in Sindh. Examining census notes that give us details of the kinship and caste groups subsumed under the label of the haris, we find a variegated and complex mix of populations. From migrating tribes, impoverished families with no ability to earn a livelihood without entering into an agreement with a zamindar, to attached families of laborers and servants, and others with no capital other than the "skin on their back"—their labor power. Haris were often made up of low-caste Hindus, ex-slaves, and other low-status kinship groups—Muslim, Hindu, and Christian. Attached to these groups were, and indeed still are, robust myths of impurity, associations with low-status occupations, and ex-slave stigmas. Some groups were subjugated based on doctrines of untouchability, but also on local myths about their eating habits, drug use, the impurity of their women, and the kinds of polluting occupations they performed.[72]

For example, Sheikh Ansari's glossary of tribes in Sindh lists the Bhils as a "menial" caste, known for eating "all kinds of wild animals. They are notorious for their habits of thieving."[73] Even when groups converted to Islam or Christianity to escape the caste system, these discourses persisted, though sometimes in a different form. Other groups that showed up frequently among the haris were *shidis, khakhelis,* or *makranis.*[74] Colonial officer H.T. Lambrick describes the khaskhelis as "old servants of the Talpurs," and Ansari explains they used to be African slaves now working as laborers or agriculturalists.[75]

Assumptions about eating habits, drug consumption, and female morality were not merely communal myths but had real consequences for access to resources, most fundamentally land and credit. Caste and kinship status made claims to land suspect in some instances, and impossible in others. Thus the logics of the feudal social structure that the colonial state reified became the foundation for the social hierarchies that continued to intensify for duration of the nineteenth century. In addition, colonial decisions to frame indebtedness as a problem was motivated by racialized judgments about the character and nature of relations between different rural subjects. Even as the colonial state saw indebtedness as a universal problem, convoluted reasoning operated to contain reforms along caste and kinship lines. Therefore racialization produced access to land and credit in the first instance but also dictated notions of worthiness for debt reform thereafter.

For instance, the extravagances of the zamindars—included their spending on *shikaar* (hunting), lavish entertainment, and women—were forgiven because of default assumptions about their moral worth. These vices were seen as the fault not of the zamindar but of the natural demands of his position, or more to the point, the loose morality of lower caste and kinship women. One report notes about the mohanas, another group who were often haris: "The mohanas are very numerous in the Muncher tract and their females, at once attractive and profligate, are a perfect curse to the idle zemindars . . . considering how abounding the temptation is... it is not wonderful that they should fall into it."[76] Therefore if the zamindar was in debt and at risk of losing his land, this was not an issue with his morality, but rather the immorality of low status women.

From the perspective of the colonial state, protecting zamindars from losing their land was of paramount concern. In fact, it was the Hindu *bania*—moneylender—who emerged as the real oppressor in Sindh, a danger to hari and zamindar alike. One revenue collector warned that if the bania was allowed to continue harassing the zamindars, "their ruin would amount to social and agrarian revolution."[77] Another frequently made argument was that the hari benefited from the labor-market shortage, putting him in a position to dictate terms to the zamindar. The haris, the argument ran, were gaining freedom from the zamindar. It was their choice to relocate or work for other zamindars if their situation became intolerable.

Colonial officials in Sindh sometimes recognized that the haris as a whole were a class of indebted landless tenants completely dependent on the zamindar.[78] One such instance is in a 1901 *Pamphlet on Relations Between Creditor and Debtor*:

> In order to live between harvests, the tenant (hari) has to borrow from the money-lender . . . the tenant is not able . . . to mortgage his right on the land and so the tenant who is established by immemorial custom as well as the tenant at will in order to feed themselves, can only borrow on their zamindar's security. The zamindar is responsible for recovering from his haris at the time of the harvest all that the banya has advanced to them during the year: he is responsible also for the debts of those who die, or abscond, or refuse to pay.[79]

The logic here is peculiar, yet typical. Even though hari indebtedness was clearly acknowledged by the colonial state, the zamindar emerged as the victim. The discourse around impoverished indebted Indians being akin to slaves from a century earlier was thus turned on its head. Indebtedness was dangerous and harmful, but some forms of indebtedness were more dangerous and harmful than others. Official reports heralded the zamindar as the defender, or an asset for the hari. While the zamindar, it was argued, was forced to pledge precious land in exchange for loans, the haris were fortunate enough to have their debts secured by the zamindar. A similar paternalistic argument is made in the Gazetteers. For example, E. H. Aitkin of the Bombay Salt Department noted in 1907 that, even though debt was common among the haris, "they were fortunate in being as a rule attached to a landlord who was debarred by his religion from taking any interest for the advances" given them by "well-to do Muslim landlords."[80]

By the late nineteenth century agrarian debt had become a crucial policy challenge confronting the colonial state. Worried that their peasant allies would lose their land to usurious moneylenders, they created credit cooperatives, passed a proliferation of legislation to protect mortgaged land from being sold, and provided relief for landowning castes and kinship groups in times of financial struggle and deficit. However, these policies did not extend to groups who had no land to lose in the first place. Even though haris were usually beholden to both the moneylender and the landlord—sometimes the same person. The veritable swaths of men and women whose indebtedness left them with limited options for survival other than to plow the lands of wealthier zamindars were notably absent from the voluminous paperwork generated on the problem of rural debt. The term debt slave thus travelled from signifying the agricultural bondage of the dispossessed, to a critique of free contract when it involved "worthy" and "moral" subject such as zamindars.

In the early twentieth century, Sindh was experiencing the transformative effect of being designated as a site of large-scale cotton production for export by the Bombay Government. This system of production could not function without a disciplined and docile labor force. Debt was wielded as a crucial, yet discrete, tool for maintaining control over labor in Sindh, integral to the region's integration into the global economy.

Conclusion

This essay has examined two distinct debt regimes that strengthened labor subordination after the abolition of slavery in India and explains how separate processes of racialization structured both. Both these regimes were enabled by the global discursive production of the Indian laborer as essentially "free" and naturally servile. By paying attention to the layers of racialization that produced truths, I have shown how local and global processes worked in tandem to place limits on what freedom could mean for the most vulnerable laboring peoples in the aftermath of abolition. Freeing bodies to join the "vast and dark" sea of human labor that Du Bois predicted a century ago was a process rooted in the feudal structures that produced their own sorting and categorizing of human life and value. These logics directed and permeated social change at the dawn of the capitalist transformations that so profoundly shaped the modern world.

Focusing on one emergent form of "racial" thinking, rooted as it was in notions of biological and inherited cultural difference, diagnoses the particularities of discourses around black, East Asian, South Asian, and Native American peoples under empire. However, to focus only on this kind of racial thinking obscures the distinct, particular, and contingent logics that shaped how capitalist transformations occurred in colonial contexts. These logics seldom conform entirely to the vocabularies and categories available in any particular historical moment. Even caste cannot be reified as the primordial building block for the feudal structure encountered here. Although caste was crucial, I have been conscious of not foreclosing other forms of social distinction by emphasizing kinship, allowing us to speak of wider processes outside the purview of the Hindu caste system that could be equally pernicious. The very logic of racial capitalism in action cuts through emergent categories such as race, or even caste, in the very moment when these categories emerge as meaningful political vocabularies of analysis—and resistance.

NOTES

1. Saidiya V. Hartman, *Scenes of Subjection: Terror, Slavery, and Self-Making in Nineteenth-Century America* (Oxford: Oxford University Press, 1997), 117.
2. Fredrick Cooper, Thomas C. Holt, and Rebecca J. Scott, *Beyond Slavery: Explorations of Race, Labor and Citizenship in Postemancipation Societies* (Durham: University of North Carolina Press, 2000), 287.
3. See Eric Foner, *Nothing but Freedom: Emancipation and Its Legacy* (Baton Rouge: Louisiana State University Press, 1983); Thomas C. Holt. *The Problem of Freedom: Race, Labor, and Politics in Jamaica and Britain, 1832–1938* (Baltimore: Johns Hopkins University Press, 1992); Hartman, *Scenes of Subjection.*
4. W. E. B. Du Bois, *Black Reconstruction in America: 1860–1880* (New York: Free Press, 1935), 16.
5. Cedric J. Robinson, *Black Marxism: The Making of the Black Radical Tradition* (Chapel Hill: University of North Carolina Press, [1983] 2000), 9.
6. Sheetal Chhabria, "Racial Capitalism in India?" (paper presented at Capital Redux: Hierarchies of Labor & Property in South Asia (Part II), Annual South Asia Studies.
7. Michael Ralph and Maya Singhal, "Racial Capitalism," *Theory and Society* 48 (2019): 851–81;
8. Jodi Melamed, "Racial Capitalism," *Critical Ethnic Studies* 1, no. 1 (2015): 76–85.
9. Ralph and Singhal, "Racial Capitalism," 864.
10. Lisa Lowe, *The Intimacies of Four Continents* (Durham, N.C.: Duke University Press, 2015); Marilyn Lake and Henry Reynolds, *Drawing the Global Colour Line: White Men's Countries and the Question of Racial Equality* (Melbourne: Melbourne University Publishing, 2008); Moon-Ho Jung, *Coolies and Cane: Race, Labor, and Sugar in the Age of Emancipation* (Baltimore: Johns Hopkins University Press, 2006).
11. Lowe, *The Intimacies of Four Continents,* 18.
12. Douglas Hay and Paul Craven, *Masters, Servants, and Magistrates in Britain and the Empire, 1562–1955* (Chapel Hill: University of North Carolina Press, 2004).
13. Uday Singh Mehta, *Liberalism and Empire: A Study in Nineteenth-Century Liberal Thought* (Chicago: University of Chicago Press, 1999); Gyan Prakash, "Colonialism, Capitalism and the Discourse of Freedom," *International Review of Social History* 41 (1996): 9–25.

14. See Gopalan Balachandran, "Making Coolies, (Un)making Workers: 'Globalizing' Labour in the Late-19th and Early-20th Centuries," *Journal of Historical Sociology* 24, no. 3 (2011): 266–96.

15. As Brown demonstrates, the British state accrued moral capital through its antislavery activities. Richard Huzzey shows the role of antislavery in advancing imperialist goals on the African continent. Christopher Leslie Brown, *Moral Capital: Foundations of British Abolitionism* (Durham: University of North Carolina Press, 2006); Richard Huzzey, *Freedom Burning: Anti-Slavery and Empire in Victorian Britain* (Ithaca, N.Y.: Cornell University Press, 2012).

16. Seymour Drescher, *Abolition: A History of Slavery and Antislavery* (New York: Cambridge University Press, 2009), 265; Orlando Patterson, *Slavery and Social Death* (Cambridge: Harvard University Press, 1982).

17. David Bryon Davis, *The Problem of Slavery in the Age of Revolution 1770–1823* (Ithaca, N.Y.: Cornell University Press, 1975), 63.

18. Regulation X of 1811 formally prohibited the import or export of slaves into or out of EIC territory but not the purchase or sale of slaves within India, which was merely regulated, not prohibited. This was followed by Regulation XIV of the revised Bombay Code of 1827, of which chapter IV lists the "illegal import, export, and transfer of slaves" in addition to kidnapping, detention, and forced labor.

19. See Howard Temperley, *British Anti-Slavery 1833–1870* (Columbia: University of South Carolina Press, 1972).

20. For an extended discussion, see in particular Andrea Major, "The Produce of the East by Free Men," in *Slavery, Abolitionism and Empire in India 1772–1843* (Liverpool: Liverpool University Press, 2012), 293.

21. William Fox, *An Address to the People of Great Britain on the Propriety of Abstaining from West Indian Sugar and Rum* (London, 1791).

22. Mahmud Tayyab, "Cheaper Than a Slave: Indentured Labor, Colonialism and Capitalism," *Whittier Law Review* 34 (2013): 215–43; Lowe, *The Intimacies of Four Continents*.

23. Sven Beckert, *Empire of Cotton: A Global History* (New York: Vintage, 2014).

24. Christopher M. Florio, "From Poverty to Slavery: Abolitionists, Overseers, and the Global Struggle for 5–24 (1006); Elizabeth Kelly Gray, "'Whisper to Him the Word "India"' Trans-Atlantic Critics and American Slavery 1830–1860." *Journal of the Early Republic* 27, no. 3 (2008): 379–406.

25. Radhika Singha, *A Despotism of L Labor in India," *Journal of American History* 102, no. 4 (2016): 100.

26. Indian Law Commission, "Reports of the Indian Law Commission Upon Slavery, with Appendices, V.1," 1841, 270.

27. Benedicte Hjejle, "Slavery and Agricultural Bondage in South India in the Nineteenth Century," *Scandinavian Economic History Review* 15, no. 1–2 (1967): 71–126.

28. Dharma Kumar, *Land and Caste in South India: Agricultural Labour in the Madras Presidency During the Nineteenth Century* (Cambridge: Cambridge University Press, 1965).

29. Indian Law Commission, "Reports," 1841, 316.

30. Indrani Chatterjee, "Abolition by Denial: The South Asian Example," in *Abolition and Its Aftermath in the Indian Ocean Africa and Asia* (London: Routledge, 2005); Indrani Chatterjee, *Gender, Slavery and Law in Colonial India* (Delhi: Oxford University Press, 1999).

31. For example, a judge in Travencore was chastised for being theatrical and prone to dramatics when he released a judgment comparing the treatment of coolies to that of slaves. See Enclosure of the Judgment of the Sessions Judge, Kottayam Sessions Case, No. 6 of 1089, in "Cooly Crimping Case," British Library, India Office Records (henceforth BL/IOR) R/3/882/108.

32. Jung, *Coolies and Cane*, 5; Moon-Ho Jung, 2017. "What Is the 'Coolie Question'?" *Labour History*, no. 113: 1–8.

33. Scholars estimate the number of Indian indentured laborers transported to have been approximately 1.2 million initially to various colonial sites, initially to sugar plantations but increasingly to a wide variety of agricultural and industrial plantations. Outside of the formal system, numbers were exponentially higher; McKeown, for instance, estimates close to 29 million Indians were transported to other parts of Asia between 1850 and 1950. See Rachel Sturman, "Indian Indentured Labor and the History of International Rights Regimes," *American Historical Review* 119, no. 5 (2014): 1439–65 (1441); Adam McKeown, *Melancholy Order: Asian Migration and the Globalization of Borders* (New York: Columbia University Press, 2008); Radhika Mongia, *Indian Migration and Empire: A Colonial Genealogy of the Modern State* (Durham, N.C.: Duke University Press, 2018); Mahdavi Kale, *Fragments of Empire: Capital, Slavery, and Indian Indentured Labor in the British Caribbean* (Philadelphia: University of Pennsylvania Press, 2010).

34. Kris Manjapra, "Plantation Dispossessions," in *American Capitalism*, ed. Sven Beckert and Christine Desan (New York: Columbia University Press, 2018), 361–87, 370.

35. See Elizabeth Kolsky, *Colonial Justice in British India: White Violence and the Rule of Law*. (Cambridge: Cambridge University Press, 2010).

36. From the Register of the Suddur Faujdari Adawlut, 17th October, 1843, No. 5785, Bombay Judicial Proceedings, BL/IOR/P/403/24 (emphasis added).

37. Prabhu P. Mohapatra, "Regulating Informality: Legal Constructions of Labor Relations in Colonial India 1814–1926," in *Global Histories of Work*, ed. Andreas Eckert (Berlin: De Gruyter Oldenburg, 2016).

38. Renisa Mawani, *Colonial Proximities: Crossracial Encounters and Juridical Truths in British Columbia, 1871–1921* (Vancouver: University of British Columbia Press, 2009);

39. Amar Wahab, "Mapping West Indian Orientalism: Race, Gender, and Representations of Indentured Coolies in the Nineteenth-Century British West Indies," *Journal of Asian American Studies* 10, no. 3 (2007): 283–311.

40. Viranjini Munasinghe, *Callaloo or Tossed Salad? East Indians and the Cultural Politics of Identity in Trinidad* (Ithaca, N.Y.: Cornell University Press, 2001), 57.

41. Johan Matthew, *Margins of the Market: Trafficking and Capitalism Across the Arabian Sea* (Oakland: University of California Press, 2016).

42. Sue Peabody, *Madeleine's Children: Family, Freedom, Secrets, and Lies in France's Indian Ocean Colonies* (New York: Oxford University Press, 2017).

43. See Mishal Khan, "Empire, Law, and Order Making after the Abolition of Slavery: Three Laboring Figures in India" (Ph.D. diss., University of Chicago, 2020).

44. See Rana P. Behal, "Coolie Drivers or Benevolent Paternalists? British Tea Planters in Assam and the Indenture Labour System," *Modern Asian Studies* 44, no. 1 (2010): 29–51.

45. Extracts from Sir Phillip Hutchins speech in the Legislative Council, 23rd March 1892, BL/IOR/L/PJ/6/364 File 2426.

46. Rana P. Behal and Prabhu P. Mohapatra, " 'Tea and Money Versus Human Life': The Rise and Fall of the Indenture System in the Assam Tea Plantations 1840-1908," in *Plantations, Proletarians and Peasants in Colonial Asia*, ed. E. Valentine Daniel, Henry Bernstein, and Tom Brass (London: Frank Cass, 1992); Ulbe Bosma, "Slavery and Labour Contracts: Rethinking Their Nexus," *International Review of Social History* 63 (2018): 503-20; Nitin Varma, *Coolies of Capitalism: Assam Tea and the Making of Coolie Labour* (Berlin: De Gruyter Oldenburg, 2016); Paul E. Baak, "About Enslaved Ex-Slaves, Uncaptured Contract Coolies and Unfreed Freedmen: Some Notes About 'Free' and 'Unfree' Labour in the Context of Plantation Development in Southwest India," *Modern Asian Studies* 33, no. 1 (1999): 121-57.

47. See Behal and Mohapatra, " 'Tea and Money Versus Human Life.' "

48. Ranajit Das Gupta, "Structure of the Labour Market in Colonial India," *Economic and Political Weekly* 16, no. 44/46 (1981): 1781–1806.

49. Robinson, *Black Marxism*, 10.

50. Manjapra, "Plantation Dispossessions," 376.

51. Neeladri Bhattacharya, "Lenders and Debtors: Punjab Countryside, 1880–1940," *Studies in History* 1, no. 2 (1985): 305–42, 325.

52. For a famous example see Sir Denzil Ibbetson, *Punjab Castes* (Lahore: Printed by the Superintendant, Government Printing, 1916).

53. There is a voluminous literature on this, but for prominent examples, see Sugata Bose, *Credit, Markets, and the Agrarian Economy of Colonial India* (Delhi: Oxford University Press, 1994); David Cheesman, *Landlord Power and Rural Indebtedness in Colonial Sind* (New York: Routledge, 2013).

54. David Hardiman, *Feeding the Baniya: Peasants and Usurers in Western India* (New York: Oxford University Press, 1996), 97.

55. Indeed, sampling records from the several regions of Sindh shows an overwhelming majority of cases heard in both Karachi and Shikarpur involved various forms of adjudicating debt.

56. Gywn Campbell, "Servitude and the Changing Face of the Demand for Labor in the Indian Ocean World, c. 1800-1900," in *Indian Ocean Slavery in the Age of Abolition*, ed. Robert Harms, Bernard K. Freamon, and David W. Blight (New Haven, Conn.: Yale University Press, 2013).

57. Hardiman, *Feeding the Baniya.*

58. "Imprisonment for Debt in India: Letter to the Editor of the Times," *Times of India*, November 16, 1878.

59. This law was designed to protect those who already paid more than 300 Rs a year in revenue—thus ending up as protection for the wealthiest and most prosperous zamindars. Two other pieces of legislation were passed for this purpose: the Agriculturalist and Land Improvements Act of 1884 and the Loans Act of 1884. See E. H. Aitken, *Gazetteer of the Province of Sind* (Karachi: Mercantile Steam Press, 1907), 338.

60. This was so in particular in the South Malabar region and in Bihar. See Rupa Viswanath, *The Pariah Problem: Caste, Religion, and the Social in Modern India* (New York: Columbia University Press, 2014); P. Sanal Mohan, *Modernity of Slavery: Struggles Against Caste Inequality in Colonial Kerela* (Delhi: Oxford University Press, 2015); Gyan Prakash, *Bonded Histories: Genealogies of Labor Servitude in Colonial India* (Cambridge: Cambridge University Press, 1990).

61. In surveys finally conducted in the 1940s, Sir Roger Thomas listed twenty possible kinds of "legitimate" fees levied against the crop that the haris were expected to deduct from their share. These included lapo, cost of carrying the grain, storage of grain in mud cabins, wage for the measurer of the grain, for the watchman, and sometimes a "hak allah" and pir jo toya—a portion simply given in the name of god and given to the jagirdar, and another to be given to the shrine. "Report of the Special Officer Appointed to Examine the Relations Between Jagirdars and Zamindars and Their Tenants and Haris," Personal Papers of Sir Roger Thomas, Agriculturalist, MSS Eur 235/470.

62. Clive Dewey, "The Influence of Sir Henry Maine on Agrarian Policy in India," in *The Victorian Achievement of Sir Henry Maine*, ed. Alan Diamond (Cambridge: Cambridge University Press, 1991), 353–75.

63. Demi-official Memorandum on the Zamindar and Cultivating Classes in Sind, 1902, 6, RSP/3210.

64. David Cheesman suggests that any zamindar with more than five hundred acres was classed as a politically significant figure. See Cheesman, *Landlord Power and Rural Indebtedness*.

65. Sind Encumbered Estates Office, *Pamphlet on Relations Between Debtors and Creditors in Sindh*, 1901, 5 RSP/3234.

66. Cheesman, *Landlord Power and Rural Indebtedness*, 60.

67. Sarah D. Ansari, *Sufi Saints and State Power: The Pirs of Sind, 1843–1947* (New York: Cambridge University Press, 1992).

68. "Sain" is a Sindhi honorific term used to signify status, honor, and power in the community. See chapter "The Zamindars Injustice towards to the Kisaan" in Abu Shaukat, *Inqilabi Dando, (Revolutionary Baton)* 1939, Translated from Sindhi by Peer Bux.

69. Indrani Chatterjee, "The Locked Box in Slavery and Social Death," in *On Human Bondage: After Slavery and Social Death*, ed. John Bodel and Walter Scheidel (Chichester, West Sussex: Wiley, 2017).

70. Minute of Dissent by G. M. Syed, *Report of the Tenancy Legislation Committee* (Karachi: Government Press, 1945)

71. Abu Shaukat, *Inqilabi Dando*.

72. Haris Gazdar, *Kinship Group and Marginalization*, Karachi: Collective for Social Science Research. *Unpublished manuscript*.

73. See Sheikh Sadik Ali Sher Ansari, *A Short Sketch, Historical and Traditional, of the Musalman Races Found in Sind, Baluchistan and Afghanistan* (Karachi: Commissioner's Press, 1901), 74–76.

74. For a history of the makranis and connections to the ex-slaves freed in the Indian Ocean and deposited by colonial sea captains in Gwadar in modern-day Baluchistan, see Hafeez Ahmed Jamali, "A Harbor in the Tempest: Megaprojects, Identity, and the Politics of Place in Gwadar, Pakistan" (Ph.D. diss., University of Texas at Austin, 2014); Behnaz A. Mirzai, "The Persian Gulf and Britain: The Suppression of the African Slave Trade," in *Abolitions as a Global Experience*, ed. Hideaki Suzuki (Singapore: National University of Singapore, 2016), 113–29.

75. Personal Papers of H.T. Lambrick, Notes and Tribes on Sind. 1941, BL/MSS EUR208/8, 9, 10; Ansari, *A Short Sketch*.

76. Papers Relating to the Indebtedness of the Zemindars of the Muncher Lake in in Sind. Madras: Scottish Press by Grave s, Cookson and Co, Popham House, 1874, 172, V/27/313/44.

77. Memorandum on Cultivating Classes, 1902, 12.

78. One report carried out a sample survey of haris and found 85–90 percent of them were using their share of the crop to credit an account; "a number of cases have been reported where the whole of the crop has been taken by the sowcar at each picking and sold." *Report on an Investigation Into the Finance and Marketing of Cultivators Cotton, Report on Investigation Carried out in Sind.* (Bombay: C. V. Thomas, 1926–1927), 11.

79. Sind Encumbered Estates Office, *Pamphlet*, 2.

80. Aitken, *Gazetteer*, 335.

CHAPTER 4

TRANSPACIFIC MIGRATION, RACIAL SURPLUS, AND COLONIAL SETTLEMENT

ALLAN E. S. LUMBA

In Cedric Robinson's analysis of the historical origins of a capitalist world system, colonialism was inextricable from racialization. In the first two parts of *Black Marxism*, Robinson cogently illustrates how colonialisms in Ireland, Africa, the Caribbean, and the Americas conditioned the twin motors of the transatlantic political economy: slave plantations and industrial manufacturing. Through displacement, poverty, or capture, colonialisms would produce a surplus of laboring bodies and a surplus of land that were racialized into a transnational exploitative and oppressive means of production.[1] Some, like the Irish, would become migrant colonial subjects working within the imperial English metropole.[2] Some, like those indigenous to the Americas, would be considered surplus to Euro-American systems and be exterminated or socially marginalized to a supposedly "vanishing presence."[3] And some, like Africans and their descendants, would be violently forced into slave labor regimes.[4] At the same time, however, through an account of uprisings, rebellions, marronage, and nationalisms, Robinson provides a necessary account of how surplus bodies and life continued to threaten the structures of racial capitalism, most acutely in the black radical tradition.[5]

Undeniably pathbreaking and influential, *Black Marxism* is nonetheless a transatlantic history. As a historian of the Philippines and Asian America, I want to shed light on how Robinson's powerful analysis of racial capitalism resonates with transpacific experiences and relations within the contemporary world system. Through Philippine and Filipino history, this essay intends to bridge transpacific and transatlantic studies of racial capitalism.

Filipino migrant labor specifically and the Philippines more broadly have been fundamental to the political economy of a capitalist world system under U.S. empire, particularly during the so-called American Century.[6] As Neferti Tadiar asserts, the colonial and postcolonial labor, resources, and "symbolic presence" of the Philippines serve as the fantasy that drives the exceptional promise of America itself as a stable, secure, and prosperous capitalist empire.[7] The history of Filipino migration under U.S. formal colonialism in particular illustrates, as Rick Baldoz declares, how "empire and migration go together."[8] Histories of Filipino migration, therefore, provides a salient window into the historical workings of a capitalist world system under U.S. imperial hegemony.

Despite existing powerful scholarship on Filipino migration, however, many in Philippine studies have not explicitly framed Filipino migrant labor through its relation to histories of U.S. settler colonialism and racial capitalism. As Nick Estes reminds us, the U.S. Indian Wars of the eighteenth and nineteenth centuries structured colonial counter-decolonization wars beyond the Americas, particularly the long Philippine American War.[9] The militarized violence of settler colonialism was also co-constitutive with the quotidian violence of "civil" settler colonial policy. As Estes shows, policy makers like Commissioner of Indian Affairs John Collier recognized the same logic of settler colonial policy at work in the governance of extractive colonies like the Philippines.[10] With this in mind, this essay trains our attention on the material conditions made possible by different U.S. colonialisms—both settler and extractive—that remain necessary to racial capitalism's "economies of dispossession."[11]

More broadly, this essay explores how and why colonialisms are necessary to thinking about transpacific racial capitalism, and how and why racial capitalism is necessary to thinking about transpacific colonialisms. I look in particular at two colonies under U.S. empire: the extractive colony of the Philippines and the settler colony of Hawai'i. I trace how authorities, across two colonies, differently conceptualized what they saw as the threatening problem of surplus. Although surplus was necessary to the production and reproduction of capitalism, it necessitated discipline and management, through constant and differing modes of racialization. Surplus threateningly manifested as an excess of both unsettling bodies and unsettled land. I examine how authorities pursued multiple strategies to spatially fix the threat of surplus, primarily through strategies of resettlement. These fixes notwithstanding, the remains of surplus land and life could always lead to something else. In Robinson's analysis of the Atlantic world, what exceeded transatlantic racial capitalism, and all its fixes, was the black radical tradition. This essay ends by gesturing to the ways a transpacific radical tradition also remained in excess to U.S. colonialisms and racial capitalism in the Pacific.

Colonialism, Settlement, Surplus

Although not a settler colony, the Philippines acts as a salient historical place for thinking through the colonial operations and global effects of racial capitalism. The first colonial encounter between natives of what is now called the Philippines and the Spanish empire occurred in 1521. Beginning in 1565, the Manila-Acapulco galleon trade would connect highly valued Asian commodities to the "New World" via the Pacific, creating a truly planetary infrastructure for global flows of capital. Through Manila Galleons, European empires and settlers in the Americas could, in the words of Andre Gunder Frank, "muscle in on and benefit from Asian production, markets, trade—in a word, to profit from the predominant position of Asia in the world economy."[12] By the early nineteenth century, however, the galleon trade would dry up, a consequence of the fall of Asian production and markets and the rise of the North Atlantic.

From the 1840s to the 1940s the Philippines would act as a crucial node in the movement of so-called coolies from mainland Asia, and many would cross the Pacific to the Americas and the Caribbean. During this period, the mass migration of Asian bodies throughout Asia and the Pacific would almost double European migration numbers.[13] Many of these transpacific migrants would end up staying and working in colonized spaces under U.S. empire. This migration had as much to do with the intensification of U.S. colonialisms across the North American continent as with the needs of North Atlantic industrial manufacturing and the supposed legal end of slavery. During the decades of high imperialism, or the scramble by North Atlantic empires to violently colonize areas of Africa and Asia not yet colonized or recolonized at the end of the nineteenth century, the United States rapidly formalized settler colonies throughout North America, annexed Hawai'i, and colonized Cuba, Puerto Rico, and Haiti. The Philippines would be its primary Asian colony, with many U.S. imperialists and capitalists fantasizing different ways to profit. But U.S. capitalists could never quite profit from the Philippines, at least not in the same way it could from its other Pacific colony, the settler colony of Hawai'i. The Philippines remained far too risky an investment for U.S. capital, because it remained far too insecure.

Insecurities were a consequence of the long history of native resistance to Spanish colonialism. Despite claiming imperial sovereignty over the archipelago for more than three centuries, the Spanish colonial state could never completely domesticate the "uncivilized" frontiers of the Philippines. Control over the northern mountains of Luzon, where the so-called Igorot headhunters lived, and the southern islands, dominated by Muslim *datus* and *sultans*, remained especially elusive.[14] The tail end of Spanish rule during the 1880s and 1890s would be shot through with native movements for decolonization, culminating in the 1896 Philippine Revolution. The material cost of suppressing native decolonization would render the Spanish colonial state highly vulnerable to U.S. military invasion during the 1898 Spanish American War. In a matter of months, the United States would easily defeat an exhausted Spanish military and quickly occupy the Philippines.[15]

In December 1898 the United States would purchase the Philippine Islands from Spain and claim sovereignty over the archipelago and its inhabitants. Philippine revolutionaries would respond by embroiling the U.S. military in wars throughout the archipelago for almost two decades. Thus, despite the American rhetoric of "freeing" Filipinos from Spanish rule, the United States would instead act as simply another imperial force of counter-decolonization. By the 1920s, most U.S. colonial authorities would consider counter-decolonization a success. As a marker of this success, movements for Filipino sovereignty were now fought mainly rhetorically in the realm of formal politics.

In Philippine historiography, the 1920s is often treated as a peacetime development era. Politically, during this era, formal decolonization was accelerated, and the status of the Philippines changed from a U.S. insular possession to a semiautonomous U.S. commonwealth in 1935. Yet this notion of war being settled, a supposed absence of official war or overt counterinsurgency, obscures the pattern of frequent economic crises and political instability throughout the vast nonurban frontiers of the archipelago. This ideological and material conception of a settled Philippine colonial life resonates with Audra Simpson's conception of settlement. As Simpson asserts, settlement can be thought of as the supposedly "smooth move to a consent-based, multicultural, and liberal society that has settled all of its accounts and has taken, successfully, legally, and ethically the land that it occupies."[16] This is not to say that the Philippines underwent a history of colonization analogous to that of indigenous life and land in the Americas. Rather, Simpson offers an intriguing conception of settlement that illustrates the tightly bound historical entanglement among colonial policies, conditions, and logics in the Philippines with U.S. settler colonialism in the Americas and the Pacific.

Furthermore, the American colonial Philippines of the 1920s was far from economically settled. Cycles of economic crisis and political destabilization would frequently unsettle plans for capital accumulation. This is especially true after the World War I economic boom, when Philippine agricultural commodities like hemp (used for rope in naval ships) and coconut oil (used for explosives) rose exponentially in value. The rush of speculative capital investment into these war-dependent agricultural commodities led to massive land accumulation by already wealthy large landowners during the late 1910s. This resulted in a shrinking population of small landowners, the proliferation and intensification of usury tactics, and greater shifts toward tenancy farming or landless transient work. The postwar reparative strategies adopted by the colonial state did little to combat land consolidation, simply redistributing land from defaulting capitalists to other large landholding capitalists.[17] The crisis also led to a combination of wage decreases, massive unemployment, colossal inflation, and rapid contraction of the money supply. These conditions drove small landowners and peasants further into precarity as they intensified borrowing from unregulated moneylenders at usurious rates just to survive. Throughout the early 1920s, everything the indebted person owned—cash, land, commodities, and labor—had become dramatically devalued.[18] By mid-decade, the loss of land, poverty, and refugees created new compositions of surplus populations scattered across the archipelago.

Colonial authorities remained anxious about surplus populations for four main reasons. First, surplus populations held the capacity for mass resistance. For Karl Marx, surplus labor in European industrial spaces routinely disrupted capitalist norms and held the potential to self-organize into a force antagonistic to capital.[19] The kinds of antagonisms in the colonial Philippines, however, is less like Marx's narrative of European capitalism and more akin to Robinson's description of resistance against slave regimes in the Americas. Robinson reveals the ordinariness of antagonism in plantation societies, especially in the responses of the African diaspora across the transatlantic. Marronage, rebellions, revolts, and uprisings were not exceptional events Robinson, but "manifest expressions of Black radicalism" that were imminent to those colonized and racialized as surplus populatons.[20] Under U.S. colonialism, Filipino surplus populations remained troubling to authorities, for they seemed to constantly unsettle the normative structures of capitalist society. Although disparate and singular to particular localities, the new social formations most threatening to both imperial and colonial authorities eventually took an organized and militant stance against: elite Filipino representational politics, American military and police occupation, unjust distribution and accumulation of land, and exploitative modes of capital accumulation.[21]

Second, U.S. colonial authorities considered surplus populations troubling because of their racial excesses. In addition to physical capacity, colonial authorities assessed the moral, psychological, or temperament characteristics to decide whether surplus bodies possessed the capacity or incapacity to become employable within a racial capitalist society. In the case of surplus labor populations in the Philippines and Hawai'i, capacity was shaped by normative notions of able-bodiedness, gender, and sexuality. Colonial authorities were especially invested in reinforcing the normative figure of the patriarchal heterosexual family.[22] In addition, colonial authorities would also judge whether bodies exhibited certain kinds of excesses, be it idleness or vices. More than mere social engineering, colonial obsessions over these supposed deviant excesses illustrates how surplus was embedded in the very bodies of those colonized through racialization.[23] Ultimately, it was race that overcoded bodies as surplus, as worthy of certain forms of living and unworthy of others.

Third, surplus populations were troubling because of their relation to space. On one hand, too little surplus in one area could lead to a breakdown of production, with workers inefficiently overworked or even a scarcity of workers. This scenario also meant labor would have an advantage in the market and therefore could demand more value for their work from capitalists. On the other hand, too much surplus in one area meant a waste of labor power, with idle bodies potentially causing unrest and, in turn, other sites of production kept idle because of a scarcity of able workers. However, the elimination of surplus labor—which is to say, the elimination of the possibility of unemployed bodies—was never the goal of authorities. Capital always needs surplus labor, excessive bodies that hold the capacity to produce more value elsewhere or in worksites, industries, and markets yet to be realized.[24] In the case of the Philippines and Hawai'i, colonial authorities scrambled to find ways to spatially fix surplus populations to surplus land.[25] One form of spatial fixing was the resettlement of racially surplus bodies to surplus lands in the non-Christian island of Mindanao. Another form of spatial fixing was the domestication of excessive Filipino migrant workers in the settler colony of Hawai'i.

Finally, because surplus labor populations connected settler and nonsettler colonies through migration, they also always threatened to exceed conceptual and spatial boundaries policed by authorities. Authorities were especially flummoxed by the unfixability of certain surplus populations, how migrants continued to find ways to refuse or escape direct colonial control. As a consequence, authorities would establish various infrastructures that encouraged entrepreneurship, property ownership, savings, and credit, attempting to settle the unsettling excesses of surplus populations.

Surplus and Settlement in a Nonsettler Colony

The 1927 report by the director of the Philippine Bureau of Labor Hermenagildo Cruz captures how unsettled colonial state authorities felt over surplus populations. The report's analysis was not limited to the colonial territory. It conceptualized the Philippine "nation" more broadly to include the diaspora in Hawai'i, the North American "mainland" United States, and elsewhere. Of special concern to authorities was the management of surplus labor in the agricultural sector, where the majority of "native" Filipinos worked. In 1925, more than 2.5 million (out of a total population of nine million) worked in the agricultural sector, dwarfing all other sectors combined.[26] Authorities sought to further entice and collaborate with agricultural capitalists by domesticating workers that remained in excess to normative capitalist society. To do so, authorities would adopt U.S. settler colonial policies and apply them to the so-called frontier spaces of the Philippines.

State authorities, such as Cruz, perceived settler colonial policies as a spatial fix to the mounting problem of Filipino surplus labor populations. At the same time, settler colonial policies were not merely a result of authorities' anxiety about the post–World War I population boom in the Philippines. Instead, it was an inheritance of U.S. colonial policy from a decade earlier, the 1913 Organic Act. The Act was established to encourage the settlement of frontier spaces, or so-called non-Christian lands. It was seen as a spatial fix for three different social and economic "problems of great magnitude." First, authorities believed that the Act would send "homeseekers from densely to sparsely populated regions." The settlement of frontier spaces would properly redistribute the growing Christian population, now recovering from more than a decade of U.S. counter-decolonization violence. Second, through "the establishment and maintenance of agricultural colonies," the Act would develop a new population of property owners and potential agriculturalists. Third, the settlement of idle lands for agricultural production would generate not only more commodities but also necessary "foodstuffs" for the reproduction of colonial and capitalist society. [27]

From 1913 to 1925, about 1.65 million pesos were spent on these objectives, enacting the policy in the form of "recruiting and transportation of colonists" and "maintenance, equipment, and operation" of ships along the traditionally non-Christian islands of Mindanao and Sulu. A whole interisland infrastructure was created. The maintenance of such an infrastructure necessitated capital to be applied toward the "purchase of equipment, administration, and salaries of officials and agents." In addition, state funds would be appropriated for financialized debt. As Cruz asserted, "the greatest parts of the appropriations were loaned to the colonists in order to assist them in the cultivation of their homesteads, in the purchase of work animals, agricultural implements, building materials, and substance prior to the first harvest."[28] The creation of shipping and transportation infrastructure and loans illustrated how settler colonial policies could not only produce agricultural commodities but could also generate capital.

Settlement policies created by the Bureau of Agriculture and Natural Resources worked in tandem with the Bureau of Lands and Non-Christian Tribes, an office notorious for producing and policing the lines between "civilized" and "uncivilized" races.[29] Settlers, or "homeseekers," when applying for land, had to fit particular criteria. For authorities, the comportment of the settler into an ideal political and economic subject was necessary to differentiate the entrepreneurial settler from the supposedly idle and unproductive "indigenous" bodies of non-Christian lands. These characteristics were based on a normative conception of a productive and moral masculine subject. Cruz, for instance, described the ideal settler as "a person of unquestionable character, not addicted to drinking and gambling, and possessed of sufficient experience in farm work or agriculturally inclined, and should be physically fitted to field work, and his records for the three previous years shall show that he is an enterprising person."[30]

The primary spatial target for settlement was the southern island of Mindanao, a space traditionally inhabited by Muslim Filipinos, also known as "Moros."[31] Authorities believed that vast tracts of land in Mindanao continued to be "sparsely settled by Moros."[32] In addition, Moros, due to being non-Christian, were racialized by authorities as uncivilized and unproductive. Both land and people were thus idly wasting away in Mindanao. Resettlement would fix this dual problem. Unlike previous Spanish colonizers, however, religious conversion would not fix the problem of idleness. Rather, authorities sought Moros' comportment to a normative kind of colonized body, one with the capacity to become a productive settler. By fixing Moros as proper productive settlers, even those racialized as uncivilized and non-Christian could be recuperated into capitalist society.

One attempt to fix Moros through settlement occurred in Cotabato, Mindanao. In 1913 the Bureau of Agriculture and Natural Resources established a colony specifically for Moros. Despite being "sparsely settled," the creation of the Catobato colony required the "removal of 96 families of Moros . . . before the land could be secured."[33] The rationale given was twofold: first, to "bring the Moros in from their widely separated holdings" and have "the Moros establish themselves in permanent, well organized communities . . . for their agricultural development along scientific lines"; and second, to place Moros "on regularly laid out adjoining homesteads . . . for the purpose of making available land for future colonization by [Christian] Filipinos."[34] For colonial authorities, the spatial rearrangement of Moros and their lands into "well organized communities" was crucial to securing any potential threat to capitalist productivity and colonial authority. Moreover, the resettlement of Moros meant the clearing out of space for "future" Christian Filipino settlers. Through the establishment of the Cotabato colony, therefore, authorities hoped to transform the Moro into a more productive kind of colonial subject, one that they believed to be closer to the domesticated Christian settler. At the same time, by reserving future colonized space for only Christian settlers, authorities also believed they could eventually stamp out Moro power in Mindanao.

Another instance of fixing a surplus population was the Momungan colony, also established in 1913. Again, Muslim Mindanao was the space of settlement. While Cotabato sought to fix those racialized as non-Christian Filipino, Momungan sought to fix those who remained in excess of racial and heteronormative norms. The colony was initially "established for the benefit of unemployed Americans in the Philippine Islands who have Filipino wives." In addition to fixing the problem of mixed-race progeny, Momungan would ideally return a sense of patriarchal power to American men, the majority of whom were racialized as white. Authorities were especially alarmed that increasingly large numbers of unemployed Americans had "fallen on evil days." In addition, Momungan was established to reinforce gendered rights to property. Surplus land was not to be distributed to Filipina women but offered solely to American men. At the same time, the colony valorized heteronormative kinship. Not every American man who had a Filipina lover would be accepted. The marriage had to fit heteronormative qualities recognizable to the state: "the qualifications of those colonists now enrolled are that they be American citizens; legally married to Filipino women; and possessing good moral character."[35] Momungan was so popular that after plans were announced, the planners almost immediately closed applications.

In addition to the above criteria, authorities demanded that American settlers comport to economic normative ideals of entrepreneurship. Deviations from this would signal to colonial authorities that an applicant did not have the capacity to properly and productively settle idle lands. This is evident in the proposal for an additional American-only colony, proposed by the Bukidnon Colony Association. Although the Bukidnon colony never came to fruition, correspondence among the director of agriculture, the governor general, and the secretary of war reveals much about how settlement entailed weeding out from the surplus those who had the normative capacity to be settlers and those who did not. Those recommended were described as "honest, sober and industrious," or "honest, industrious and of good habits." Those rejected were perceived as suffering from excesses, described as "addicted to intoxicants, inefficient and incompetent," "unmarried and has no dependent on him," and "ex-convict; irresponsible, inefficient, and incompetent." Most significantly, however, were descriptions of those who the association believed could be rehabilitated: "formerly drank to excess but is said to be an abstainer now," "formerly drank considerably but not believed to drink immoderately at present," or "imprisonment . . . for homicide. Pardoned by the Governor-General July 2, 1913."[36] These descriptions illustrate that settler colonial policies could always offer white Americans a path toward redemption and recuperation, no matter what "evil days" had befallen them.

Thus, as the vetting of applications show, for some, the colonial government of racial capitalist surplus entailed the expulsion of those deemed excessive; for others, governing surplus entailed the possibility of rehabilitation. Those who received recommendations as normative settlers with the capacity to become economically productive were mainly U.S. military veterans or those who had worked for the colonial state in some way. Once the long Philippine American War was considered "settled," the colonial government attempted to rehabilitate those who seemed excessive to normative Philippine society. At the same time, settlement entailed repurposing and incorporating some of the disorderly surplus into the social order, through the fixing of supposedly idle land. This logic is especially acute when authorities grappled with what to do with what they saw as the unsettling problem of mixed-race progeny. Another dimension of the Momungan colony (and the potential colony in Bukidnon), therefore, was its particular sociality, a kinship founded on miscegenation. In this instance, the Momungan colony was an attempt to recuperate mixed-race children and, through settler colonialism, to create a settled place for those who were considered racially surplus to the social order of both the American and Philippine nations.[37]

Despite public opinion that "colonies [we]re a failure from the economic standpoint," there was a "general consensus" from authorities that Mindanao colonization was a success. Cruz believed resettlement "brought about the peaceful penetration into vast tracts of public land which would otherwise lie idle, by the most enterprising and progressive elements of Luzon, the Visayan islands, and the Moro region." Moreover, the material consequences of past settler logic proved to Cruz that resettlement was the most viable spatial fix to the problem of Philippine surplus land and labor. As he argued, settler colonial policies led to "the migration of over 8,700 colonists from the different provinces [. . .] to unsettled portions of the country," thus leading "the way to a proper redistribution of the inhabitants of this Archipelago."[38]

Although Cruz cast the resettlement policies in Mindanao as a viable spatial fix, the scale was too small to properly deal with one of the major concerns of Filipino colonial authorities during the 1920s: the hemorrhaging of Filipino surplus labor to other Pacific colonies of the U.S. empire. As labor commissioner, Cruz remained constantly anxious over the threatening potential of a restive surplus agrarian labor population. As Cruz claimed, the agrarian sector had witnessed an increasingly "alarming . . . number of strikes and suspension of work" and greater antagonism toward capitalists, landowners, and the government.[39] During the mid-1920s, these economically precarious and politically unsettling conditions were forcing vast numbers of Filipinos to migrate to the settler colony of Hawai'i. In the eyes of colonial authorities, Filipino surplus labor was benefiting non-Filipino capitalists in non-Philippine lands. At the same time, despite being at first heavily recruited to Hawai'i by settler capitalists, Filipino workers would be quickly perceived as excessive to settler society, thus demanding new forms of racial and colonial capitalist fixes.

Unsettling Surplus in a Settler Colony

The history of Filipino migration to the Hawaiian colony was structured by centuries old histories of anti-indigenous racial capitalism and settler colonialism. Beginning in 1778, colonial encounters with European settlers and missionaries decimated the Hawaiian population, enabling American capitalists to create lucrative sugar plantations throughout the islands and chip away at indigenous claims to sovereignty. Colluding with U.S. military forces, settlers overthrew the Hawaiian monarchy, setting the stage for eventual U.S. annexation in 1898. The fates of Hawai'i and the Philippines soon became intertwined as the Hawaiian islands became a crucial military base to launch the U.S. colonial occupation of the Philippines. To further weaken indigenous claims to economic control and political sovereignty, plantation labor was imported from elsewhere, quickly establishing a racialized regime of migrant labor.[40]

Yet the organization of settler capitalists, the Hawaiian Sugar Planters' Association (HSPA), was in a constant state of crisis regarding its surplus of imported labor. By maintaining a migrant labor regime grounded in racial hierarchy and apartheid, the HSPA hoped to weaken any kind of worker solidarity that could counter settler dominance. This necessitated the recruitment of a continuous stream of differently racialized labor populations to constantly break up any possible organized resistance that could arise from any one nonnative and nonwhite community. This is the juncture where Filipino migrant workers enter the colonial story of Hawai'i.

Filipino recruitment to Hawai'i had long been a primary concern for both Philippine and U.S. authorities. Initially unregulated by any government, as early as the Philippine American War, sugar planters had made inquiries about importing Filipino labor to Hawai'i. It was not until 1909, however, that HSPA recruitment in the Philippine colony intensified. The focus on the

Philippines was a response to a crisis of surplus labor for the HSPA—mainly, a surplus population consisting of Japanese workers, increasingly organized and restive.[41] Consequently, a seemingly more domesticated and legally convenient surplus labor supply was identified in the Philippine colony.

Filipino recruitment was greatly aided by the contradictions within and between U.S. colonial and immigration policy. The geopolitical position of the Philippine colony as an insular possession legally designated Filipinos as nonforeign migrants, unintentionally allowing Filipino citizens to be categorized as nationals and not subject to existing exclusionary immigration laws.[42] Because of their nebulous legal categorization within the U.S. empire, Filipinos were able to slip past long instituted bans on Asian migration. The great success of private recruitment (and eventual state sponsorship) led to an intensification of exploitative labor practices, leaving Filipino workers with few legal protections and in a consistently precarious state. Despite both official and literary accounts of the brutal conditions of agribusiness plantations in Hawai'i, the flow of Filipino migration to Hawai'i did not slow, and soon an entire logistical and financial infrastructure emerged in response to mass recruitment to Hawai'i. Consequently, Philippine colonial state authorities would be constantly frustrated by their lack of authority over this efflux of workers and the capital they produced elsewhere.

From the founding of the American colonial state in the Philippines, authorities debated placing restrictions on the migration of newly colonized Filipino labor to the Hawaiian colony. In 1901, both colonial civil governor William H. Taft and Secretary of War Elihu Root argued against any restrictions on Filipino bodies. The colonial state would eventually take a quasi-formal stance on Filipino migration to Hawai'i in 1906. Despite protestations from the Philippine Chamber of Commerce about the loss of Filipino labor power, the colonial state created a policy that sought to "protect those Filipinos who desired to go" to Hawai'i and refrained from officially discouraging migration.[43] Over the next decade, American colonial authorities would adopt this hands-off approach, touting the laborer's "best interest," until a 1915 act granted the Bureau of Labor authority to regulate contracts of Filipino migrant laborers. Looking back, Bureau of Labor director Cruz believed that this "constant drain of Filipino agricultural hands" ended up being "a great subtraction from the productive energy of the country." By creating more collaboration between Philippine labor and capital, Cruz hoped that Filipinos would refrain from migrating and instead expend "their energies in their native country rather than in foreign lands."[44]

Anxieties over losing the potential spoils of Filipino surplus labor to foreign capital was even articulated by Philippine Senate president Manuel Quezon. During debates over Philippine independence and Filipino exclusion from Hawai'i, the logic of surplus would be at the core of his statements on worker migration. In a letter to the secretary of war in 1930, Quezon wrote, "I hope no Filipino ever left the Islands to help enrich with his labor another land, when most of our natural resources await development."[45] Moreover, for Quezon, the loss of Filipino surplus left the Philippines itself vulnerable to an invasion of foreign surplus populations. He articulated this threat during the 1930 U.S. congressional hearings by arguing that "the problem of conserving the race is more important than political freedom of the country, for independence will be useless if it will only benefit another race who come to take the place of our laborers."[46]

By 1926, Filipino migration to Hawai'i was not merely a symbolic concern for Filipino and American authorities; it had become an alarming material reality as Filipinos made up almost two-thirds of the laboring population on Hawaiian sugar plantations.[47] There were several intertwining reasons for this intensification in migration. First, as mentioned earlier, the legal status of Filipinos as U.S. colonial subjects enabled workers to bypass anti-Asian immigration bans. The second reason was the aforementioned increased militancy of Japanese Americans, the most dominant labor community from the 1910s to the early 1920s. Third, the World War I boom in global sugar demand and consumption led to increased labor needs in the Hawaiian colony, a policy strongly encouraged by the U.S. Food Administration. The final reason was the post–World War I economic crisis in the Philippines. "Again," Cruz argued, "the general business depression after the world war and the consequent unemployment of many contributed in no small degree to the increase of the number of Filipinos emigrating to Hawaii [sic]." According to the official numbers, migration in the years from 1921 to 1925 surpassed the total number of Filipino migrants since recruitment began in 1909.[48]

The population increase of Filipino migrants was immediately racialized as a problem of excessive surplus. Imperial and colonial authorities mainly obsessed over the Filipino body's emotional, biological, and cultural excesses, which was perceived as a constant unsettling threat to the political economy of the Hawaiian territory and the U.S. mainland. To authorities, the problem of Filipino surplus was clearly evident in their militant labor organizing during the multiracial Sugar Strike of 1920 (led mostly by Japanese and Filipino organizers), as well as the mainly Filipino strike in 1924. Rather than consider organized labor actions as responses to the injustices of racial capitalist production, colonial authorities and planters turned to U.S. academia to pathologize Filipinos as suffering under "temperamental disorders."

In the early 1920s, American psychology experts Stanley Porteus and Marjorie Babcock were encouraged by planters and officials to conduct research on different racialized communities of workers. Their goal was to identify the mental capacity and social underdevelopment of different races in Hawai'i and justify the existing racial hierarchy and segregation of workers on plantations.[49] In their findings, Filipinos were pathologized as having "racial defects" such as "super-sensitiveness, poor emotional control and unstable moods," "alternate obstinacy and suggestibility," and "impulsiveness."[50] Evidence of these racial defects lay in the failed labor strikes of 1920 and 1924. For Porteus and Babcock, the Filipino's restiveness and resistance to existing labor regimes was not a response to unjust working, social, and political conditions. Instead, this rebelliousness was a result of belonging to a "race in an adolescent stage of development." Because of their emotional and mental immaturity, Filipino migrants could not normatively adjust to conditions new to them and thus lashed out at settler society and institutions.[51]

In addition to temperamental excesses, anxieties over the excess of diseased and disabled Filipino bodies saturated U.S. colonial policy. These anxieties drew from longer histories of anti-Asian discourses that cast particular races as sickly. Racial capitalism in this instance created dichotomies between laboring bodies: racialized workers who were hygienic and healthy versus racialized workers who were diseased and prone to sickness and disability.[52] A 1910 article in the *San Francisco Chronicle*, for instance, panicked that "diseased and infected and dangerous" laborers from the Philippines would soon flood Hawai'i. The fear of colonized bodies colonizing another U.S. colony led to demands for restrictions and increased surveillance of Filipino migration.[53] Throughout the early 1910s, different U.S. authorities within the Bureau of Immigration and Naturalization and the Department of Commerce and Labor would frequently butt heads with the War Department over the restriction of Filipino migration on the basis of "disease." Different strategies were deployed, such as requiring a Filipino migrant to possess a "certificate of a quarantine officer" or undergo a physical examination upon arrival in Hawai'i. Ultimately, anxious American authorities and publics saw Hawai'i as a vulnerable gateway to the U.S. North American mainland. The imperial metropole, in this case, had to be protected from Filipino racialized bodies that were not only "indolent" but biologically "afflicted with, or subject to, dangerous contagious diseases."[54]

Finally, Filipino migrant workers were perceived as culturally excessive, idle bodies prone to pursuing irrational pleasures and leading lives of impermanence. These perceptions were grounded in longer colonial discourses on the Filipino as naturally idle and excessive. According to American officials in the early twentieth century, the Filipino submitted easily to base desires of consumption and waste and thus did not possess the capacity to save or invest.[55] One colonial authority, Resident Filipino Labor Commissioner of Hawai'i Cayetano Ligot, wrote of his disapproval of the excessive habits of Filipino workers in Hawai'i. In his 1924 report to the colonial governor of the Philippines, Ligot argued that the idle nature of Filipinos led them to be more susceptible to immoral social ties and illicit activities. This, according to Ligot, had "produced a class of gamblers and collectors who visit the plantations and disturb the working conditions very much, while at the same time imposing upon the Filipino laborers considerable burdens in the way of monetary losses, most of which are pure losses, because the collections are seldom used for the purpose for which are collected." Unlike the normative economic subject, the Filipino was "much inclined to lay off and rest with no good and sufficient reason, except that they feel like it, particularly during the days after the pay day." In addition, this excessiveness led to a life of transience, of refusing to settle. As Ligot remarked, "the habit of Filipinos in moving from one plantation to another was a deterrent to their progress and their usefulness."[56]

To Ligot, one solution to fix the excesses of the Filipino was the institution of savings and thrift. Investment in capitalist security would endow Filipinos with a sense of futurity wedded to a capitalist world and, of course, deter any disorder caused by labor organizing. To accomplish this, Ligot suggested the establishment of a banking institution, the Filipino Laborers' Bank.[57] According to Ligot, most of the local establishments that offered banking services like savings, loans, or remittances were stores run by supposedly alien capitalists, Japanese or Chinese owners. In his proposed Filipino Laborers' Bank, most of the capital would not be held in Hawai'i but would instead be "distributed to the Provincial Treasurers of the Philippines with the instruction of using it for exchanging money orders and drafts issued to Filipino laborers."[58] The bank would also find a way to domesticate Philippine surplus labor and migrant surplus wealth, through the capture of Filipino worker savings and remittances from Hawai'i to the Philippines.

"The Bank," reasoned Ligot, "can help the government, and avoid unnecessary losses of the owners of money orders or drafts, and we can improve the character of the laborers in saving money."[59] Through the dispersion of local credit, the bank would additionally differentiate the Filipino from "alien" Asian settlers and make the Filipino a normative junior collaborator in the maintenance of white settler colonialism in Hawai'i.

Although Ligot's fantasy of capturing Filipino savings and remittances through a state-backed bank never came to fruition, he did correctly apprehend its possibility for profit. Several newspapers during the Great Depression touted the supposed success of Filipino migrant workers in Hawai'i in terms of thrift and hard work, quantified mainly through their savings and remittances of wages. During the peak of Filipino migration to Hawai'i, from 1915 to 1929, more than twelve million dollars were remitted to the Philippine colony. Even during the initial years of the Depression, remittance numbers remained steady, with an average of three million dollars a year from 1930 to 1932. Additionally impressive to the authors of these articles was the consistency of saving by Filipino workers in Hawai'i. Filipinos saved more than $4.6 million in various territorial banks from 1927 to 1932. These numbers were striking in comparison to other racially marginalized communities in the United States. The HSPA, by providing banking and remittance services, was often the prime beneficiary of this intercolonial flow of cash. Although the fees were not stated, the HSPA would have taken a percentage of all money remitted to the Philippine colony, which from 1925 to 1932 totaled more than $23 million.[60] Thus U.S. empire created conditions in which plantation companies could doubly exploit Filipinos: first, by exploiting their labor through low wages and, second, by taking a cut of those wages through remittance fees.

During the early 1930s, savings and remittances of Filipino migrant workers in Hawai'i would play a significant part in U.S. congressional hearings about instituting a Filipino immigration ban. On one hand, those who advocated for Filipino exclusion used Filipino remittances as evidence of the ways migrants removed money from the U.S. economy and instead used it to prop up their "native" economy elsewhere.[61] On the other hand, both employers and colonial officials held up Filipino savings and remittances as evidence of the "racial" capacity of Filipinos to become fixed by capitalism. Through intercolonial banking networks, Filipino migrant workers held the potential to improve themselves and significantly benefit both colonial economies. This narrative of Filipino migrant workers as supporting two colonial economies under U.S. empire positioned Filipino workers as potentially postcolonial national heroes, enabling security during times of political and economic insecurities, to both the U.S. and Philippine publics.[62]

In Hawai'i, authorities and plantation capitalists racially fixed surplus populations into a settler colonial division of labor. Over time, however, waves of racially surplus populations, such as Japanese migrant workers, would unsettle the racial capitalist status quo. Like others before them, Filipino migrants were seen as racially excessive and thus threats to settler colonial norms in Hawai'i. At the same time, Filipino migrants created a unique problem for the HSPA and colonial authorities because, as subjects of U.S. empire, their movements to and from Hawai'i were legally protected. As a consequence, authorities sought to domesticate and fix the excesses of Filipino migrants through banking, to resettle their accumulated wages in capitalist infrastructures of savings accounts and remittances. Once settled within financial institutions owned and operated by the HSPA or transimperial banks, these savings could be remitted and resettled to the Philippine "homeland" and rendered accessible to the Philippine state and Filipino capitalists for expropriation. For Philippine authorities, the development of a banking infrastructure connecting the colonies fixed the initial problem of Filipino migration, the seeming loss of labor power to the benefit of non-Filipino capital. Through remittances, the accumulation of Filipino migrant work (congealed as wages) would be recaptured back in the Philippine colony, a seeming intercolonial fix for the problem of escaped surplus labor.

What Remains

Despite all of the colonial fixes implemented, the excesses of racialized surplus populations in Hawai'i never became completely settled. What remained in excess of racial capitalist, settler colonial, and intraimperial discipline and management was a transpacific radical tradition. Stretching from the provinces of the Philippines to the plantations of Hawai'i were ongoing organized struggles for liberation and justice. An episode that expresses this radical tradition is contained within Luis Taruc's 1953 autobiography, *Born of the People*.

Taruc was a key public figure of the Philippine anticolonial communist group *Hukbong Mapagpalaya ng Bayan* [The People's Liberation Army], or *Hukbalahap*. The foreword of *Born of the People* was written by Paul Robeson, one of the most internationally famous black entertainers of the mid-twentieth century, who was widely known (and later punished) by global publics for his antiracist, anticolonial, and anticapitalist activism. Robeson reminisces about his time with workers in Hawai'i, when he was able to get to know a large community of Filipino migrant organizers, become acquainted with their songs, and learn more about their struggles for economic justice and decolonization.

> When I was in Hawaii a few years ago it was my privilege to sing for and with sugar and pineapple workers, to clasp their hands in firm friendship, to share for a short time their way of life. Truly, here was unity, amazingly broad—Hawaiians, Japanese-Americans, Portuguese, black and white workers from the United States, Chinese and Chinese-Americans, and many workers from the Philippines. [...] We had long discussions with my brothers and sisters from the Philippines about artists and others serving the people in their struggles toward a better life. They talked of their land, of the Hukbalahap, of the fight to survive against Japanese fascism, and later against the vicious forces of American imperialism and against their own collaborators.[63]

These talks about collective struggles for economic justice and decolonization would enable Robeson to the think about the year of his birth, 1898, the time of U.S. colonial occupation of the Philippines and other places across the Pacific and Caribbean. Robeson would then connect this memory to ongoing struggles for decolonization, within and against other global empires. "The real story of that time has been recorded," he writes, "one of the most shameful periods of United States history, comparable to the British in India and South Africa, the Belgians in the Congo, or for that matter, the United States in almost any section of Latin America, beginning with Mexico and Panama."[64]

On one hand, Robeson's story unsettles the story of Hawai'i as the American fantasy of multiculturalism. It does not allow the celebration of immigration as a process that enabled migrant workers to "freely" choose where to sell their labor across global markets. Instead, it underlines that migration is structurally shaped by racial, colonial, and imperial violence. Hawai'i may have been a fantasy for both plantation capitalists espousing year-round "full" employment or liberal tourists espousing multicultural harmony, but for workers it was a nightmare, a place where race determined where they fell within a hierarchy of valuation and determined to what degree they would be exploited by capitalism. Robeson's brief analysis of the historical making of the Hawaiian labor regime was an implicit critique of the logic of racial surplus and colonial settlement in the management of bodies in the Philippines and Hawai'i.

On the other hand, Robeson's story gestures to what Stefano Harney and Fred Moten call an undercommons history of Filipino surplus and settlement.[65] It illustrates that the story of surplus is also a story of the coming together of those who may have historically been disaggregated by time and space but were brought into unforeseen intimacy through racial capitalism and colonial regimes.[66] Although what they held in common was certainly exploitation, Robeson illustrates that through struggle, different histories of resistance and the multiplicity of singular desires for justice became intertwined and intensified through proximity to one another. It is through Robeson, too, that the resonance between transpacific collective resistance and the black radical tradition is articulated.

> Often we talk of the struggles of colonial peoples, of the early struggles here in the days of our nation's birth. We are daily in touch with the sufferings and strivings of 15 million Negro Americans for nationhood in the South and full freedom in all the land. We follow the surging forward of the emergent African nations, all over that vast continent.[67]

To Robeson, the scene of friendship in struggle in Hawai'i reverberates with the echoes of transatlantic struggles for liberation, past and pending.

It was this undercommon history of surplus and settlement that remained unsettling to racial capitalist and colonial fixes. Robeson's account is of collective life, generous hospitality, and brief yet meaningful encounters: "to clasp their hands in firm friendship, to share for a short time their way of life." As migration increases proximity and contact between bodies for racial capitalist exploitation and continuing colonialism, perhaps these preserved histories of friendship and sharing each other's way of life (even for a short time) can serve as a reminder of the ongoing echoes and connections between the transpacific and black radical traditions.

NOTES

1. Cedric J. Robinson, *Black Marxism: The Making of the Black Radical Tradition* (Chapel Hill: University of North Carolina Press, 2000).
2. Robinson, *Black Marxism*, 39.
3. Robinson, *Black Marxism*, 127.
4. Robinson, *Black Marxism*, 129.
5. Robinson, *Black Marxism*, 72.
6. For more on the relation between Filipino migrant workers and a capitalist world system dominated by the United States, see Caroline S. Hau, *On the Subject of the Nation: Writings from the Margins, 1981 to 2004* (Quezon City, Philippines: Ateneo de Manila University Press, 2007), 228; Vicente L. Rafael, *White Love and Other Events in Filipino History* (Durham, N.C.: Duke University Press, 2000), 205; Neferti X. M. Tadiar, *Things Fall Away: Philippine Historical Experience and the Makings of Globalization* (Durham, N.C.: Duke University Press, 2009), 103. The significance of migrant labor to postcolonial economies under U.S. empire is especially apparent through the lens of Filipino cash remittances. Personal remittances from Filipino migrant workers accounted for 10 percent of the Philippine economy in 2017. This, of course, does not include under-the-table flows of money. Chris Schnabel, "PH Remittances Beat Gov't Target, Hit Record in 2017," *Rappler*, February 15, 2018, https://www.rappler.com/business/196148-philippines-ofw-remittances-december-2017.
7. Neferti X. M. Tadiar, *Fantasy-Production: Sexual Economies and Other Philippine Consequences for the New World Order* (Quezon City, Philippines: Ateneo de Manila University Press, 2004), 26.
8. Rick Baldoz, *The Third Asiatic Invasion: Migration and Empire in Filipino America, 1898–1946* (New York: New York University Press, 2011), 45.
9. Nick Estes, *Our History Is the Future: Standing Rock Versus the Dakota Access Pipeline, and the Long Tradition of Indigenous Resistance* (Brooklyn, N.Y.: Verso, 2019), 91.
10. Estes, *Our History Is the Future*, 138.
11. Jodi A. Byrd, Alyosha Goldstein, Jodi Melamed, and Chandan Reddy, "Predatory Value: Economies of Dispossession and Disturbed Relationalities," *Social Text* 36, no. 2 (June 2018): 1–18. See also Manu Vimalassery, "The Wealth of the Natives: Toward a Critique of Settler Colonial Political Economy," *Settler Colonial Studies* 3, nos. 3–4: 295–310; Glen Coulthard, *Red Skin, White Masks: Rejecting the Colonial Politics of Recognition* (Minneapolis: University of Minnesota Press, 2014).
12. Andre Gunder Frank, *ReORIENT: Global Economy in the Asian Age* (Berkeley: University of California Press), 5.
13. Adam McKeown, "Global Migration, 1846–1940," *Journal of World History* 15, no. 2 (June 2004): 155–89.
14. Datus and sultans are native forms of chief or sovereign in the Philippine archipelago.

15. For more on revolutionary thinking in the Spanish colonial Philippines, see Benedict Anderson, *Under Three Flags: Anarchism and the Anti-Colonial Imagination* (New York: Verso, 2006); Reynaldo Ileto, *Pasyon and Revolution: Popular Movements in the Philippines, 1840–1910* (Quezon City, Philippines: Ateneo de Manila University Press, 1997); Vicente Rafael, *The Promise of the Foreign* (Durham, N.C.: Duke University Press, 2005).

16. Audra Simpson, "Sovereignty, Sympathy, and Indigeneity," in *Ethnographies of U.S. Empire*, ed. Carole McGranahan and John F. Collins (Durham, N.C.: Duke University Press, 2018), 72–89.

17. Peter W. Stanley, *A Nation in the Making: The Philippines and the United States, 1899–1921* (Cambridge, Mass.: Harvard University Press, 1974), chap. 9.

18. William Pomeroy reports interest rates of up to 300 percent during the early 1920s. William Pomeroy, *The Philippines: Colonialism, Collaboration, and Resistance* (New York: International, 1992), 59.

19. Karl Marx saw this potential in the "industrial reserve army" that, through the highly disciplined industrial division of labor, could self-organize into a conscious force antagonistic to capital. Karl Marx, *Capital Vol. 1* (New York: Penguin, 1990), 791.

20. Robinson, *Black Marxism*, 311.

21. During the 1920s, there was an explosion of organized peasant movements. Some of these were radical organizations, with direct relation to the Comintern or the Communist Party of the United States; others were millenarian fraternities or secret organizations that were considered cults. Pomeroy, *The Philippines*, 59–67.

22. The feminist, queer, and disability studies critique of patriarchy and heteronormativity is especially salient. Some recent studies of note are Mel Chen, *Animacies: Biopolitics, Racial Mattering, and Queer Affect* (Durham, N.C.: Duke University Press, 2012); Alison Kafer, *Feminist, Queer, Crip* (Bloomington: Indiana University Press, 2013); Jasbir Puar, *The Right to Maim: Debility, Capacity, Disability* (Durham, N.C.: Duke University Press, 2017).

23. On social engineering and colonialism, see Glenn May, *Social Engineering in the Philippines: The Aims, Execution, and Impact of American Colonial Policy, 1900–1913* (Westport, Conn.: Greenwood, 1980); Michael Adas, *Machines as the Measure of Men: Science, Technology, and Ideologies of Western Dominance* (Ithaca, N.Y.: Cornell University Press, 1989). For more on how surplus could become both deviant and excessive, see José Muñoz, *Cruising Utopia: The Then and There of Queer Futurity* (New York: New York University Press, 2009), 147.

24. For more on the necessity of surplus laboring bodies for capitalist accumulation, see Karl Marx, *Capital Vol. 1* (New York: Penguin, 1990), 791.

25. Ruth Wilson Gilmore, *Golden Gulag: Prisons, Surplus, Crisis, and Opposition in Globalizing California* (Berkeley: University of California Press, 2007), 55–78.

26. Hermenegildo Cruz, *Labor Conditions in the Philippine Islands* (Manila: Government of the Philippine Islands, 1927), 9.

27. Cruz, *Labor Conditions in the Philippine Islands*, 18.

28. Cruz, *Labor Conditions in the Philippine Islands*, 32.

29. Cruz, *Labor Conditions in the Philippine Islands*, 40.

30. Cruz, *Labor Conditions in the Philippine Islands*, 42.

31. Moro is an umbrella term for Muslim ethnolinguistic communities native to Mindanao, Sulu, Palawan, and other parts of the Visayas.

32. "E. Dworak to Pershing, April 17, 1913," Box 130, Folder 873, Records of the Bureau of Insular Affairs, Record Group 350, National Archives and Records Administration (hereafter BIA RG350, NARA), 10.

33. "E. Dworak to Pershing, April 17, 1913," 10.

34. "E. Dworak to Pershing, April 17, 1913," 9.

35. "W. E. Cobey, Acting Director of Agriculture, July 28, 1916," Box 1165, Folder 26874, BIA RG350, NARA.

36. "Bukidnon Colony Association, August 24, 1916," Box 1165, Folder 26874, BIA RG350, NARA.

37. Cruz, *Labor Conditions in the Philippine Islands*, 35.

38. Cruz, *Labor Conditions in the Philippine Islands*, 38.

39. Cruz, *Labor Conditions in the Philippine Islands*, 83–84.

40. For more on indigenous struggles and decolonization in Hawai'i, see J. Kehaulani Kauanui, *Hawaiian Blood: Colonialism and the Politics of Sovereignty and Indigeneity* (Durham, N.C.: Duke University Press, 2008); Noenoe K. Silva, *Aloha Betrayed: Native Hawaiian Resistance to American Colonialism* (Durham, N.C.: Duke University Press, 2004); Haunani-Kay Trask, *From a Native Daughter: Colonialism and Sovereignty in Hawaii* (Honolulu: University of Hawai'i Press, 1999). For relations of Asian settlement in Hawai'i, see Candace Fujikane and Jonathan Okamura, *Asian Settler Colonialism: From Local Governance to the Habits of Everyday Life in Hawaii* (Honolulu: University of Hawai'i Press, 2008)

41. For more on the history of Japanese migrant workers and organized struggles in Hawai'i, see Moon-Kie Jung, *Reworking Race: The Making of Hawaii's Interracial Labor Movement* (New York: Columbia University Press, 2010); Gary Okihiro, *Cane Fires: The Anti-Japanese Movement in Hawaii, 1865–1945* (Philadelphia: Temple University Press, 1992); Ronald Takaki, *Pau Hana: Plantation Life and Labor in Hawaii* (Honolulu: University of Hawai'i Press, 1983).

42. Baldoz, *The Third Asiatic Invasion*, 12.

43. "Early Records on the Emigration of Filipino Laborers to Hawaii or the United States, November 5, 1931," Box 459, Folder 3037, BIA RG350, NARA, 3.

44. Cruz, *Labor Conditions in the Philippine Islands*, 18.

45. "Early Records on the Emigration of Filipino Laborers to Hawaii or the United States, November 5, 1931," 3.

46. "Early Records on the Emigration of Filipino Laborers to Hawaii," 2.

47. R. A. Duckworth, *Report on Hawaiian Sugar Plantations and Filipino Labor* (Manila: Government of the Philippine Islands, 1926), 5.

48. "Hermenegildo Cruz correspondence with James Wood," April 23, 1929, James Woods Collection, Box 1, Folder 1.1, Bancroft Library, University of California.

49. S. D. Porteus and Marjorie Babcock, *Temperament and Race* (Boston: Gorham, 1926).

50. Porteus and Babcock, *Temperament and Race*, 66.

51. Porteus and Babcock, *Temperament and Race*, 62.

52. Neel Ahuja, *Bioinsecurities: Disease Interventions, Empire, and the Government of Species* (Durham, N.C.: Duke University Press, 2016); David Arnold, *Colonizing the Body: State Medicine and Epidemic Disease in Nineteenth-Century India* (Berkeley: University of California Press, 1993); Warwick Anderson, *Colonial Pathologies: American Tropical Medicine, Race, and Hygiene in the Philippines* (Durham, N.C.: Duke University Press, 2006); Alfred Crosby, *Ecological Imperialism: The Biological Expansion of Europe, 900–1900* (Cambridge: Cambridge University Press, 2015); Mark Harrison, *Climates and Constitutions: Health, Race, Environment, and British Imperialism in India, 1600–1850* (Oxford: Oxford University Press, 2000); Nayan Shah, *Contagious Divides: Epidemics and Race in San Francisco's Chinatown* (Berkeley: University of California Press, 2001).

53. "Early Records on the Emigration of Filipino Laborers to Hawaii," 4.

54. "Early Records on the Emigration of Filipino Laborers to Hawaii," 5.

55. Allan Lumba, *Monetary Authorities: Capitalism and Decolonization in the American Colonial Philippines* (Durham, N.C.: Duke University Press, forthcoming), chap. 3.

56. Cayetano Ligot, *Filipino Laborers in Hawaii: Report of Honorable Cayetano Ligot to Governor General Leonard Wood* (Manila: Government of the Philippine Islands, 1924), 16.

57. Ligot, *Filipino Laborers in Hawaii*, 32.

58. Ligot, *Filipino Laborers in Hawaii*, 34.

59. Ligot, *Filipino Laborers in Hawaii*, 34.

60. This data was compiled from various newspaper clippings, including "Filipinos in Hawaii Able to Save Money," *Manila Bulletin*, July 28, 1933; "Hawaii Filipinos Save more Money," *The Philippines Herald*, September 9, 1932; "Why Filipinos are Lured to Hawaii," *The Philippines Herald*, January 13, 1934. Box 459, Folder 3037, BIA RG350, NARA.

61. Committee on Immigration and Naturalization, *Exclusion of Immigration from the Philippine Islands* (Washington, D.C.: U.S. Government Printing Office 1930), 49.

62. This narrative rehearses the way twenty-first century overseas Filipino workers within an exploitative hyerglobalized world system are narrated as heroes by the present-day Philippine government. Joyce Ann L. Rocamora, "OFWs: Modern-Day Heroes Still," Philippine News Agency, August 27, 2018, https://www.pna.gov.ph/articles/1046084.

63. Luis Taruc, *Born of the People* (New York: International Publishers, 1953), 7.

64. Taruc, *Born of the People*, 8.

65. Stefano Harney and Fred Moten, *The Undercommons: Fugitive Planning and Black Study* (Brooklyn, N.Y.: Autonomedia, 2013).

66. I borrow this notion of intimacy from Lisa Lowe, *The Intimacies of Four Continents* (Durham, N.C.: Duke University Press, 2015).

67. Taruc, *Born of the People*, 8.

CHAPTER 5

THE COUNTERREVOLUTION OF PROPERTY ALONG THE 32ND PARALLEL

MANU KARUKA

It turned democracy back to Roman Imperialism and Fascism; it restored caste and oligarchy; it replaced freedom with slavery and withdrew the name of humanity from the vast majority of human beings.

—W. E. B. Du Bois, *Black Reconstruction*, 1935

D oes the work of W. E. B. Du Bois offer guidance for a critique of settler colonialism, and for an anti-imperialist politics? I argue that it does. In this essay, I engage the fourteenth chapter of *Black Reconstruction*, "Counter-Revolution of Property," to examine the history of the Southern Pacific Railroad. In *Black Reconstruction*, Du Bois demonstrated the centrality of colonial and racial violence to the history of capitalism. Moreover, he historicized a program of racial justice, which he referred to as the dictatorship of labor.

In the epigraph to "Counter-Revolution of Property," Du Bois provided an outline for his core arguments in the chapter, charting the combination of "triumphant industry" with "privilege and monopoly," together driving "an orgy of theft." This theft, Du Bois insisted, "was the natural child of war." The ensuing "anarchy" augured an antidemocratic reaction, delivering "the land into the hands of an organized monarchy of finance while it overthrew the attempt at a dictatorship of labor in the south." The fulfillment of emancipation and the achievement of a genuine multiracial democracy were defeated when concentrated finance capital successfully captured control of the land. This defeated program, "a dictatorship of far broader possibilities than the North had at first contemplated," had placed political power "in the hands of Southern labor . . . confiscated and redistributed wealth, and built a real democracy of industry for the masses of men." The defeat of this political program, the counterrevolution of property, Du Bois argued, would set the terms of the struggles for democracy, racial justice, and decolonization in the following era, both in North America and in the world at large.[1]

In this essay, I focus on the southern transcontinental railroad line in the United States and its role in the development of an industrial capitalist economy centered on mining and agriculture, where the contradiction between free land and free labor was resolved through the counterrevolution of property. Along the Colorado River basin, the counterrevolution of property manifested through the interrelationship of the U.S. Army and finance capital. After the Civil War, Du Bois noted, northern industry controlled a "vast organization for production, new supplies of raw material, a growing transportation system on land and water, and a new technical knowledge of processes."[2] How to mobilize these resources, and to what ends?

The dictatorship of labor, as Du Bois analyzed it, sought to marshall the U.S. Army and financial institutions toward politically and economically empowering freedpeople, so as to finalize the defeat of the slaveholder oligarchy. In the counterrevolution of property, "Reform became liberal . . . calling for freedom of the South from military control." Losing sight of "the radical revolution of controlling capital and forcing recognition of the rights of labor by government control" resulted in labor war in the North and serfdom in the South.[3] In this defeat, the outlet for both the U.S. Army and finance capital became U.S. industrial and military expansion west of the Mississippi River. The New South and the American West pieced together inheritances of the slaveholder aristocracy. As this essay seeks to demonstrate, the "counterrevolution of property" that defeated Reconstruction can help us understand the historical development of Arizona and southern California as deep wellsprings of the far right.

Du Bois would have us understand land's centrality to the abolition of slavery. Land, he wrote, was "the most pressing" problem that freedpeople faced. It was "absolutely fundamental . . . to any real emancipation of the slaves." The necessity of land for establishing a material basis for emancipation extended far beyond the wartime requisition of Confederate property that had come into the possession of the occupying Union Army. Du Bois assessed a need for an additional twenty-five to fifty million acres "if the Negroes were to be installed as peasant farmers." Opposing this policy was the "settled determination" of the planter oligarchy to constrict the majority of black people to the position of landless workers, alongside the "deep repugnance" of many in the North against the confiscation of individual property. Such a policy would contradict what Du Bois called "the American Assumption"—the idea that "any American could be rich if he wanted to, or at least well-to-do"—an assumption that "stubbornly ignored the exceptional position of a freed slave." The U.S. government declared that land would be restored to its "original owners" after they received presidential pardon. President Johnson's 1865 Proclamation of Amnesty declared a "restoration of all rights of property, except as to slaves," to "all persons who have directly or indirectly participated in the existing rebellion."[4] This policy amounted to a restoration of the oligarchy that had controlled the United States, by controlling the South.

The politics of land was at the heart of the counterrevolution of property. Distributing land to freedpeople, Du Bois writes, would have "made a basis of real democracy in the United States that might easily have transformed the modern world." The failure to abolish the landed property of the slaveholding oligarchy alongside the abolition of their property in slaves would shape the history of capitalism in the period after the U.S. Civil War, the age of imperialism. Du Bois noted that freedpeople's demand for land "was met by ridicule, by anger, and by dishonest and insincere efforts to satisfy it apparently."[5] This ridicule, anger, dishonesty, and lack of sincerity imprinted the historiography of the period, and it persists in our day, in readings of this history that refuse to acknowledge its relevance to the analysis of settler colonialism and imperialism.

The counterrevolution of property, to follow Du Bois, involves the conquest of an "empire of rich land," through which "all of the national treasure of coal, oil, copper and iron had been given away for a song to be made into the monopolized basis of private fortunes with perpetual power to tax labor for the right to live and work." Railroads, he noted, were central to this process, turning vast public resources over "to individuals and corporations to use for their profit."[6] The counterrevolution of property can help us understand the interrelationship of military occupation and capital accumulation.[7]

Black Reconstruction provides keys for understanding settler colonialism and U.S. expansion west of the Mississippi River. I draw from Du Bois's argument about the counterrevolution of property as the historical and political context for the completion of the southern transcontinental railroad route. Following the historically intersecting paths of the Colorado River and the Southern Pacific Railroad, we can trace the historical development of a regional economy rooted in monopoly control of agriculture, transportation, and mining.[8] This regional economy tied together agricultural and industrial oligarchies, linking the Imperial Valley with the former Cotton Kingdom through agribusiness, armaments, and finance. This regional economy has provided fertile ground for far-right reaction that has violently opposed movements for genuine democracy and self-determination, in the world at large.[9]

The essay begins with the military occupation of the Colorado River against indigenous nations and against Mexico. Military occupation furnished a context for planning a southern transcontinental railroad route to extend and maintain slaveholders' political and economic power. The region's mining economy preceded the irresolvable crisis separating the interests of slaveholding and industrial capital. In the Colorado River region, the resolution of this crisis arrived, in part, on the southern transcontinental route. In this area, military dictatorship stabilized the production and realization of capital, shaping the nature of the counterrevolution of property and resulting in a new synthesis of agrarian capital, industrial capital, and war.[10] The essay ends in the fields of southern California, the seat of this new synthesis, a heartland of monopoly agribusiness for the next era. The counterrevolution of property in the Colorado River region marked a transition from the interests of a slaveholder oligarchy to those of an agribusiness oligarchy. Understanding this transition, with its implications for the strangulation of democracy, ecological crisis, and the violent abrogation of collective well-being, is of the highest urgency in the present crisis.

Rivers

Struggles over land have historically taken place along rivers. Following the course of rivers, claiming control of river crossings and flood plains, colonialists first imposed private property relations over indigenous relationships in and with land. Europeans first reached the confluence of the Gila and Colorado rivers, the Quechan homeland, in 1541. By the 1780s, colonists had violently seized the most productive land in the area. In July 1781, Quechans spearheaded a revolt to expel Spanish colonial authority from the area. Quechans and neighboring communities won independence for the next seventy years, while their land nominally passed from Spain to Mexico in 1821. This respite occurred amid a regional intensification of colonial violence. St. Louis–based merchants unleashed a new round of regional violence, drawing New Mexico into their economic orbit and away from Sonora. In the 1830s, Mexicans moved through independent Quechan territory on their way to California from Sonora, their safety ensured only by the acquiescence of their Quechan hosts. In the Treaty of Guadalupe Hidalgo, Mexico ceded Quechan territory to the United States, layering a new colonialism atop the existing colonialism. Quechans recognized the sovereignty of neither Mexico nor the United States over their lands.[11]

Imperialism in North America, as elsewhere, had long followed rivers, but by the 1840s, imperialists had begun to anticipate railroads for cementing territorial control. Article VI of the Treaty of Guadalupe Hidalgo projected the construction of a railroad along the Gila River. Part of the U.S. slaveholder class advocated railroad construction to connect the Cotton Kingdom with the Pacific, hoping to facilitate the economic and geographic growth of slaveholder power. According to the boundaries outlined in the treaty, the most felicitous course of railroad construction to the Pacific coast would cross through Mexican territory. The drive to build a southern rail route to the Pacific fueled lingering controversy within the United States about the actual location of the U.S.-Mexico border a decade after the treaty. By invading and occupying Mexico, the United States gained territory that included productive farmlands as well as rich stores of gold, silver, copper, oil, and uranium, raw materials for industrial development.[12]

The colonization of the region rapidly intensified after the discovery of gold in California in 1849. The Colorado River became a favored route for westward travel. Gold-rush traffic trampled and despoiled Quechan fields while polluting the waters. To offset this damage, Quechans charged travelers a toll to ferry goods and animals across the river. A gang of Americans wandered in from Sonora, where they had been collecting bounties on "Apache scalps," and joined a rival ferry operation. The Quechans had hired a man named Callahan to operate one of their boats. His body was later found floating in the river. Santiago, a Quechan leader, visited John Glanton, the leader of the gang, seeking to forge a reasonable compromise over the ferry business. Glanton responded to his overtures by beating him severely. After Santiago returned home, the Quechans waited until an April night in 1850, after Glanton's gang had gotten drunk on a liquor shipment from San Diego. After Glanton and his men had fallen asleep, a group of Quechans quietly entered their cabin. They clubbed the whole gang to death, thus asserting their control over trade and diplomacy at the river crossing.[13]

The colonialist reaction to Quechan control sought to steer trade and diplomacy in other directions. Settlers in California, identifying the scalp hunters as fellow honest businessmen, clamored for revenge. Responding to pressure from mass meetings in San Diego, Gen. Persifor Smith, the regional U.S. Army commander, issued orders on July 4, 1850, authorizing a military post at the juncture of the Gila and Colorado rivers. The State of California marshalled a volunteer force of 142 men, recruiting among recent immigrants from the United States, who found the promised daily five-dollar wage (plus rations) better than their weekly wages. This hastily assembled military force attempted to invade Quechan lands, where they were promptly chased into a defensive location, periodically wandering out to rob Mexicans returning to Sonora with gold from California.[14]

The U.S. Army established Fort Yuma in 1850 to administer the military occupation of Quechan territory. Fort Yuma was about a mile from the mouth of the Gila River, at an ideal site for crossing the river. In the words of Lt. Sylvester Mowry, "Fort Yuma is a hell of a place. More than 200 miles from anywhere in the midst of an Indian country—hotter than hell—and not a sign of anything for amusement."[15] Soldiers frequently deserted the fort, but San Diego, the nearest town, was 180 miles away, across desert and mountain terrain. The U.S. Army paid villagers at Temecula, an Indian village in California, thirty dollars a head to capture deserters. Military occupation would provide the foundation for the formation of profitable businesses. In this way, the U.S. Army scaled up and formalized the presence of Glanton's gang of bounty hunters.[16]

Following Lt. Mowry's perspective, we should understand that Fort Yuma was not located in the United States. By this time, Cupeño women sold flour and performed laundry work for white settlers in southern California, even as they continued the work necessary to maintain their traditional relationships with their lands and their communities. As a materialization of U.S. sovereignty, the fort remained highly unstable. Fresh produce was scarce, and scurvy was common among the soldiers stationed there. Wagon trains that departed from San Diego with thirty thousand pounds of barley and water often arrived at Fort Yuma with only five thousand pounds, having consumed the rest during the monthlong journey. This cost the army five hundred to eight hundred dollars per ton. The military budget covered the preconditions for private profit, and for state revenue.[17]

The founding officer at Fort Yuma, Maj. Samuel Heintzelman, who had received a brevet promotion to lieutenant colonel for a skirmish with Cahuillas in 1851, sought to profit from his assignment. In the isolation of his command, Heintzelman attempted to blend the functions of military occupation with the imperative of capital accumulation. While stationed at Fort Yuma, Heintzelman joined the Gila Association, a group of speculators led by John Weller. As the U.S. boundary commissioner, Weller represented the U.S. government in talks to set the U.S.-Mexico border, from the Pacific Ocean to the confluence of the Colorado and Gila rivers, where Ft. Yuma was situated. Where Quechans had dealt with the Glanton gang in a way that asserted the primacy of their own trade and diplomatic protocols, a mere three years later, the Gila Association asserted a very different set of trade and diplomatic protocols over the river crossing. Colonial occupation was a precondition for the accumulation of capital.[18]

The Gila Association delegated Heintzelman to lobby Judge John Hays of San Diego County for land rights at Fort Yuma. Judge Hays insisted on a five thousand dollar bond and a five hundred dollar annual fee in return for his acquiescence. Unable to quickly raise the money, Heintzelman instead returned to Yuma and surveyed the military reservation, making sure to include the ferry landing within its boundaries. Heintzelman then ordered all newly designated "trespassers" to remove themselves from the vicinity. After asserting control over his junior officers, who had themselves pooled money to establish a ferry at the fort, Heintzelman and three associates formed the Colorado Ferry Company in April 1851. State revenue and personal profit blended in a colonial situation. Military hierarchy, within military occupation, shaped the colonial monopoly as a precondition for a "free market."[19]

Amid these negotiations, the San Diego County Sheriff's Department imposed taxes on Cupeños, seizing and selling their cattle after they refused to pay. Sheriff Agoston Harazsthy (a pioneer of California viticulture) approached this as a question of state revenue collection. Cupeños had a different understanding of the relationship between the United States and their homelands. The sheriff's actions constituted a declaration of war. Cupeños therefore began forging alliances with neighboring tribes, including Quechans and Cocopahs. Amid these nascent coalitions, Heintzelman threatened violent retribution against indigenous people seeking respite from famine conditions at Fort Yuma after the crops failed that summer.

The fort provided no security for indigenous lives; instead, it provided security for colonial property claims. In June 1851, the army ordered the abandonment of Fort Yuma and the occupation of Santa Isabel, an Indian village 125 miles to the west. Heintzelman ordered a small detachment to remain, in order to maintain his claim on the ferry business. Witnessing the departure of U.S. soldiers from their lands, Quechans joined the larger insurrection against colonial power. By the end of the year, the army had abandoned the Yuma crossing entirely. In the coming months, traffic from San Diego was severely disrupted.[20]

The U.S. Army issued orders to reoccupy Fort Yuma on February 3, 1852, this time with a substantially larger force. The army also began shipping supplies by schooner on the river. Heintzelman and his soldiers returned to face a situation of low-grade guerilla resistance. Indigenous forces concentrated their power for an action in early March, when several hundred Quechans successfully attacked a schooner delivering supplies to Fort Yuma, making away with the cargo. Bereft of food and other crucial supplies, U.S. soldiers retaliated by systematically raiding and burning Quechan villages and fields and imprisoning Quechan women. Heintzelman rebuffed Quechan peace overtures until October, when he imposed a general submission to U.S. Army rule, replacing Quechan political leadership. The destruction of food and assault on civilians preceded stable capitalist relations of accumulation, and the corresponding profits for Heintzelman and his associates.[21]

Heintzelman planned to stabilize U.S. power over the area by maintaining "a sufficient garrison" at the fort. The occupation pursued political ends. Heintzelman believed that Quechans would "soon learn to respect our strength, if they have not already done so." The occupation also pursued economic ends. Heintzelman anticipated that Quechans would "become accustomed to get from us things they now consider luxuries, but which will become necessities." The political economy of occupation, Heintzelman concluded, would serve the ends of genocide. "The vices of contact with whites," he wrote, "will cause them to dwindle rapidly away, and another race soon occupy their places."[22] In Heintzelman's vision, capital accumulation would result in a racial replacement of the indigenous peoples of the place. A lengthy ethnographic report on the tribe, duly submitted to the Congressional Record, provided a programmatic case for this replacement.[23]

With the 1854 Gadsden Purchase, the U.S. government acquired 29,640 square miles of land south of the Gila River for ten million dollars. Ostensibly a land purchase for building a railroad connecting Texas and the Pacific coast, mineral wealth in this part of Sonora drove U.S. interests in controlling the land. James Gadsden, U.S. Ambassador to Mexico, threatened that if Mexico refused to sell the land, the United States would simply take it. The Gadsden Purchase, and the corresponding development of a regional mining industry, compelled railroad construction in order to ease the importation of labor, mitigate the region's isolation, and transport the products of the mines. These processes would significantly increase the value of real estate in northern Mexico, leading to distrust among wealthy and powerful Sonorans that the Mexican government was preparing to sell off even more land to the United States. The migrating border powerfully destabilized the relations of production, and state formation, in northern Mexico.[24]

A U.S.-based group of mining speculators reached the Yuma crossing in 1854, after locating a number of rich silver veins in the mountains west of Tubac, in the Sonoran Desert. Charles Poston, a member of this group, noted the competing ferry companies at the river crossing and the "good subjection" of indigenous people in the vicinity. At the crossing, the speculators surveyed a site they christened Colorado City, which would provide the foundation for the town that became Yuma. Incorporating Colorado City, they began seeking land investments, anticipating the passage of a transcontinental railroad through the townsite.[25] Incorporation was a condition for real estate investments, which preceded settlement and a productive economy.

In May 1855, the *Mining Magazine* described the valley where "the deserted town of Tubac" was located. The journal's correspondent suggested that hundreds of settlers would move there from California, if only "they be free from the hostility of the Apaches." The mineral wealth of the country remained "undiscovered" and undeveloped, "without the aid of a party sufficiently strong to repel the hostile attacks of the Navajo and Apache." The major obstacles to accumulation on these newly acquired lands, therefore, were "the difficulty of procuring supplies, and the hostility of the Indians."[26] The stabilization of capitalist development, according to the *Mining Magazine*, required a violent colonial assault on Navajo and Apache life. The railroad, as a vehicle for commerce, settlement, and war, offered a potential solution for these requirements.

Railroad

In 1855, in his capacity as the U.S. secretary of war, Jefferson Davis submitted a report on Pacific railroad explorations. Teams of engineers reported on topography, climate, geological resources, and plant and animal life, mapping territories west of the Mississippi River. Crucially, the engineers were also directed "to obtain statistics of the Indian tribes which are found in the regions traversed." The teams rarely strayed far from the vicinity of U.S. Army outposts. The fact of military occupation imprinted the geological and geographic knowledge that was a precondition for U.S. claims of sovereignty over these lands. According to the final report, the southernmost route, on the 32nd parallel, marked "the most practical and economical route for a railroad from the Mississippi to the Pacific ocean," because of shorter distance, relatively benign climate, and easy topographical conditions for grading and laying track. The 32nd parallel route would connect San Francisco with New Orleans, benefiting the expansionist interests of the slaveholding oligarchy.[27]

The 1855 Charter of the Texas Western Railroad Company charged the completed railroad with transporting "a vast amount of cotton" from east Texas. The charter insisted on the uniqueness of Texas among the U.S. states, in that it owned and could appropriate "lands sufficient to aid in the construction of a railroad to the Pacific." Texas state-owned lands were legacies of a history of colonialism, annexation, and particular regimes of capital accumulation mixing slavery, finance, and industrial production with a distinctly Texan watermark. Railroad construction, the charter predicted, would make Texas "the wealthiest and most populous State of the Union," transferring "the command of the exchanges and commerce of the world" from London to New York.[28] Infrastructure development in Texas and along the 32nd parallel in North America, according to the railroad's boosters, would expand the production of cotton under the organization of chattel slavery, and it would thereby facilitate the ascendancy of the United States in interimperialist competition with Great Britain. Advocates imagined the railroad as a means to expand slavery westward from Texas and enforce the containment of Comanches, Kiowas, and Apaches by facilitating a major escalation in the regional presence of the U.S. Army. In 1856, the Texas Western Railroad renewed its charter and changed its name to the Southern Pacific Railroad. The Southern Pacific had received a Louisiana charter the previous year, part of a network of railroads chartered throughout the state. New Orleans city leaders had initially envisioned a rail network to solidify the city's links with Nashville, but Southern Pacific directors were unable to raise sufficient capital and failed to build track within the time allotted in their charter. As the charter lapsed and creditors forced its sale, it was auctioned off in 1858 to a Texas buyer. Louisiana's rail network would end up solidifying trade within the trans-Mississippi region, especially with Texas. Further west, the Southern Pacific Railroad would drive the development of a regional mining economy, at the confluence of cotton and copper.[29]

Mines

Heintzelman, commanding officer at Fort Yuma and ferry operator, added the presidency of the Sonora Exploring and Mining Company, with principal backing from the head of the Texas Western Railroad, to his portfolio. In its first stockholders' report, the company explained that it planned to deploy "an armed party of sufficient strength to protect itself against the Indian tribes." This group would explore the area and "recover and hold possession of old Spanish mines." By "recovering" these mines, the Company suggested, it would restore the cycles of capital accumulation that had been interrupted by "the Apache War and Mexican Revolution." The Sonora Exploring and Mining Company would reverse the legacies of indigenous resistance and Mexican independence by reversing the "withdrawal of the Presidios or garrisons then stationed there."[30] The restoration of military occupation was a precondition for the expected profits of Maj. Heintzelman and his associates.

The mining company's 1856 shareholder report wildly exaggerated the quantity and quality of mineral resources in Sonora, describing the company's landholdings along the line of the Southern Pacific Railroad as "the most favorable point for a seat of government for the proposed new Territory of Arizona, and of a branch railroad to the Gulf of Mexico."[31] The mining company attempted to entice investment by dangling future possibilities of state and corporate formation on the land it claimed to own. Because of the capital requirements for mining equipment and labor, most Mexicans were locked out of mine ownership, and most who owned claims ended up selling to U.S.-based mine operators.[32] In the relationship between the mining industry and military occupation, we can see the concentration of capital in fewer hands, and the corresponding institutional development of U.S. governance.

In 1857, Oliver Wozencraft, the southern California Indian agent, visited Heintzelman. Wozencraft advocated a southern transcontinental railroad as a tool of expansion; he also argued that the Colorado River should be diverted and apportioned to irrigate agriculture in southern California. Wozencraft believed the railroad would enable military and administrative expansion, which would in turn enable the development of large-scale industrial agriculture. The Southern Pacific Railroad could be a vehicle to adapt and expand the monocrop plantation economy of the Cotton Kingdom into southern California.[33]

In 1858, the Sonora Exploring and Mining Company reported that extracting rich silver ore from the Salero mine in the Santa Rita Mountains had stalled until machinery could be imported to pump water "by a less laborious and tedious process than the Mexican method of carrying it up on men's shoulders."[34] Transforming these mountains from Mexican to U.S. control, the mining company suggested, manifested in the means of production employed at the mine. The company presented a transition from men's shoulders to mechanical water pumps as one laced with implications for racial and colonial sovereignty. The company located its headquarters in Tubac, "an old Mexican town," noting that it had constructed buildings to conduct business and to protect its employees "in case of attack by the Indians."[35] The company's claims to control over production took place in an ongoing context of colonial occupation. The mining company mobilized prior colonial infrastructure toward the accumulation of capital, an inheritance involving a colonial transfer of capital and assets. After subsisting on supplies delivered from Fort Yuma, two hundred miles away, shipped by wagon trains under military escort, the company began obtaining cheaper and more regular supplies from Mexican towns and villages just south of the border, about fifty miles away. A filibuster led by Col. Henry Crabb, met with a blind eye from the local U.S. administrator, disrupted this trade. As a banking crisis broke out in 1857, the mining company's directors placed emergency funds at Fort Yuma, to be disbursed as necessary. Cash and food sustained the mines by way of Fort Yuma.[36]

The company announced an unambiguous investment in the rapid colonization of Sonora. "It is . . . our true interest to secure the early settlement of the country by as good a class of citizens as it is possible to induce to go there." Colonization would facilitate the development of mining, industry, and agriculture. Colonialism was a basis for the realization of the mining company's profits. Moreover, the company's directors argued, given the capital outlays necessary to open mine shafts, to invest in the necessary machinery, to organize smelting and amalgamation, and to employ and organize a large workforce, mining in Arizona would be "the peculiar province of associated capital."[37] In southern Arizona, according to the directors of the Sonora Exploring and Mining Company, stable capital accumulation would begin in monopoly form.

For Heintzelman, military administration of the U.S.-Mexico borderlands marked a business opportunity. In August, a mining engineer at the Tubac headquarters of the Sonora Exploring and Mining Company reported that the company paid Mexican workers twelve to fifteen dollars per month. It paid those working the furnace one dollar per day, for a twelve-hour day. The mining company paid "American laborers" thirty to seventy dollars per month, including board. Labor had become scarce, Heintzelman complained in his journal.[38] One September morning in 1858, he visited two German settlers living in the ruins of the Tumacacori Mission, gathering intelligence on Apache movements and sniffing out "the slag of old furnaces where the Padres smelted silver ore."[39] Later that month, in Cerro Colorado, chastened by the difficulty in finding workers, he doubted the productivity of the mine, where the work did not yet cover operational expenses. By December, the company had learned of some other promising prospects in the area, but reports of gold on the banks of the Gila River had drawn away Mexican mineworkers. A few black mineworkers remained behind, building adobes, their wives handling laundry. Some Yaquis also rode through the mines, driving wagons.[40]

Stabilizing colonial occupation was a precondition for the stabilization of capital accumulation. By the end of the 1850s, a Quechan-Mohave alliance continued to resist the imposition of U.S. colonial authority. In reaction, U.S. politicians called for the annexation of Sonora by the United States, and the army installed new posts deep in Mohave territory. The United States claimed legal jurisdiction over Arizona Territory, but practically speaking, this was not the case. In his journal entry of January 2, 1859, Heintzelman recorded his hope that people heading to prospect gold in California would instead stop in Arizona to mine copper, silver, lead, and other metals. "The country has not been thoroughly explored," he noted. Earlier in the same journal entry, he noted that a cook and his assistant had been taken captive on a branch of the Sonora River, an area he described as "overrun with Apaches. They live in the mountains and kill and steal at liberty and seldom meet with any resistance." Claims to private property in land and ore, let alone the fruits of labor, met the hard fact of ongoing indigenous control. In practical terms, Arizona continued to be a foreign country for people from the United States.[41]

By 1860, Heintzelman's mining camps in southern Arizona relied primarily on Mexican and Native workers. Samuel Colt, the Connecticut-based firearms manufacturer who made his fortune with a bulk firearms order during the U.S. war against Mexico, was the largest stockholder of the Sonora Exploring and Mining Company and was elected its president in April 1859. Advocates for the southern transcontinental route argued that it would suppress the resistance of Apaches, Navajos, and other indigenous nations in western Texas, New Mexico, and Arizona. Some imagined that spreading slavery and crushing indigenous autonomy could be accomplished through the same vehicle. Others, hoping to utilize and enflame Apache conflict with Mexicans in Sonora, supported low-grade warfare to facilitate an easy, cheap conquest of the region, "leaving to us (when the time is ripe for our possession)," in the words of Sylvester Mowry, "the territory without its population."[42]

Crisis

After the slaveholding oligarchy launched the Civil War, emigrants to California from the southern states attempted to forge concrete links with the Confederacy, opening a crisis of property and territorial jurisdiction. The leadership of Arizona's territorialization movement sympathized with the southern planter class. One prominent advocate of territorial organization in Arizona, Lansford Hastings, approached Jefferson Davis with a plan to seize Arizona. Confederate Arizona, in turn, would be a launching point for a campaign to gain control of California. Hastings would later serve as a major in the Confederate Army.[43]

In August 1861, John Baylor, commanding Confederate soldiers from Texas, proclaimed the establishment of the Confederate Territory of Arizona, including all of southern New Mexico Territory, from the Rio Grande to California. Amid sporadic fighting with Union soldiers, Confederate troops faced attacks from Apaches. In mid-July, Baylor ordered the Arizona Guards not to engage in indigenous diplomacy, reporting that "the Congress of the Confederate States has passed a law declaring the extermination of all hostile Indians." He urged that the Arizona Guards should "use all means" to persuade Apaches and other Native people to come to them, "for the purpose of making peace." Once they came in, he continued, "kill all the grown Indians and take the children prisoners and sell them to defray the expense of killing the Indians." Baylor's letter caused an uproar after it was leaked, forcing Jefferson Davis, who had been attempting to forge alliances with Indian nations in Oklahoma, to remove Baylor from his position.[44]

During the Civil War, Quechans, Cocopahs, Pimas, and Maricopas all aided the Union Army. Quechans, for example, carried sensitive communications and provided intelligence on movements across the Colorado River. Fort Yuma served as a prison for people suspected of Confederate sympathy. In October, Col. Joseph West, then the commanding officer at Fort Yuma, received orders describing the significance of Fort Yuma for the United States as "an outpost of all Southern California." Any possible "menace" from Confederate troops based in Texas or Arizona would have to pass through Yuma. West was instructed to seize all ferryboats on the Colorado River. "All the crossing of the river must be done at the one point under the guns of the fort." Anyone crossing the river in either direction would have to swear allegiance to the United States before passing.[45]

In earlier years, Heintzelman had asserted military occupation in order to establish his own control of the ferry crossing, in pursuit of personal wealth. Six months into the Civil War, Fort Yuma had become a place for the centralization of political authority through military occupation, not only to defeat slavery, but also to reassert control of the land against indigenous peoples and Mexicans. These were the military conditions, in Arizona, to defeat the treason of the planter class. Unlike the former Confederate States, these military conditions were never followed by a dictatorship of labor. Instead, military dictatorship would shape the development of industrial capitalism, and the corresponding division of the working class, in the years to come.

Upon territorialization in 1863, the Sonora Exploring and Mining Company notified its shareholders that its property "is in full and undisputed possession, and no adverse claims exist," only to contradict itself a paragraph later. The company warned of the need for territorial organization, "to insure law and order," and soldiers "in adequate numbers to put down these marauding thieving Indians." Under current conditions, the "outbreak of the present unfortunate civil war" rendered the company "barely able by great concessions, to protect and hold its property." The establishment of U.S. sovereignty through troop deployments was a precondition for functioning property rights in the area. Colonial occupation, implemented through military dictatorship, provided the foundation for capital accumulation.[46]

In Louisiana, the Southern Pacific posted increasing losses over the course of the war, shipping Confederate soldiers and war material at discounted fares or for free.[47] In 1864, Sylvester Mowry grimly warned that failure to build a railroad on the 32nd parallel would make the United States vulnerable to "the great maritime powers of Europe." Mowry anticipated transformations in global political economy. The people of the United States, he warned, would feel "the shame and the sorrow" if they lost "a territory of innumerable treasure." They would forfeit more than money. They would forfeit "the prestige of stability, progress, and invincibility."[48] Stabilizing capital accumulation, asserting private property in land, and managing associated labor in southern Arizona were all predicated on a colonial monopoly that emerged out of military occupation.

The long history of Indian slavery in the Sonoran Desert persisted in 1866, after the end of the Civil War. Apache oral histories remember the capture and imprisonment of four women by Mexican troops in the Santa Rita Mountains, then in Arizona Territory. The women, the youngest of whom was seventeen, were taken to Sonora and sold to the owner of a maguey plantation. The older women were sent to the fields, while the youngest, Idistana, was forced to do housework and to nurse the plantation owner's children. The ordeal of their captivity lasted for five years, until the women escaped together one night after religious services, walking at night and subsisting on nopales.[49]

John Lauderdale, stationed as a doctor at Fort Yuma in the autumn of 1868, noted the arrival of daily emigrant trains of "poor jaded people" passing through from Texas, heading to southern California. They came to Fort Yuma without provisions or money, "so are dependent upon government" for their needs. "I saw one today who had been in the Confederate army. He looked rather crest fallen but the poor fellow looked hungry and said he had a young family with him who were likewise begging for bread."[50] A few days later, Lauderdale saw someone drive a large herd of cattle over the river, en route to California. These emigrants from Texas, he maintained, "are refugees from negro supremacy . . . they go to a country where the negro is not considered quite so good as a white man."[51] In the years of Reconstruction, westward migration from the southern United States became a safety valve for refugees from multiracial democracy. The counterrevolution against

Reconstruction, the birth pangs of a new hegemonic bloc in the United States, would drive the colonization and settlement of territories between Texas and the Pacific Ocean after the Civil War.[52] This phase of colonialism proceeded in reaction to the revolutionary possibilities of Reconstruction, forming under the auspices of a dictatorship of industrial capital. Colonialism and racist reaction would shape the concentration of industrial capital in the following era, setting the stage for what Du Bois referred to as a "new imperialism which is subjecting the labor of yellow, brown and black peoples to the dictation of capitalism organized on a world basis," whereby the United States "was turned into a reactionary force."[53]

Resolution

In the 1870s, Du Bois wrote, the U.S. Army became "the representative of the party of political corruption," facing political opposition from "land monopoly and capitalistic reaction in the South." The attack on corruption weakened the only forces that "could support democracy in the South."[54] Toward the west, the army, with all of its corruption, was able to achieve a different kind of relationship with land monopoly and capitalist reaction. The Southern Pacific Railroad would drive through the heart of this compact.

During its wars against Apaches after the Civil War, one-third of all U.S. Army forces were posted in Arizona. Fort Yuma continued to rely on river traffic for supplies, and the army contracted out its supplies to a ferry company that charged exorbitant rates. A group of powerful settlers monopolized state offices, federal contracts for military administration, and Indian administration in Arizona. As the United States invaded the area after the Civil War, it established an economy concentrated in a few hands, in direct coordination with state and federal government. This control continued to push southward into Mexico. In the late 1860s, U.S. authorities established Puerto Isabel, a town at the mouth of the Colorado River. It served as a customhouse for goods moving between Mexico and the United States. Although located in Mexico, the town was under U.S. control, especially after 1870, when a group of people from the United States expelled the Mexican customs officer, murdering three of his assistants who resisted the expulsion. U.S. soldiers stationed at Fort Yuma patrolled the area around Puerto Isabel and, according to Mexican officials, enforced different laws for Mexicans and for people from the United States. The moving border was profitable for the United States. Such profits were a precondition for railroad construction.[55]

In March 1877, the *Weekly Arizona Miner* reported on the Southern Pacific Railroad's progress, anticipating that the railroad would reach the Colorado River by April 15. The Southern Pacific had purchased steamboats, planning to run a daily ferry between Yuma and Ehrenberg. "The attention of capitalists from every direction is being drawn to Arizona," the *Weekly Miner* declaimed. The railroad channeled attention to the "vast mineral deposits of our Territory" by promising "an easy entrance" and "quick communication" with the outside world." The *Weekly Miner* projected the immigration of fifty thousand people to Arizona within a year and the incorporation of Arizona as a U.S. state before the end of the Hayes administration. In the same issue, the paper noted that the Southern Pacific Railroad had dug a three-hundred-foot well fifteen miles east of Indian Wells, providing "plenty of flowing water," which was "of excellent quality for engine purposes." After 1879, the Southern Pacific would build a regional water infrastructure around Yuma. The railroad necessitated new ways to manage and distribute water in the desert, with the Colorado River itself a primary resource for a functioning railroad.[56] Water constituted a core element of the colonial monopoly in its newly industrial form.

In April, three pages after an article on "The Murderous Apache: The Red Devils Laying Waste the Fairest Valleys of Arizona," the *Weekly Arizona Miner* published a dispatch from the "front" of the Southern Pacific Railroad construction, about fifty miles west of Yuma. Twelve hundred Chinese men and forty white men toiled in the sun, sleeping, cooking, and eating in railroad cars moving along the line of construction. Water was a primary concern. The Southern Pacific shipped drinking water by rail from wells at least fifty miles away. Horses were given water from deep wells, sunk past the saline water at the surface.[57]

The Southern Pacific Railroad reached Yuma on May 23, 1877. Once at Yuma, the geography of military occupation put a brake on construction. The necessity of gaining permission from the U.S. Department of War to build through the military reservation at Fort Yuma delayed completion of a bridge spanning the river until September 30. During this delay, many of the Southern Pacific's Chinese workers left the line of construction. The remaining workers later raised their wages through a series of work stoppages. After the Southern Pacific bridged the Colorado River (charging tolls to the army for crossing the river by rail), it reached Tucson in 1880, quickly rendering Fort Yuma obsolete for military purposes. The strategic significance of the fort, asserting direct control over the Colorado River, was less pressing once a rail link had been established. The army closed the fort, turning it over to the Interior Department. Its buildings initially served as a boarding school for Indian children; they now house the Quechan tribal government. The completion of the southern transcontinental railroad network, and the construction of branch lines connecting to it, spurred a land boom from southern California to Texas, hastening immigration from the United States and Europe while contributing to the further consolidation of land claims under a decreasing number of hands. In the process, the corporation rose to the forefront as a core institutional form of the emergent political economy and its corresponding social arena.[58]

Historians estimate that by its completion, the Southern Pacific employed six thousand workers, of whom five thousand were Chinese. Southern Pacific directors relied principally on Chinese migrant labor, segregated into specific types of skilled and unskilled task labor and paid well below the standard wage rate for white workers at comparable tasks. The Chinese workers' camps were far from the line of construction, perhaps to minimize possible confrontations, or possible unities, with non-Chinese workers (primarily Mexicans and whites). The distance increased the dependence of Chinese work camps on merchants and labor contractors for supplies, especially water, serving the interests of maintaining a low-wage, pliable workforce. After the Southern Pacific crossed the Colorado River, copper mining in nearby Clifton boomed, resulting in a skyrocketing demand for Mexican mine workers. Copper bosses began bringing in Chinese workers, seeking to tamp down the cost of labor. In response to violent reactions from white and Mexican workers, management agreed to employ Chinese workers only in work "that neither white men nor Mexicans would accept." The counterrevolution of property in Arizona Territory was predicated on the splintering effect of racial distinctions that headed off workers' unity, shaped the division of labor in railroad and mining, and depressed wages in the area's core industries.[59]

Counterrevolution

As Du Bois noted, the years from the end of the war to the Panic of 1873 were characterized by a "wild freebooting," informing a new common sense that "free competition in industry was not going to bring proper control and development." Rather than "surrendering power either into the hands of labor or of the trustees of labor," power was instead concentrated in a "trusteeship of capital . . . which would dominate the government of the United States." After the overthrow of the old planter oligarchy, this resulted in "a new feudalism based on monopoly . . . of [the land's] wealth in raw material, in copper, iron, oil and coal, particularly monopoly of the transportation of these commodities on new public iron roads privately sequestered." This new feudalism "was destined to crush the small capitalist as ruthlessly as it controlled labor." Massive corporations "began to establish a super-government," drawing in the petty bourgeoisie by guaranteeing income on their investments while removing their control over industry, and drawing in sections of the working class through divisions between skilled and unskilled labor and the intensification of racial and ethnic divisions. Control by major corporations tied together the regions of the South and the West. This regional alliance was "fattened upon the perversion of democracy in the South," offering lower freight prices, improved markets, and rising land values to the West.[60]

The new common sense that justified this new feudalism did not involve any disturbance of what Du Bois referred to as "the American assumption" of equal economic opportunity for all. To the contrary, politics was infected with "the idea that individual wealth spelled national prosperity." The aim of "this new American industrial empire" was not national well-being but, instead, "the individual gain of the associated and corporate monarchs," through the concentrated control of finance capital, through managerial and engineering efficiency, and through access to raw materials and market demand that engulfed competitor nations. "Profit, income, uncontrolled power in My Business for My Property and for Me—this was the aim and method of the new monarchical dictatorship."[61] This new feudalism and its corresponding common sense would be the prerequisites for the rise of the United States to a position of global hegemony.[62]

The 1881 completion of the Southern Pacific Railroad facilitated the profitability of Arizona's giant copper mines. In this period, land speculators realized their investment "through railways to the Solid South."[63] The mines devoured a workforce comprised primarily of Mexicans from Sonora, as well as new immigrants from Europe's peripheries. Throughout this era, Mexicans worked the mines seasonally, their lives remaining anchored to their fields in Arizona and Sonora. Tohono O'odham and Yaqui men, generally relegated to the lowest-paid unskilled jobs, also participated in the industrial workforce. The railroads and mining corporations of Arizona increasingly turned to El Paso as a primary site to recruit Mexican workers.[64]

Arizona copper mines quickly established a position as raw material suppliers for long-distance electrical transmission cables, a core infrastructure for commercial and military communications and a vital part of the railroad's ancillary telegraph technology. Once completed, the transcontinental railroad transformed the regional geography, pulling southern Arizona away from northern Mexico, increasing its reliance on the Pacific and Atlantic seaboards as sources of capital and machinery. As a result, mining, agriculture, and cattle ranching in Arizona were increasingly concentrated under the control of large corporations, resulting in what Du Bois referred to as a "new feudal monopoly" based on the control and transportation of raw materials.[65] Corporate concentration devastated the area's historic Mexican elite, driving many into the ranks of the working class. Colonial occupation sustained the regional economic boom. Army forts and Indian reservations provided government contracts, ensuring profits for ranchers and farmers. At Yuma, five companies ferried goods up the Colorado River. Quechans, who had controlled the river crossing not even fifty years earlier, were now relegated to low-paying jobs on these ferries and in the small towns that sprouted like weeds downstream. Local elites covetously eyed Quechan lands on the river bottoms, some of the best agricultural land in the area.[66]

By this time, through a process that "began with fighting, stealing, and cheating," Stephen Jay Gould had succeeded in consolidating the southwestern rail network in his grip.[67] Predicated on colonial violence, military occupation, and the abrogation of treaties, the rail network congealed the ooze and muck of the era. Gould commanded nearly all rail traffic moving eastward from the western United States. He worked out a compromise with the Southern Pacific directors. Texas was the fulcrum. The Gould network would control the northern and eastern portions of the state while the Southern Pacific would control everything west of Fort Worth. By suspending market competition, the rail networks gained the ability to coordinate rates for shipping freight, enabling them to dictate terms for farmers and shippers as well as railroad workers. Colonial occupation provided the framework and ballast for monopoly capitalism.[68]

By late 1884, the Mexican Central Railroad, constructed along the old Camino Real, connected Chihuahua with El Paso. The Mexican Central, built and operated under U.S. financial and corporate control, facilitated a massive influx of foreign capital to northern Mexico, further concentrating landholdings in the hands a few large companies, solidifying U.S. control of the Mexican mining industry, and facilitating the shipping and exploitation of Mexican labor on both sides of the border, to the advantage of U.S. corporate profits. While industrial mining transformed the circulation of workers, colonial occupation continued to constrict the movements of indigenous people on their lands. In 1885, the U.S. Army exiled a group of Apache men to Florida by train, ostensibly as prisoners of war. The group included men who had worked for the U.S. Army as scouts. Two of these men, Gray Lizard and Massai, successfully planned their escape after overhearing plans for their execution upon their arrival in Florida. They jumped from the train, made their way on foot, and arrived home two years later.[69]

Across the South, a process of industrialization was taking place, with the manufacture of pig iron, cotton and textiles, and lumber and the rebuilding of railroads destroyed during the war.[70] In Texas, the construction of an industrial infrastructure enabling the modernization of agriculture relied on leased convict labor. Black, Mexican, and white convicts were leased to farms and to railroad companies. Farm and railroad management systematically worked convicts to death, calculating the costs of buying new leases against the costs of maintaining individual laborers over an extended time. In 1885 and 1886, the Texas Knights of Labor organized around a dual antipathy to convict laborers and Chinese workers, associating both groups with scab labor. By accepting these divisions, the Texans failed to follow the lead of the Louisiana Knights of Labor, which had begun organizing thousands of black agricultural workers alongside railroad workers in 1883. By 1887, the Louisiana Knights of Labor launched a public campaign demanding higher and regular wages, paid in currency rather than scrip. In reaction, planters organized vigilante "defense committees," terrorizing camps of evicted strikers and targeting black workers suspected of strike affiliations. At the behest of planters, white paramilitaries executed somewhere between thirty-five and three hundred black workers that November. The bloodshed, rembered as the Thibodaux Massacre, broke organized working-class resistance to Louisiana sugar planters for at least a generation. Terrorism provided a bedrock for bourgeois hegemony in Gilded Age Louisiana.[71]

This period saw the consolidation of industrial production and finance capital in the hands of "a few strong purposeful kings with vast power of finance and technique in their hands," who promised law and order and steady income on investments. Du Bois described it as "a new Empire of

Industry" that "was offering to displace capitalistic anarchy and form a dictatorship of capital to guide and repress universal suffrage." In this process, the working class was divided, with black workers placed "not in but beneath the white American labor movement." In time, "the better-paid skilled and intelligent American labor," in coordination with "capitalist guild-masters," formed "closed guilds," which "fought to share profit from labor and not to eliminate profit."[72]

In 1903, the strike wave along the southern transcontinental railroad route reached Arizona, where it took the form of a major strike in the mines and mills of the copper and gold industries. Following the passage of an eight-hour law in the Arizona Territorial legislature, the Phelps Dodge controlling interests in the mines at Morenci and Metcalf agreed to follow the letter of the law, but only by imposing a wage reduction. Since Anglo and Irish miners in the region had already effectively achieved ten hours' pay for eight hours' work, the wage reduction applied primarily to Mexican workers, mostly immigrants, relegated to less desirable and lower-paid work. The Clifton-Morenci strike began on June 1. The entire community, including large numbers of women and children, joined adult men, mostly Mexicans, with a smaller contingent of Italians, in crowds estimated to be between two and three thousand. The press, identifying fifteen strike leaders, warned of "outside agitators," but Mexican and Italian mutual aid societies had built up to the strike with painstaking organization. Their demands included union recognition and wage parity with Anglo and Irish miners. On June 6, the governor sent the Arizona Rangers, and on June 11, President Theodore Roosevelt deployed U.S. cavalry to help break the strike. In all, a force of eight hundred police, Arizona Rangers, National Guard, and U.S. cavalry enforced a return to work. Even under this pressure, the strikers held out for another three weeks. Afterwards, ten men were arrested and sentenced to the Yuma Territorial Prison; several of them died in the prison. One, Weneslado H. Laustannau, an immigrant from Mexico, died of "heat prostration" after repeated bouts of solitary confinement in dark, sweltering cells that sheltered rattlesnakes. The prison was also a site of radicalization. The Mexican revolutionary Ricardo Flores Magón, a major leader of the Partido Liberal Mexicano (PLM), was imprisoned there a few years later. Abrán Salcido, who served a two-year sentence at Yuma, emerged from the prison as a dedicated revolutionary and PLM member.[73]

Fields

This essay has tracked the interrelationship between the Colorado River and the Southern Pacific Railroad. More than providing a source of water to power steam locomotives or a gradient for laying track on relatively flat ground, the river shaped the path of the railroad and its usefulness for late nineteenth-century U.S. capitalism. The river's water enabled the mining and agricultural economies that developed along the railroad's tracks. The development and consolidation of railroad monopolies also enabled the expansion of finance capital, through what Du Bois referred to as "the new method of stock-watering," whereby "actual invested capital was doubled and trebled in face value by issuing stock, and the public was compelled to pay fabulous interest on fictitious investments." By enhancing the capitalization of land, the railroad intensified the politics of water.[74]

Since the 1880s, canal companies had applied for rights-of-way through Quechan land. Diverted water resulted in new landscapes, providing the basis for industrial agriculture in California. In the 1890s, former engineers of the Southern Pacific worked with the company to build an irrigation system in the Mojave River valley, culminating in the transformation of the Salton Sink into the Imperial Valley. In Arizona, irrigation projects led to the formation of an enormous industrial agriculture complex in the Salt River valley, dependent on a seasonal tide of tens of thousands of Mexican workers. Industrial agriculture and railroads continued to seek sources of cheap labor, renewing colonial labor structures predicated on the violent control of land. Amid a policy of widespread, targeted persecution intended to cleanse Sonora of Yaquis, successive generations of Yaqui men worked on the Southern Pacific Railroad, establishing their expertise in skilled steelwork. By 1900, Mexican workers provided the major pool of unskilled labor on the Southern Pacific and other railroads in the region.[75]

The maintenance of the Southern Pacific, both as a physical infrastructure and as a profitable corporation, steered canalization and large-scale irrigation along the Colorado River, remaking the so-called American Nile into an industrial river. In 1904, Congress passed a law declaring all irrigable parts of the Quechan reserve to be public-domain lands, violating an 1893 agreement with Quechans. In 1909, a number of Quechan men worked on building a dam several miles north of Yuma. Once completed, the dam prevented the annual floods that had deposited rich river silt on

Quechan farmlands, hacking at the roots of Quechan agriculture. Allotment of Quechan lands began in 1912. Land transactions, beginning in 1910, had already sold prime Quechan farmland to Anglos. The remaining land, isolated in the most barren parts of the reservation, all but worthless for farming, was allotted to individual Quechans. Sold at low rates without competitive bidding, prime farmland on the reservation would balloon in value after the construction of irrigation. Having been legally dispossessed of title to their lands, Quechans watched profits line outsiders' pockets. When the United States initiated the construction of irrigation works, Quechans drew wages for irrigation construction, but only for three years. Indian Bureau officials expected Quechan allottees to dig and maintain their own irrigation ditches. In 1914, the Indian Agent at Fort Yuma began leasing Quechan allotments to Anglo farmers, charging Quechans with the operation and maintenance costs for irrigation.[76]

Where the river meets the land, capital found fertile ground to develop mining, agriculture, and railroads along industrial lines. By the 1930s, such acquisitive fecundity would contribute to the calcification of yet another infrastructure: the border, a mechanism to resolve the preceding division between agrarian and industrial capitalists.[77] The Imperial Valley saw a wave of strikes in 1930 among Mexican and Filipino vegetable and fruit pickers, as well as white packers. Workers lost their demands for higher wages, better housing, and a grievance procedure, but their strike organization helped drive the formation of the Trade Union Unity League, an industrial union bringing workers from different racial backgrounds into a single organization. Growers reacted through vigilante violence against workers and their representatives, developing Associated Farmers, a trade organization that agreed to coordinate labor during strikes and to actively assist police activity during strikes. The corresponding rise of what Carey McWilliams referred to as "farm fascism" in the Imperial Valley centered on growers' assertion of a "right to harvest."[78] Between 1931 and 1934, California deported tens of thousands of Mexicans, from as far north as Los Angeles County. The Southern Pacific earned $14.70 for each passenger taken from Los Angeles to the border. A decade later, the Southern Pacific and several other southern railroad systems posted bonds to recruit men from as far south as Mexico City to work under the bracero program.[79]

During World War II, the Southern Pacific paid $48 million in wages to Mexican men working under the bracero program.[80] The border facilitated the capitalization of indigenous lands and waters, and it facilitated the circulation of labor, including large numbers of indigenous people, such as Tohono O'odhams, whose nation was cleaved in half by the border.[81] In the counterrevolution of property along the 32nd parallel, we can see the concentration of capital in fewer hands across key economic sectors. We see a shifting history of class rule, predicated on intense colonial and racial violence—violence that is foundational to our own time.

"Property involves theft by the Rich from the Poor," wrote Du Bois. "Labor, black labor," he continued, "must be either enfranchised or enslaved." The emancipation of black workers from slavery, he insisted, was meaningless before an ongoing land monopoly and a "merely nominal" wage contract. "Force, therefore, and outside force, had to be applied or otherwise slavery would have persisted in a but slightly modified form." This force, necessary to fulfill the promise of emancipation, was the dictatorship of labor, which established "democratic control over social development, education and public improvements." The counterrevolution of property was a reaction to the dictatorship of labor. "The overthrow of Reconstruction," Du Bois insisted, "was in essence a revolution inspired by property, and not a race war."[82]

The counterrevolution of property was not driven by race and culture. "It was property and privilege, shrieking to its kind, and privilege and property heard and recognized the voice of its own."[83] Privilege and property reacted against the theory that the wealth and income of the "wealthy ruling class . . . is the product of the work and striving of the great millions."[84] Reaction shut the door on the promise of emancipation. "Abolition-democracy," Du Bois noted, was itself "largely based on property, believed in capital and formed in effect a powerful petty bourgeoisie," believing in a "general dictatorship of property." The leaders of Northern abolition, living on proceeds from investments, would resist the confiscation and redistribution of property, even on a democratic basis. "While they seized stolen property in human bodies," Du Bois continued, "they never could bring themselves to countenance the redistribution of property in land and tools, which rested in fact on no less defensible basis." The refusal to redistribute land and technology fatally limited emancipation. The failure to redistribute income and transform property relations, Du Bois argued, was "a disaster to democratic government in the United States." Du Bois insisted that a new dictatorship of labor would be necessary to fulfill the revolutionary promise of emancipation. He anticipated that, before the end of the twentieth century, "the deliberate distribution of property and income by the state on an equitable and logical basis will be looked upon as the state's prime function."[85]

The failure to redistribute land and technology, to fulfill the promise of emancipation, was a historical antecedent of imperialism, resulting in world war. Du Bois charged that it was in "the very echo of that philanthropy which had abolished the slave trade" that a "new industrial slavery of black and brown and yellow workers in Africa and Asia" would arise.[86] "The world wept and is still weeping and blind with tears and blood," wrote Du Bois, of the counterrevolution of property. This process, he continued, led to the rise of "a new capitalism and a new enslaved of labor," a worldwide system of trade and production that enabled the dictatorship of capital to expand its power from Europe and North America, to Asia and Africa, driving a fierce competition culminating in the outbreak of World War I. From his vantage in the early 1930s, Du Bois charted "grotesque Profits and Poverty, Plenty and Starvation, Empire and Democracy, staring at each other across World Depression." The task of rebuilding society, he insisted, "whether it comes now or a century later," would necessitate a return to the core principles of Reconstruction: "Land, Light and Leading for slaves black, brown, yellow and white, under a dictatorship of the proletariat."[87]

NOTES

I thank Jordan T. Camp and Destin Jenkins for their critical engagement with earlier drafts of this essay.

1. W. E. B. Du Bois, *Black Reconstruction* (New York: Free Press, [1935], 1992), 580.
2. Du Bois, *Black Reconstruction*, 581.
3. Du Bois, *Black Reconstruction*, 597.
4. Andrew Johnson, *Prest. Johnson's Amnesty Proclamation . . . Done at the City of Washington, the Twenty-Ninth Day of May, in the Year of Our Lord One Thousand Eight Hundred and Sixty-Five . . .* Washington, 1865. https://www.loc.gov./item/rbpe.23502500/.
5. Du Bois, *Black Reconstruction*, 601–3.
6. Du Bois, *Black Reconstruction*, 581.
7. Manuel Barrera, *Race and Class in the Southwest: A Theory of Racial Inequality* (Notre Dame, Ind.: University of Notre Dame Press, 1979); Cedric Robinson, *Forgeries of Memory and Meaning: Blacks and the Regimes of Race in American Theater and Film Before World War II* (Chapel Hill: University of North Carolina Press, 2007), xii–xiii.
8. Barrera, *Race and Class in the Southwest*, 35–37; Rodolfo F. Acuña, *Occupied America: the Chicano's Struggle Towards Liberation*, (San Francisco: Canfield Press, 1972), 1. This essay might be read in conversation with Elliot West's arguments about a "Greater Reconstruction," which draws out continuities between

"far western expansion and the Civil War." West's analysis focuses more on the Northern Rockies and western edge of the Great Lakes, whereas this essay focuses on the Colorado River basin and lands to its south. One distinction between our approaches is that whereas West focuses on questions of national consolidation and citizenship, my emphasis is on imperialism and class power. See Elliot West, *The Last Indian War: The Nez Perce Story* (New York: Oxford University Press, 2009).

9. Michal Kalecki, "The Fascism of Our Times," in *The Last Phase in the Transformation of Capitalism* (New York: Monthly Review Press, 1972).

10. Du Bois, *Black Reconstruction*, 591–92, 620–21.

11. Frank Love, *Hell's Outpost: A History of Fort Yuma* (Yuma, Ariz.: Yuma Crossing, 1992), 5; Jack D. Forbes, *Warriors of the Colorado: The Yumas of the Quechan Nation and Their Neighbors* (Norman: University of Oklahoma Press, 1965), 201–20, 266–70, 295; Joel R. Hyer, *"We Are Not Savages": Native Americans in Southern California and the Pala Reservation, 1840–1920* (East Lansing, Michigan State University Press, 2001), 30–31; Barrera, *Race and Class in the Southwest*, 8; Robert A. Sauder, *The Lost Frontier: Water Diversion in the Growth and Destruction of Owens Valley Agriculture* (Tucson: University of Arizona Press, 1994), 29, 48–53. Walter Johnson, *The Broken Heart of America: St. Louis and the Violent History of the United States* (New York: Basic Books, 2020), 26–36.

12. C. Gilbert Storms, *Reconnaissance in Sonora: Charles D. Poston's 1854 Exploration of Mexico and the Gadsden Purchase* (Tucson: University of Arizona Press, 2015), 22–23; Acuña, *Occupied America*, 20.

13. Forbes, *Warriors of the Colorado*, 297–319; Hyer, *"We Are Not Savages"*, 57–58.

14. Love, *Hell's Outpost*, 6–8; Jerry D. Thompson, "'Near 106 Yesterday. It Has Been a Cool Summer': Samuel P. Heintzelman Views Yuma Crossing and Arizona Territory," *Journal of Arizona History* 41, no. 3 (Autumn 2000): 241–66 (242); Arthur Woodward, *Feud on the Colorado* (Los Angeles: Westernlore Press, 1955), 26–30; Douglas D. Martin, *Yuma Crossing* (Albuquerque: University of New Mexico Press, 1954), 141–52; Arthur Woodward, ed., *Journal of Lieutenant Thomas W. Sweeny, 1849–1853* (Los Angeles: Westernlore Press, 1955).

15. Love, *Hell's Outpost*, 1; Mowry letter to Ned Bicknell, October 29, 1855, in New York Westerners *Brand Book*, Vol. 15, #2.

16. Love, *Hell's Outpost*, 2.

17. Hyer, *"We Are Not Savages"*, 56–57; Samuel P. Heintzelman and E. D. Townsend, "Official Report of Samuel P. Heintzelman, 1853," *Journal of California and Great Basin Anthropology* 28, no. 1 (2008): 89–102. On Quechan life near the fort, and their wage labor, see Robert Bee, *Crosscurrents Along the Colorado: The Impact of Government Policy on the Quechan Indians* (Tucson: University of Arizona Press, 1981), 18–19; Love, *Hell's Outpost*, 17.

18. Diane M. T. North, *Samuel Peter Heintzelman and the Sonora Exploring and Mining Company* (Tucson: University of Arizona Press, 1979), 6.

19. Love, *Hell's Outpost*, 9–12; Woodward, *Feud on the Colorado*, 25, 40–44, 77; Janet L. Hargett, "Pioneering at the Yuma Crossing: The Business Career of L. J. F. Jaeger, 1850–1887," *Arizona and the West* 25, no. 4 (Winter 1984): 329–54; Manu

Vimalassery, "The Wealth of the Natives: Towards a Critique of Settler Colonial Political Economy," *Settler Colonial Studies* 3, no. 3 (2013): 311–26.

20. Love, *Hell's Outpost*, 17–21. Thompson, " 'Near 106 Yesterday,' " 243, 247. Hyer, *"We Are Not Savages,"* 61–67.

21. Thompson, " 'Near 106 Yesterday,' " 242–43, 251–53; Richard E. Lingenfelter, *Steamboats on the Colorado River, 1852–1916* (Tucson: University of Arizona Press, 1978), 11–15; Love, *Hell's Outpost*, 22–26; Roxanne Dunbar-Ortiz, *An Indigenous Peoples' History of the United States* (Boston: Beacon, 2014).

22. North, *Samuel Peter Heintzelman*, 6; U.S. Congress, House, Message from the President . . ., Transmission Report in Regard to Indian Affairs on the Pacific, H. Exec. Doc. #76, 34th Cong., 3rd sess., 1854, 34–58.

23. Thompson, " 'Near 106 Yesterday,' " 256; "Message from the President . . .," 112–14.

24. Samuel Peter Heintzelman, *Fifty Miles and a Fight: Major Samuel Heintzelman's Journal of Texas and the Cortina War* (Austin: Texas State Historical Association, 1997), 12; Martin, *Yuma Crossing*, 178–79; B. Sacks, *Be It Enacted: The Creation of Arizona Territory* (Phoenix: Arizona Historical Foundation, 1964), 9; Thompson, " 'Near 106 Yesterday,' " 257; Storms, *Reconnaissance in Sonora*, 85–94; Acuña, *Occupied America*, 73–74; Love, *Hell's Outpost*, 35–39; James Woodall Taylor, "Geographic Bases of the Gadsden Purchase," *Journal of Geography* 57 (1958): 402–10 (406–7); Rodolfo F. Acuña, *Corridors of Migration: The Odyssey of Mexican Laborers, 1600–1933* (Tucson: University of Arizona Press, 2007), 74–75; Miguel Tinker Salas, *In the Shadow of the Eagles: Sonora and the Transformation of the Border During the Porfiriato* (Berkeley: University of California Press, 1997), 52–53. Over time, Acuña writes, this "internal chaos" in Sonora, spurred by the development of mining and railroads in Arizona, would impel Mexican migration from Sonora into Arizona, New Mexico, and California, which would provide a core labor force for the further development of mining, railroads, and agricultural industries. Acuña, *Occupied America*, 78.

25. Heintzelman, *Fifty Miles and a Fight*, 12. See also Heintzelman Journal, July 11, 1854; Martin, *Yuma Crossing*, 178–79; Sacks, *Be It Enacted*, 9; Thompson, " 'Near 106 Yesterday,'" 257; Storms, *Reconnaissance in Sonora*, 85–94. In the summer of 1871, after the defeat of the Paris Commune, Poston would submit a proposal to the Thiers government for shipping Communist prisoners, including craftsmen and mechanics, to the mouth of the Colorado River. Alexander Saxton, *The Rise and Fall of the White Republic: Class Politics and Mass Culture in Nineteenth-Century America* (New York: Verso, 1990), 218.

26. *Mining Magazine* 4, no. 5/6 (May–June 1855), 392.

27. *Report of the Secretary of War on the Several Pacific Railroad Explorations* (Washington, D.C.: Nicholson, 1855), 9, 15, 37–38. See Megan Kate Nelson, "Death in the Distance: Confederate Manifest Destiny and the Campaign for New Mexico, 1861–1862," in *Civil War Wests: Testing the Limits of the United States*, ed. Adam Arenson and Andrew R. Graybill (Oakland: University of California Press, 2015), 35–36. Matthew Karp suggests that "a broad and powerful combination of southern elites, from Andrew Jackson and John Tyler to Jefferson Davis and Alexander Stephens, insisted on the centrality of slavery in American international relations."

These elites imprinted international relations with Mexico, as well as with Indian nations. Matthew Karp, This Vast Southern Empire: Slaveholders at the Helm of American Foreign Policy (Cambridge, Mass.: Harvard University Press, 2016), 6–7.

28. *Charter of the Texas Western Railroad Company and Extracts from Report of Col. A. B. Gray and Secretary of War on the Survey of Route: From Eastern Borders of Texas to California* (Cincinnati: Porter, Thrall & Chapman, 1855), 4, 6, 10, 24. Cotton would become a major crop in the Salt River Valley fields after World War I. The fields were worked primarily by Mexicans, who moved between them and the copper mines. The farms were major industrial concerns fueled by a demand for cotton to provide threading for tire manufacturing. Acuña, 217–19.

29. Storms, *Reconnaissance in Sonora*, 100; Alvin M. Josephy, Jr., *The Civil War in the American West* (New York: Knopf, 1991), 10–13; Merl E. Reed, *New Orleans and the Railroads: The Struggle for Commercial Empire, 1830–1860* (Baton Rouge: Louisiana State University Press, 1966), 78–79.

30. *Report of the Sonora Exploring and Mining Co. Made to the Stockholders*, December 1856 (Cincinnati: Railroad Record Print, 1856), 5.

31. North, *Samuel Peter Heintzelman*, 14–15, 20–27.

32. Salas, *In the Shadow of the Eagles*, 88.

33. Heintzelman, *Fifty Miles and a Fight*, 227. See also William B. Secrest, "Wozencraft," *Real West* 24, no. 180, 181 (October, December 1981), 6–13, 56; 36–40, 54; Heintzelman, *Samuel Peter Heintzelman papers*. December 31, 1851; January 8, 1852; April 15, 1857; April 6, 1869. For Wozencraft's role in the Treaty of Temecula, see Hyer, *"We Are Not Savages"*, 67–71.

34. *Second Annual Report of the Sonora Exploring & Mining Co.*, March 29, 1858 (Cincinnati: Railroad Record Print, 1858), 4.

35. *Second Annual Report of the Sonora Exploring & Mining Co.*, 5. Acuña, *Occupied America*, 77.

36. *Second Annual Report of the Sonora Exploring & Mining Co.*, 6–7, 9; Salas, *In the Shadow of the Eagles*, 94. Acuña, 75.

37. *Second Annual Report of the Sonora Exploring & Mining Co.*, 12–13.

38. North, *Samuel Peter Heintzelman*, 40–41; Sylvester Mowry, *Arizona and Sonora: The Geography, History, and Resources of the Silver Region of North America* (New York: Harper, 1864), 166; Heintzelman Journal, Tubac G. P., August 24, 1858; North, *Samuel Peter Heintzelman*, 61.

39. North, *Samuel Peter Heintzelman*, 80.

40. Heintzelman Journal, Cerro Colorado, November 1, 1858; December 1, 1858; December 22, 1858; December 23, 1858. North, *Samuel Peter Heintzelman*, 115, 137, 151–52.

41. Love, *Hell's Outpost*, 44–45; Heintzelman Journal, Cerro Colorado, January 2, 1859; North, *Samuel Peter Heintzelman*, 160–61.

42. Samuel Truett, "The Ghosts of Frontiers Past: Making and Unmaking Space in the Borderlands," *Journal of the Southwest* 46, no. 2 (Summer 2004): 321, 326; "Cost of Indian Wars," *Miner*, November 30, 1877; Salas, *In the Shadow of the Eagles*, 64; Mowry, *Arizona and Sonora*, 35.

43. Sacks, *Be It Enacted*, 32–33, 40, 42, 57–63.

44. As cited in Alvin M. Josephy, Jr., *The Civil War in the American West*, (New York: Knopf, 1991), 50–51; Andrew E. Masich, *Civil War in the Southwest Borderlands, 1861–1867* (Norman: University of Oklahoma Press, 2017), 50–53.

45. Arthur A. Wright, *The Civil War in the Southwest* (Denver: Big Mountain Press, 1964), 32, 37–38; Love, *Hell's Outpost*, 47; Ray Colton, *The Civil War in the Western Territories* (Norman: University of Oklahoma Press, 1959).

46. Heintzelman, *Fifty Miles and a Fight*, 73, n. 32, n. 33; North, *Samuel Peter Heintzelman*, 15–20, 32, 172–85; Sacks, *Be It Enacted*, 61; Charles D. Poston, *Building a State in Apache Land: The Story of Arizona's Founding Told by Arizona's Founder* (Tempe, Ariz.: Aztec Press, 1963), 102–5; Sonora Exploring and Mining Company, *Heintzelman Mine*, Arizona, New York, 1863, 5–6.

47. Lawrence E. Estaville, Jr., *Confederate Neckties: Louisiana Railroads in the Civil War* (Ruston: Louisiana Tech University, 1989), 78.

48. Mowry, *Arizona and Sonora*, 231.

49. Sherry Robinson, *Apache Voices: Their Stories of Survival as Told to Eve Ball* (Albuquerque: University of New Mexico Press, 2000), 27–28.

50. Robert M. Utley, ed., *Army Doctor on the Western Frontier: Journals and Letters of John Vance Lauderdale, 1864–1890* (Albuquerque: University of New Mexico Press, 2014), 36–37.

51. Utley, *Army Doctor on the Western Frontier*, 37.

52. On hegemonic blocs, see Clyde Woods, *Development Drowned and Reborn: The Blues and Bourbon Restoration in Post-Katrina New Orleans*, ed. Jordan T. Camp and Laura Pulido (Athens: University of Georgia Press, 2017), 2, 292–93.

53. Du Bois, *Black Reconstruction*, 631.

54. Du Bois, *Black Reconstruction*, 624.

55. Love, *Hell's Outpost*, 56–59; Salas, *In the Shadow of the Eagles*, 114–15.

56. "The Railroad and Immigration," "Transfer of the Colorado Steam Navigation Company's Steamers to the Southern Pacific Railroad Company," and "Water in the Desert," *Weekly Arizona Miner*, March 23, 1877; Orsi, 176–78.

57. "Southern Pacific Railroad and the Front," *Weekly Arizona Miner*, April 13, 1877.

58. See *Letters from Mark Hopkins, Leland Stanford, Charles Crocker, Charles F. Crocker and David D. Colton, to Collis P. Huntington, from August 27th, 1869, to December 30th, 1879* (New York: John C. Rankin, 1891): Charles Crocker to Collis Huntington, September 3, 27, 1877, October 1, 2, 5, 8, 10, 1877, November 8, 13, 20, 23, 1878; Love, *Hell's Outpost*, 56–69; Barrera, *Race and Class in the Southwest*, 21, 24.

59. Barbara L. Voss, "The Historical Experience of Labor: Archaeological Contributions to Interdisciplinary Research on Chinese Railroad Workers," *Historical Archaeology* 49, no. 1 (2015): 4–24 (4, 12, 13); Alton King Briggs, "The Archaeology of 1882 Labor Camps Along the Southern Pacific Railroad," PhD. diss., University of Texas at Austin, 1974), 31, 197–204. See Andrew Griego, ed., "Rebuilding the California Southern Railroad: The Personal Account of a Chinese Labor Contractor, 1884" *San Diego Historical Society Quarterly* 25, no. 4 (Fall 1979). In November 1878, Charles Crocker, head of Southern Pacific construction, complained that a labor

contracting firm, Sisson, Wallace & Co., was controlling the availability of Chinese workers. *Letters from Mark Hopkins . . .*: Charles Crocker to Collis Huntington, November 13, 1878. Lyle M. Stone and Scott L. Fedick, "The Archaeology of Two Historic Homestead and Railroad-Related Sites On the Southern Pacific Main Line Near Mobile, Maricopa County, AZ. Report to Dibble and Associates, Phoenix, AZ, From Archaeological Resources Services, Inc, Tempe, AZ, 1990, 144–45; Acuña, *Corridors of Migration*, 56–57.

60. Du Bois, *Black Reconstruction*, 583–84, 596.

61. Du Bois, *Black Reconstruction*, 55–586.

62. Aijaz Ahmad, "Fascism and National Culture: Reading Gramsci in the Days of Hindutva." *Social Scientist* 21, no. 3/4 (1993): 32–68, 38–39; Alan Shandro, *Lenin and the Logic of Hegemony : Political Practice and Theory in the Class Struggle.* (Leiden: Brill), 3–10.

63. Du Bois, *Black Reconstruction*, 634.

64. Eric V. Meeks, *Border Citizens: The Making of Indians, Mexicans, and Anglos in Arizona* (Austin: University of Texas Press, 2007), 26–30; Lawrence A. Cardoso, *Mexican Emigration to the United States, 1897–1931* (Tucson: University of Arizona Press, 1980), 13–14; Eric Meeks, *Border Citizens: The Making of Indians, Mexicans, and Anglos in Arizona* (Austin: University of Texas Press, 2007), 74; Acuña, *Occupied America*, 85.

65. Du Bois, *Black Reconstruction*, 583–84.

66. On the politics of race, class, and copper in ensuing decades, see Philip J. Mellinger, *Race and Labor in Western Copper: The Fight for Equality, 1896–1918* (Tucson: University of Arizona Press, 1995); Neil Foley, *Mexicans in the Making of America* (Cambridge, Mass.: Harvard University Press, 2014), 41–43; Acuña, *Occupied America*, 81. During this time, the Southern Pacific Railroad began to search for coal supplies in northern Mexico and across the U.S. southwest. Roberto R. Calderón, *Mexican Coal Mining Labor in Texas and Coahuila, 1880–1930* (College Station: Texas A&M University Press, 2000), 33; Acuña, *Corridors of Migration*, 54, 58, 90, 94; Bee, *Crosscurrents Along the Colorado*, 19.

67. Du Bois, *Black Reconstruction*, 582–83.

68. Theresa A. Case, *The Great Southwest Labor Strike and Free Labor*, (College Station: Texas A&M University Press, 2010), 30–31.

69. Acuña, *Occupied America*, 39–40, 55–57, 81; Sherry Robinson, *Apache Voices: Their Stories of Survival as Told to Eve Ball*, (Albuquerque: University of New Mexico Press, 2000), 87–92.

70. Du Bois, *Black Reconstruction*, 589.

71. Ethan Blue, "A Parody on the Law: Organized Labor, the Convict Lease, and Immigration in the Making of the Texas State Capitol," *Journal of Social History* 43, no. 4 (Summer 2010): 1023, 1024, 1026; Theresa Case, "The Radical Potential of the Knights' Biracialism: The 1885–1886 Gould System Strikes and Their Aftermaths," *Labor: Studies in Working-Class Histories of the Americas* 4, no. 4 (2007): 83–107, esp. 96–99; Rick Halpern, "Solving the 'Labour Problem': Race, Work, and the State in the Sugar Industries of Louisiana and Natal, 1870–1910,

Journal of Southern African Studies 30, no. 1 (March 2004): 23. A later phase of African American railroad workers' organization in Texas and Louisiana proceeded in the World War I era. See Joseph Kelly, "Showing Agency on the Margins: African American Railway Workers in the South and Their Unions, 1917–1930," *Labour/Le Travail* 71 (Spring 2013): 123–48.

72. Du Bois, *Black Reconstruction*, 596–97.
73. Philip J. Mellinger, *Race and Labor in Western Copper* (Tucson: University of Arizona Press, 1995), chap. 2; Acuña, *Corridors of Migration*, 116–17; Acuña, *Occupied America*, 98–99. On U.S. prisons as sites where Mexican revolutionary consciousness was produced, see Christina Heatherton, *Making Internationalism: The Color Line, the Class Struggle, and the Mexican Revolution* (Berkeley: University of California Press, forthcoming).
74. Du Bois, *Black Reconstruction*, 582.
75. Sauder, *The Lost Frontier*, 40, 46, 69–70, 173; Richard J. Orsi, *Sunset Limited: The Southern Pacific Railroad and the Development of the American West, 1850–1930*, (Berkeley: University of California Press, 2005), 189, 226–28; Acuña, *Corridors of Migration*, 101; Refugio Savala, *Autobiography of a Yaqui Poet* (Tucson: University of Arizona Press, 1980), 5–7, 33, 51, 54; Barrera, *Race and Class in the Southwest*, 45.
76. Water diversions also influenced the consolidation of Quechan villages. Bee, *Crosscurrents Along the Colorado*, 65–72; Sauder, *The Lost Frontier*, 55, chap. 5. On the interplay of canalization and allotment, see Sauder, *The Lost Frontier*, 63.
77. Du Bois, *Black Reconstruction*, 614.
78. Carey McWilliams, *Factories in the Field: The Story of Migratory Farm Labor in California* (Berkeley: University of California Press, 2000), 213, 231–32. The Imperial Valley sustained specific connections with Arizona into the late 1930s. As McWilliams noted, Arizona was a primary source of migrant workers for Imperial Valley fields during the Dust Bowl era. McWilliams, *Factories in the Field*, 308.
79. Barbara A. Driscoll, *The Tracks North: The Railroad Bracero Program of World War II* (Austin: University of Texas Press, 1999), 47, 99–100, 112, 141; Don Mitchell, *They Saved the Crops: Labor, Landscape, and the Struggle Over Industrial Farming in Bracero-Era California* (Athens: University of Georgia Press, 2012), chap. 8.
80. Foley, *Mexicans in the Making of America*, 145; Erasmo Gamboa, *Bracero Railroaders: The Forgotten World War II Story of Mexican Workers in the U.S. West* (Seattle: University of Seattle Press, 2016), 191–95.
81. Geraldo L. Cadava, "Borderlands of Modernity and Abandonment: The Lines Within Ambos Nogales and the Tohono O'odham Nation," *Journal of American History* 98, no. 2 (September 2011): 362–83 (377).
82. Du Bois, *Black Reconstruction*, 618–22.
83. Du Bois, *Black Reconstruction*, 630.
84. Du Bois, *Black Reconstruction*, 604.
85. Du Bois, *Black Reconstruction*, 591.
86. Du Bois, *Black Reconstruction*, 632.
87. Du Bois, *Black Reconstruction*, 634–35.

CHAPTER 6

RACIAL CAPITALISM AND BLACK PHILOSOPHIES OF HISTORY

JUSTIN LEROY

Ruins of Emancipation

Four months after the U.S. Senate passed the Thirteenth Amendment in 1864, setting in motion the abolition of slavery in the United States, a remarkable editorial appeared in one of the nation's leading antislavery newspapers. It read, "There is neither in the political, nor religious, nor philanthropic worlds of the America people, any agency at work that can encompass the entire abolishment of slavery. . . . In slave society, labor lies prostrate, and capital dictates its own terms, which are perpetual subjugation; in other words, perpetual slavery."[1] The author's use of the words "capital" and "labor" might suggest that he was a utopian socialist or a German Marxist émigré—two groups that took great interest in American slavery. The author was in fact James McCune Smith, a black physician, writer, and social reformer who traveled in New York's elite abolitionist circles—an unlikely candidate, in other words, to rail against perpetual subjugation under capital. Yet at the height of the Civil War, by this time widely acknowledged as a battle over slavery, Smith confidently declared, "Far from this war diminishing the wish or power of capital to own labor, it will increase both. Colossal monopolies are parceling out even the free States for their ownership. The slave in the South will have namesakes in fact, if not in title, North of Mason and Dixon's line." By likening the power of capitalism to the Slave Power itself, Smith warned of the expansion of slavery by another name at the very moment chattel slavery was set to disappear.

Four million enslaved souls were freed in the aftermath of the Civil War; it was a momentous achievement, despite Smith's reservations. Freedpeople took control over their own destinies in ways that would have been unimaginable just a few years earlier. And yet, by the turn of the century, Frederick Douglass, Smith's close friend and the nation's preeminent black orator, was also wary about the terms of emancipation: "The negro is physically, in certain localities, in a worse condition to-day than in the time of slavery."[2] Douglass made these remarks as part of his last major public address, "The Lessons of the Hour," which he delivered in 1894 at the Metropolitan AME Church in Washington, D.C. Born enslaved in Maryland, Douglass was an abolitionist, reformer, writer, and occasional statesman. His spectacular language and fiery rhetoric made him a transatlantic celebrity, and he was among the most famous Americans of the age. In the 1840s, Douglass, like most other black abolitionists, considered slavery to be categorically different from other forms of economic and social disadvantage. Yet by the 1890s, freedom, when marred by labor exploitation and racial terror, began to look uncomfortably similar to slavery. Douglass concluded: "It comes of the determination of slavery to perpetuate itself, if not under one form, then under another. It is due to the folly of endeavoring to put the new wine of liberty in the old bottle of slavery."

Douglass's language is instructive. He recognized the often substantive differences between slavery and freedom, yet acknowledged that the very structure of slavery—the bottle—could exercise firm boundaries around freedom: slavery could survive its apparent demise to live on in new forms. While the impetus behind Douglass's address was to argue that lynching exposed freedpeople to a degree of arbitrary violence that dwarfed even what they had experienced under slavery, he was also concerned with the economic structure of the postwar South: "The landowners of the South want the labor of the Negro on the hardest terms possible. They once had it for nothing. Now they want it for next to nothing." For Douglass, as for Smith before him, freedom bore an uneasy resemblance to slavery.

Smith's and Douglass's formulations are in many ways difficult to take at face value. Their words—"capital dictates its own terms, which are perpetual subjugation; in other words, perpetual slavery;" "a worse condition to-day than in the time of slavery"—challenge our most fundamental understanding about historical change over time and the moral urgency of abolition. How could Douglass, who spent the first two decades of his life enslaved and a quarter century in the abolitionist movement, so casually compare the disappointments of freedom to the horrors of slavery? After a lifetime spent working to make slavery the central issue in American public life, how could Smith interrupt the significance of widespread recognition that the Civil War was a contest over bondage rather than reunification to interject concerns about so-called wage slavery? Quite simply, when approached with the assumption that freedom, no matter how truncated or limited or violent, represented the first step toward something better than slavery, Smith's and Douglass's words do not make sense except as metaphor, analogy, or hyperbole. Wrestling with these words on the terms that they lay out—the perpetuation and expansion of slavery over time, rather than its abatement—means suspending our deeply held (if not always explicitly articulated) notions about the inevitability of historical progress and the inexorable forward march of history. To take these words seriously necessitates a philosophy of history that can bear the weight of black life under racial capitalism.

Toward Black Philosophies of History

The relationship between blackness and the philosophy of history began with disavowal. Amos Beman, a black reverend from Connecticut, was determined to find information on the history of Africa and its people. In 1843, he wrote to Noah Webster, the famous editor and dictionary compiler, no doubt hoping that one of the nation's most learned men could give him the answers he was searching for. Webster replied, "of the wooly-haired Africans . . . there is no history and can be none."[3] Although Webster would not have been aware of it, Georg Wilhelm Friedrich Hegel had systematized this rejection of the possibility for African history in a series of lectures at the University of Berlin in the 1820s. Hegel concluded, "The Negro . . . exhibits the natural man in his completely wild and untamed state," and that Africa "is no historical part of the World; it has no movement or development to exhibit."[4] For Hegel, history "shows the development of the consciousness of Freedom on the part of Spirit, and of the consequent realization of that Freedom."[5] This process unfolded across both time and space, beginning with what he described as despotism in the ancient Orient (freedom only for the despot), progressing through Greek and Roman antiquity (freedom for some), and culminating with the modern nations of Prussia and England (freedom for all). Hegel's Negro, however, had "not yet attained to the realization of any substantial objective existence" and could have no awareness of the nature of freedom; he thus stood outside of history, "only as on the threshold."[6] Despite his ejection of blackness, Hegel's philosophy of history remains foundational to commonsense understandings of how history works. In fact, his sense of the link between moral and historical progression has at times seemed to speak *especially* to black history—consider Martin Luther King, Jr.'s paraphrase of the abolitionist Theodore Parker, "the arc of the moral universe is long, but it bends toward justice."[7]

For Amos Beman and for many who came after, seeking out the archives of black history was not merely about correcting factual omissions or writing more complete narratives. The recovery of such histories would have moral force, providing crucial tools in the struggle for racial justice. These archives would write black history and, in doing so, write blackness into history, thus bringing black people closer to freedom. The collector and bibliophile Arthur Schomburg captured this sentiment when he wrote, in 1925, "The American Negro must remake his past in order to make his future. . . . History must restore what slavery has taken away."[8] Recovering black history would be the bridge between the slave past and a freedom yet to come. Nearly a century after Schomburg wrote these words, there is a body of work on black history more magnificent than he probably could have imagined. Yet there is little doubt that this work has not—and cannot—restore what slavery took away.

While figures such as Hegel and Webster attempted to cast Africa and Africans out of history, the production of countless black historical narratives has seemed to militate against their ultimate success. It has been the tireless work of two centuries to recover the archives of black history and reject this foundational exclusion, rendering Africans and their descendants fit for the long march through history and toward freedom.[9] Following this logic, black people enter history precisely (perhaps only) at the moment that they confirm its forward movement by claiming a place within its trajectory. Black history begins when there is progress from slavery toward freedom— recall Schomburg's rhetorical opposition, "history must *restore* what slavery has *taken away.*" Even though this type of historical progress seems to combat the violence of being excluded from history, it nonetheless confirms Hegel's argument that history consists of the very movement toward freedom. Although many aspects of black history are illuminated by adhering to Hegel's framework (King did, after all, successfully organize actual marches for freedom), others, such as Smith's and Douglass's hesitations about emancipation, are obscured and rendered illegible. And accounts of black history that boldly claim Africans' and Africa's historical importance remain contentious when they would trouble the story of history's forward movement.[10] Thus, it might be instructive to dwell on what it means to linger at the threshold, remaining on the edges of history (at least certain kinds of history). If what links King and Hegel is a faith that through the unfolding of history a freedom yet unrealized will be forthcoming, it is a faith that cannot account for the intractability of blackness. In other words, the perpetual movement closer to freedom, the moral arc of the universe bending toward justice—these models of history are not the only ways, or even the most useful ways, for making sense of slavery and its abolition.

Reckoning with slavery and what came after requires new philosophies of history. Saidiya Hartman has used the term "afterlife of slavery" to describe the ways "black lives are still imperiled and devalued by a racial calculus and political arithmetic that were entrenched centuries ago."[11] It is an apt formulation that suggests a different, counterintuitive relationship between past and present, slavery and freedom. To ponder slavery's afterlife is to be open to the possibility that "the distinction between the past and the present founders on the interminable grief engendered by slavery and its aftermath . . . then and now coexist; we are coeval with the dead."[12] The notion of the afterlife is an interruption of progressive historical time. Things are supposed to live and then die, and if they live again or don't quite die, it distorts any sense of proper sequence. That sense of distortion is productive. In the words of Michel-Rolph Trouillot, "slavery here is a ghost, both the past and the living presence; and the problem of historical representation is how to represent the ghost."[13] Ian Baucom has argued that contemporary finance capitalism is a repetition or iteration of the financialized slave trade of the eighteenth century and that, by extension, "the present time . . . inherits its nonimmediate past by *intensifying* it."[14] Each of these philosophies of history is a reminder that history can move in a multitude of ways, whether cyclical, static, cumulative, palimpsestic, or something else entirely.

It is important to emphasize that nothing inherent to black history is resistant to the movement toward freedom, and nothing inherent to blackness makes it coterminous with the unending violence of slavery. To insist otherwise would be to reinscribe Hegel's beliefs about the historical stasis of Africa and the impossibility of black freedom. Rather, the historical formation of racial capitalism has bequeathed slavery an afterlife and rendered the forward movement of emancipation fraught. Racial capitalism places slavery within a broad, protean set of conditions that emerged out of but were not reliant upon slavery. These conditions continued to shape black freedom after emancipation. Racial capitalism's adaptability—operating through the idiom of freedom as easily as it did through that of slavery—is what makes it so useful for theorizing a black philosophy of history. Using the language of racial capitalism to describe what came both before and after emancipation emphasizes historical continuities over breaks, without disavowing historical dynamism or making slavery itself the only determinant of black history.

At times, the failures of emancipation were so great that black writers used the language of slavery even in its legal absence as a way of articulating a philosophy of history. Each emancipatory moment in the nineteenth-century British Atlantic world, whether in the U.S. North, the British West Indies, or the U.S. South, was premised on a form of freedom that transformed the primary vehicle for black subjugation from a relationship between capitalism and slavery into one between capitalism and freedom. Using an archive composed of black disappointment with freedom, the remainder of this chapter challenges the moral claims embedded within narratives about the progress from slavery to freedom and argues that racial capitalism ensured the transferability of systems of inequality beyond the slavery/freedom divide.[15]

The Poverty of Slavery and Freedom

The autobiography of Venture Smith (not to be confused with James McCune Smith, whose words opened this chapter) may be disappointing to readers familiar with nineteenth-century slave narratives.[16] Flights to freedom, the evils of slavery, the unparalleled personal transformation effected through emancipation, and other staples of the genre are nowhere to be found in Smith's narrative. These themes are so absent, in fact, that scholars have regarded the text as a deracinated celebration of liberal capitalism, with nothing to tell us about the operation of slavery or the limits of black freedom.[17] Smith was born into West African nobility, endured the Middle Passage, lived enslaved in New England and New York, and claimed his freedom at a time when the antislavery movement was still nascent. He knew nothing of abolitionists, or the Slave Power. Yet his distance from the antebellum plantation system and the conventions of later writers offered distinct insights: because Smith did not write with antislavery intentions, he unknowingly catalogued the hardships of freedom more openly than the next generation would.

When Smith was eight years old, he was captured, marched to the coast, and sold to British slave traders. The ship he boarded was bound for Barbados and then Rhode Island. Smith would have likely been sold in Barbados if a crewman, himself from Rhode Island, had not taken an interest in him. Smith wrote, "I was bought on board by one Robertson Mumford, steward of said vessel, for four gallons of rum, and a piece of calico, and called Venture, on account of his having purchased me with his own private venture. Thus I came by my name."[18] Smith's account of how he got his name—as an investment, or a good business venture—sets the tone for the rest of the narrative.

Smith was eventually sold to the Long Island merchant Oliver Smith, who would come to prominence as a lieutenant colonel in the Continental Army, and whose name Venture would eventually adopt.[19] The Colonel agreed to allow Smith to purchase his freedom, working for others when the Colonel didn't require him. Despite providing a pathway to freedom, the colonel was still a businessman, and the price he charged Smith for his freedom was steep indeed. For five years, Smith fished and farmed when he could find scraps of time, and the Colonel hired him out during the winter months, taking one quarter of Smith's wages. Smith eventually complained that this arrangement prevented him from working during the more profitable warmer months, and after some debate, the Colonel agreed to hire Smith out on Fishers Island and Long Island during the summer, but required more than half of Smith's wages in exchange for this generosity. Smith ultimately paid the "unreasonable sum" of more than seventy pounds for his liberty in 1765, more if his garnished wages were counted.[20] "The reason of my master for asking such an unreasonable price, was he said, to secure himself in case I should ever come to want."[21] Smith was referring to the fact that in colonial Connecticut, slave owners bore financial responsibility if their manumitted slaves could not find economic security and became beggars or vagrants.[22] Colonial legislators were happy to reap the rewards of slavery, but did not wish to bear the financial burdens of emancipation.

The fact that Smith could so freely labor toward his self-purchase perhaps suggests that Northern society was less reliant on slavery than its West Indian or Chesapeake counterparts. But the promiscuity of Smith's work is not evidence of slavery's lack of importance so much as it is evidence of a racialized labor flexibility that has long functioned as a marker of developed capitalism. On the plantation, enslaved property functioned both as labor and as capital. In the urban North, enslaved labor could provide just enough capital and security to slave owners to make their engagements with the riskiness of capitalism less fraught. The Colonel's investment in Smith was essentially without risk: he could command Smith's labor in his shipyard for life, he could allow Smith to work in whatever capacity he requested and collect a portion of wages until his initial investment was recouped, or he could manumit Smith after receiving a sum that would inure him against Smith's future economic failure. Racial vulnerabilities produced by but not limited to slavery allowed whites to leverage blackness, avoiding the very risk taking that supposedly made them deserving of profit and riches under capitalism.[23] It was this flexibility in the way Smith's labor was exploited that made freedom seem unmomentous. "Being thirty-six years old, I left Col. Smith once and for all. I had already been sold three different times, made considerable money with seemingly nothing to derive it from, had been cheated out of a large sum of money, lost much by misfortunes, and paid an enormous sum for my freedom."[24] Smith's refusal to mark his freedom in anything but sober and somber terms foreshadows the disappointments with freedom that would continue to grow sharper as he built a life after slavery.

Similar forms of labor, coercion, and economic vulnerability shaped Smith's life in freedom, despite the fact that he was able to keep all of his wages. The more successful Smith became, the more egregious the forms of economic exploitation he was vulnerable to. As he attempted to build economic stability in freedom, Smith's constant setbacks and failures exposed the impossibility for economic success to negate the vulnerabilities of race. This reality became clear only after Smith purchased himself, for while he was enslaved, his condition and his exploitation slipped into one another. Emancipation may have increased Smith's ability to accumulate capital, but it did not decrease his vulnerability to expropriation and exploitation. In both slavery and freedom, whites hedged against economic risk by transferring it to Smith.

One incident in particular stands out. Smith was traveling along the Connecticut River from East Haddam to New London "in an Indian's boat," and on the return trip, the Indian agreed to transport a hogshead of molasses for Elisha Hart, a wealthy merchant from nearby Saybrook. Smith and the Indian stopped in Saybrook to unload the molasses, but it was lost in the river in the process. "Although I was absent at the time, and had no concern whatever in the business, I was nevertheless prosecuted by this conscientious gentleman, (the Indian not being able to pay for it) and obliged to pay upwards of ten pounds lawful money, with all the costs of court."[25] Smith was well-off, but Hart, an officer in the Continental Army, had married into one of Connecticut's wealthiest families.[26] Hart "threatened to carry the matter from court to court till it would cost me more than the first damages would be," and so, after consultation with friends, Smith agreed to "pay the sum and submit to the injury."[27] Smith recounted that after Hart's victory, he often taunted Smith about this "unmerited misfortune."[28] The incident with Hart broke Smith's usually measured tone. "Such a proceeding as this, committed on a defenceless stranger, almost worn out in the hard service of the world, without any foundation in reason or justice, whatever it may be called in a christian land, would in my native country have been branded as a crime equal to highway robbery. But Captain Hart was a *white gentleman*, and I a *poor African*, therefore it was *all right, and good enough for the black dog*."[29] Smith's sense of being "worn out in the hard service of the world" was not about being enslaved or free, but how his blackness produced a similar— though not identical—relationship to labor and capital that transcended the fact of his emancipation.

Racial Freedom as Racial Capitalism

As part of a government commission to Santo Domingo in 1871, Frederick Douglass had the opportunity to visit Jamaica and witness firsthand the coolie system, an experiment in racialized labor that emerged after emancipation. Touted as a free labor alternative to slavery, tens of thousands of Indian and Chinese workers traveled from Britain's Asian imperial outposts to its West Indian colonies on indenture contracts that were functionally little less coercive than slavery.[30] Douglass noted that they had "expressions which might be worn by convicts serving out a sentence in a penal colony," which likely reminded him of his first exposure to Irish workers under British colonial rule a quarter century earlier. Douglass reported on his experiences in a series of editorials in his newspaper, the *New National Era*. "This Coolie trade—this cheap labor trade, as now called and carried on—is marked by all the horrible and infernal characteristics of the slave trade." He went on, "There is nothing in the details of the African slave trade, either in the manner of procuring its victims or of treatment of them in transit, more revolting and shocking to the sense of decency, justice, and humanity than are seen in this foul, harrowing, sickening, and deadening Coolie trade." Douglass realized that the neutral, neat language of free buying and selling of labor covered over a trade that looked like slavery by another name. In the coming years he would witness the total collapse of Reconstruction, and Douglass's evolving views on the coolie trade likely contributed to his understanding of black laborers' situation in the South as part of a larger global labor problem in the struggle against capitalist exploitation.[31]

Douglass followed up his initial writing on the coolie trade with a broader critique of cheap labor. "How vast and bottomless is the abyss of meanness, cruelty, and crime sometimes concealed under fair-seeming phrases," he wrote. "Cheap labor . . . seems harmless enough, sounds well to the ear, and looks well upon paper," but in actuality it meant "ease and luxury to the rich, wretchedness and misery to the poor." The idea of cheap abundant labor promised advancement and progress for all, but Douglass wrote that such progress was but an illusory veneer that contained "dead men's bones within." Early in his abolitionist career, Douglass was loathe to make overly direct connections between chattel slavery and so-called wage slavery, but by 1871—the height of Reconstruction—he could not help but draw them closer and closer together: "The African slave trade with all its train of horrors, was instituted and carried on to supply the opulent landholding inhabitants of this country with cheap labor; and the same lust for gain . . . which originated that infernal traffic, discloses itself in the modern cry for cheap labor and the fair seeming schemes for supplying the demand." In a flash, Douglass assimilated slavery into a history of class conflict, of the demand for cheap labor overtaking any concerns with justice or humanity. He reiterated his conviction that the coolie trade was "kindred in character and results to the African slave trade of other days." He noted that at the dawn of the British slave trade in the sixteenth century, Queen Elizabeth "professed great abhorrence of bringing away the Africans without their 'consent,' " and that "the same scrupulous regard for the rights of volition appears in the contracts and schemes by which Coolies are transported from India, China, and other parts of the globe." He implied that feigned concern with consent could hide neither the coercive nature of such "free" labor nor its resemblance to slavery.[32]

Seeing the condition of Asian coolies forced Douglass to think differently about black Southern workers. A common abolitionist refrain was the notion that after the abolition of slavery, lingering color prejudice would be the only thing preventing black people from taking an equal place in American society. The simplicity of the word *prejudice* belies the expansive and often complex ways black thinkers understood the term. It was sometimes a matter of individual white people's racist ideas about black people, but more often it referred to the calculus of justifications for denying black people legally mandated rights and committing violence against their property and bodies. Writing in this more expansive mode after the fall of Reconstruction, Douglass claimed:

> The workshop denies him work, the inn denies him shelter; the ballot-box a fair vote, and the jury-box a fair trial. He has ceased to be the slave of an individual, but has in some sense become the slave of society. He may not now be bought and sold like a beast in the market, but he is the trammeled victim of prejudice, well calculated to repress his manly ambition, paralyze his energies, and make him a dejected and spiritless man, if not a sullen enemy to society, fit to prey upon life and property and to make trouble generally.

Ever-popular ideas about black indolence and criminality, Douglass argued, were the result of psychic and physical violence that prevented black people from participating in political and economic life. Prejudice, then, was not a matter of individual attitudes, but an afterlife of slavery, rendering black life subject to the whims not of one master or household, but to all of white society.[33]

Before the Civil War, Douglass was reluctant to draw too many comparisons between slavery and free wage labor, no matter how exploitative. After the war, comparing the condition of free black laborers and coolies provided Douglass the opportunity to unleash the full force of his voice and pen upon the capitalist order. Writing that the cause of black laborers in the South was "one with the labor classes all over the world," he supported labor unions, predicting that the laborer "will develop what capital he already possesses— that is the power to organize and combine for [his] own protection." Such combinations were necessary because "experience demonstrates that there may be slavery of wages only a little less galling and crushing in its effects than chattel slavery, and that this slavery of wages must go down with the other." Douglass was particularly distressed that the exploiters of labor shifted the blame for these slavelike conditions from their own exploitative practices to cultural and mental deficiencies in black laborers. He asked, "How happens it that the land-owner is becoming richer and the laborer poorer?" There was no ambiguity in Douglass's answer, no reluctance to fully indict the power of capital: "This sharp contrast of wealth and poverty . . . can only exist in one way, and from one cause, and that is by one getting more than its proper share of the reward of industry, and the other side getting less, and that in some way labor has been defrauded or otherwise denied its due portion." Douglass fully cast off the antebellum illusion that slavery was the antithesis of free labor, and replaced the unambiguous progress from slavery to freedom with a continuum of labor exploitation.[34]

Abolition is Another Term for Communism

There is little left to learn from thinking of the abolition of slavery as an epochal break with what came before, and much still to learn from dwelling on the dreadful power of racial capitalism to distort and conscript emancipation for its own ends. When Douglass proposed that freedpeople in the 1890s could be "in a worse condition...than in the time of slavery," he interrupted the notion of historical progress. Douglass's words rejected the neat distinction between then and now. In his provocation, the injustices of the past did not exist as mere echoes cast into the present, slowly fading over time. Nor did they linger statically—they amplified ("worse than"). If what came after was worse than slavery, black reformers could not be sure that the march away from slavery was inevitably a march toward freedom. By asking his audience to imagine a freedom so conscripted that it was more terrible than slavery, Douglass challenged them to think of the fight against slavery as but one battle in a larger war to wrest black freedom from the dynamics of racial capitalism.

Racial capitalism is not just hyperexploitation; it is how race naturalizes the tensions inherent to capitalism's logic of forward progress. As we wrote in the introduction to this volume, the "violent dispossessions inherent to capital accumulation operate by leveraging, intensifying, and creating racial distinctions." If "race serves as a tool for naturalizing the inequalities produced by capitalism, and this racialized process of naturalization serves to rationalize the unequal distribution of resources, social power, rights, and privileges," then race fills a space torn open by the contradictions of capital. Africa could not be part of Hegel's philosophy of history, not because Africans lack the reason necessary to apprehend their own capacity for freedom, but because to acknowledge the violence wrought in the name of European development would render Hegel's theory of history and freedom a farce. Racial capitalism, then, is more than an analytic to consider questions of labor and capital. It offers itself as a black philosophy of history, a rebellion against strict periodization, against facile distinctions between slavery and freedom, and against the idea that movement forward in time must also mean moral or humanistic progress.

There can be a violence to the ways black people are written into history just as surely as there is a violence to the ease with which they are written out of it. But the purpose of such a claim is not that conditions can never improve, or that all of black history is reducible to slavery. Rather than stubbornly insisting that history does indeed exhibit forward movement (evidenced by the fact that, no matter how constricted by racial capitalism, black life in the present cannot be described as slavery), openness to other trajectories of historical movement can help better diagnose the problem of why freedom has at times looked altogether too much like slavery despite the fact that it is not. This openness can also provide a path to finding new language to describe a more full, aspirational form of freedom than that which emancipation provided. Take, for example, the words of T. Thomas Fortune, who was born enslaved in 1856 and became editor of one of the most influential and radical black newspapers of the late nineteenth century, the *New York Age*. In the pages of that paper he wrote, "We are opposed to all tyranny, because we have and do now feel its blighting influence. We are with the people. Nihilism in Russia, Communism in Germany and in France, Irish contention in Great Britain, and Abolitionism (another term for Communism) in the United States, are only synonyms for resistance by the people to the tyranny and corruption of the Government,—whether it be imperial, monarchical, or constitutional government."[35] Abolition as another term for communism. Like James McCune Smith's statement about the Civil War being utterly unable to end slavery, Fortune's is one whose meaning is not immediately clear when evaluated by the standards of progressive historical time. But viewed through the lens of racial capitalism and slavery's afterlife, then it becomes something quite different.

If slavery is capitalism, then of course abolition would be communism. Allowing these histories to collide with each other—or at least being open to the possibility of such a collision—is the only way to make sense of the archives of black freedom. It is a different way of bringing blackness into history: the collision makes slavery a counterpoint against Hegel's philosophy of history, and emancipation a necessary precondition for any form of historical progress, rather than evidence that such progress has already taken place. If abolition is another term for communism, then abolition is an ongoing yet incomplete process, and Smith was right to claim that there was no force at play in the nineteenth century that could encompass the *entire* abolishment of slavery. Smith's claim did not invalidate the achievements of emancipation so much as draw different conclusions from them. His claim offers a way of writing black history that does more than simply prove Africa and Africans do have a history, despite Hegel and Webster's objections; instead, it gestures toward a black philosophy of history that can account for both the enduring nature of slavery and the perpetually unfolding potential of abolitionist thinking.

NOTES

1. James McCune Smith, *Weekly Anglo-African*, August 27, 1864.
2. Frederick Douglass, "The Lessons of the Hour," *The Life and Writings of Frederick Douglass* Vol. 4, *Reconstruction and After*, ed. Philip Sheldon Foner (New York: International, 1955), 525–27.
3. Noah Webster to Amos G. Beman, 27 April 1843, in *Speak Out in Thunder Tones: Letters and Other Writings by Black Northerners, 1787–1865*, ed. Dorothy Sterling (New York: Doubleday, 1973), 291. For another reading of this anecdote, see Laura Helton et al., "The Question of Recovery: An Introduction," *Social Text* 33, no. 4 (2015): 1–18.
4. Georg Wilhelm Friedrich Hegel, *The Philosophy of History*, trans. John Sibree (New York: Colonial, 1857), 93, 99.
5. Hegel, *The Philosophy of History*, 63.
6. Hegel, *The Philosophy of History*, 93, 99.
7. Theodore Parker, "Of Justice and Conscience," in *Ten Sermons of Religion* (Boston: Crosby, Nichols, 1853); James Melvin Washington, ed., *A Testament of Hope: The Essential Writings of Martin Luther King, Jr.* (New York: Harper and Row, 1986).
8. Arthur Schomburg, "The Negro Digs Up His Past," *Survey Graphic*, March 1925.
9. On the notion of being unfit for history, see Stephen Best, *None Like Us: Blackness, Belonging, Aesthetic Life* (Durham, N.C.: Duke University Press, 2018).
10. There is a veritable cottage industry of scholarship dedicated to debunking Eric Williams's *Capitalism and Slavery* (Chapel Hill: University of North Carolina Press, [1944] 1994) and Martin Bernal's *Black Athena: The Afroasiatic Roots of Classical Civilization* (New Brunswick, N.J.: Rutgers University Press [1987] 2020). More recently, Judith Carney has come under similar criticism for her *Black Rice: The African Origins of Rice Cultivation in the Americas* (Cambridge, Mass.: Harvard University Press, 2001). For a criticism of this tendency, see Cedric J. Robinson, "Capitalism, Slavery, and Bourgeois Historiography," *History Workshop Journal* 23 no. 1 (1987): 122–40.

11. Saidiy Hartman, *Lose Your Mother: A Journey Along the Atlantic Slave Route* (New York: Farrar, Straus, and Giroux, 2007), 6.

12. Saidiya Hartman, "The Time of Slavery," *South Atlantic Quarterly* 101, no. 4 (2002): 757–77 (758, 759).

13. Michel-Rolph Trouillot, *Silencing the Past: Power and the Production of History* (Boston: Beacon, 1995), xx.

14. Ian Baucom, *Specters of the Atlantic: Finance Capital, Slavery, and the Philosophy of History* (Durham, N.C.: Duke University Press, 2005), 29 (emphasis added).

15. Britt Rusert, "Disappointment in the Archives of Black Freedom," *Social Text* 33, no. 4 (2015): 19–33.

16. Venture Smith, *A Narrative of the Life and Adventures of Venture, a Native of Africa; But Resident Above Sixty Years in the United States of America* (New London, Conn.: Holt, 1798).

17. James Brewer Stewart, ed., *Venture Smith and the Business of Slavery and Freedom* (Amherst: University of Massachusetts Press, 2010); Chandler B. Saint and George M. Krimsky, *Making Freedom: The Extraordinary Life of Venture Smith* (Middletown, Conn.: Wesleyan University Press, 2009); Robert E. Desrochers Jr., "'Not Fade Away': The Narrative of Venture Smith, An African in the Early Republic," *Journal of American History* 84, no. 1 (1997): 40–66; Philip Gould, "Free Carpenter, Venture Capitalist: Reading the Lives of the Early Black Atlantic," *American Literary History* 12, no. 4 (2000): 659–84.

18. Smith, *Narrative*, 13.

19. Saint and Krimsky, *Making Freedom*, 60–61.

20. Smith, *Narrative*, 24.

21. Smith, *Narrative*, 24.

22. Saint and Krimsky, *Making Freedom*, 59.

23. Walter Johnson, *Soul by Soul: Life Inside the Antebellum Slave Market* (Cambridge, Mass.: Harvard University Press, 1999); Karen Ho, *Liquidated: An Ethnography of Wall Street* (Durham, N.C.: Duke University Press, 2009).

24. Smith, *Narrative*, 24.

25. Smith, *Narrative*, 30.

26. Henry Whittermore, *History of Middlesex County, Connecticut, with Biographical Sketches of Its Prominent Men* (New York: J. B. Beers, 1884), 478–87.

27. Smith, *Narrative*, 30.

28. Smith, *Narrative*, 30.

29. Smith, *Narrative*, 30.

30. Walton Look Lai, *Indentured Labor, Caribbean Sugar: Chinese and Indian Migrants to the British West Indies, 1838–1918* (Baltimore: Johns Hopkins University Press, [1993] 2004), Ashutosh Kumar, *Coolies of the Empire: Indentured Indians in the Sugar Colonies, 1830–1920* (Cambridge: Cambridge University Press, 2017), Moon-Ho Jung, *Coolies and Cane: Race, Labor, and Sugar in the Age of Emancipation* (Baltimore: Johns Hopkins University Press, 2006), and Lisa Lowe, *The Intimacies of Four Continents* (Durham, N.C.: Duke University Press, 2015).

31. "The Coolie Trade," *New National Era*, August 10, 1871.

32. "Cheap Labor," *New National Era*, August 17, 1871.
33. Frederick Douglass, "The Color Line," *North American Review*, June 1881, in *The Life and Writings of Frederick Douglass*, 4:344.
34. Frederick Douglass, "Address to the People of the United States," in *The Life and Writings of Frederick Douglass*, 4:381–85.
35. "Who Is the Parasite?," *New York Globe*, February 16, 1884.

CHAPTER 7

GHOSTS OF THE PAST

Debt, the New South, and the Propaganda of History

DESTIN JENKINS

The history of racial capitalism is often treated as coterminous with the transatlantic slave trade and chattel slavery. This is understandable. Scholars have detailed the violent processes of commodification on slave ships leaving the Gold Coast of Africa. They have revealed how the "permanent" labor of enslaved black women underlay fiscal policy in parts of Colonial America. And they have shown how "the entire 'pyramid' of the Atlantic economy of the nineteenth century . . . was founded upon the capacity of enslaved women's bodies: upon their ability to reproduce capital."[1] Clearly, then, the trade in and commodification of enslaved black women, men, and children was essential to the coherence, if not emergence, of racial capitalism. But in focusing primarily on slavery, we undertheorize what came after. Indeed, the synecdoche comes with important theoretical and political consequences. It often means either treating the end of slavery as the end of racial capitalism or treating emancipation, one of "the most radical redistributions of property in history," as a "non-event."[2] To insist that emancipation marks the end of racial capitalism assumes that what followed was race-neutral. That assumption is ahistorical. Although emancipation did not level social hierarches, it was a momentous event that brought an end to the direct ownership of human beings. Emancipation abolished a dominant mode of governance that helped power violent racialized modes of extraction. Yet racial capitalism persisted as a wide-ranging system and enduring structure.

How, then, do we explain the reproduction of racial capitalism, including its constitutive elements of racial governance and the entanglements of racial differentiation and accumulation? We might look to the reparations paid to British slave owners in the wake of abolition, and how those funds were invested.[3] We might also focus on new instruments of financial governance. Emancipation generated new answers to older questions of who rules and through what means. How to constrain large territories and the choices of huge swaths of the world's laboring population? At one level, the new forms of rule between empires and their colonies, and within imperial nation-states, were expressed through violence, coercion, and labor impressment. At another level, modern forms of indebtedness recreated conditions of bondage, dependence, and discipline that made contemporary observers question whether slavery had truly ended.[4] To be clear, neither debt in general nor governance through debt was new.[5] What was new was the proliferation of debt of all types—agrarian and sharecropping, foreign, state, and local—and the powerful ways credit-debt relations were articulated through race.[6] To that end, I am interested in the historical continuities and repetitions of racial capitalism between the 1870s and late 1920s, a moment we might call Imperial Jim Crow.

Scholars have long seen the scramble for Africa and the rise of the United States as an imperial power as the upshot of the overaccumulation crises of the late nineteenth century. Increased industrial and agricultural mechanization, the story goes, led to the overproduction of manufactured goods, and consumption could not keep pace. New and old imperial powers increasingly relied on territorial possessions to resolve recurring economic depressions, surplus goods, and labor violence.[7] Racial ideology and racism shaped and were shaped by these imperial resolutions. As the old category of "slave" ceased to organize agricultural production, "racial types" served new economic functions, helping to stabilize currencies in some cases and to power racially segregated enclave economies in others.[8] During the Age of Empire, imperialists in Western Europe, the United States, Japan, and Latin America used biological notions of absolute human difference to justify continental inequality and facilitate the extraction of the materials essential to mass production and consumption.[9] W. E. B. Du Bois offered perhaps the most powerful synthesis in his 1915 essay, "The African Roots of War." For Du Bois, prosperity was not incidental to, but predicated on, racial inequality within the global North and in the global South. This was the essence of "democratic despotism."[10]

I want to emphasize the importance of government debt to the rise of new modes of racial capital accumulation. For starters, public debt rechanneled "the prodigious surpluses of capital" into large-scale physical infrastructure projects, as geographer David Harvey notes.[11] Debt-financed infrastructure also meant contracts for engineering firms and concrete companies. Debt-financed schools and parks were the infrastructural backbone of "separate but equal," the artifacts of Jim Crow segregation. Scholars have gotten great mileage from Du Bois's claim that white workers secured "a sort of public and psychological wage."[12] They have not considered the analytical promise of his argument about race and *dividends*. The concurrent rise of racial segregation and imperial expansion signaled a worldwide investment in "color prejudice. The 'Color Line' began to pay dividends."[13] Whereas the wage evokes images of the factory floor, fever-pitched battles between industrial employers and employees, and how whiteness mediates income differentials and the exclusion of the mass of the world's workers from the formal economy, dividends point us toward the domain of stocks and bonds, rents, and interest payments. Government debt unlocked profits for underwriting investment banks, made for new roads and streets that separated black from white, and delivered interest payments to wealthy bondholders.[14]

This essay tries to tackle an admittedly large story by focusing on something small. It considers what the financial, political, and labor history of Alabama's Port of Mobile teaches us about racial capitalism at the turn of the twentieth century. I say that with a few qualifications. To focus on the role of debt in the redevelopment of the Port of Mobile necessitates linking that history to that of the city of Mobile, the state of Alabama, and the South as a whole. This interdependence is rooted in two historical relationships. First, Alabama's credit stood behind Port bond issues. Second, older reputational harms that clung to the city of Mobile, the state of Alabama, and southern debt were brought to bear on Port bonds during the 1920s. The Port of Mobile is the center of gravity in this story, but following the life of a bond and excavating the historical memory of bondholders demands movement across local, state, and regional scales within the broader Atlantic world.

This chapter will raise more questions than it will answer, mostly because the social, political, and economic history of municipal debt has received little attention. Indeed, how the repudiation of debt during the late nineteenth century conditioned the credit reputations of southern municipal borrowers long after demands more research.[15] What follows, then, is a preliminary exploration of the historical memory of bondholders, and how the sins of the fathers fifty years prior snapped back on New South boosters in the 1920s.

New South boosters and Port of Mobile promoters faced two challenges in their efforts to attract bond buyers. The first was the paradox of Jim Crow. On the one hand, the stability of southern debt was effectively backed by a modern regime of racial totalitarianism; employers' ability to restrict mobility and extract surplus value was sanctioned by and exercised through the state. On the other hand, racial violence, domination, and segregation could become a liability. Black longshoremen working along the Port of Mobile repeatedly struck, and other black workers migrated to the North. Labor agitation and black migration could disrupt dependence on a steady labor force, the circulation of goods, and fees charged on incoming vessels, and undermine the overall value of Port debt. The second challenge was that they not only had to persuade bond buyers that Jim Crow governance would protect their capital, but also that defaults were unlikely, that repudiation was a thing of the past, and that the South was and would remain politically stable. This was, in no small part, a narrative challenge. Development often hinges on the stories borrowers tell about their present condition and future forecasts, and whether lenders are convinced by those projections. Equally critical is how the past is engaged, remembered, and deployed. City officials, boosters, manufacturers, bankers, and others depended on racist narratives of carpetbagger excesses, the saturnalia of debt, and the valiant return of ex-Confederates. That is, they depended on what Du Bois termed the "propaganda of history" to enhance municipal creditworthiness and expand borrowing channels.[16]

Redemption

The Civil War and emancipation had an enormous impact on southern municipal finance. Take New Orleans, for example, where the total assessed value of property was a little more than $125 million in 1861. By 1865, it fell to less than $99 million. Part of the decline was caused by the wartime destruction and devaluation of real estate. Another "item of $6,609,210 was taken off assessment rolls at one stroke when the slaves were emancipated."[17] During the antebellum period, enslaved black people were property. Along with real estate, they were treated as taxable assets, and some of the revenue was ultimately routed to repay bondholders.[18] With soil exhausted in large parts of the rural South, buildings and physical infrastructure leveled during the war, and human capital liquidated, post–Civil War southern municipalities faced the problem of economic prosperity in the absence of slave labor. Who would rebuild decrepit streets and install vital infrastructure? How could that be done without pushing expenditures beyond politically palatable levels, in the midst of depleted revenues?

These postbellum fiscal dilemmas were compounded by the heavy weight of debt. This was not the first time that southern borrowers had run into debt troubles. But whereas antebellum debt woes were rooted in state-level borrowing practices, northern and international finance, slavery, and indigenous dispossession, postbellum debt woes were especially pronounced at the local level.[19] The economic depression and bond defaults of the 1840s precipitated the passage of strict limits on state indebtedness, and local governments assumed an increasingly large share of government debt throughout the remainder of the nineteenth century.[20] This structural shift in the distribution of government debt implied that questions of whether to repay debt and through what means were placed at the doorstep of municipal officials. As corruption and the horrors of Reconstruction emerged as dominant motifs, some attributed municipal debt woes to the machinations of a "greedy band of creditors" who partnered with fraudulent and corrupt radical Republicans.[21] Who or what to blame remained a source of contention, but bankruptcy, declining tax revenues, missed debt-service payments, and striking taxpayers were undeniable realities for cities like Mobile, Alabama.[22]

Southern cities dealt with fiscal pressures through prison labor and retrenchment. Sarah Haley has recently underscored the importance of chain-gang labor to agricultural production. These new arrangements between the state and private capital were promising for another reason: the violation of yearlong contracts and vagrancy laws allowed post–Civil War elites to commandeer black labor power to fix decrepit city streets.[23] Mobile mayor Cleveland F. Moulton concluded that "working prisoners on the streets" amounted to just sixteen cents per day in additional costs. The city's Democratic Party also imposed severe fiscal constraints, limiting municipal spending to one hundred thousand dollars annually. Officials who authorized expenditures exceeding this amount were "criminally liable."[24]

Municipal officials adapted to a world of diminished revenues through prison labor and retrenchment, but such tactics could not resolve the problems of indebtedness. Having missed renegotiated interest payments, in the face of federal lawsuits, and unable to make payroll, by late 1878 lawyers, powerful business leaders, and the *Mobile Register* settled on repudiation as a way out of its debt crisis.[25] Difficult though it may seem in our current political moment of bondholder supremacy, Mobile was one of many local and state governments throughout the South to repudiate debt.[26] The rationales were diverse, but North Carolina's former governor and senator Zebulon Vance offered perhaps the most bombastic justification. Vance insisted that his state had no "moral obligation" to pay back its debt because "one-half of our property, upon which one-half of our bonds were based, was wantonly destroyed by consent of a large majority of those who held them." The state would be of no help to bondholders and "no court of conscience on the earth would permit a creditor to destroy one-half of his security and claim full payment out of the remainder." By declaring their opposition to slavery and fighting a war against the Confederacy, Vance maintained, northern creditors were themselves to blame for destroying the security—"slave property"—on which North Carolina's debt rested.[27] Repudiation was no small step in the escalating conflict with creditors. Whereas a default could be read as an unfortunate consequence of poor fiscal planning, repudiation was a defiant rejection of the debtor-creditor arrangement.

A detailed account of bondholder power is beyond the scope of this essay. Suffice to say that the ability of bondholders to strike back depended on the kinds of government debts they owned and the terrain of struggle on which they fought. Not long after the Civil War, federal bondholders fought to resume the gold standard and worked to defeat farmers in the West and planters in the South. The monetary system, then, was the crucial battleground for federal bondholders. The Eleventh Amendment and the inability of bondholders to sue states circumscribed their power in profound ways. Holders of partially repudiated Alabaman debt, and state debts more generally, had no legal standing; legal action was not realistic. By contrast, the federal courts had become "the [municipal] bondholders' great defender," in the words of one observer.[28] As jurist John F. Dillon explained in 1876:

The Supreme Court of the United States has upheld the rights of the holders of municipal securities with a strong hand, and has set a face of flint against repudiation even when made on legal grounds termed solid by the State courts, by municipalities which had been deceived and defrauded. That such securities have any general value left is largely due to the course of adjudication in respect thereto by the Supreme Court, and the reliance which is felt by the public that it will stand firmly by the doctrines it has so frequently asserted.[29]

Yet judicial support was often little more than a moral victory. The poor tax-collection machinery in defaulting and repudiating municipalities and losses on readjusted debt obligations meant that bondholders who turned to, and secured judgment from, the judiciary walked away with a "hollow remedy."[30] The *New York Times* appeared exasperated, explaining in 1879, "there is practically no way of enforcing their [creditor] rights." Municipal "revenues are exempt from seizure." Although the property "held for profit and not for public trusts or uses" could be pledged toward repayment, "in fact" municipalities reeling from economic depression "have no property of such sort." Put simply, if a city "does not pay, the courts will order it to pay; if it will not do so then, why, it need not."[31]

Arguably, the origins of municipal bondholder power can be traced back to this position of weakness. Unable to fully rely on the courts and private collection officers, creditors began to develop a recollective, perceptional power that increasingly assumed institutional form. In September 1877, one Bostonian suggested a novel approach to stemming the tide of repudiation: He pledged one hundred dollars to start a fund that would permit the *Nation* "to keep the names of these repudiating counties and States constantly before the public." This "Black List of Repudiation," he continued, might be included as "a standing advertisement on the first page," indicating the failure of borrowers to "pay their obligations at maturity."[32] A blacklist, affirmed another creditor, would not only deter "capitalists and business men" from lending to recalcitrant cities and counties but also discipline all borrowers. They "will be taught . . . the simple but eternal lesson that 'honesty is the best policy.' "[33] This shaming technique, and the attempt to broadcast the activities and actions of cities like Mobile, proved to have the most lasting, disciplinary effect.

The Alabama state legislature did more than mediate the battle between Mobile bondholders and local advocates of repudiation. In the spring of 1879, Mobile officials looked to commit state-assisted municipal suicide. Repealing the city's charter, officials hoped, would strengthen the position of the new government over bondholders. By the end of March 1879, the city of Mobile was a thing of the past. It was now known as the Port of Mobile.[34] The city's creditors were incensed. In early October 1879, many of them gathered to hear the terms of a renegotiated settlement from the "Commissioners of Mobile." By then, more than $1.8 million in bonds issued in 1875 were in default. The city had few revenue sources pledged to service another $385,000 in debt, and more than $115,000 in interest payments was past due. Led by

W. H. Hays, a president of the Bank of the State of New York, creditors resolved that the Alabama legislature had "inflicted injury on the financial standing, not only of the City of Mobile, but also of the great State of Alabama itself, one which . . . hinders her future financial operations." Their response to state-assisted municipal suicide was to attack the reputation of Mobile and Alabama, making it more difficult for them to borrow in the future. Aware of the long-term consequences of reputational injury, Mobile's commissioners became "exceedingly active in their endeavors to prevent the reporters from obtaining copies of the resolution and details of the proceeding."[35] By December 1886, the Alabama General Assembly assisted once more in Mobile's affairs, bringing an end to the Port of Mobile municipality and placing Mobile under a new charter.[36]

Despite attempts to suppress information and the revival of the city of Mobile, bondholders would not soon forget. Even as southern municipalities emerged from the fiscal troubles of the 1870s, cities like Mobile would continue to run up against the historical memory of bondholders, an increasingly potent recollective power that could undermine the dreams and ambitions of the New South.

New South

W. E. B. Du Bois rejected the suggestion that the Civil War reoriented the United States toward "petty bourgeois development." Rather, the end of Reconstruction marked a transition from one feudal order to another, from "agrarian feudalism in the South" based on slave labor to continental neo-feudalism "based on monopoly" of raw materials, "the transportation of these commodities on new public iron roads privately sequestered," and "the manufacture of goods by new machines and privileged technique." Leaving aside the transition question, Du Bois's emphasis on monopoly control of raw materials, infrastructure, and the instruments of production helps to frame the economic ambitions of a new breed of southerners.[37] Through the Mobile Commercial Club (MCC), the Mobile Chamber of Commerce, the Cotton Exchange, and similar associations, a new generation sought to elevate the place of the New South within a global project of imperial extraction.[38]

The MCC thought the potential of Alabama hinged on extracting resources from the earth and directing the commodifying eye toward minerals and timber. Its boosters claimed that Alabama's coal area was larger than the entire state of Maryland and that coal output increased from 320,000 tons in 1880 to 4,000,000 tons in 1889. Iron output was equally impressive, if not fantastic, jumping from more than 62,300 tons in 1880 to more than 890,000 tons in 1889. The MCC looked to sell investors on Alabama by pointing to the "immense deposits of red Hematite and Black Band ore, inexhaustible in quantity and of inestimable value." Nearby were known deposits of marble, flag, slate, and limestone. The recent "discovery of petroleum opens up a boundless field for new enterprises and profit." Millions of acres offered everything from yellow pine to white oak, cottonwood to cypress, gum to juniper, "all accessible, both by rail and water ways." Mobile's potential was also seemingly limitless. Along with mineral wealth, the climate "should make Mobile a Mecca for all fugitives from the rigorous blasts and icy blizzards of the North."[39] Within the booster's imaginary, the minerals, trees, even the climate itself, were commodified into objects and experiences of consumption.

Not everything was new about the New South program. There was some continuity between proslavery political economists who insisted on free trade, and New South boosters.[40] "America is gradually learning the truth which is as fixed as fate, that the *world's competition must be met or our factories abandoned*," the MCC proclaimed in 1891. Free trade and competition with the manufacturing centers of the world were "inevitable laws of trade." The MCC outlined a program that would increase domestic cultivation and consumption of cotton "by spindles . . . of our own Southland." Infrastructural improvements would not only shrink the distance between coal deposits and the Port of Mobile; it would also allow Alabama to undercut Sydney, Australia, "the cheapest coal port in the world."[41]

The Mobile Commercial Club projected an image of the South as immune to the kinds of battles between labor and capital sweeping other parts of the country. Part of the supposed peace was due to Mobile's climate. The "mild and healthful climate" allowed for "healthful food." Both meant that workers required "less clothing, less fuel, less medicine than any other manufacturing centre in the world. Living expenses are thus reduced to a minimum." And whereas striking industrial workers in the North were forced to endure freezing temperatures, in Mobile a lockout or strike meant instead that "a garden spot at a nominal cost would enable an artisan to maintain his family in independence and comfort."[42] Another reason for southern tranquility was white labor's racial and class consciousness. As the *Manufacturers'*

Record (*MR*) explained, white workers felt a sense "of race superiority," a "consciousness" that "excites a sentiment of sympathy and equality on their part with the classes above them."[43] If there was some truth to the first part of the *MR*'s claim (white supremacy), the second part was propaganda. At every step, attempts by eastern financiers to integrate the trans-Mississippi West into the nation's broader political economy were met by populist critiques of absentee investors and agitation against unjust agrarian debts.[44] In response to the populist challenge, New South boosters responded by affirming the safeguard of racial hierarchy.

But this was labor as an abstraction. Coal output did not "somehow" increase, and mineral deposits did not just rise to the surface. Contrary to the MCC's bland descriptions, black longshoremen were the foundation on which these commercial visions rested. Mobile was one of many cities to which newly freed African Americans migrated. Black longshoremen quickly "displaced" their Irish predecessors as the laboring mainstay of the Port of Mobile, struck for higher wages in 1867, and again during the 1870s. Labor peace and harmony would have been news to white workers who organized and lobbied city officials to exclude black longshoremen from loading lumber and timber. Whatever harmony did exist was doubtlessly due to the International Longshoremen's Association's (ILA) policy of Jim Crow segregation between black and white workers. And it is hard to imagine black workers who controlled their own locals in full agreement with their upper-class employers.[45] Through passive voice and romanticism, by treating workers as interchangeable inputs who shared the same racial and class outlook as rich merchants and manufacturers, New South boosters erased the actual racialized workers who extracted raw materials and the essential men who loaded the vessels moving in and out of the Port of Mobile.

Port cities had become essential to war preparation, water transportation, and, in the words of the U.S. Maritime Commission, advancing "commercial and shipping interests in the uplifting of American trade."[46] From the river and harbors just below New Orleans to the harbors of Galveston and Mobile, the federal government provided millions in appropriations for these ocean shipping and port cities between 1891 and 1906.[47] The U.S. chief of engineers helped secure an appropriation of five hundred thousand dollars to improve Mobile's harbor and ship channel, and in August 1888 the city's leaders persuaded Congress to help dredge the harbor further.[48] Federal support might enable newly consolidated firms to strengthen their position in the tropical fruits trade. Take, for instance, the United Fruit Company of Boston, which purchased the Snyder Banana Company in 1898. A much-improved Port of Mobile would allow the firm to accommodate greater imports from Cuba, Haiti, and other parts of the West Indies.[49] Federal funds were supplemented by state legislative action. In 1921, the Alabama legislature adopted an amendment to the state constitution to undertake waterfront improvements under strict fiscal limits. Two years later, the State Docks Commission assumed the power to acquire, control, and operate terminal facilities.[50]

As junior partners, New South boosters strengthened ties with the northern bourgeoisie. The merchants and manufacturers who emerged from the merger movement could rely on vital state assistance in developing the Port of Mobile.[51] However, with debt a central means by which cities raised huge chunks of funds for infrastructure projects, New South boosters confronted the problem of bondholder memories.

Municipal bondholders of the 1920s were not nearly as weak as their late-nineteenth-century counterparts. The Sixteenth Amendment certified their claim to tax-exempt interest income, a critical exception to the broader attempt to tackle wealth inequality through progressive income taxation. Thereafter municipal debt became the preserve of wealthy elites and such institutional investors as savings banks and insurance companies.[52] Prospective bond buyers had multiple investment outlets, could secure various tax privileges and government guarantees, and, just as important, could rely on firms like the Bond Buyer, Moody's Investors Service, and Poor's Publishing to keep tabs on the deficits, debt limits, expenditures, and other behaviors of government borrowers.[53] And with municipal governments borrowing to fulfill the infrastructural promises of progressivism, investors had a plethora of debt from which to choose. So why buy southern municipal bonds instead of those issued by local governments elsewhere, most of which had neither defaulted nor repudiated bonds in years past?

Navigating these concerns and the wide range of bondholder power fell to people like Sydney J. Bowie. Born in Talladega, Alabama, as the Civil War came to an end, Bowie graduated from the University of Alabama School of Law at age twenty. He practiced law in his hometown, served as city clerk, as an alderman, and then as Democratic congressman between 1901 and 1907. After declining to run once more, Bowie moved to Birmingham, where he practiced law and engaged in business.[54] He was part of a new middle class that helped guide the South into the mainstream of American life.[55] And part of that responsibility meant appealing to bond buyers and financiers from around the country. To that end, Bowie turned to the *Daily Bond Buyer* (*DBB*) in July 1922. Founded in 1891, by the 1920s the *DBB* had become the "technical organ of the municipal bond business," national in scope and reaching "every bond house of consequence."[56] Clerks, supervisors, and other municipal finance officers from around the country paid the *DBB* to advertise information about upcoming bond offerings. Municipal borrowers far removed from major financial centers along the East Coast had long struggled to reach lenders. The culture of mass investment, modern communicative technologies, and the blossoming world of advertising allowed local governments to secure bids for everything from county jails to schools, roads to parks.[57] Serving as a member of the Alabama harbor commission, Bowie drew attention to a forthcoming ten-million-dollar bond issue to develop the Port of Mobile.[58]

At a most basic level, Bowie's job was to project confidence in a relatively new species of municipal debt—revenue bonds. Whereas the more familiar general obligation bond was backed by property tax revenue, payments to revenue bondholders were based on the success of revenue-producing enterprises (water systems, streetcar railways, and other utilities). But beyond that, Bowie had to underscore the strength of the administrative machinery behind the bonds. This meant pointing to government guarantees, insulated revenues, and limits to democracy.

The 1920s may have marked the eclipse of progressivism, but the call for state ownership of vital infrastructure persisted.[59] Bowie implied that if left to private enterprise, fares and operational expenses would be costlier. Instead, Alabama was to own and control the Port of Mobile with charges set and regulated at a rate "sufficient to pay the expenses of the port" and, crucially, to ensure timely debt service payments.[60] In much of the American South, Brazil, India, and elsewhere, the system of crop liens had enmeshed tenant farmers in a system of indebtedness. Merchants were guaranteed something of a steady stream of payments, if not in cash then in title to agricultural commodities.[61] Analogously, Sydney Bowie assured bond buyers that the port itself was yet another guarantee: bonds were "secured by a prior lien upon the facilities created and erected."[62] The harbor improvement bonds, as they became known, were effectively state bonds backed by the credit of Alabama. Interest-rate ceilings were common; the bonds would be offered "at a rate not exceeding 5 percent." (By the late 1930s, the actual rate was around 4.27 percent.) In case of a revenue shortfall, the State Docks Commission could borrow again "for the payment of interest on outstanding bonds or other indebtedness."[63] Although bondholders could not count on tax revenues, Bowie clarified that the bonds would "not involve any additional charge or burden upon the treasury of the state." Existing holders of Alabaman debt thus need not worry about port bonds as an extra claim on state and local revenues. Finally, Bowie made clear that democracy was circumscribed: debt administration would remain insulated from day-to-day politics and confined within a narrow three-man sphere of governor appointees.[64]

Equally critical in Bowie's appeal was what went unsaid, intimations that point to the concerns of a specific type of capitalist. According to investment profiles developed by bankers, bond theorists, and sellers of financial information just after World War I, the typical municipal bond buyer was conservative. Almost universally a "he," this investor differed from the gambler who traded stocks, differed even from other lenders who took more risks by buying corporate bonds. The municipal bond buyer preferred lower average yields, between 4 and 4.5 percent, to higher-yielding but riskier investments.[65]

Bond buyers had to be confident that the government to which they lent funds for an extended period of time was politically stable. As two bond theorists explained in March 1920:

> It will be recognized at once that the bonds of unstable governments are much harder to market and bring a lower price than bonds of stable governments; but, in truth, the matter goes much further than this. In a country known to be subject to revolutionary outbreaks and whose political future seems uncertain there is a greater element of risk, not only in government bonds but in the bonds of railroads or industrial enterprises as well. Investors demand a higher return if they are to loan their money where a political upheaval may destroy either the actual physical structures or the property rights which stand as security for the loans. The bonds of enterprises in Central and South America, excepting Chile, Brazil, and the Argentine, have always constituted obvious evidence of this fact.[66]

Although principally an analysis of international investment, the basic point about risk and stability also applied to governments within the United States. Political upheavals, such as the wave of strikes across the United States in 1919, might undermine the secondary market for a municipal bond, limiting the ability to resell a bond to other investors without offering a premium. The destruction of debt-financed physical infrastructure might make collection of revenues, and payments to bondholders, impossible.

Municipal bondholders were concerned with steady interest payments, and they prioritized governmental stability too. Considered in this light, Jim Crow was more than an insulated system of gendered and racial violence within a wider democratic system; it was the basis of stability expected of borrowers, key to the revitalization of the South's credit profile, and a structuring condition of the municipal bond market during the early twentieth century.

Drawing from a familiar playbook of abstracting labor, Bowie stressed the economic potential of the Port of Mobile without saying a word about black workers. By the 1920s, "African Americans constituted more than 90 percent of dockworkers," as one historian has observed. Black foremen selected and supervised black longshoremen, workers on whom the Mobile, Oceanic, and Ryan stevedoring companies relied to load and unload cargo. This was backbreaking work where trust among a gang was critical, where human labor was only partially mediated by machinery:

> The general practice at this port is to work all hatches simultaneously with one gang of longshoremen assigned to a hatch. The size of the gang varies according to the type of commodity to be handled, the average usually being 17 men including the foremen. Practically all general cargo handled to and from off-shore vessels is handled by ship's tackle, and usually the loading and unloading of small coastwise and river vessels and covered barges is done by hand. Open barges or closed ones equipped with top hatches are unloaded by locomotive cranes at some terminals, where apron railway tracks permit their use.[67]

It was this labor that ultimately allowed the State Docks Commission to collect various harbor dues from towboats and vessels and fees charged for bunker refueling. Without black labor, then, there would be no proceeds from the operation of the port "applied toward payment of interest on out-standing bonds, [and] installments of principal as they mature."[68]

Black longshoremen illustrated the paradox of Jim Crow, a source at once of stability and volatility. Black longshoremen were critical to the reproduction of racial capitalism: through segregated locals, they loaded and unloaded the commodities that circulated throughout the United States, the Atlantic world, and beyond. At the same time, they posed a serious threat to racial capital accumulation. Indeed, black longshoremen had already staged a dramatic walkout in 1913. Not long after Bowie appealed to bond buyers, "waterfront employers instituted the open shop and used strikebreakers, many of them white, to defeat a walkout" by the black-led International Longshoremen's Association. Nor was this the last instance of black labor agitation and the reliance of employers on city police to crush labor strikes.[69] Unionization held the seeds of worker solidarity in ways that might threaten employer dominance; to strike was to disrupt the timely offloading of commodities, the ability to charge fees, and debt service payments. It is no wonder that Bowie threaded the needle between reference to abstract labor and omission of black workers.

"Fictionality," writes economic sociologist Jens Beckert, "is a constitutive element of capitalist dynamics." Fictional expectations assume "narrative form" in ways that "coordinate action, have performative effects, help to create newness, and are contested in four key fields of the capitalist economy: money and credit, investment decisions, innovation processes, and consumption choices."[70] Current affairs and future forecasts in narrative form are no doubt essential to persuading prospective bond buyers. But so too is history, the third temporality on which municipal debt sales turn. Fifty years after the overthrow of Reconstruction and repudiation, Sydney J. Bowie had to contend with the reputational harm that still clung to Mobile debt. He had to tell a story about the past with many inconvenient truths: he had to work between reverence for, and soft criticism of, his forefathers; he had to explain why such respectable men violated the debtor-creditor arrangement.

By the 1920s, Reconstruction was seen as a noble but failed overstep in federal power at best, and a disastrous experiment in racial governance at worst. Modern film hardened these sentiments among white Americans. As historian David Blight notes, the many Civil War films released during the 1910s "virtually all followed ritual plots full of nostalgia, reconciliation, brave if defeated Confederates surrounded by their virtuous women." In *Birth of a Nation*, Thomas Dixon Jr. and D. W. Griffith went further, depicting Reconstruction as "directed by deranged radicals and sex-crazed blacks" and the Ku Klux Klan as protectors of civilization.[71] Sydney J. Bowie remixed this propaganda in the pages of the *Daily Bond Buyer*.

"For ten years," Bowie declared, "we had suffered under the influence of aliens or those worse than aliens who monopolized our offices, who filched our substance." Americans "lately enfranchised and lately freed who had never shown the ability to rule any free state anywhere" had assumed political office throughout the South. In a sense, Bowie's was a global history of "Negro" governance. He furthered the myth of black political ineptitude and showed how white supremacists assimilated Haiti, the first independent black republic, into their thinking, obscuring the centurylong consequences of France's extractive indemnity, turning poverty and mismanagement into a natural law of blackness.[72]

Prospective bond buyers needed to know that 1874–75 saw the reestablishment of "the rule of the white men of the state in control of their own affairs." But this "glorious event" presented a problem. Northern creditors might share in racist banter, but the fact was that Mobile's defaults, repudiations, state-assisted suicide, and years of retrenchment occurred under white Democratic rule. The native sons impaired development and placed the city in fiscal shackles. Here, then, was the wrinkle in the otherwise standard story of Reconstruction: Bowie could not displace the problems of municipal finance onto black people. So he asked creditors to give his forefathers a pass. They had no choice but to do things that, in hindsight, were unwise.

The point of Bowie's story was not simply to excuse the poor decisions of redeemers. Bowie was also making a point about the continuity of white racial governance. He maintained that the three major fears of the 1870s had long since been allayed. The redeemers initially feared the return of federal "bayonets," but from the 1880s onward the federal government refused to challenge southern racial rule.[73] Black governance was put to rest through violent intimidation and severe legal voting restrictions. The third fear of being "governed again by white men without property interest" was slightly more complicated. It required navigating the class politics of white supremacy. When Bowie told readers of the *DBB* that elite white men were in control of port debt administration, he clarified that not all white Alabamans were equal. He said what northern readers of the *DBB* surely thought: Only white men of property could govern honestly, shield the state from despoliation, and manage fiscal affairs.[74] With all three fears—federal intervention, black political power, and nonelite white rule—sufficiently dealt with, Bowie encouraged prospective bond buyers to have full confidence in the political, economic, and social stability of Mobile.

Bowie's propaganda of history proved an important step toward upgrading the Port of Mobile. In August 1924, the Merchants Bank of Mobile partnered with financiers from Birmingham and Nashville, Tennessee, to lend one million dollars at an interest rate of 4.5 percent.[75] On March 10, 1927, the *Manufacturers' Record* announced that another batch of bonds in the amount of one million dollarswould soon hit the market, "making a total of $6,000,000 of State-guaranteed docks securities that will have been issued and sold." Others were encouraged to bid for the right to construct a transit shed just "north of the cotton compress and warehouse."[76] The successful offerings of port bonds were then used to sell still more debt. In June 1927, for instance, New York investment bank Brandon & Waddell looked to resell debt issued by the city of Mobile. As part of its pitch, the bank pointed to the Port of Mobile, the ten-million-dollar development project that would accelerate the movement of "cast iron pipe, cement and other products" and that was not too far from "Louisville, Cincinnati, St. Louis, Chicago and other important cities."[77]

Indeed, a glance at the finance section of the *MR* during the winter and summer of 1927 reveals countless southern municipal bond offerings for lights, roads, streets, bridges, water improvement systems, schools, highways, and playgrounds.[78] "Devoted to the Upbuilding of the Nation Through the Development of the South and Southwest," the *MR* monitored debt issued by counties large and small, as well as major cities and states, and the purchase of those bonds by banking firms from around the country.[79] Some of the more reputable investment banks, such as Chicago's Halsey, Stuart & Co., took an interest in Houston debt.[80] Other, more regional investment banks, such as M. W. Elkins & Co. of Little Rock, Arkansas, declared, "We are interested in the purchase of Southern Municipals including road, school, county, drainage and levee bonds."[81] Although Sydney J. Bowie and others might decry carpetbagging capitalists, by the 1920s southern statesmen and manufacturers welcomed foreign investment. "Capital has confidence in Alabama," declared the Alabama Power Company, which supplied electric current for the Port of Mobile. In late 1926, the governor and governor-elect of Alabama both affirmed the state's "fair and cordial attitude . . . before an audience of Eastern investment and commercial bankers meeting at a luncheon in Montgomery." With white elites firmly in charge, Bowie might have added, "outside funds invested in this state would always be safeguarded and protected."[82]

Reputation

Institutionalized through bond ratings, the sale of financial information, and internal deliberations of bond financiers, municipal creditworthiness was not a fixed determination but a fluid assessment that changed depending on the type of information with which creditors had to work. What's more, creditworthiness was more than a technocratic question of revenues, expenditures, and manageable capital outlays. The image of the South as "purely American," as one New England attorney claimed in the *MR*, or the *MR*'s claim of improved relations between whites and "the negro who behaves himself," might also affect a borrower's reputation.[83]

But there was something curious about the municipal bond market during the early twentieth century. Writing in 1936, one historian of bond finance explained, "Southern municipalities have the worst reputation . . . because, like some guests, they came to the default 'party' early and stayed late." Defaults and repudiations in one municipality had "prejudiced investors against southern municipals, despite the fact that municipal credit in that section cannot be regarded as a homogenous whole."[84] Other borrowers would soon experience the pitfalls of guilt by association. During the late 1920s, this southern phenomenon necessitated that an individual locality simultaneously improve its own borrowing reputation, that of the state, and that of the South as a whole.

Throughout the decade, the *DBB* encouraged municipal officials to submit information that might enable a bond sale.[85] This created room for local officials and their banker allies to present their cities in a positive light, quieting, for instance, concerns about the impact of natural disasters (earthquakes in California, or the great flood of the Mississippi River) on fiscal health and the ability to meet debt-service payments.[86] In other cases, the *DBB* recirculated information published elsewhere. The importance of financial information to bond buyers, and the *DBB*'s reliance on municipal officials to procure information, permitted interested stakeholders to deodorize what remained of the South's odious borrowing reputation. In effect, the centrality of information to the early-twentieth-century bond market and modern print technologies made easier the spread of racist propaganda.

Racist historians repeated the same story so many times, it is almost as if they forgot how to locate synonyms for plunder and ignorance or lost their ability to embellish the propaganda in which they specialized. It is either that or the banality was itself part of the ritual of antiblackness. One historian of the American South, J. G. de Roulhae Hamilton of the University of North Carolina, added a few punch lines in October 1927. Reconstruction debts were illegitimate; the extension of suffrage to Negroes, "who had no conception of law, no tradition of organized government, and who had acquired in their relatively brief contact with white people no knowledge of government and no capacity for participation in it," had made it so. By and large, however, Hamilton repeated the same tropes, citing other racist histories to justify repudiated debt.[87] In this respect, historian Matthew Page Andrews stood out.[88]

His 1927 essay, "American Responsibility for Reconstruction Debts," which first appeared in the *Landmark* and was reprinted in the *MR* and later the *DBB*, situated Reconstruction within a global context.[89] Andrews invoked the Soviet Union's repudiation of foreign loans, a move, he claimed, that was indicative of the broader attempt by the "Russian regime of Lenin and Trotsky" to violate the divine right of property. In one sense, the new Soviet regime was analogous to Reconstruction: "the very lowest elements of Southern whites" had come to power. In another sense, at least "the same race or people" led the Russian Revolution. What made Reconstruction much worse was that southern "governments were turned over to ignorant and illiterate negroes." Whereas Reconstruction and the Russian Revolution both challenged property rights, Reconstruction also inverted racial hierarchy. To understand the horrors, Andrews encouraged his readers to imagine South Africa "overrun by the armies of some other part or portion of the British Empire." He asked them to think of the evils of "radical partisans" disenfranchising "the best whites in order to place negroes, agitators, levelers and riffraff of every previous condition of ignorance or criminality in control of the conquered section."

The turning point in Andrews's history was essential to his larger attempt to blame black people for the decisions made by white people. Reconstruction officially came to an end when President Hayes "wisely withdrew the troops" and those bent on self-government arose. To this familiar narrative of white manhood, Andrews added something new. Whereas Bowie spoke of the "native sons," Andrews maintained that Reconstruction governments were "overthrown by a people representing the purest British stock." Andrews not only held onto class distinctions among white people but suggested a racial hierarchy among whites as well. Differences had not yet metastasized into a global category of whiteness. It was not the facts of his history that mattered but what Andrews hoped that history would do. He hoped that turning southern whites into Anglo-Saxons could improve the reputation of the South. Andrews implied that although the redeemers (now cast as white southerners of British stock) violated the creditor-debtor agreement, they ultimately stabilized the South. They had no choice but to "repudiate all the acts of their predecessors who had also been their ignorant and venal oppressors."[90]

These were colorful stories, but the key question is why these and other essays appeared in the financial press. Why did the *Daily Bond Buyer* reprint a moral tale justifying the repudiation of older debts? The *DBB*'s raison d'être was in part to monitor various challenges (from threats to tax exemption to municipal socialism) that might undermine bondholder investments and in part to coordinate action among bondholders when confronted by those challenges. Although repudiation was a much older challenge, aspiring lawyers had begun working to mobilize holders of repudiated debts. The *DBB* was thus a forum for creditor action and debtor defense. The propaganda of history was essential to both sides.

Legal action remained a considerable threat to the stability of southern debt and the South's borrowing reputation. In April 1927, Kinnear & Falconer of Stonehaven, Scotland, delivered a notice to the U.S. Congress on behalf of holders of select repudiated southern state debts.[91] The law firm methodically undercut the "Various excuses." Some claimed that debt was contracted during the Civil War and was thus nullified. To the contrary, the firm replied, the debts were "contracted for industrial and similar purposes, such as railways, banks, etc., before or after the Civil War." Just because "the money was placed in investments which ultimately proved unremunerative" or "misappropriated by the States' own officials" did not mean borrowers were not responsible. And as long as the bonds bore the "Seal of the State and the signatures of the States' responsible officials," the debts were surely legitimate.[92]

Kinnear & Falconer found only one excuse worth considering. If propagandists were right that Reconstruction debts had been issued by governments led by aliens and illiterate Negroes, sanctioned by the federal government and backed by federal bayonets, "it surely follows that there is a moral obligation on the Federal Government to see that they are paid." It was a point on which the *MR* and Matthew Page Andrews agreed. The *MR* did not blame "recreant" bankers for buying bonds issued by "unscrupulous scoundrels" and "negroes, many of whom could neither read nor write." Demanding that financiers foot the bill might signal an older hostility to finance capital that New South boosters worked hard to smother. Rather, because Reconstruction gave rise to "a wild saturnalia" of debt, a scourge of corruption backed by "Washington," the *Manufacturers' Record* insisted the federal government settle with holders of repudiated debt.[93] Bailing out foreign creditors, Andrews suggested, would finally rid the South of these reputational blemishes.[94]

In the end, neither bondholders nor repudiating spokesmen got their wish. In August 1930, the Corporation of Foreign Bondholders of London and the Association of British Chambers of Commerce demanded "the

Foreign Secretary bring to the attention of the United States Government the matter of the repudiated bonds." However, with the world reeling from the opening shock of a global economic depression, calls for creditor-debtor relief on late-nineteenth-century obligations did not go far. The wave of defaults on corporate and foreign bonds and debts issued by thousands of cities, towns, and districts around the United States (including Mobile), meant that the $390 million due to holders of repudiated southern debt paled in comparison to the billions of dollars lost and impaired during the 1930s.[95]

That Which Lingers

Despite the momentous ruptures, perhaps the most colorful thread running through the history of racial capitalism is the distinct yet consistent ways in which black workers remain the source of stability and volatility.

That the black worker was essential to slavery was obvious to W. E. B. Du Bois. The fact could be measured through the metrics of industry (sugar prices, bales of cotton, imports and exports between the North and South, and across the Atlantic); seen through the majestic forms of modernity ("new cities were built on the results of black labor"); noted in terms of life and death ("in America without a slave trade, it paid to conserve the slave and let him multiply"); and by the cruel efforts of slaveholders to maintain profits ("neglect and the breaking up of families").[96] Within the plantation household, enslaved black women nursed the babies of white women. Through "the appropriation of their breast milk and the nutritive and maternal care," as historian Stephanie Jones-Rodgers has explained, black women's biological capacities were further commodified and harnessed to the growth of racial capitalism.[97] As the keystone, black workers threatened the entire system by running away. Indeed, "there were grave losses to the capital invested in black workers."[98]

We have already seen how Mobile's black longshoremen threatened and reproduced racial capitalism. Long after emancipation black women also remained essential workers; in Atlanta, their domestic supervision of white children allowed white parents to partake "in other remunerative and social activities." Quitting was more than just an individual exercise. As Tera Hunter has brilliantly shown, quitting "accumulated into bigger results as workers throughout the city repeatedly executed this tactic, frustrating the nerves of employers."[99]

By the early 1960s, the black political activist and autoworker James Boggs thought automation and cybernation would render factory work unnecessary "for the great majority." Boggs was particularly concerned for black industrial workers who, by that point, had become unevenly integrated into the Fordist model of capitalism.[100] That argument has some merits, but looking back from 2020, it is clear Boggs's prediction of black disposability did not come to pass. Think of black public sector workers who remain key to shuffling white gentrifiers within the city to high-paying tech jobs, and who, as conductors and train operators, help transport workers from the suburbs to downtown corporate offices. Think of the essentiality of black football workers, on whom NFL team owners depend to secure the spoils from massive television contracts, and on whom local businesses depend for a steady stream of customers on game day. Think of the reliance of local college towns on the labor of black college football workers. And finally, to come full circle, we might think of black dockworkers and their allies who disrupted the Port of Oakland, the 8th busiest container port in the United States, to commemorate Juneteenth 2020. Like their predecessors in Mobile, this time they interrupted the movement of valuable goods throughout the Bay Area, Asia, and beyond.

Black workers have been and remain essential workers across a range of industries and sectors. They help power racial capital accumulation, yet, through an exercise of collective labor power can disrupt the system and upend that order. There is something about finance that helps obscure the essentiality of black labor—something about how financial instruments launder income; how municipal bonds allow investors to collect payments without ever having visited the issuer; how financial information flattens the contentious struggles between black workers and their employers into streamlined discussions of yield, revenues, and expenditures. But as a lens, racial capitalism brings these connections into view.

NOTES

I have benefited from conversations with members of the Old History of Capitalism workshop. Thanks to members of the Race and Capitalism working group, and participants in the Race and Ethnicity Workshop at the University of Illinois, Chicago, and the Modern America Workshop at Princeton University. Special thanks to Michael Dawson, Megan Ming-Francis, Adom Getachew, Ryan Jobson, and Michael Ralph for providing essential feedback at different stages of this project.

1. Stephanie E. Smallwood, *Saltwater Slavery: A Middle Passage from Africa to American Diaspora* (Cambridge, Mass.: Harvard University Press, 2007); Jennifer Morgan, *Laboring Women: Reproduction and Gender in New World Slavery* (Philadelphia: University of Pennsylvania Press, 2004), 70–72; Robin L. Einhron, *American Taxation, American Slavery* (Chicago: University of Chicago Press, 2006); Walter Johnson, "To Remake the World: Slavery, Racial Capitalism, and Justice," *Boston Review*, 2016.

2. David A. Bateman, Ira Katznelson, and John S. Lapinski, *Southern Nation: Congress and White Supremacy After Reconstruction* (Princeton, N.J.: Princeton University Press, 2018), 11. For historical events, see William H. Sewell, Jr., "Historical Events as Transformations of Structures: Inventing Revolution at the Bastille," *Theory and Society* 25, no. 6 (December 1996): 841–81.

3. Moon-Ho Jung, "Outlawing 'Coolies': Race, Nation, and Empire in the Age of Emancipation," *American Quarterly* 57, no. 3 (September 2005): 679–80.

4. Given the huge mass of racialized workers in the global North and South excluded from formal wage relations, pushed and pulled beyond wage labor into the informal and illicit economies, the rise of wage labor cannot fully account for new forms of unfreedom and bondage. In many ways, then, to focus exclusively on wage labor contributes to the tendency to treat racial capitalism as a variety of, and moment in, capitalism's more "general" history. For postemancipation financial governance, see Peter James Hudson, *Bankers and Empire: How Wall Street Colonized the Caribbean* (Chicago: University of Chicago Press, 2017), 17.

5. David Graber, *Debt: The First 5,000 Years* (New York: Melville House, 2011); Tim di Muzzio and Richard H. Robbins, *Debt as Power* (Manchester: Manchester University Press, 2016).

6. Arguably one can trace the emergence of racial governance through debt to the indemnity imposed by France on the first black independent republic of Haiti. Liliana Obregón, "Empire, Racial Capitalism, and International Law: The Case of Manumitted Haiti and the Recognition Debt," *Leiden Journal of International Law* 31 (2018): 597–615.

7. Walter LaFeber, *The New Empire: An Interpretation of American Expansion, 1860–1898* (Ithaca, N.Y.: Cornell University Press, 1963); William Appleman Williams, *The Tragedy of American Diplomacy* (Cleveland: World, 1959).

8. Andrew Zimmerman, *Alabama in Africa: Booker T. Washington, the German Empire, and the Globalization of the New South* (Princeton, N.J.: Princeton University Press, 2012), 14; Allan E. S. Lumba, "Imperial Standards: Colonial Currencies, Racial Capacities, and Economic Knowledge During the Philippine-American War," *Diplomatic History* 39, no. 4 (September 2015): 603–28; Abram L. Harris, *The Negro as Capitalist: A Study of Banking and Business* (Philadelphia: American Academy of Political and Social Science, 1936).

9. Eric Hobsbawm, *The Age of Empire, 1875–1914* (New York: Vintage, 1989), 32; Thomas C. Holt, *The Problem of Race in the Twenty-First Century* (Cambridge, Mass.: Harvard University Press, 2000), 21–22, 60.

10. W. E. B. Du Bois, "The African Roots of War," *Atlantic*, May 1915, 707–14 (708–9).

11. David Harvey, *The Urban Experience* (Baltimore: Johns Hopkins University Press, 1989), 33, 36, 62–64.

12. W. E. B. Du Bois, *Black Reconstruction in America, 1860–1880* (New York: Free Press, [1935] 1998), 700–701. See especially David R. Roediger, *The Wages of Whiteness: Race and the Making of the American Working Class* (New York: Verso, 1991).

13. Du Bois, "The African Roots of War," 708.

14. Thomas Piketty, *Capital in the Twenty-First Century* (Cambridge, Mass.: Harvard University Press, 2013), 113–14, 132.

15. For potentially productive leads on how the propaganda of history was entangled with the study of both municipal debt and debt management during the early twentieth century, see A. M. Hillhouse, *Municipal Bonds: A Century of Experience* (New York: Prentice-Hall, 1936), 55–56.

16. Du Bois, *Black Reconstruction*, esp. chap. 17.

17. Hillhouse, *Municipal Bonds*, 48.

18. Harriet E. Amos, *Cotton City: Urban Development in Antebellum Mobile* (Tuscaloosa: University of Alabama Press, 1985), 128–30.

19. As Claudio Saunt has explained, during the 1830s financiers and speculators understood that even if the domestic slave trade continued, there could be neither internal improvements nor productive plantation lands without indigenous dispossession. Along with fraud, violence, and racist indifference, speculators in London, New York, and Boston employed joint-stock companies to liquidate property titles granted to the Creeks and Choctaws. Alabama did its part by issuing debt to capitalize state banks. As foreign and northeastern capital triggered Indian removal, white settler colonialism within a racial state meant that theft was virtually ignored, if not condoned. When treasury secretary Levi Woodbury placed funds promised indigenous nations in municipal debt, the Chickasaw Nation were conscripted into financing their own dispossession. The Panic of 1837 wiped out much of these investments, and creditors "lay claim to the mortgaged land" when state banks faltered. Claudio Saunt, "Financing Dispossession: Stocks, Bonds, and the Deportation of Native People in the Antebellum United States," *Journal of American History* 106, no. 2 (September 2019): 315–37 (319, 324, 328–30).

20. John Joseph Wallis, "American Government Finance in the Long Run: 1790 to 1990," *Journal of Economic Perspectives* 14, no. 1 (Winter 2000): 61–82 (69–70).

21. Michael W. Fitzgerald, *Urban Emancipation: Popular Politics in Reconstruction Mobile, 1860–1890* (Baton Rouge: Louisiana State University Press, 2002), 219, 220, 231–32; Hillhouse, *Municipal Bonds*, 47–58; First National Bank of Mobile [FNBM], *Highlights of 75 Years in Mobile* (1940), 29.

22. Fitzgerald, *Urban Emancipation*, 206–7.

23. Alex Lichtenstein, *Twice the Work of Free Labor: The Political Economy of Convict Labor in the New South* (New York: Verso, 1996); Sarah Haley, *No Mercy Here: Gender, Punishment, and the Making of Jim Crow Modernity* (Chapel Hill: University of North Carolina Press, 2016); Bateman, Katznelson, and Lapinski, *Southern Nation*, 13.

24. Fitzgerald, *Urban Emancipation*, 203, 214, 253.

25. Fitzgerald, *Urban Emancipation*, 219, 220, 231–32.

26. Hillhouse, *Municipal Bonds*, 145–67; C. Van Woodward, *Origins of the New South, 1877–1913: A History of the South* (Baton Rouge: Louisiana State University Press, [1964] 1981), 23–24, 48–49.

27. Vance quoted in John F. Hume, "Are We a Nation of Rascals?," *North American Review* 139, no. 333 (August 1884): 127–44 (138).

28. Hillhouse, *Municipal Bonds*, 290, 351; "Agricultural Dishonesty," *Nation* 25, no. 637 (September 13, 1877): 166.

29. Dillon quoted in Hillhouse, *Municipal Bonds*, 291.

30. Federal revenue was mostly derived from taxes on alcohol, tobacco, and imports during the 1870s, and federal revenue collection agents were mostly concentrated in "the major commercial centers of the Northeast." U.S. marshals located in the South were mostly focused on policing evasion "rather than on collecting revenue." The upshot was a weak network of federal collectors of tax revenue in southern states and municipalities. Hillhouse, *Municipal Bonds*, 276–77; Richard Franklin Bensel, *Yankee Leviathan: The Origins of Central State Authority in America, 1859–1877* (New York: Cambridge University Press, 1991), 401–3.

31. "Compromise of Public Debts," *New York Times*, January 20, 1879, 4. Note also the amusing example of bondholder weakness: "Lee County [Iowa] has begun to pay her bonds, a surplus mule being the first article offered in liquidation of the debt. The mule was seized by the officer, and although a large number of persons were present, no one bid on that mule. Of course, no bidders, no sale; so the mule was remanded to the stable, to eat himself up at the public expense." *Commercial and Financial Chronicle* 11, no. 266 (July 30, 1870): 145.

32. "The Black List of Repudiation," *Nation* 25, no. 637 (September 13, 1877): 166.

33. "Repudiated Municipal Debts," *Nation* 26, no. 661 (February 28, 1878), 151.

34. Mobile was not alone in trying to evade creditors through municipal suicide and new municipal incorporation: "Default by Duluth, Minnesota, in the late seventies and early eighties grew out of real estate speculation and promotion of the eastern terminus of the Northern Pacific Railroad. With a population of only about 3,000 in 1877, the city had already piled up a debt of $400,000. But the Duluth default is remembered primarily because of an abortive attempt to defeat creditors' rights by the creation of a new municipal corporation. On February 23, 1877, the legislature carved the Village of Duluth out of the city's territory, embracing in the village the entire business section, the harbor, railroad depots and tracks, nearly all the dwelling houses, nineteen-twentieths of all the taxable property and all the population except about 100 inhabitants. No provision was to be made for payment of the city's debts by the village unless creditors agreed to a drastic reduction in their claims." It is unclear just who was part of the one hundred inhabitants left in the emaciated community. Hillhouse, *Municipal Bonds*, 57–58, 74.

35. "Mobile's Indebtedness," *New York Times*, October 7, 1879, 10; Hillhouse, *Municipal Bonds*, 52–53.

36. FNBM, *Highlights of 75 Years in Mobile*, 34.

37. W. E. B. Du Bois, *Black Reconstruction*, 583–84.

38. Mobile Chamber of Commerce and Maritime Exchange and Shipper's Association, "Mobile Statement of Water-Borne Commerce of Port and Rivers," December 1908.

39. Mobile Chamber of Commerce, "Mobile Statement of Water-Borne Commerce," 2, 9, 12.

40. Walter Johnson, *River of Dark Dreams: Slavery and Empire in the Cotton Kingdom* (Cambridge, Mass.: Harvard University Press, 2013), 11.

41. Commercial Club, "Geometrical Proof of the Superiority of the Port of Mobile," January 1891, 7–9, 20.

42. Commercial Club, "Geometrical Proof," 21.

43. *Manufacturers' Record* cited in Woodward, *Origins of the New South*, 221–22, 249, 291.

44. Charles Postel, *The Populist Vision* (New York: Oxford University Press, 2007); Noam Maggor, "To Coddle and Caress These Great Capitalists: Eastern Money, Frontier Populism, and the Politics of Market-Making in the American West," *American Historical Review* 122, no. 1 (February 2017): 55–83.

45. Robert H. Woodrum, "The 'Culture of Unity' Meets Racial Solidarity: Race and Labor on the Mobile Waterfront, 1931–1938," *Journal of Southern History* 84, no. 4 (November 2018): 883–924 (891–92); Lester Rubin, William S. Swift, and Herbert R. Northrup, *Negro Employment in the Maritime Industries: A Study of Racial Policies in the Shipbuilding, Longshore, and Offshore Maritime Industries* (Philadelphia: University of Pennsylvania Press, 1974).

46. U.S. Maritime Commission and U.S. Board of Engineers for Rivers and Harbors, "The Ports of Mobile, Ala., and Pensacola, Fla.," Rev. 1937, https://catalog .hathitrust.org/Record/011245197, ix.

47. Woodward, *Origins of the New South*, 125.

48. FNBM, *Highlights of 75 Years in Mobile*, 16, 37; "Mobile Statement of Water-Borne Commerce."

49. Charles Grayson Summersell, *Mobile: A History of a Seaport Town* (Tuscaloosa: University of Alabama Press, 1949), 52; Hobsbawm, *The Age of Empire*, 64.

50. U.S. Maritime Commission, "The Ports of Mobile, Ala., and Pensacola, Fla.," 11.

51. Sven Beckert, *The Monied Metropolis: New York City and the Consolidation of the American Bourgeoisie, 1850–1896* (New York: Cambridge University Press, 2001), 300; Naomi R. Lamoreaux, *The Great Merger Movement in American Business, 1895–1904* (New York: Cambridge University Press, 1985).

52. Roy C. Osgood, "The Effect of Taxation on Securities," *Annals of the American Academy of Political and Social Science* 88 (March 1920): 156–68 (163).

53. For the institutionalization of the "black list" of defaults and repudiations, see "State of Bahia, Brazil, Now in Full Default," *Daily Bond Buyer* [DBB] 86, no. 10,050 (June 15, 1922): 1452; "Elizabeth Ready to Pay Off Adjustment Bonds," *DBB* 86, no. 10,049 (June 14, 1922): 1441; "Municipal Bond Default Report No. 7," *DBB* 100, no. 11,522 (April 27, 1927): 1230. For examples of the surveillance of finances more generally, in the United States and beyond, see "Finances of Cities: 1918," *DBB* 78, no. 8540 (October 20, 1919): 1858–59; "Manitoba Province Has Large Deficit in 1921,"

DBB 85, no. 9958 (February 27, 1922): 429; "Syracuse Approaching Debt Limit," DBB 85, no. 9970 (March 13, 1922): 545; "A Friendly Warning to Canada," DBB 85, no. 9970 (March 13, 1922): 553; "Cleveland's Debt," DBB 85, no. 9977 (March 21, 1922): 623.

54. "Sydney Johnston Bowie (1865–1928)," *Biographical Directory of the United States Congress*, http://bioguide.congress.gov/scripts/biodisplay.pl?index=B000695.

55. Sheldon Hackney, "Origins of the New South in Retrospect," *Journal of Southern History* 38, no. 2 (May 1972): 191–216 (196).

56. Fraser Brown, *Municipal Bonds: A Statement of the Principles of Law and Custom Governing the Issue of American Municipal Bonds with Illustrations from the Statutes of Various States* (New York: Prentice-Hall, 1922), 180.

57. For a few examples of the kinds of information municipal officials provided, see "San Francisco, CAL.," under "Bond Sales," *DBB* 77, no. 8431 (June 11, 1919): 905; "$81,250 Town of Montclair New Jersey 5 percent Playground Bonds," *DBB* 85, no. 9980 (March 24, 1922): 648; "$200,000 Shelby County Tennessee Jail Bonds," *DBB* 85, no. 9980 (March 24, 1922): 648.

58. Sydney J. Bowie, "Alabama's Port Amendment," *DBB* 86, no. 10,070 (July 10, 1922): 1695–96. For the full text of the amendment, see "Alabama Port Amendment," *DBB* 87, no. 10,148 (October 10, 1922): 2466.

59. Daniel T. Rodgers, *Atlantic Crossings: Social Politics in a Progressive Age* (Cambridge, Mass.: Harvard University Press, 1998); Daniel J. Johnson, "'No Make-Believe Class Struggle': The Socialist Municipal Campaign in Los Angeles, 1922," *Labor History* 41, no. 1 (February 2000): 25–45; Douglass E. Booth, "Municipal Socialism and City Government Reform: The Milwaukee Experience, 1910–1940," *Journal of Urban History* 12, no. 1 (November 1985): 51–74; Gail Radford, "From Municipal Socialism to Public Authorities: Institutional Factors in the Shaping of American Public Enterprise," *Journal of American History* 90, no. 3 (December 2003): 863–90.

60. Bowie, "Alabama's Port Amendment," 1695–96.

61. Sven Beckert, "Emancipation and Empire: Reconstructing the Worldwide Web of Cotton Production in the Age of the American Civil War," *American Historical Review* 109, no. 5 (December 2004): 1405–38.

62. Bowie, "Alabama's Port Amendment," 1695–96.

63. U.S. Maritime Commission, "The Ports of Mobile, Ala., and Pensacola, Fla.," 13.

64. "Scope of Alabama's Port Development," *Wall Street Journal*, August 28, 1924, 5.

65. "Municipal Bond Average at New Peak," *DBB* 102, no. 11,719 (December 20, 1927): 4590; "Comparative Yields on 'Prime' Municipal and Corporate Bonds, 1900–1965," in U.S. Congress, Joint Economic Committee, Subcommittee on Economic Progress, "State and Local Public Facility Needs and Financing: Volume II," 89th Cong., 2nd sess., December 1966, 280.

66. Hermann F. Arens and James R. Bancroft, "Causes Affecting the Value of Bonds," *Annals of the American Academy of Political Science* 88 (March 1920): 208.

67. Woodrum, "The 'Culture of Unity,'" 888, 891; U.S. Maritime Commission, "The Ports of Mobile, Ala., and Pensacola, Fla.," 17–22.

68. U.S. Maritime Commission, "The Ports of Mobile, Ala., and Pensacola, Fla.," 13.

69. Woodrum, "The "Culture of Unity,' " 883, 893.

70. Jens Beckert, *Imagined Futures: Fictional Expectations and Capitalist Dynamics* (Cambridge, Mass.: Harvard University Press, 2016), 10–12.

71. David W. Blight, *Race and Reunion: The Civil War in American Memory* (Cambridge, Mass.: Harvard University Press, 2001), 394–95.

72. Obregón, "Empire, Racial Capitalism, and International Law," 605, 612–13.

73. Bateman, Katznelson, and Lapinski, *Southern Nation*, 16, 19.

74. Bowie, "Alabama's Port Amendment," 1696.

75. "Scope of Alabama's Port Development," 5.

76. "Progress on Port Terminal Facilities at Mobile," *Manufacturers' Record* 91, no. 10 (March 10, 1927): 65.

77. Brandon & Waddell, "$200,000 City of Mobile, Alabama Bonds," display ad in *New York Times*, June 6, 1927, 28.

78. "$394,500,000 in Bond Sales South in 1926," *Manufacturers' Record* 91, no. 7 (February 17, 1927): 81; "$36,716,000 Southern Municipal Securities Sold in 10 Days Bring Aggregate Premium of $794,000," *Manufacturers' Record* 91, no. 2 (June 16, 1927): 87.

79. *Manufacturers' Record* 91, no. 1 (January 6, 1927).

80. "$36,716,000 Southern Municipal Securities Sold in 10 Days Bring Aggregate Premium of $794,000," *Manufacturers' Record* 91, no. 24 (June 16, 1927): 87; "Southern Securities in Active Demand," *Manufacturers' Record* 91, no. 25 (June 23, 1927): 83.

81. "Financial News" section of *Manufacturers' Record* 91, no. 1 (January 6, 1927): 151.

82. Alabama Power Company advertisement in *Manufacturers' Record* 91, no. 1 (January 6, 1927): 252; U.S. Maritime Commission, "The Ports of Mobile, Ala., and Pensacola, Fla.," 25.

83. "A New England View of the People of the South in Relation to America," *Manufacturers' Record* 91, no. 13 (March 31, 1927): 58; "South Recognizes Colored People of Merit," *Manufacturers' Record* 91, no. 18 (May 5, 1927): 70.

84. Hillhouse, *Municipal Bonds*, 42, 420, 423.

85. For a few example of the *DBB*'s entreaty to municipal officials, see "How Umatilla Co., Oregon, Advertises a Bond Sale," *DBB* 77, no. 8401 (May 6, 1919): 664; " 'Fine Results,' " *DBB* 77, no. 8427 (June 6, 1919): 868; "Canadian City Uses the Daily Bond Buyer," *DBB* 77, no. 8468 (July 25, 1919): 1252; "Attention Municipal Officials," *DBB* 86, no. 10,042 (June 6, 1922): 1356.

86. "California Gets Back at Us," *DBB* 101, no. 11,553 (June 3, 1927): 1686; "NOTICE to Bond Buyers, Bond Holders—and To Whom It May Concern," *DBB* 101, no. 11,569 (June 22, 1927): 1925.

87. J. G. de Roulhac Hamilton, "Those Southern Repudiated Bonds," *Virginia Quarterly Review* 3, no. 4 (October 1, 1927): 490–506. W. E. B. Du Bois identified Hamilton as among those "authors [who] believe the Negro to be sub-human and congenitally unfitted for citizenship and the suffrage." For Du Bois, Hamilton's *Reconstruction in North Carolina* was "Standard-Anti Negro" propaganda. Du Bois, *Black Reconstruction*, 731.

88. Matthew Page Andrews, *The Dixie Book of Days* (J. B. Lippincott, 1912); *The American's Creed and Its Meaning* (Doubleday, Page, 1919); *History of the United States* (J. B. Lippincott, 1914); *A Heritage of Freedom: The Political Ideals of the English-Speaking Peoples* (George H. Doran, 1918); *The Women of the South in War Times* (Norman, Remington, 1920); *The Soul of a Nation: The Founding of Virginia and the Projection of New England* (C. Scribner's Sons, 1943).

89. A monthly publication of the English-Speaking Union, the *Landmark* looked to improve "the knowledge of one another possessed by the English-speaking peoples. The English-Speaking Union aims at no formal alliances; it has nothing to do with governments, but is merely an attempt to promote good fellowship among the English-speaking democracies of the world." https://babel.hathitrust.org/cgi/pt?id =inu.30000093219271;view=1up;seq=12. "The Repudiated Reconstruction Debts of Some Southern States," *Manufacturers' Record* 91, no. 12 (March 24, 1927): 45–46; "The Repudiated Reconstruction Debts of Some Southern States," *DBB* 100, no. 11,500 (April 1, 1927): 933–34.

90. "The Repudiated Reconstruction Debts of Some Southern States," 933–34.

91. Namely, Alabama, Arkansas, Florida, Georgia, Louisiana, Mississippi, North Carolina, and South Carolina. "Appeal to Congress on Defaulted Bonds," *New York Times*, February 18, 1927, 12; "Britons Ask Confederate Debt Payment," *China Press*, February 12, 1928, 7.

92. "English Bondholders Fighting for Payment of Repudiated Bonds," *Manufacturers' Record* 91, no. 15 (April 14, 1927): 58–59.

93. "English Bondholders Fighting for Payment of Repudiated Bonds," 58–59.

94. "The Repudiated Reconstruction Debts of Some Southern States," 933–34.

95. "Old Repudiated Debts That Stir the British," *New York Times*, August 10, 1930, X12; Philip Hampson, "Happy Days Budgets Now Full of Grief," *Chicago Daily Tribune*, April 17, 1932, A9.

96. Du Bois, *Black Reconstruction*, 2–3, 7.

97. Stephanie Jones-Rodgers, *They Were Her Property: White Women as Slave Owners in the American South* (New York: Oxford University Press, 2019), xiii, 102.

98. Du Bois, *Black Reconstruction*, 9.

99. Tera W. Hunter, *To 'Joy My Freedom: Southern Black Women's Lives and Labors after the Civil War* (Cambridge, Mass.: Harvard University Press, 1997), 54, 60.

100. James Boggs, *The American Revolution: Pages from a Negro Worker's Notebook* (New York: Monthly Review Press, 1963), 34–35; Michael C. Dawson, "Then and Now: On Racial Capitalism and Racial Conflict," *SSRC Items Series* (November 2016), https://items.ssrc.org/reading-racial-conflict/then-now-on-racial-capitalism -and-racial-conflict/.

CHAPTER 8

DEAD LABOR

On Racial Capital and Fossil Capital

RYAN CECIL JOBSON

By means of its conversion into an automaton, the instrument of labor confronts the laborer, during the labor-process, in the shape of capital, of dead labor, that dominates, and pumps dry, living labor-power.

—Karl Marx, *Capital*, Vol. 1

Out of the exploitation of the dark proletariat comes the Surplus Value filched from human beasts which, in cultured lands, the Machine and harnessed power veil and conceal.

—W. E. B. Du Bois, *Black Reconstruction in America, 1860–1880*

A Story of the Economic Development of Inanimate Things

Alongside his many titles, W. E. B. Du Bois is a critical theorist of energy, race, and capital. In his personal papers, archived at the University of Massachusetts, Amherst, a handwritten note dated to 1925 reads as follows: "A story of the economic development of inanimate things—land, coal, steel, etc., in which men are things" (figure 8.1). The note is not attributed to a specific manuscript. In fact, when weighed against his expansive oeuvre, the story to which the fragment refers could reasonably assume the form of historical narrative, personal memoir, sociological treatise, or speculative fiction.

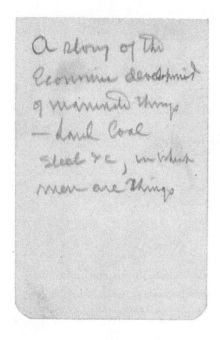

8.1 "A story of the economic development of inanimate things—land, coal, steel, etc., in which men are things" (1925).

W. E. B. Du Bois Papers (MS 312), Special Collections and University Archives, University of Massachusetts, Amherst

As Adrienne Brown and Britt Rusert observe, Du Bois indulged literature as a leisure activity and a professional enterprise, often using "fiction to test out and amplify his developing philosophical and sociological positions."[1]

It requires a leap in logic and historiography to conclude that the story he conceived in 1925 culminated in his *magnum opus* published a decade later, *Black Reconstruction in America, 1860–1880*. Rather than insist on a definite link between them, however, I consider what can be derived from the later manuscript when read against the fragment from his private archive. In other words, to what extent does *Black Reconstruction* constitute a story of the economic development of inanimate things, and how does this alter conventional understandings of its contributions to the study of race and capital?

In the years surrounding the publication of *Black Reconstruction*, Du Bois grew increasingly preoccupied with the science of carbon-based fuels and the labor enlisted for their extraction. In February 1932, he ventured to Harlan County, Kentucky, where he observed the violent repression of striking coal miners by private security forces and law enforcement. The scene struck an already seasoned Du Bois, who confided that he had never encountered "so much persecution, so much constant repression, ruthlessness, brutality, and utter disregard of human life and property" in his sixty-four years.[2]

As political scientist Timothy Mitchell observes, the expansion of coal in the second half of the nineteenth century produced a specialized class of labor that governed the production of energy. While this endowed labor with an unprecedented ability to disrupt channels of distribution and exact concessions from private capital and state authorities, it also threatened to conceal this essential labor in enclaves far removed from the blinkered landscape of cities and industrial centers.[3] Du Bois sought to remedy this distance in his writings. In an October 1936 column for the *Pittsburgh Courier*, he reviewed the collections of the German Museum in Munich, reserving special praise for its instructional facsimile of a coal mine and survey of the evolution of hauling techniques, from elementary manual hauling to the steam and electric methods of his contemporaries. Perhaps lamenting the suppression of the striking workers in Harlan County, he opined, "We know, of course, how much we depend on coal and iron and salt and metals. . . . But how many people see and know about a coal mine?"[4]

Appearing less than a year after the initial publication of *Black Reconstruction*, Du Bois's contribution to the *Courier* offers a window into his preoccupations at a moment of world energy transition. His praise for the museum display, in which visitors "penetrate story after story until you are four or five stories under the ground," provides an instructive foil for the narrative structure of *Black Reconstruction*.[5] In *Black Reconstruction*, Du Bois posits the foreclosure of Reconstruction democracy as the foundation of "a new feudalism based on monopoly . . . in raw material, in copper, iron, oil and coal."[6] Ephemeral items from his papers further underscore this concern. Presaging his argument in the monograph's fourteenth chapter, "Counter-Revolution of Property," a hand-sketched graph dated to 1933 charts the exponential rise in U.S. coal, iron, cotton, and tobacco production from 1860 to 1930 (figure 8.2). Looking backward from a global economic depression, Du Bois turned to the history of Reconstruction for a diagnostic of his political present.

Penned at a moment when carbon-based fuels began to dominate the U.S. energy complex, *Black Reconstruction* offers an early contribution to the study of "fossil capital" that enjoys greater purchase in the contemporary moment of anthropogenic climate change.[7] Recent studies of this ilk, however, either neglect the genealogies of race and capital offered by Du Bois and his interlocutors or limit an engagement with racial capital to an epoch of chattel slavery prior to the advent of fossil energy. In *Black Reconstruction*, Du Bois resists this tendency by narrating the history of capital as a

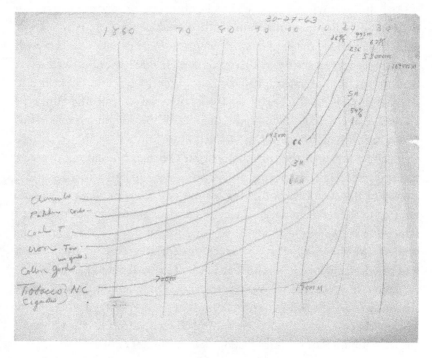

8.2 "Goods production, 1933."

W. E. B. Du Bois Papers (MS 312), Special Collections and University Archives, University of Massachusetts, Amherst

racialized production of dead labor in which dynamic human labor is reduced to instrumental labor power.

Following Marx, all capital is extracted from human labor: "*Capital is dead labor* which, vampire-like, lives only by sucking living labor, and lives the more, the more labor it sucks."[8] As a concept, dead labor attunes us to the "dominance of past, materialized, accumulated labor over immediate living labor."[9] Even so, the relationship between dead labor and living labor is mediated by a racial calculus that Du Bois elaborates in his archetypal formulations of "the black worker" and "the white worker." In what follows, I frame *Black Reconstruction* as a history of fossil capital. As a story of the economic development of inanimate things, *Black Reconstruction* demonstrates how the production of coal and oil came to be narratively detached from prior accumulations of dead labor that consolidated the spoils of plantation slavery in the form of capital and the machine. Heeding Du Bois, the imperative of fossil capital to replace living labor with dead labor is secured alongside a false premise in which the white and black worker comprise ontologically distinct categories of labor—a fiction enforced by antiblack violence and the dispensation of a public and psychological wage of whiteness. But as Du Bois reminds us, to accept this premise uncritically is a fatal error.

Racial Capital / Fossil Capital

The indivisible histories of slavery and capitalism are at once histories of energy. The historical formation of the proletariat—the forcible separation of humans from their means of subsistence and reproduction—constitutes the foundational gambit of capital, which Marx christens as "so-called primitive accumulation." Yet, as careful readers of Marx demonstrate, this process is not confined to a foundational moment of colonial violence and expropriation.[10] Indeed, this violence of "war capitalism" persists in efforts to compel living labor to emulate the qualities of dead labor as inert and machinelike.[11] The transmutation of dynamic human labor into instrumental labor power, then, is one in which human labor is rendered in thermodynamic terms as a reserve of potential energy.[12]

But this subjection of labor is never total. For this reason, Karl Polanyi classifies human labor alongside land and money as "fictitious commodities" whose aims are to "annihilate all organic forms of existence and to replace them by a different type of organization, an atomistic and individualistic one."[13] Nevertheless, the dictates of capital insist upon treating labor as an uncomplicated commodity, reserves of energy called upon to compete with the spoils of prior labor and the organic remains of prior life—namely, automated machinery and carbon-based fuels.

For Du Bois, this transmutation of labor necessarily begins in the plantation Americas and "the most extreme case of theft of labor that the world can conceive; namely, chattel slavery."[14] Marx likewise maintained the history of so-called primitive accumulation as one of racial capital. In an oft-cited passage, Marx opines: "The discovery of gold and silver in America, the extirpation, enslavement and entombment in the mines of the aboriginal population, the beginning of the conquest and plunder of India, the conversion of Africa into a preserve for the commercial hunting of blackskins, are all things which characterize the dawn of the era of capitalist production."[15] Despite his insistence that racial violence constitutes the basis of a capitalist mode of production, select cohorts of Marxist critics have relegated the production of race to a moment either prior to or constitutively outside of capitalism, which is eclipsed by the formation of an undifferentiated working class comprised of free labor. Or, in the eyes of political Marxists such as Robert Brenner and Ellen Meiksins Wood, the centrality of the colonial theater is disputed and the English countryside is recast as the staging ground for the historical genesis of the proletariat. By this account, proletarian labor is necessarily free labor and emerges concurrent with, but independent from, chattel slavery.

Recent works in the new history of capitalism echo earlier scholarly treatments of slavery and capitalism in their challenge to prescribed metropolitan narratives of the origin of capitalism. Narratives of the latter sort, however, have found renewed conceptual purchase in an emergent body of criticism loosely assembled under the banner of "fossil capital." Although the ideological leanings of its chief architects are by no means uniform, their writings are united in their framing of fossil capital as a distinct and unprecedented epoch in the history of capitalism. As Andreas Malm puts it, "industrial capital hinges upon a popular exodus from the countryside," in which "the fossil fuel of coal was coupled to the machine through the rise of stationary steam power in the mills of Britain."[16] Steam, rather than slavery, is offered as the decisive variable in the genesis of the industrial capitalist. Companion texts, including Mitchell's *Carbon Democracy*, refuse an explicit fidelity to political Marxism but nonetheless stop short of a substantive engagement with histories of race and capital. My intention is not to dispute the value of this literature, but to offer a critical addendum. In doing so, I follow Du Bois in my contention that any genealogy of fossil capital necessarily departs from an earlier moment in which human labor was first rendered in thermodynamic terms as labor *power*—a productive machine fated to compete with nonhuman machines.

The slave is the original expression of human labor as labor power. In the form of enslaved labor, the black worker was transfigured as pure labor power divorced of all human characteristics. It is this premise—of labor as a genuine rather than a fictitious commodity—on which the category of wage labor is later elaborated. As Marx puts it, "the veiled slavery of the wage workers in Europe needed for its pedestal, slavery pure and simple in the new world."[17] Race, in other words, amounts to more than an unscrupulous plot devised by propertied classes *ex post facto* to drive a wedge between segments of an otherwise uniform working class. Rather, race supplies the premise on which select classes of labor are appraised for their thermodynamic capacity for work, rather than their material needs and creative potential.

Marx cautions us to distrust accounts of original accumulation that laud the spendthrift and ingenuity of the industrialist in his fortuitous inheritance of the means of production. Rather, the cult of private ownership is a product of deception such that in "the tender annals of political economy, the idyllic reigns from time immemorial."[18] The perpetuation of fossil capital is made possible by a context in which human labor is regarded as machine-like and the dead labor accumulated as capital and machinery is regarded as the natural province of private property. The victory of capital in the age of carbon energy was not guaranteed. After all, fossil fuels held the potential to emancipate labor rather than further its subjugation. It is only when human labor is taken for granted as an inert reserve of energy and work that the spoils of fossil capital are narratively detached from the prior accumulations, or dead labor, on which they depend.

The Old History of Fossil Capital

The burgeoning literature on fossil capital, epitomized by Malm's monograph of the same title, attributes the production of an undifferentiated and atomized class of proletarian labor to the rise of steam power and fossil fuels. In *Fossil Capital*, Malm traces the historically contingent origins of a fossil economy characterized by "a cementation of fossil fuel–based technologies, deflecting alternatives and obstructing policies of climate change mitigation: a poisoned fruit of history." The question at the heart of this narrative, then, is how potentially labor-saving technologies of carbon-fueled automation came to serve the interests of capital rather than of labor. For Malm, the answer lies in steam. While hydropower was easily accessible, less capital intensive, and more sustainable, it did not suit the requirements of capital. It was not "stock" energy; it could not be stored and accumulated in private reserves. Steam, on the other hand, lent itself to a "division and organisation of labour that we recognise as typically capitalist . . . a certain cast of capitalists and workers, foremen and assistants." Malm reasons that coal-fired steam engines occasioned the spatial and temporal characteristics that water could not: "The engine was a superior medium for extracting surplus wealth from the working class, because, unlike the waterwheel, it could be put up practically anywhere. . . . Conditioned by the properties of the landscape, supplies of moving water were found only in some places; impossible to detach from the surface of the earth."[19] In its reliance on stocks of carbon-based energy that could be transported from country to city, capital was liberated from the strictures of absolute space. Striving for an ever "greater annihilation of space by time," steam liberated capital from its reliance on spatially contingent reserves and created new impediments to subversion by organized labor.[20]

Malm entices us with a passage from *The Poverty of Philosophy*: "The hand-mill gives you society with the feudal lord; the steam-mill society with the industrial capitalist." He later adduces, "steam begets capital—not the other way around."[21] Although Malm successfully demonstrates how steam was called upon to serve the basic objectives of capital accumulation, he does not sufficiently justify steam as a worthy point of origin. Akin to his political Marxist compatriots, Malm lionizes Marx in certain instances while discarding elements that, even if they do not disprove, would necessarily complicate his thesis. In this respect, Malm's analysis is not incorrect, but incomplete. Malm observes that the "diffusion [of self-acting machinery] in the cotton industry would coincide with a general revolution in energy use: the triumphal procession of the self-acting mule—or the 'Iron Man', as it would be known among the operatives—was also that of steam."[22] But what "revolution" was necessary to generate the raw material, the cotton, required to make this development possible in the first instance?

Thanks to black critiques of political economy, there is little occasion to rehearse critiques of political Marxism that posit the centrality of Atlantic slavery to the rise of modern industrial capitalism.[23] Scholars in this tradition return to Marx to demonstrate that the colonial Americas served as a principal theater of primitive accumulation in which the forced and unrequited labor of enslaved Africans generated the necessary injection of capital and raw materials that culminated in the industrial revolutions of the North Atlantic. In tandem with the concluding chapters of *Capital*, Volume 1, Marx's 1846 letter to Pavel Annenkov is where he advanced this argument in clearest terms: "Without slavery there would be no cotton, without cotton there would be no modern industry. It is slavery which has given value to the colonies, it is the colonies which have created world trade, and world trade is the necessary condition for large-scale machine industry."[24]

Despite renewed attention to this passage, it is my contention that this observation is not limited to the expropriation of land and raw materials via chattel slavery, but extends to the production of unprecedented and distinctly racialized subjects as the ideal form of commoditized labor power. Whereas the "new histories of capitalism" and their discontents focus their competing claims on the question of whether slavery was essential to the rise of the Industrial Revolution in Europe, my objective in this essay is not to substantiate or repudiate this thesis. In turning attention to colonial theaters of proletarianization as the foundation of racial capital, I am less interested here in the extent to which slavery generated the requisite productive surplus to supply English textile factories than I am in the production of racial laboring subjects that underwrite the fossil economy of the present.

Mintz reminds us that the distinction between the plantation slave and the proletarian is one of appearance rather than substance: "Like proletarians, slaves are separated from the means of production; but of course, it is not that they have nothing but their labor to sell. Rather, they are *themselves* commodities . . . they themselves appear to be a form of capital, though they are human beings."[25] The plantation slave, then, is the figure in which the fictitious commodification of human labor appears and is accepted as total. Under this false projection, the slave is pure labor power, an ideal type against which the category of free labor is later elaborated. When Malm describes the expropriation of the commons in the English countryside as a historical process in which "ex-farmers and ex-artisans no longer own anything but a capacity to perform labour, or labour power, naked and unequipped, a mere potential screaming for tools with which to work," he unfortunately neglects the ways chattel slavery provided a staging ground for the subsequent degradation of free labor.[26]

Malm's framework resonates with our present conjuncture of expanded and unconventional fossil-fuel extraction, disputes over pipelines, and heightened frequency and intensity of adverse climatic impacts. His framework is not wrongheaded so much as it is belated. Rather, it is my hope that a revision to his genealogy of proletarianization, one that departs from the plantation Americas rather than the British countryside, will generate new insights into a theory of fossil capital. In the most basic terms, *Fossil Capital* is impoverished by a perspective in which raw material and machine, but not the human, can be reduced to property. With this in mind, we might recall that this imperative of capital reaches its highest form in the black worker as "the ultimate exploited . . . that mass of labor which has neither power to escape from labor status, in order to directly exploit other laborers, or indirectly, by alliance with capital, to share in their exploitation."[27]

Race Against the Machine

In the "Fragment on Machines" from the *Grundrisse*, Marx imagines mechanical automation as a harbinger of the end of capitalist work and the emancipation of labor from wage slavery. In this instance, the surplus of prior labor fixed in capital and machinery creates the conditions for "the general reduction of the necessary labour of society to a minimum."[28] Yet he cautions that this could be achieved only through the abolition of private property. Under the dictates of capital, machinery instead degrades labor, as living labor is "cast merely as its conscious linkages" in a matrix of automated production.[29]

Malm regards the steam engine similarly. His is not a technologically deterministic narrative of fossil capital. Instead, he is motivated by "the question of the steam engine . . . the question of why it was adopted and diffused."[30] While coal and the steam engine may have supported the immediate interests of capital better than the water mill, Malm awards less consideration to the organization of labor under steam. What explains the persistence of capital under a fossil economy?

Du Bois supplies an answer in his history of Reconstruction in the United States. Indeed, at this moment, "the opportunity for real and new democracy in America was broad." Dispensing with the idealist propositions of nineteenth-century liberalism, Du Bois insists that genuine democracy would involve a comprehensive reparations. Here, the demand for land is fundamental: "to have given each one of the million Negro free families a forty-acre freehold would have made a basis of real democracy in the United States that might easily have transformed the modern world."[31]

The specter of automation haunts the narrative of *Black Reconstruction*. In the chapter "Counter-Revolution of Property," Du Bois uncovers how a new regime of racial capital thwarted the march toward this real and new democracy. During the transition from an economy dominated by enslaved labor to one of nominally free labor, working-class consciousness across racial lines threatened to raise the "question as to whom this wealth was to belong and for whose interests laborers were to work."[32] The liminal period of Reconstruction, then, was a pivotal one in which the endurance of private property could not be guaranteed. The emancipation of enslaved peoples abolished one regime of chattel property, and the new political subjects it produced posed an imminent challenge to the dictatorship of property in general.

For Du Bois, the foreclosure of the question of property redistribution and its eventual abolition hinges fundamentally on the fossil economy.

Writing in the throes of the Great Depression, Du Bois enjoyed the luxury of hindsight in his historical treatment of the abolition of slavery and the dawn of a new epoch of capital in the United States. By 1930, domestic fossil-fuel consumption—including coal, natural gas, and petroleum—had reached a number thirty-three times greater than in 1865. Under the genuine democracy that the end of Reconstruction foreclosed, this new fossil economy held the potential to further emancipate labor from the dictates of capital.

But it was not to be. The corrupt end of Reconstruction in the United States was a world historical event. It did not simply foreclose the possibility of democracy under the guardianship of a unified working class through crude racial violence that served to suppress the black vote and to embolden segments of white workers across the South. It enabled the persistence of private property and the dominance of capital over labor through what Du Bois describes at several junctures as either a "new feudalism," a "new imperialism," or a "new enslavement of labor." As he writes:

> Far from turning toward any conception of dictatorship of the proletariat, of surrendering power either into the hands of labor or the trustees of labor, the new plan was to concentrate into a trusteeship of capital a new and far-reaching power which would dominate the government of the United States. This was not a petty bourgeois development, following the overthrow of agrarian feudalism in the South. It was, on the contrary, a new feudalism based on monopoly—but not monopoly of the agricultural possibilities of the land so much as of its wealth in raw material, in copper, iron, oil and coal, particularly monopoly of the transportation of these commodities on new public iron roads privately sequestered, and finally, of the manufacture of goods by new machines and privileged technique.[33]

How, then, was labor consigned to this "new feudalism," in which living labor was once again forced to compete irrevocably with the residual surplus of its predecessors? Marx tenders a clue when he asserts that "past labor always disguises itself as capital."[34] However, Du Bois reminds us that it is the projection of enslaved people as laboring machines that first permits their labor to be disguised as capital. The subjection of labor to capital under a fossil economy can only be guaranteed if labor is treated as machinelike—in which *men are things*. That Du Bois opens *Black Reconstruction* with a chapter titled "The Black Worker" rather than "The Plantation Slave" provides us with the clearest evidence of this thesis. Lifting the veil on the proverbial secret of primitive accumulation, Du Bois refuses to conflate the appearance of plantation slaves as "a series of investments in fixed capital" with the fact of "the Negro . . . [as] an average and ordinary human being."[35]

For Du Bois, the treatment of the black worker *qua* plantation slave as fixed capital—or, *dead labor*—is a distortion of their status as an ordinary human being in service of the accumulation of surplus value. At present, the dilemma facing black studies involves whether to more thoroughly occupy this distortion or to demystify its troubled origins. Not only did black workers generate the surplus value fixed in the machine that they would later be forced into competition with, but they also served as the "founding stone of a new economic system" in which free labor is also degraded. In *Black Reconstruction*, Du Bois disputes that the black worker is unthinkable as an ordinary worker, rather than as a fixed capital investment. It is only by approaching the slave as the black worker—and analytically, as equivalent with the proletarian—that we can avoid the hazards of this illusion that beleaguered organized labor and provided the conditions necessary for the defeat of Reconstruction democracy by fossil capital.

The enslavement of African peoples constituted the broadest effort to consolidate stores of energy under private ownership. This fact should serve as a cogent reminder that the private ownership of energy necessitates extractive violence, whether the source of that energy is fossil fuels, the harnessed energy of solar, wind, or water, or human labor power. A principal feature of capitalism is the imperative to reduce the creative capacities of human labor to the thermodynamic principles of human labor power. As philosopher Amy Wendling puts it, "In the paradigm of production, the body is reconceived as a productive machine, and, as such, a unit whose contribution to the production process comes in the form of measurable work."[36] On the plantations of the Americas, labor was first conceived of in these terms. The plantation is the origin ground of machine fetishism, in which the surplus value generated by machinelike human labor came to be regarded as the exclusive property of planter-capitalists. In turn, our critique of capital cannot proceed from a critique of the peculiar forms of capital forged under the fossil economy. Any alternative to capital must necessarily proceed on the basis of a critique of racial capital that refuses to cast human labor in thermodynamic terms; that is, as a mere linkage in a matrix of automated production. Du Bois takes this as his starting point when he reanimates the labor of the black worker not as dead labor but in its highest expression of political potential: the general strike.

The defeat of Reconstruction foreclosed the potential for radical democracy not only in the United States, but the world over.[37] Du Bois reminds us that its tragic defeat was not inevitable. The refusal to treat the black worker as a worker, or more fundamentally as an ordinary human being, signaled that this defeat was imminent. Subsequently, "the United States was turned into a reactionary force. It became the cornerstone of that new imperialism which is subjecting the labor of yellow, brown, and black peoples to the dictation of capitalism organized on a world basis; and it has not only brought nearer the revolution by which the power of capitalism is to be challenged, but also it is transforming the fight to the sinister aspect of a fight on racial lines embittered by awful memories."[38] As a historian of capital, Du Bois demonstrates how contingent relations of production came to be understood as timeless and inevitable consequences of racial difference. In turn, the present conjuncture of fossil capital, in which human labor power is further displaced by the bounty of prior accumulations of capital—namely, industrial technologies and extractive fuels—can only be understood alongside constitutively older histories of racial capital.

Therefore, when Sven Beckert and Seth Rockman draw a parallel between the plantation economy and the fossil economy, in which "enslaved workers grew the cotton that made the United States into the nineteenth-century version of what Saudi Arabia would become with respect to oil in the twentieth,"[39] I want to extend the observation a step further to demonstrate that such contexts are not merely analogous but genealogically linked. Race not only pervades the labor regimes of contemporary extractive ventures[40] but permits the fruits of prior labor to be consolidated under the private domain of multinational capitalists and elite state actors. On the backs of the black worker arose "a new capitalism and a new enslavement of labor" founded in the dictatorship of capital, private property, and a monopoly over the resources that would come to define the age of fossil fuels.[41]

Instructively, racial capitalism has found renewed purchase in a series of festschrifts for the work of Cedric Robinson and his most widely engaged work, *Black Marxism: The Making of the Black Radical Tradition.* Unfortunately, this renaissance is tempered by misguided readings of racial capitalism as a peculiar variant of capitalism in general. In Robinson's account, all capitalism is necessarily racial capitalism in that its fundamental "tendency . . . [is] not to homogenize but to differentiate—to exaggerate regional, subcultural, and dialectical differences into 'racial' ones."[42] As such, he does not presuppose an unchanging ontology of racial difference. On the contrary, racial capitalism incorporates dynamic regimes of accumulation driven by technologies of putatively racial differentiation. With an eye toward Robinson's original intent, I return to the extractive calculus of racial capital to trouble the totalizing suffix attached to racial capitalism. Rather than an economic system defined by a fixed logic of racial difference, racial capital attunes us to the always contingent relations of race, capital, and extraction that pervade ongoing regimes of accumulation by dispossession.

That racial capital exceeds the normative categories of bourgeois or Marxist political economy does not endorse the dubious conclusion that "work is a white category."[43] In fact, to do so is to be complicit in purging the uncredited labor of the dead from memory. The exploitation of black labor is neither natural nor invariable. As such, we must avoid an analytical conflation in which we consider the black worker as nothing more than dead labor in the same fashion as planters' logs and accounting ledgers. Indeed, the dead lurk among us in the capital and machines extracted from the labor of prior generations: "we suffer not only from the living, but from the dead."[44] Our task after Du Bois is no less than a redoubled critique of political economy. It is to reanimate the accumulated labor that sits frozen in the form of surplus capital and machinery. As such, the concept of social death describes a material relation, not an ontological condition.[45] Or more precisely, social death indexes a material relation between living labor and dead labor—in which the latter preys ever more completely upon the former—that deceptively appears as an ontological predicament.

We have not eclipsed racial capital. Racial capital forms the contractual basis on which fossil capital came to pervade the extractive complexes of the twentieth and twenty-first centuries. Fossil capital continues to rest on a racial logic that, as Peter Hudson reminds us, "dislodges the pretension of a universal working-class subject, who is invariably white."[46] Yet, when confronted with an oil rig, a nuclear cooling tower, or a wind farm, scholars of energy armed with attendant neologisms—the Anthropocene, Capitalocene, and fossil economy—are eager to allow racial capital to fall out of view. In *Black Reconstruction*, Du Bois demonstrates the fixed capital of machinery and the dead labor of surplus capital supplanted the possibility of real and genuine democracy after emancipation. Indeed, it is the failure of Reconstruction that gave rise to this new imperialism in which the very capacity to imagine democratic futures is beholden to the expansion of carbon energy. It was a "splendid failure," however, because the history of Reconstruction demonstrates that another future was, and is, possible.[47]

NOTES

1. W. E. B. Du Bois, Adrienne Brown, and Britt Rusert, "The Princess Steel," *PMLA* 130, no. 3 (May 2015): 819–29 (819).
2. David Levering Lewis, *W. E. B. Du Bois: 1919–1963: The Fight for Equality* (New York: Henry Holt, 2000), 296.
3. Timothy Mitchell, *Carbon Democracy: Political Power in the Age of Oil* (London: Verso, 2011), 19.
4. W. E. B. Du Bois, "56: Forum of Fact and Opinion," in *Newspaper Columns by W. E. B. Du Bois*, Vol. 1, *1883–1944*, ed. Herbert Aptheker (White Plains, N.Y.: Kraus-Thomson, 1986), 120.
5. Du Bois, "56," 120.
6. W. E. B. Du Bois, *Black Reconstruction in America, 1860–1880* (New York: Free Press, [1935] 1998), 583.
7. See Andreas Malm, *Fossil Capital: The Rise of Steam Power and the Roots of Global Warming* (London: Verso, 2016).
8. Karl Marx, *Capital*, Vol. 1, *A Critique of Political Economy*, trans. Ben Fowkes (New York: Penguin Classics, 1990), 342 (emphasis added).
9. Salvatore Veca, "Value, Labor and the Critique of Political Economy," *Telos* 1971, no. 9 (Fall 1971): 48–64 (48).
10. Silvia Federici, *Caliban and the Witch* (Brooklyn, N.Y.: Autonomedia, 2004); David Harvey, *The New Imperialism* (Oxford: Oxford University Press, 2003); Nikhil Pal Singh, "On Race, Violence, and So-Called Primitive Accumulation," *Social Text* 34, no. 3 (September 2016): 27–50.
11. Sven Beckert, *Empire of Cotton: A Global History* (New York: Vintage, 2014).
12. Amy Wendling, *Karl Marx on Technology and Alienation* (New York: Palgrave Macmillan, 2009).
13. Karl Polanyi, *The Great Transformation: The Political and Economic Origins of Our Time* (Boston: Beacon, [1944] 2001), 171.
14. Du Bois, *Black Reconstruction*, 604.
15. Marx, *Capital*, Vol. 1, 915.
16. Malm, *Fossil Capital*, 298, 16.
17. Marx, *Capital*, Vol. 1, 925.
18. Marx, *Capital*, Vol. 1, 874.
19. Malm, *Fossil Capital*, 7, 33, 124.
20. Karl Marx, *Grundrisse: Foundations of the Critique of Political Economy* (London: Penguin, [1939] 1993), 539. Here, Malm lends a worthy preamble to Mitchell's musings of the material properties of coal and oil, in which the relatively light and malleable properties of oil permitted greater ease of transport across long distances and undermined the capacity for labor to disrupt production and articulate broader claims for social and economic justice. See also Mitchell, *Carbon Democracy*.
21. Marx cited in Malm, *Fossil Capital*, 32, 33.
22. Malm, *Fossil Capital*, 66.

23. Peter James Hudson, "The Racist Dawn of Capitalism," *Boston Review*, March 2016, http://bostonreview.net/books-ideas/peter-james-hudson-slavery-capitalism.

24. Letter from Marx to Pavel Vasilyevich Annenkov in *Karl Marx, Frederick Engels: Collected Works*, Vol. 38, trans. Peter Ross and Betty Ross (New York: International Publishers, [1846] 1975).

25. Sidney W. Mintz, "Was the Plantation Slave a Proletarian?," *Review (Fernand Braudel Center)* 2, no. 1 (Summer 1978): 81–98 (90).

26. Malm, *Fossil Capital*, 280.

27. Du Bois, *Black Reconstruction*, 15.

28. Marx, *Grundrisse*, 706.

29. Marx, *Grundrisse*, 692.

30. Malm, *Fossil Capital*, 17.

31. Du Bois, *Black Reconstruction*, 17, 591, 602.

32. Du Bois, *Black Reconstruction*, 591.

33. Du Bois, *Black Reconstruction*, 583.

34. Marx, *Capital*, Vol. 1, 757.

35. Tomich cited in Mintz, "Was the Plantation Slave a Proletarian?," 91; Du Bois, *Black Reconstruction*, xix.

36. Wendling, *Karl Marx on Technology and Alienation*, 64.

37. On the relevance of Du Bois's *Black Reconstruction* to the study of Latin America and the Caribbean, see Jason P. McGraw, "A Tropical Reconstruction," *Labor* 12, no. 4 (December 2015): 29–32.

38. Du Bois, *Black Reconstruction*, 631.

39. Sven Beckert and Seth Rockman, eds., *Slavery's Capitalism: A New History of American Economic Development* (Philadelphia: University of Pennsylvania Press, 2016), 13.

40. See Hannah Appel, *The Licit Life of Capitalism: US Oil in Equatorial Guinea* (Durham, N.C.: Duke University Press, 2019).

41. Du Bois, *Black Reconstruction*, 634.

42. Cedric J. Robinson, *Black Marxism: The Making of the Black Radical Tradition* (Chapel Hill: University of North Carolina Press, [1983] 2000), 26.

43. Frank Wilderson III, "Gramsci's Black Marx: Whither the Slave in Civil Society?," *Social Identities* 9, no. 2 (2003): 225–40 (238).

44. Marx, *Capital*, Vol. 1, 91.

45. In a new preface to *Slavery and Social Death*, Orlando Patterson underscores social death as a historical, rather than ontological, condition: "Social death was not a theory I imposed upon the historical realities of slavery. It is there screaming in the facts of life under slavery for any historian who cares to look with eyes unfiltered by agentic romance." Orlando Patterson, *Slavery and Social Death: A Comparative Study* (Cambridge, Mass.: Harvard University Press, [1982] 2018), xiv.

46. Peter James Hudson, "Racial Capitalism and the Dark Proletariat," *Boston Review*, February 2018, 64.

47. Du Bois, *Black Reconstruction*, 708.

CHAPTER 9

"THEY SPEAK OUR LANGUAGE . . . BUSINESS"

Latinx Businesspeople and the Pursuit of Wealth in New York City

PEDRO A. REGALADO

In April 1982, Banco Popular de Puerto Rico published an advertisement in the *New York Times* showing Johnny Torres, the owner of Metro Spanish Food Wholesalers (Metro) in the South Bronx. Cross-armed, in formal attire, and in front of his products, Torres mused, "In 1966, we saw an opportunity to create a wholesale food distribution cooperative to supply the many small grocery stores that serve New York's Hispanic community." He added, "[Banco Popular] listened and provided us with funds for a 1,000-square-foot warehouse and inventory. They kept on listening as we grew to 5,000, 7,500, 15,000, 25,000, and finally 40,000 square feet today."[1]

Together, Banco Popular and Metro weathered the shift from the urban liberalism of the 1960s to the fiscal conservatism of the 1970s with great success. By 1980, Banco Popular boasted nearly a dozen branches in New York City while Metro became one of the twenty-five largest Latinx businesses in the country.[2] Torres, whose enterprise supplied the hundreds of *bodegas* that dotted New York's cityscape, would have experienced great difficulty in expanding his company if not for Banco Popular's loans, especially in an economically slumped metropolis where Latinx-owned ventures garnered little backing from the city's major banks. In a pun that alluded to the ethnic and economic bonds uniting Metro and Banco Popular, Torres concluded, "They speak our language . . . business."[3]

Since Cedric Robinson published *Black Marxism*, scholars have generally associated racial capitalism with plunder, theft, dispossession, and enslavement.[4] It has largely been a story of white people, or white-people-in-the-making, using various expressions of structural, state, and bodily violence to accumulate wealth and to unload risk onto other racialized groups.[5] Expanding this formulation, this chapter traces how, beginning in the 1960s, an elite group of Latinx businesspeople—such as Banco Popular's executives and the large Latinx-owned businesses they supported—embraced capitalism, both as the sword that would lead toward upward economic mobility and the shield that would ostensibly insulate their communities from the racialized consequences of urban decline and rapid deindustrialization.

High rates of poverty and unemployment plagued most African American and Latinx New Yorkers during the 1970s.[6] Their lives were worsened when the municipal response to the city's 1975 fiscal crisis included laying off thousands of public workers, raising transportation fares, and turning toward a privatization agenda that deteriorated public infrastructure.[7] Even so, the evolving alliance of banking executives and business owners explored in this chapter yielded unprecedented profit and power for New York's emergent Latinx elite. It argues that they did so by taking advantage of, and helping to develop, a political culture that promoted business-oriented solutions to the concentrated poverty of rapidly growing Latinx neighborhoods, including those in the South Bronx. Beginning with Banco Popular's first bank branch in the borough in 1961, Latinx business communities and their advocates worked at the federal and local levels to secure subsidies for nonwhite-owned businesses and to leverage favorable lending terms for start-up business owners like Johnny Torres. The success of this cohort set an important new precedent for Latinx New Yorkers. By the 1980s, elected officials, including Mayor Ed Koch, increasingly extended funding and government appointments to Latinx residents contingent on their adherence to notions of empowerment that emphasized individual ability, "financial knowhow," and the goal of escaping poverty over upending its causes. In turn, New York's elite Latinx businesspeople (a group of mostly men) often facilitated the defunding of social service programs, crowding out nonelite individuals and community organizations that did not trumpet business ownership as the primary vehicle for Latinx urban revitalization.

The story of Latinx entrepreneurship, read in conjunction with emergent literature on black capitalism, broadens our usual ways of charting racial capitalism in U.S. cities by demonstrating how an elite network of Latinx Americans capitalized on two pivotal developments during this period: the rapid growth of Latinx immigrants to U.S. cities, including New York, and the national turn toward fiscal conservatism.[8] Far from pulling themselves up by their bootstraps, Latinx capitalists often achieved success thanks to municipal, state, and federal investment in their ventures. In the process, they manipulated the racial malleability of "Hispanicity"—one that disassociated them from African Americans and black Latinxs within their respective communities—to achieve high profits and seize bureaucratic power during an era when the policy options of diverse Latinx national groups became increasingly tied.[9] During the 1980s, Banco Popular and its peers, including New York National Bank, offered banking services to thousands of Latinx residents who formerly had none. At the same time, they produced a municipal politics that positioned the entrepreneurial pursuit of wealth as a vital element of Latinx culture and civic participation locally and nationally.

Banking on Empire

Banco Popular de Puerto Rico's 1961 arrival in New York marked a turning point for the future of Latinx commerce in the city, as well as for Latinx representation and influence in municipal government. However, the commercial bank's "foreign" designation by the New York State Legislature concealed Banco Popular's much longer history of collaboration with U.S. lawmakers. Beginning in the early twentieth century, their partnership triggered the rapid growth of Banco Popular's lending capital, which, for its part, helped to structure the massive movement of Puerto Ricans away from the island during the post-World War II period.[10]

Banco Popular was established in 1893, when it began focusing on deposits and small loans for the Puerto Rican public.[11] By the 1930s, its executives helped finance some of Puerto Rico's central sugar mills, which were owned by American corporations that implemented a sugar plantation system on the island soon after U.S. colonial occupation.[12] The products they generated often exceeded the yields of other significant sugar-manufacturing states, including Hawai'i, Florida, and Louisiana.[13] The system's vast scale, in turn, conditioned the employment and migration patterns of a large share of Puerto Rican workers, many of whom were displaced from their small landholdings.[14]

Whereas Wall Street banks retreated from the Caribbean in the wake of the Great Depression, Banco Popular capitalized on the shifts in U.S. policy brought about by the New Deal.[15] San Juan residents leafing through the pages of the newspaper *El Mundo* in December 1934, for instance, learned that Banco Popular had been "appointed and authorized to proceed to receive applications and make loans within the terms of Title I of the Congress law known by the National Housing Act."[16] Although the law only allowed Banco Popular to issue loans for home repairs, the Federal Housing Authority (FHA) went further four years later when Congress approved U.S.-backed mortgage loans in Puerto Rico, with Banco Popular at the helm of lending. The agency and the bank were on such close terms that when the FHA established an office in Puerto Rico, it was housed on the seventh floor of Banco Popular's building in the narrow streets of old San Juan.[17] Banco Popular approved 221 loans for homes in its first year of mortgage lending.[18] Still, the vast majority of Puerto Ricans—including those displaced by U.S.-driven transformations to the country's agriculture production—were left out, far from affording even the most modest of the country's newly constructed homes.[19]

Banco Popular's assets continued to grow just as Puerto Ricans increasingly absorbed the shocks of colonial dispossession and macroeconomic transformations.[20] During the 1940s, tens of thousands of residents experiencing high levels of unemployment searched for livelihoods away from the island.[21] By the time the Puerto Rican "Great Migration" to New York subsided in 1960, Gotham's Puerto Rican population had grown by roughly six hundred thousand—a figure that far surpassed the number of residents living in San Juan, Puerto Rico's capital.[22]

The bank's executives soon followed the diaspora, seeking to find their footing in an emerging market that they helped to generate. During the summer of 1961, a state decision enabled Banco Popular to open a new branch in the South Bronx.[23] Despite the Bronx's fraught reputation as an emerging symbol of urban decline, the borough's dense concentration of Puerto Ricans—reinforced by decades of city-sponsored racial and ethnic steering, ranging from the New York City Housing Authority's racially discriminatory practices to urban renewal "slum clearance"—proved bountiful for Banco Popular.[24] Nearly a decade into its venture, the bank boasted more savings accounts at its office in the South Bronx than at any other branch in New York City or any of its sixty-one branches in Puerto Rico.[25] Moreover, 7 to 8 percent of its overall deposits were accounted for by the bank's five New York branches.[26]

The relationships that Banco Popular (and its peer Banco de Ponce) fostered with city officials as a result of its success transformed Latinx representation in local governance. As early as 1964, Mayor Robert Wagner attended the opening ceremony of the bank's new branch, where he told onlookers, "I believe [Banco Popular] will make a great contribution to the welfare of our city as you have to the Commonwealth. We fight shoulder-to-shoulder in the war against poverty."[27] A year later, an assistant to Wagner's successor, John Lindsay, wrote to a Banco de Ponce branch manager requesting the names of employees who might like to be part of the mayor's administration.[28] In 1967, Lindsay enlisted thirty-nine-year-old Puerto Rican Banco Popular branch manager Nick Ortiz as a salaried housing aide when he formed a New York City unit of the Urban Coalition—a body intended to attack the problems of the city's poor nonwhites. Before taking on the new job, Ortiz was the branch manager who had first helped to fund Johnny Torres's Metro Spanish Food Wholesalers in the South Bronx.[29]

At his swearing-in ceremony, Ortiz announced to a crowd of more than two hundred people at City Hall that he sought to "bring the multiple services being offered by the city, state and Federal agencies to ghetto *businessmen*."[30] The city government had deposited four million dollars in African American and Puerto Rican banks (including Banco Popular) earlier that year, expecting that business ownership would multiply in the city's poor neighborhoods of color.[31] When the program fell short of expectations, the Lindsay administration shifted its focus toward training and consulting services for nonwhite entrepreneurs. For Ortiz, the ability "to provide business know-how" was an essential element to the success of Latinx New Yorkers hoping to escape poverty. Moreover, he believed that nonwhite businesspeople were "the only ones that will effectively develop their own business people." He added, "This is how the Puerto Rican has done it in Puerto Rico."[32]

By the end of the 1960s, Banco Popular had successfully steered local government's agenda in its favor through the work of probusiness advocates like Ortiz. According to one business leader, there were approximately ten thousand Latinx businesses in New York City by the time Ortiz was sworn in.[33] Most of them were owned by Puerto Rican New Yorkers; they included small food retail stores called *bodegas*, as well as restaurants, jewelry stores, record shops, beauty salons, and more. Their growth, along with Banco Popular's unexpected economic windfall, signaled to the city's highest-ranking officials—who often perceived Latinx residents as burdensome to postindustrial economic development—that "Spanish-speaking" capitalists were among those best suited to represent the city's racially and nationally diverse Latinx community of roughly 1.2 million in 1970.[34] Meanwhile, this cohort's efforts to become spokespeople for the community were further empowered by the slow eclipse of Great Society programs, which opened greater opportunities for nonwhite entrepreneurs nationwide.

Hispanic Capitalism

Beginning in 1969, a group of Mexican American, Puerto Rican, and Cuban American representatives in President Richard Nixon's administration established "Hispanic" businesspeople as reliable partners in the public-private alliances that prevailed during the 1970s.[35] Similar to Banco Popular officials in New York City, this group became favored for its potential ability to shore up Latinx support for the president's governing agenda while outweighing more progressive claims emanating from the left-wing Puerto Rican and Chicano social movements that had developed during this period. In return, this assemblage of entrepreneurs, politicians, and industrialists normalized the primacy of nonwhite business ownership as a silver bullet for the looming crises of poverty, unemployment, and racial inequity in U.S. cities.

Among other initiatives for Latinx-centered advocacy, the Cabinet Committee on Opportunities for Spanish Speaking People (CCOSSP), created in 1969, was intended to ensure that federal programs reached "all Spanish speaking and Spanish surnamed Americans."[36] Consternation about which Spanish-speaking constituencies would be represented in the CCOSSP abounded among Latinx leaders. After all, their efforts were to prove decisive in constructing a federally recognized Hispanic peoplehood.[37] In a letter to Nixon, Puerto Rico's governor, Luis A. Ferré, emphasized, "A necessary qualification for the new Chairman is that he be favorably oriented toward all Spanish speaking Americans—not just one particular group. It would be a great mistake, for example, if a Mexican-American Chairman were not sufficiently conscious of Puerto Ricans and concerned about them."[38] New York's Puerto Rican congressional representative, Herman Badillo, shared similar sentiments, as did Cuban American officials in Florida, who lamented their lack representation on the committee. These tensions highlighted the important regional differences among Latinx national group constituencies and were at the heart of a collective struggle to shape a top-down notion of Hispanicity—one that, as Neil Foley writes, reached toward an aspirational whiteness that obscured the racial diversity that actually constituted these groups.[39] Ultimately, the CCOSSP's advisory council was comprised of nine individuals (mostly men) of Mexican, Puerto Rican, and Cuban descent.

Given that many of them touted experience in commerce, it was unsurprising that the CCOSSP, in its broad scope, regularly emphasized the importance of the private sector to Latinx social progress. The committee worked closely with federal agencies, including the Small Business Administration (SBA), which made more than two thousand loans totaling nearly $41 million to Latinx businesses in 1971.[40] It similarly partnered with the newly established Office of Minority Business Enterprise (OMBE), which funneled much of the Office of Economic Opportunity's reduced antipoverty budget toward agendas that reinforced the goal of Latinx, and other nonwhite, business ownership.[41] This included funding business resource center offices in cities across the country to provide free technical advice and consulting services for Latinx business owners; providing low-rent leases to Latinx-owned businesses in federal buildings; and helping Latinx contractors secure section 8(a) contracts, bonding, and lines of credit.[42] Present at the OMBE's signing in 1969 was a small group of entrepreneurs including Banco Popular's president Rafael Carrión Jr. and his client, influential South Bronx businessman Johnny Torres, who stood over Nixon's shoulder and whose advertisement would later adorn the pages of the *New York Times*.[43]

According to the administration, the OMBE also played an important role in enabling the creation of eleven new Latinx-owned banks and thirteen Latinx-owned savings and loan corporations in just four years.[44] These banks benefited from the president's Minority Bank Deposit Program in 1970, which sought to pump one hundred million dollars into nonwhite-owned banks, with two-thirds coming from the private sector and one-third from federal government agencies. The rationale seemed simple: In a memorandum to the heads of federal departments and agencies, Office of Management and Budget director George Shultz wrote, "Minority banks are, by their very nature, small minority businesses. . . . Furthermore, these banks serve a useful function in the minority community in spreading the *financial knowhow* which is essential in any business enterprise."[45] Within a year of its launch, the program increased deposits in nine Latinx banks by roughly seventy million dollars.[46]

The combined efforts of elite "Hispanic" businesspeople, their advocates, and government officials during the early 1970s institutionalized and made popular the business-centered approach to Latinx urban poverty that had picked up steam during the previous decade. Few embodied this rags to riches ideal as well as Romana Bañuelos, who Nixon appointed as the first Latinx Treasurer of the United States in 1971.[47] Bañuelos, a Mexican American woman, owned one of the largest Latinx food processing businesses in California and also co-founded the Pan American National Bank of East Los Angeles. More than helping to establish programs that outlasted Nixon's presidency, the entrepreneurial group that Bañuelos formed part of helped to cement "financial knowhow" as an essential element of respectable Latinx civic participation, urban revitalization, and social mobility. Back in New York City, Latinx business and finance continued to grow even as the city teetered on the brink of bankruptcy in 1975.[48] Moreover, the political networks they had groomed since Banco Popular's arrival positioned them as ideal partners during New York's ostensible economic bounce-back of the 1980s.

"When I Look at a Hispanic, I Want Him to Be a Businessperson"

South Bronx banker Serafin Mariel was among those who reaped the benefits of policies and political alliances that an earlier generation of Latinx businesspeople had fostered. The Puerto Rican businessman (a former banker at Bankers Trust) founded New York National Bank (NYNB) in 1982 with an investment of $1.6 million. "We bought our first branch from one of the major banks in the area. They were going to close it," he stated.[49] Three years later, his bank grew to roughly $47 million in assets.[50] Commenting on Mariel as the "improbable godfather" of Bronx entrepreneurship, one business magazine article read, "If you are a responsible Bronx business person and you need a helping hand with a permit, why not meet the head of the Department of Buildings or the Port Authority or the Urban Development Corporation? Mariel will make the introductions."[51]

By the 1980s, the South Bronx had been scarred by decades of severe disinvestment exacerbated by the tens of thousands of arson fires that wreaked havoc on the area's buildings, mostly home to Latinx and African American residents.[52] For Mariel, the borough's distress could be tackled with the "practical" business measures that the private sector offered. "When I look at a Hispanic, I want him to be a business person" he remarked.[53] Just as New York's major banks gazed outward toward global markets (the Caribbean once again among them), Mariel advertised that part of the NYNB's purpose was to revive the Bronx's economic vitality. Like Banco Popular before it,

NYNB touted its familiarity with the language and customs of its Latinx client base. And whereas many of the city's major banks required a minimum income of between fifteen and twenty thousand dollars for consumer loans, NYNB only required a minimum of nine thousand dollars, just below the median income of roughly ten thousand dollars for Latinx residents in the state.[54]

In addition to consumer lending, NYNB also formed a management and technical assistance corporation, which provided the area's small businesses with financial advice, planning for mergers and acquisitions, and assistance in obtaining venture capital.[55] NYNB's limited lending capacity meant that it was required to partner with other banks and state entities to expand its large-scale clientele.[56] In such events, the bank obtained loans from larger financial institutions initially unwilling to invest in companies located in poor, nonwhite neighborhoods. NYNB's officers thus served as translators for the viability of Latinx entrepreneurial practice.

Bronx-based G&M Sportswear, which operated a garment factory with more than two hundred workers, according to its owner John Marquez, was among the businesses that NYNB advocated for. After determining that G&M required five hundred thousand dollars in financing to increase its sales from four million to seven million, NYNB's venture capital company made an investment, the bank made a loan, and the New York State Development Agency provided the rest.[57] The first of the three investors, NYNB's venture capital company, was made possible by a Nixon-era program that created and funded Minority Enterprise Small Business Investment Companies (MESBICs), which operated as investment capital entities partly funded by the SBA.[58] The program's goal was to alleviate institutional gaps in the availability of finance capital for nonwhite-owned businesses, a self-help approach to addressing unemployment and curing poverty in low-income urban neighborhoods across the country.[59]

As with Banco Popular, part of the NYNB's success was rooted in the bank's ability to tap into federal legislation to increase its assets. It similarly relied upon its ability to position itself as a vital partner to community businesses and to a city government that had increasingly shifted toward private-sector models of urban revitalization. NYNB mastered this balancing act between city government and local neighborhoods, for instance, by placing its officers on local boards such as the Chamber of Commerce. At the same time, the bank financed local housing projects, working with grassroots organizations such as the Mid-Bronx Desperados that grew out of the Community Development Corporation movements of the 1960s—but which had become increasingly dependent on private money.[60] Speaking to a group of retail bankers in 1985, Mariel concluded, "The lesson is clear: you can make money in some of these so-called—and I say so-called—disadvantaged areas."[61]

The networks that Mariel and his high-earning cohort across the nation developed also reinforced a cultural narrative that associated Latinx population growth with an ethnically distinct well of economic opportunity during the 1980s.[62] Nationwide, corporations, including McDonald's, Coca-Cola, and most famously Coors, which proclaimed itself "the beer for the Decade of the Hispanic," increasingly courted what they perceived as a massive increase to their potential consumer bases. Advertising media highlighted this push as marketing expenditures directed toward the Latinx consumer market nationwide doubled between 1982 and 1985.[63] Magazines like *Hispanic Business* documented and promoted this trend, publishing business and political news stories oriented toward Latinx professionals and entrepreneurs in similar ways to *Black Enterprise*, its African American counterpart.[64]

Despite promoting analogous messages about the free market's emancipatory potential, contributors to *Hispanic Magazine* frequently differentiated the importance of their so-called Hispanic heritage, one that they distanced from blackness both within and outside of the Latinx community. In one feature comparing Latinx and African American firms, the magazine asserted a refrain that had become common among many Latinx businesspeople: "The black community generally does not have a heritage of entrepreneurship, and this nation's history of slavery and discrimination against blacks is primarily to blame."[65] Latinx strides within the U.S. economic system were thus believed to be rooted in the group's supposed and inherent entrepreneurial spirit. Black heritage within the Latinx community was erased. If they were to become an enriching element of American society, the logic presumed, then Hispanic Americans needed to become active participants in the free enterprise system.

Desirables

The continued rise of Latinx business and finance coincided with the arrested development of Latinx electoral politics in the city during the 1980s. Just as NYNB distinguished itself among South Bronx businesses, many of

New York's Puerto Rican political leaders lamented the unactualized representational gains that they believed the city's Latinx population warranted. In 1979, one Puerto Rican official bemoaned, "We had hopes that there would be maybe half a dozen to a dozen positions that would be ours, to affect programs and policy and hiring right up and down the line."[66] Yet by the mid 1980s, Puerto Ricans held only ten city and state elected offices, even as the group's population rose over 850,000.[67] Their political urgency was magnified by a Latinx community that expanded with the arrival of other Caribbean and Latin American groups, particularly those from the Dominican Republic, Colombia, Ecuador, and Mexico.[68]

Although hopes of increased governing power stalled, elite Latinx businesspeople capitalized on a political machine that remained amenable to ethnic patronage. When Ed Koch ran for a third term as mayor in 1985, he sought the backing of Latinx business leaders, who had grown in number and influence since Banco Popular's arrival in 1961. New Yorkers sitting in front of their television sets during Koch's campaign may have watched John Marquez (president of G&M Sportswear and one of NYNB's most successful clients) standing in his Bronx factory sporting a tan suit and a gold watch as he shot a campaign commercial for the incumbent mayor.[69] Marquez leaned on a wooden ladder and remarked, "With Koch, I'll tell you one thing, I'm very comfortable. . . . He's really for the small businessman."[70] Koch indeed championed the private sector as a catalyst for economic growth and urban revitalization. The increase in city budgets under his administration signaled a recovery from the austerity years of the late 1970s, but the recovery was uneven.[71] As John Mollenkopf argues, the Koch administration placed a disproportionate share of spending into expanding development activities while failing to restore education and property services to pre–fiscal crisis levels.[72]

Koch's approach gained him financial favor from high-earning Latinx businesspeople, particularly in the form of campaign contributions. The majority of Latinx donations to Koch's 1984–85 campaign came from a small cluster of contractors, bankers, consultants, and business owners. Their donations comprised more than half of total Latinx contributions to his campaign.[73] In return for their support, Koch provided this group with business subsidies by way of below-market-rate loans, relocation grants, industrial development bond financing, Urban Development Action Grants, and real estate tax abatement.[74] Koch also granted businesspeople substantial control in representing the community's concerns when he created the

Commission on Hispanic Affairs in 1986. The mayor charged the body with identifying the problems faced in the areas of education, employment, economic development, housing, health, and criminal justice.[75] The commission's board included a familiar set of characters. Its chairman was Banco Popular's senior vice president, Edgardo Vasquez, who looked to propose "ways in which the city and state can work with the private sector and community groups in a joint effort to serve needs in the Hispanic community which cannot be served by the city alone."[76] Other members included NYNB founder Serafin Mariel and food wholesaler Johnny Torres.

In the commission's first of many public hearings across the city, Angelo Falcón of the Institute for Puerto Rican Policy rebuked Koch, labeling the commission a "mockery" and asserting that community members had long expressed their concerns directly to the mayor's office: "You will find that close to two decades later we are still discussing the same ignorance and insensitivity from city government," he lamented.[77] At the eight-hour hearing at Columbia Teachers College, other local elected officials and community activists highlighted the prevalence of increased drug usage among Latinx youth and escalating rents in East Harlem that forced many Latinxs from their homes.[78] At the Brooklyn hearing two weeks later, director of housing for Brooklyn Legal Services, Roger Maldonado, reiterated the prevalence of housing abuses against underrepresented Latinx tenants, who faced unwarranted evictions and were poorly represented in landlord-tenant cases. Latinx tenants who lacked translators or bilingual lawyers faced an uphill battle in the city's overcrowded housing courts, Maldonado explained. "It is the landlord's attorney, not the courts who explains to the tenant what his or her rights are." He concluded, "This system is absolutely unfair."[79]

By the end of the two-month hearings, more than one hundred Latinx community organizations and individuals had testified before city leaders, including Ed Koch. They called for city resources to combat income and housing insecurity, to repair a failing educational system, and, in some cases, to end the exploitation of undocumented immigrants who became "targets for those who prey on the helpless."[80] The commission submitted its report the following year.[81] When Koch disbanded it in 1987, residents were disappointed that key recommendations were rejected.[82] Though widely considered a political ploy to court and retain Latinx voters, the commission offered Latinx residents the rare opportunity to address city leaders collectively. Ultimately, their testimonies made clear that the gains touted by New York's Latinx business leaders remained far from representative of life for most Latinx residents. The Latinx poverty rate grew to roughly 32 percent by the end of the decade, far above the national average of 13 percent.[83] For at least one third of the 1.7 million Latinx New Yorkers, economic subsistence remained dire.[84]

Loaning Dreams

Koch's Commission on Hispanic Affairs empowered a group of elite businesspeople who prioritized incentives for business growth as a cure for their community's problems. Keen on fulfilling the economic potential that the "Decade of the Hispanic" held in the public imagination during the 1980s, this group exercised its power in service of a vision of community advancement that emphasized individual ability. They shaped and deployed a notion of Hispanicity that distanced them from African Americans and black Latinxs while promoting a middle-class orientation which, as Sonia Song-Ha Lee writes of other political leaders of the era, focused on "escaping poverty rather than its eradication."[85] That even the commission's recommendations were mostly dismissed reflected the limits of Latinx business leadership in achieving that goal. Instead, their political positioning obscured dissent emanating from a broad range of community organizations and activists whose proposals might have required upending the public-private partnerships that wealthy Latinx communities had cultivated at the local and national level since the 1960s. Acceptable Latinx governance required *not* advocating for transformative community investment, let alone grappling with the capitalist roots of social inequality in New York City.

Historians have generally understood the 1970s turn toward privatization as detrimental for Latinx groups across the board. This chapter has introduced an understudied cast of Latinx characters who generated great wealth during this era and whose unexpected success helped to institutionalize racial capitalism as the main avenue for Latinx empowerment in New York City politics. For Banco Popular de Puerto Rico, soaring profits grew on the heels of U.S. colonial administration and dispossession on the island, not in spite of it. When the bank opened its first branches in New York during the 1960s, it manipulated its "foreign" status to appear not only as a politically neutral institution but also as symbolic of, and essential to, the idea of Latinx social progress. During the 1970s, the Nixon administration's constellation of capitalist-oriented programs enabled the "Hispanic" business elite to which these bankers belonged to reinforce business ownership as the primary solution to the growing crisis of poverty and unemployment in U.S. cities. In the process, this group of bankers, consultants, business owners, and politicians positioned themselves as respectable models of Latinx civic participation.

Their efforts reverberated at the local level, both in policy and in rhetoric, during the 1980s. In the South Bronx, NYNB's operations thus embodied a form of urban revitalization facilitated by two decades of Latinx businesspeople's campaigns for the essential role of ownership. Like its predecessors, the bank sparked the economic imaginations of aspiring Latinx businesspeople in the region, loaning dreams of upward mobility as much as they loaned money. As Koch's Commission on Hispanic Affairs demonstrated, racial capitalism promised individuals like Johnny Torres, Serafin Mariel, John Marquez, and others a level of municipal access that earlier political leaders had struggled to gain. Moreover, they lacked accountability to the communities who they claimed to represent, preconditioning the economic possibilities of Latinx New Yorkers for whom poverty and anti-immigrant sentiment remained potent during the 1990s—even as Latinx business activity flourished.

NOTES

1. "Display Ad 48—No Title," *New York Times*, April 26, 1982, D10.
2. In this chapter, I use "Latinx" when broadly referring to immigrant groups from Latin America and the Caribbean, as well as their descendants. This term is used contemporarily to encompass individuals who do not identify with binary gender pronouns, but also, as Nicole Guidotti-Hernández writes, to transcend "boomer-generation nationalist-formations." I use "Hispanic" in particular moments throughout the chapter to describe the businesspeople who would have referred to themselves as such during the 1970s, when the term first emerged. For more on the history and uses of "Latinx," see Nicole M. Guidotti-Hernández, "Affective Communities and Millennial Desires: Latinx, or Why My Computer Won't Recognize Latina/o," *Cultural Dynamics* 29, no. 3 (August 2017): 141–59; Richard T. Rodriguez, "X Marks the Spot," *Cultural Dynamics* 29, no. 3 (August 2017): 202–13; Urayoán Noel "The Queer Migrant Poemics of #Latinx Instagram," *New Literary History* 50, no. 4 (Autumn 2019): 531–57.
3. "Display Ad 48."
4. Cedric Robinson, *Black Marxism: The Making of the Black Radical Tradition* (Chapel Hill: University of North Carolina Press, 2000).
5. Among many other secondary texts, see Jennifer Morgan, *Laboring Women: Reproduction and Gender in New World Slavery* (Philadelphia: University of

Pennsylvania Press, 2004); Sven Beckert and Seth Rockman, *Slavery's Capitalism: A New History of American Economic Development* (Philadelphia: University of Pennsylvania Press, 2016); Stephanie Smallwood, *Saltwater Slavery: A Middle Passage from Africa to American Diaspora* (Cambridge, Mass.: Harvard University Press, 2007); Walter Johnson, *Soul by Soul Life Inside the Antebellum Slave Market* (Cambridge, Mass.: Harvard University Press, 1999).

6. Mark K. Levitan and Susan S. Wieler, "Poverty in New York City, 1969-99: The Influence of Demographic Change, Income Growth, and Income Inequality," *RFBNY Economic Policy Review*, July 2008, 22.

7. For the history of New York City's 1975 fiscal crisis, see Kim Phillips-Fein, *Fear City: New York's Fiscal Crisis and the Rise of Austerity Politics* (New York: Metropolitan Books, 2017). For grassroots response to the crisis, see Lana Dee Povitz, *Stirrings: How Activist New Yorkers Ignited a Movement for Food Justice* (Chapel Hill: University of North Carolina Press, 2019).

8. See N. D. B. Connolly, *A World More Concrete: Real Estate and the Remaking of Jim Crow South Florida* (Chicago: University of Chicago Press, 2016); Marcia Chatelain, *Franchise: The Golden Arches in Black America* (New York: Liveright, 2020); Keeanga-Yamahtta Taylor, *Race for Profit How Banks and the Real Estate Industry Undermined Black Homeownership* (Chapel Hill: University of North Carolina Press, 2019). For studies on Latinx migration during this period, see A. K. Sandoval-Strausz, *Barrio America: How Latino Immigrants Saved the American City* (New York: Basic Books, 2019); Llana Barber, *Latino City Immigration and Urban Crisis in Lawrence, Massachusetts, 1945–2000* (Chapel Hill: University of North Carolina Press, 2017). For history of fiscal conservatism, see Kim Phillips-Fein, *Invisible Hands: The Making of the Conservative Movement from the New Deal to Reagan* (New York: Norton, 2009); Julilly Kohler-Hausmann, *Getting Tough: Welfare and Imprisonment in 1970s America* (Princeton, N.J.: Princeton University Press, 2017).

9. I engage here from Sonia Song-Ha Lee's discussion of Hispanicity in *Building a Latino Civil Rights Movement: Puerto Ricans, African Americans, and the Pursuit of Racial Justice in New York City* (Chapel Hill: University of North Carolina Press, 2014). See also Neil Foley, "Becoming Hispanic: Mexican Americans and the Faustian Pact with Whiteness," in *Reflexiones: New Directions in Mexican American Studies*, ed. Neil Foley (Austin: University of Texas Press, 1998); Benjamin Francis-Fallon, *The Rise of the Latino Vote: A History* (Cambridge, Mass.: Harvard University Press, 2019); Arlene M. Dávila, *Latino Spin: Public Image and the Whitewashing of Race* (New York: New York University, 2008).

10. "Puerto Rican and Israeli Banks Get Approval for Branches Here," *New York Times*, June 8, 1961.

11. Guillermo Baralt, *Tradición de Futuro: El Primer Siglo del Banco Popular de Puerto Rico* (San Juan: Banco Popular de Puerto Rico, 1993), 23, 24.

12. Sánchez Korrol writes, "Between 1889 and 1929, the total acreage devoted to sugar production increased 230 percent, going from 72,000 acres to 237,758 acres." Virginia E. Sánchez Korrol, *From Colonia to Community: A History of Puerto*

Ricans in New York (Berkeley: University of California Press, 1983), 20, 22; Baralt, *Tradición de Futuro*, 109, 111.

13. Baralt, *Tradición de Futuro*, 113.

14. Jorge Duany, "From the Bohio to the Caserio: Urban Housing Conditions in Puerto Rico," in *Self-Help Housing, the Poor, and the State in the Caribbean*, ed. Robert B. Potter and Dennis Conway (Knoxville: University of Tennessee Press, 1997), 195.

15. See David Freund, *Colored Property: State Policy and White Politics in Suburban America* (Chicago: Chicago University Press, 2007); Peter James Hudson, *Bankers and Empire: How Wall Street Colonized the Caribbean* (Chicago: Chicago University Press, 2017), 7.

16. Baralt, *Tradición de Futuro*, 135. Translation by author.

17. Baralt, *Tradición de Futuro*, 136.

18. Baralt, *Tradición de Futuro*, 137.

19. Whether the bank participated in the practice of redlining is difficult to determine with extant sources, though the bank was likely subject to the FHA's *Underwriting Manual* guidelines. See Federal Housing Administration, *Underwriting Manual: Underwriting and Valuation Procedure Under Title II of the National Housing Act*, Washington, D.C., 1934, 1936, 1938.

20. During the 1940s, the island's political leaders, including businessman Teodoro Moscoso, worked with Banco Popular's principal owner, Rafael Carrión, to help pass bills that would lead to the development of Operation Bootstrap, an ambitious economic program that overhauled the island's economy toward modern manufacturing. A. W. Maldonado, *Teodoro Moscoso and Puerto Rico's Operation Bootstrap* (Gainesville: University of Florida Press, 1997), 30; Rita M. Maldonado, "The Role of the Financial Sector in the Economic Development of Puerto Rico" (Ph.D. diss., New York University, 1969), 136, 138.

21. Sánchez Korrol, *From Colonia to Community*, 27, 38; César J. Ayala and Rafael Bernabe, *Puerto Rico in the American Century: A History Since 1898* (Chapel Hill: University of North Carolina Press), 181.

22. *1950 Census of Population*, Vol. 4, Special Reports, Part 3, Puerto Ricans in the Continental United States, table 1, 3d/11; *1960 Census of Population*, Subject Reports, Puerto Ricans in the United States: Social and Economic Data for Persons of Puerto Rican Birth and Parentage, table 1, 9; *1960 Census of Population*, Supplementary Reports: Population Counts and Selected Characteristics for Puerto Rico, 1960, table 5 (Washington D.C.: Bureau of the Census, 1961), 3.

23. "Puerto Rican and Israeli Banks."

24. For recent work on the Bronx, see Peter L'Official, *Urban Legends: The South Bronx in Representation and Ruin* (Cambridge, Mass.: Harvard University Press, 2020); Bench Ansfield, "Born in Flames: Arson, Racial Capitalism, and the Reinsuring of the Bronx in the Late Twentieth Century" (Ph.D. diss., Yale University, forthcoming); Evelyn Gonzalez, *The Bronx* (New York: Columbia University Press, 2006).

25. Robert J. Cole, "Puerto Rican Bank Here Stresses Public Service," *New York Times*, July 25, 1970.

26. Cole, "Puerto Rican Bank Here Stresses Public Service."

27. The Economic Opportunity Act helped to create Small Business Development Corporations, which offered nonwhite businesspeople low-interest loans and consulting for their business ventures. Latinx businesspeople were often intermediaries between government and fund allocation. See Pedro A. Regalado, "Where Angels Fear to Tread: Latinx Work and the Making of Postindustrial New York" (Ph.D. diss., Yale University, 2019). "Text of Speech—At Inaugural Ceremonies for the Banco Popular De Puerto Rico," December 4, 1964, Box 060055W, Folder 9, Robert F. Wagner Documents Collection; Speeches Series, LaGuardia & Wagner Archives, City University of New York.

28. Remarks by Mayor John V. Lindsay of New York City Before the Conference: "Puerto Ricans Confront the Problems of the Urban Society; A Design for Change," April 15, 1967, Box 69, Folder 364, Puerto Rican Community Conference, John V. Lindsay Papers; Letter to Richard Rosen, December 20, 1965, Box 388, Folder 34, Puerto Rican Correspondence, John V. Lindsay Papers, Yale University Manuscripts and Archives, New Haven, Connecticut.

29. U.S. Congress, Senate, Hearings Before the Committee on Small Business, "The Role of the Federal Government in the Development of Small Business Enterprises in the Urban Ghetto," 99th Cong., 2nd sess., 1968, 107–12.

30. Charles G. Bennett, "Lindsay to Form Urban Unit Here," *New York Times*, August 26, 1967 (emphasis added).

31. Seth S. King, "City Acts to Spur Ghetto Business," *New York Times*, October 29, 1967. For more on African American banking, see Mehrsa Baradaran, *The Color of Money: Black Banks and the Racial Wealth Gap* (Cambridge, Mass: Harvard University Press, 2017).

32. U.S. Congress, "The Role of the Federal Government," 108.

33. U.S. Congress, "The Role of the Federal Government," 115.

34. *1970 Census of Population*, Vol. 1, Characteristics of Population, New York, Part 34, table 119, 34/607, 34/611. For more on middle-class Puerto Rican professionals and politics in New York, see Lee, *Building a Latino Civil Rights Movement*.

35. For more on the formulation of the term "Hispanic" and Latinx politics during this period, see Geraldo Cadava, *The Hispanic Republican: The Shaping of an American Political Identity, from Nixon to Trump* (S.I.: Ecco Press, 2020); Benjamin Francis-Fallon, *The Rise of the Latino Vote: A History* (Cambridge, Mass.: Harvard University Press, 2019); Cristina Beltran, *The Trouble with Unity: Latino Politics and the Creation of Identity* (New York: Oxford University Press, 2010); Cristina Mora, *Making Hispanics: How Activists, Bureaucrats, and Media Constructed a New American* (Chicago: University of Chicago Press, 2014).

36. Other significant initiatives included National Economic Development Agency and Project Alpha. "Cabinet Committee to Increase Hispanic Businesses," *Hoy*, January 31, 1974, 2. "The Cabinet Committee on Opportunities for Spanish Speaking People," Box 71, Folder 70 "Spanish Speaking," Anne L. Armstrong, Series XIII, White House Central Files: Staff Member and Office Files, Richard M. Nixon Presidential Library and Museum, Yorba Linda, California; Mora, *Making Hispanics*.

37. Francis-Fallon, *The Rise of the Latino Vote*, 4.
38. Luis A. Ferré, "Letter to Richard M. Nixon," April 27, 1971, Box 2, FG 145-Cabinet Committee on Spanish Speaking People, White House Central Files: Subject Files, Richard M. Nixon Presidential Library and Museum, Yorba Linda, California.
39. Foley, "Becoming Hispanic: Mexican Americans and the Faustian Pact with Whiteness."
40. Anne L. Armstrong, Series XIII, Box 71, Folder "Spanish Speaking," April 1973, White House Central Files: Subject Files, Richard M. Nixon Presidential Library and Museum, Yorba Linda, California; Baradaran, *The Color of Money*, 180, 191.
41. Baradaran, *The Color of Money*, 180, 191.
42. U.S. Department of Commerce, Office of Minority Business Enterprise, *MBE Outlook*, July 1972.
43. Dean J. Kotlowski, *Nixon's Civil Rights: Politics, Principle, and Policy* (Cambridge, Mass: Harvard University Press, 2001), 145; "Nixon Sets Up Agency to Help Blacks Own, Manage Businesses," *Jet*, March 20, 1969, 20; Johnny Torres, interview by author, Union City, New Jersey, September 4, 2018.
44. "The Cabinet Committee on Opportunities for Spanish Speaking People," Box 71, Folder 70.
45. George Shultz, "Deposit Program for Minority Banks," Memorandum for Heads of Departments and Agencies, October 2, 1970, Box 21, Folder "Spanish Speaking Confidential," Robert H. Finch Series II: Cabinet Committee on Opportunities for the Spanish Speaking, White House Central Files: Staff Member and Office Files, Richard M. Nixon Presidential Library and Museum, Yorba Linda, California (emphasis added).
46. "Bank Deposit Program Exceeds $100 Million Goal," *MBE Outlook*, July 1972, 6.
47. See Cadava, *The Hispanic Republican*.
48. Juan Guedella, "A New Benchmark," *Hispanic Business*, January 1987.
49. "The Changing Shape of Retail Banking: Responding to Customer Needs," Summary of a Conference Sponsored by the Office of Comptroller of the Currency (Darby, Pa.: Diane, 1993), 40.
50. Larry Rohter, "New York's Thriving Hispanic Banks," *New York Times*, August 11, 1985.
51. James S. Howard, "Where Angels Fear to Tread . . . Call in the Entrepreneurs," *D & B Reports*, July/August 1987.
52. See Bench Ansfield, "Born in Flames: Arson, Racial Capitalism, and the Reinsuring of the Bronx in the Late Twentieth Century" (Ph.D. diss., Yale University, forthcoming); Lizabeth Cohen, *Saving America's Cities: Ed Logue and the Struggle to Renew Urban America in the Suburban Age* (New York: Farrar, Straus, and Giroux, 2019), 349–84.
53. Rohter, "New York's Thriving Hispanic Banks."
54. Rohter, "New York's Thriving Hispanic Banks"; "The Changing Shape of Retail Banking"; *1980 Census of Population*, Vol. 1, Characteristics of Population, chapter C, General Social and Economic Characteristics, New York, part 34, table 91, 34/188.

55. Juan Guedella, "Getting the Bucks the Mesbic Way," *Hispanic Business* 7, no. 8 (August 1985).

56. "We still make the $5,000 and $10,000 loan to the small-business man in our community," stated one official of Banco Popular's New York district in 1985. "But the number of $300,000 to $800,000 loans we make has grown dramatically in the last few years," he added. While equity return of "nonminority" banks averaged just over 10 percent, Banco Popular reported an impressive 15 percent rate of return from 1980 to 1985. Rohter, "New York's Thriving Hispanic Banks."

57. "The Changing Shape of Retail Banking."

58. Walter L. Sorg, "MESBIC's: The Blend of Private Initiative and Governmental Encouragement," *New Dimensions in Legislation*, Paper 7, June 1, 1972.

59. NYNB's company was called the Triad Capital Corporation; it invested in a range of other minority-owned businesses. Timothy Bates, "Financing the Development of Urban Minority Communities: Lessons of History," *Economic Development Quarterly* 14, no. 3 (2000): 227–41. Howard, "Where Angels Fear to Tread."

60. Themis Chronopoulos, "The Rebuilding of the South Bronx After the Fiscal Crisis," *Journal of Urban History* 43, no. 6 (2017): 932–59; "The Changing Shape of Retail Banking."

61. "The Changing Shape of Retail Banking."

62. For more on middle-class Latinxs, consumerism, and race, see Dávila, *Latino Spin*.

63. For more on Coors and Latinx people, see Allyson P. Brantley, "Building a Boycott, One Bumper Sticker at a Time: Coors Boycott Ephemera, 1977–1978," *Ephemera Journal* 17, no. 2 (September 2014); Harold Jacobson, "Trends in Hispanic Market Advertising Expenditures," *Hispanic Business*, December 1986.

64. Cissy Ross, "A Voice for Hispanics: Unknown Business Magazine Gets Noticed," *Gainesville Sun*, October 16, 1994.

65. "The Nation's Top 100 Hispanic & Black Firms—How They Compare," *Hispanic Business*, September 1985.

66. David Vidal, "Many Hispanic Leaders, Disillusioned with Koch Policies, Seek New Paths to Progress," *New York Times*, May 13, 1979.

67. Llorin R. Thomas and Aldo A. Lauria Santiago, *Rethinking the Struggle for Puerto Rican Rights* (New York: Routledge, 2019), 226; *1980 Census of Population*, Vol. 1, Characteristics of Population, chapter C, General Social and Economic Characteristics, New York, part 34, table 59, 33/93.

68. See Jesse Hoffnung-Garskof, *A Tale of Two Cities: New York and Santo Domingo After 1950* (Princeton, N.J.: Princeton University Press, 2008); Laird W. Bergad, "The Latino Population of New York City, 1990–2010," Latino Data Project, Report 44, November 2011, Center for Latin American, Caribbean & Latino Studies, Graduate Center, City University of New York.

69. Lagarchvist, "Ed Koch Campaign Commercials 1985," September 18, 2013, https://www.youtube.com/watch?v=GfGPx62llaY.

70. Lagarchvist, "Ed Koch Campaign Commercials 1985."

71. Chronopoulos, "The Rebuilding of the South Bronx After the Fiscal Crisis," 936.

72. John Mollenkopf, *Phoenix in the Ashes: The Rise and Fall of the Koch Coalition in New York City Politics* (Princeton, N.J.: Princeton University Press, 1992), 139.

73. "Press Release: Study Reveals Top Puerto Rican–Latino Contributors to Koch and Cuomo Businessmen Dominate Campaign-Giving," Institute for Puerto Rican Policy, June 12, 1986, Edward I. Koch Collection, Departmental Correspondence Series, La Guardia and Wagner Archives, La Guardia Community College, New York.

74. Esteban Velez, "Getting Ahead in the Big Apple," *Hispanic Business*, May 1986.

75. "Memorandum to Agency Heads, June 8, 1979," Edward I. Koch Collection, Commission on Hispanic Concerns Affairs Subject Files, La Guardia and Wagner Archives, LaGuardia Community College, New York.

76. Velez, "Getting Ahead in the Big Apple."

77. David Medina, "Koch Hearing—Power-Play for Future Votes," *San Juan Star*, March 24, 1986. Three days later, the *New York Daily News* asked, "What good is a hearing if nobody listens?" Miguel Perez, "What Good Is a Hearing If Nobody Listens?," *New York Daily News*, March 27, 1986.

78. Patricia Hurtado, "Hispanics Decry Rising Rents," *Newday*, March 20, 1986. "Master List, March 3, 1986," Box 12, Folder 8, Edward I. Koch Collection, Commission on Hispanic Concerns Affairs Subject Files, La Guardia and Wagner Archives, LaGuardia Community College, New York.

79. Leslie Schwerin, "Mayor's Commission Listens to the Concerns of Hispanic Community," *Starrett Sun*, April 11, 1986.

80. Roger Sanjek, *The Future of Us All: Race and Neighborhood Politics in New York City* (Ithaca, N.Y.: Cornell University Press, 1998), 149; Milagros Ricourt and Ruby Danta, *Hispanas de Queens: Latino Panethnicity in a New York City Neighborhood* (Ithaca, N.Y.: Cornell University Press, 2003), 95. John Murtaugh, "Testimony: Commission on Hispanic Concerns," Box 12, Folder 8, Edward I. Koch Collection.

81. Lydia Chavez, "Mayor's Response to Report on Hispanic Concerns Criticized," *New York Times*, March 10, 1987.

82. Chavez, "Mayor's Response to Report on Hispanic Concerns Criticized,"

83. Justine Calcagno, "Trends in Poverty Rates Among Latinos in New York City and the United States, 1990–2011," Latino Data Project, Report 55, November 2013, Center for Latin American, Caribbean & Latino Studies, Graduate Center, City University of New York.

84. Bergad, "The Latino Population of New York City, 1990–2010."

85. Lee, *Building a Latino Civil Rights Movement*, 248.

CONTRIBUTORS

Destin Jenkins is the Neubauer Family Assistant Professor of History at the University of Chicago. His research interests include urban history, twentieth-century African American history, and crime and punishment. He is the author of *The Bonds of Inequality: Debt and the Making of the American City* (The University of Chicago Press, forthcoming).

Ryan Cecil Jobson is the Neubauer Family Assistant Professor of Anthropology at the University of Chicago. His research engages questions of sovereignty and extractive resource development in the colonial and postcolonial Americas. He is at work on his first book manuscript, a historical ethnography of the Caribbean petrostate of Trinidad and Tobago.

Manu Karuka is an assistant professor of American studies at Barnard College. He is the author of *Indigenous Nations, Chinese Workers, and the Transcontinental Railroad* (University of California Press, 2019). He is also co-editor of *Futures Held Hostage: Confronting US Hybrid Wars and Sanction in Venezuela* (Pluto Press, 2020) and co-editor of *The Sun Never Sets: South Asian Migrants in an Age of U.S. Power* (New York University Press, 2013).

Mishal Khan is a postdoctoral fellow at the Bernard and Audre Rapoport Center for Human Rights and Justice at The University of Texas at Austin, after completing her PhD in Sociology at the University of Chicago. Her work examines slavery and abolition in South Asia and the wider British Empire, linking these histories to the emergence of global legal labor regimes during the twentieth century.

Justin Leroy is an assistant professor of history at the University of California, Davis. His research focuses on the intellectual history of the U.S. and Atlantic world, and the problem of slavery and empire in the nineteenth century. He is the author of The Lowest Freedom: Slave Emancipation, Racial Capitalism, and the Black Radical Tradition (Columbia University Press, forthcoming).

Allan E. S. Lumba is an assistant professor of history at Virginia Tech. His work explores the intersections between race, sovereignty, and capitalism in the U.S. Pacific empire and the Philippine colony. He is the author of *Monetary Authorities: Capitalism and Decolonization in the American Colonial Philippines* (forthcoming).

K-Sue Park is an associate professor of law at Georgetown University Law Center. Her work examines the creation of the American real estate system through the history of colonization. Her publications have appeared in the *Harvard Law Review, The University of Chicago Law Review, The History of the Present, Law & Social Inquiry, Law & Society Inquiry,* and the *New York Times.*

Pedro Regalado is a Junior Fellow of the Society of Fellows at Harvard University. He researches the history of race, Latinx immigration, and capitalism in American cities. His forthcoming book examines the history of twentieth century New York through the lens of Latinx workers in the city's rapidly evolving industries, recuperating Latinx residents as active agents in the remaking of the city's economy and landscape.

Shauna J. Sweeney is an assistant professor of women's and gender studies and history at the University of Toronto. Her work focuses on early modern political economy, transnational feminisms, and slavery and freedom in the Atlantic world. She is the author of *A Free Enterprise: Market Women, Insurgent Economies and the Making of Caribbean Freedom* (forthcoming).

ACKNOWLEDGMENTS

This volume is a collective endeavor and the result of several years of work. We are indebted to everyone whose work appears here, and to those whose does not. *Histories of Racial Capitalism* began while we both held fellowships at Harvard's Charles Warren Center for Studies in American History, where Walter Johnson first convinced us of the project's viability. The Radcliffe Institute for Advanced Study at Harvard and the Stevanovich Institute on the Formation of Knowledge at the University of Chicago also provided support for two in-person collaborative discussions among the contributors. We extend thanks to Stephanie Smallwood, Peter James Hudson, Megan Ming Francis, Jackie Wang, and Michael Ralph, who also participated in those discussions.

We are especially indebted to the Race and Capitalism project housed jointly at the University of Chicago and the University of Washington. Michael Dawson and Megan Ming Francis not only provided essential funding; they also created opportunities for us to secure constructive criticism from Adom Getachew, Ashleigh Campi, Jodi Melamed, Mark Golub, John Robinson III, Emily Kazenstein, Amna Akbar, Shatema Threadcraft, Alfredo Gonzalez, Tania Islas, Leach Wright Rigeur, Rutger Ceballos, and Federico Navarrete Linares. We have also benefited immensely from Mark Jerng and the Mellon Initiative on Racial Capitalism at the University of California, Davis.

Columbia University Press has been an extraordinary partner throughout this process. The History of U.S. Capitalism series editors, Julia Ott, Devin

Fergus, Bethany Moreton, and Louis Hyman, have believed in the importance of this volume from the earliest stages. Bridget Flannery-McCoy, and later Stephen Wesley and Christian Winting, took on much of the work of managing production, allowing us to focus on the volume itself.

Lastly, we are grateful to our students who entertained early versions of our interpretive claims and helped us sharpen our ideas.

INDEX

Page numbers in *italics* indicate figures.

CPSIA information can be obtained
at www.ICGtesting.com
Printed in the USA
JSHW040856160621
15945JS00003B/12